DATE DUE

Kristin Luker

DUBIOUS CONCEPTIONS

THE POLITICS OF TEENAGE PREGNANCY

HARVARD UNIVERSITY PRESS
Cambridge, Massachusetts, and London, England

First Harvard University Press paperback edition, 1997

Library of Congress Cataloging-in-Publication Data

Luker, Kristin.
Dubious conceptions : the politics of teenage pregnancy /Luker.
p.   cm.
Includes bibliographical references and index.
ISBN 0-674-21702-0 (cloth)
ISBN 0-674-21703-9 (pbk.)
1. Teenage pregnancy—United States.   2. Teenage pregnancy—
Government policy—United States.   3. Teenage pregnancy—
United States—Prevention.   I. Title.
HQ759.4.L85   1996
306.874'3—dc20   95-52833

TO JOAN DUNLOP

ACKNOWLEDGMENTS

Scholarly books are simultaneously an intensely personal and a deeply collective enterprise. They are personal products, since a single mind ultimately must decide what to leave in and what to leave out and a single mind must stand behind what has been written. But the raw material that becomes a book is, if the author is as lucky as I am, profoundly shaped by the acumen and generosity of numerous friends, colleagues, and experts. Most impressive to me is the way in which this generosity is sustained, even in the face of a new social movement that is busily trying to erect boundaries around "intellectual property." Like all academics, I have great respect for the hard work involved in getting something as evanescent as an idea down on paper, and the notes and bibliography of this book clearly show how indebted I am to the written scholarship of others.

But among the most valuable parts of academic life are the impromptu discussions, the shared ideas, the suggestions for new sources of data, the willingness to read yet one more draft of a chapter. This book has, if anything, profited even more from this second, invisible kind of scholarship. I now understand better than ever why scholars often make a point of declaring that they alone are responsible for any errors in their book: it is a way of acknowledging that the book the reader holds was actually produced by a great many people, but that the final decisions—for better or worse—are the author's own.

I have been fortunate enough to have the support of some outstanding institutions. The Commonwealth Fund and the Ford Foundation supplied funding for most of the research represented here, and the University of California at Berkeley and Princeton University offered a congenial intellectual atmosphere in which to analyze that research. In particular, the

Women's Studies Program and the Office of Population Research at Princeton University provided an ideal setting in which to reflect on an issue so closely connected with both demography and gender. While at Princeton, I was privileged to hold the Doris Stevens Chair in Women's Studies, which granted funds that helped make this book possible. Also at Princeton I met Mary Ann Belanger, librarian at the Office of Population Research, who went far beyond the call of duty and reminded me once again that librarians are academia's most valuable—and undervalued—resources.

A number of committed and brilliant graduate students brought fresh vision and energy to this project. Eleanor Bell, Cynthia Harper, Deborah Kang, Rich Kaplan, Chris Rhomberg, Arlene Stein, and Laura Weide wrote dozens of thoughtful and intelligent memos that contributed immeasurably to the book. Likewise, I have had the assistance of some extraordinarily capable undergraduate assistants. Elaine Villamin helped shepherd this book through its final hectic months with calmness, good cheer, and efficiency. She deserves the academic equivalent of combat pay. In earlier years, I was aided by Lisa Bass, Lissa Bell, Kara Hatfield, Vandana Sipahimalani, and Stephanie Petit.

Colleagues in a range of disciplines offered their thoughts and criticisms. I cannot begin to thank them enough, but I can at least list them. Had I taken all of their advice to heart, this might have been a wiser book. Jim Cramer, Paul DiMaggio, Michelle Fine, Frank Furstenberg, Arline Geronimus, Arlie Hochschild, Christopher Jencks, Jerome Karabel, David Kirp, Richard Lincoln, Kelly Luker, Wendy Luttrell, River Malcolm, Sara McLanahan, Peter Morrison, Karen Padget, Sam Popkin, Lillian Rubin, Paul Starr, and James Trussell all read drafts of the manuscript, some of them many times. Other colleagues took the time to argue with me, think with me, and force me to be more precise. Although some of these conversations were episodic, they were nonetheless vital. I can only hope that my contributions to the work of others will be as useful. The professionals at Harvard University Press—most notably Joyce Seltzer and Maria Ascher—did a tremendous job of transforming the overall argument into something clearer and finer.

The long, hard, often lonely task of shaping a book from hundreds of musings and notes was made infinitely more bearable by my husband, Jerome Karabel, who provided emotional as well as intellectual support, and by Magic, who brought joy wherever he went and whose time with us was much too short.

CONTENTS

DUBIOUS
CONCEPTIONS

1

THE PROBLEM

AND ITS

HUMAN FACE

At the Eileen Sullivan Daycare Center, in the sunny playroom for toddlers, young David Winters sits entranced in front of a colorful bead-and-wire toy.[1] His chubby fingers tease the beads up and across the bright red, blue, and green wires, his solemnity lightened by rare and dazzling smiles as he conquers a particularly tricky corner in the game.

Born a month prematurely, David has gone on to flourish at the Sullivan Center after a rocky start. Across the street, in the high school to which the daycare center belongs, David's mother, Michelle Brown, is taking her algebra exam. If all goes well and Michelle gets the B she hopes for, she may well succeed at being the first member of her family to graduate from high school. And if she does, she has every intention of crossing that auditorium stage three months from now, dressed in her graduation robes and holding baby David in her arms.

Meanwhile, beyond the walls of the school and the daycare center, Michelle and her baby are at the heart of important and troubling questions that are being asked by people from all walks of life. In the United States, although teenagers give birth to only 12 percent of all babies, they represent about a third of all unmarried mothers. These young mothers are somewhat less likely than older mothers to start prenatal care on time, and are slightly more likely to have low-birthweight babies and complications during pregnancy and childbirth—all of which are factors associated with medical and sometimes developmental problems in their children.[2]

Michelle is not sure she's old enough to get married, though she never

I

considered herself too young to have or to raise David, despite the fact that she was only seventeen when he was born. She did think briefly about having an abortion, but both her mother and grandmother were adamantly opposed; and truth to tell, Michelle was secretly happy they were. Their support, combined with her own experiences and those of many of her friends, makes her sure that she can successfully handle being both a young mother and a student. Being a wife is another story, though.

Michelle's reluctance to marry is strengthened by some harsh economic realities. The father of her baby works full time at McDonald's, but his minimum-wage salary of $684 a month just won't support the three of them. He's a diligent and even desperate worker (he competed against more than a hundred other applicants for his job), and he's been promised a promotion to manager. Even managers don't get medical benefits at McDonald's, however, and David's health still calls for frequent and expensive visits to the pediatrician. Although Michelle squirms under what she sees as the shame attached to welfare, she can't afford to give up the money (and especially the medical services that come with it) in order to marry.

Michelle and David's situation illustrates a host of important questions about age, sex, and marriage. To many people over forty, the idea of pregnant teenagers walking openly down school corridors, not to mention the existence of high school daycare centers, is something that outstrips the imagination. Until the mid-1970s visibly pregnant *married* women, whether students or teachers, were formally banned from school grounds, lest their swelling bellies cross that invisible boundary separating the real world (where sex and pregnancy existed) from the schools (where they did not). The idea that a pregnant *unmarried* woman would show herself not only in public but in schools, where the minds of innocent children could be corrupted, was more unthinkable still.

And what role does David's father play in all this? Like many of the fathers in discussions of early pregnancy, he is largely invisible to the public eye. We do know that most fathers are relatively young themselves (about 80 percent of teenage mothers have a partner who is within five years of their own age).[3] And we also have reason to suspect that this young man's faithful visits to the neonatal intensive care unit during David's lengthy stay there and his eager willingness to be a good father mark him as more typical than the stereotype would have it. Still, some twenty-five years after the most recent round of feminist activism, most people focus on teenage mothers instead of on young parents, so our knowledge about such men is surprisingly limited. This book will try to focus on both men and women as much as possible, but the available data force us to speak more often and with more authority about young women. The focus on young women in a book about early pregnancy should not, however, be taken as "natural."

For similar reasons, this book focuses largely on blacks and whites. Despite the fact that the U.S. Census gathers data on a number of races, and despite the fact that pregnancy among teenagers has been a national concern for the past two decades, reasonably comparable data exist only for whites and African Americans. More problematically, "race" is a social rather than a biological category and as such is defined differently in different historical eras.[4] Furthermore, the National Center for Health Statistics and the Bureau of the Census, which provide the data that underlie studies such as this, use different systems of racial classification.[5] Thus, for the sake of accuracy, the discussion that follows will center on blacks and whites (providing data on other groups where possible), but readers should keep in mind that this dichotomy only partly reflects the rich tapestry of modern America.

The changes that have occurred over the last twenty years are more far-reaching than most people, even those most intimately involved, can appreciate. For example, Michelle and David raise questions not only about sex, age, and marriage but about other issues that Americans are currently struggling with—issues such as poverty, dependency, and the difficulties of getting ahead in the increasingly competitive global economy. More subtly, they raise questions about "family values," about the relationship of individuals to the community, and about the competing claims of rights and obligations in this new economy. For example, have doors already been closed to David because his mother is a teenager and has not married his father? Has an inevitable sequence of life events—premature birth, impaired health, failure in school, poverty, perhaps even a tendency to violent behavior—been set in motion for David by his mother's behavior? In the opinion of many people, David's future is already blighted and his right to participate as an equal in the pursuit of the American dream has already begun to diminish, all by virtue of decisions in which he has had no say. The little boy whose imagination is fired by a colorful bead-game is, in the eyes of many, already well on the way to a life of trouble and failure.

A great number of Americans think that children like young David are being lost in a particularly painful and troubling fashion which has important implications for the larger society. One way of reading the story of Michelle

3

and her baby is to say that David's future is being compromised by the selfishness of his mother, by her inability to put the long-term needs of a vulnerable baby before her own longings and desires. According to the most generous interpretation, Michelle is doing this out of youth and ignorance. The liberal view of Michelle's actions—from having sex in the first place, to not using contraception when she does have sex, to not getting an abortion despite the fact that she is young and poor, to trying to raise David without bothering to marry his father—is that she is simply too immature to appreciate the consequences of her actions. The harm is being done unwittingly, and Michelle is as much a victim as David.[6]

This view has the virtue of protecting Michelle from moral censure for her actions (when advocates speak of "babies having babies," they imply that Michelle cannot be held to the standards expected of adults any more than David can). At the same time, however, it denies her the status of full personhood, exempting her from the obligations of being a moral actor held accountable for the choices she makes. In turn, people deemed incapable of making meaningful moral choices often find themselves the targets of those who would make choices for them. The problem is that Americans have a rather mixed history of doing bad things to young or otherwise vulnerable people "for their own good," of confusing an unwillingness to make the "right" choice with an incapacity to do so.

A darker reading of Michelle's actions and motives exists alongside the narrative of the young mother as innocent victim who unwittingly harms her baby. According to this reading, Michelle is the calculating, knowing, "rational actor" of neoclassical economics: she coolly assesses the costs of having a baby, analyzes the benefits of welfare, and "invests" in a course of action that will get her what she wants. This view at least has the virtue of granting her the status of a real decisionmaker whose choices must be taken seriously. But when looked at closely, the dilemma of early pregnancy highlights the limitations of rational-actor theory as a useful way of looking at human behavior. Part of what makes economic theories of human interaction so elegant and parsimonious is that all motives are reduced to the easily observed ones of the marketplace. Passion, conviction, altruism, and morality become, in this view of the social world, either "externalities" or "revealed preferences" and are reduced to the status of "utilities."[7]

Yet careful scrutiny makes it clear that the rational actor of neoclassical economics is not an *individual* in the generic sense of the word, but rather a *male individual:* the concepts of "work" and "family" have assumptions about gender deeply embedded within them. In the nineteenth century, American society came to rely on a cultural division of labor whereby men went out into the marketplace and engaged in the kind of selfish, disconnected, amoral, and autonomous behavior lauded in economic theory. Bruised and tattered by the harshness of this dog-eat-dog world, they then came home to the pious, altruistic, caring, connected, and profoundly moral world of women where the values of the marketplace were held at bay and older, more humane values were honored.[8]

Part of the cultural schizophrenia of our own time is that this old division of moral labor is breaking down. We have come to expect women to emulate competitive, "selfish" male behavior in the workplace but to carry on their traditional roles of altruistic nurturers everywhere else.[9] Michelle and the problem of early pregnancy highlight these dilemmas in particularly compelling ways. At some level we intuit that teenage mothers are doing things that in another time and place would be acceptable and often praiseworthy, because they are just doing the same things that earlier generations of women did from time immemorial. Teenage mothers often get pregnant because they *aren't* being rational actors who put self first—they may have sex to please a man, and they may fail to use contraception because the man either actively objects or makes it difficult by complaining that a condom reduces his pleasure. And filled with images from movies and magazines, young women may read a man's unwillingness to use contraception as a tacit commitment to the consequences, namely a baby. Teenage mothers, like other mothers, have also been known to get pregnant hoping that the pregnancy will solidify a partnership, making a couple out of two individuals. Many of them choose to forgo an abortion because they have moral objections, and because they feel a commitment to this new person in the making. Most poignantly, in the vast majority of cases, giving birth while still a teenager is a pledge of hope, an acted-out wish that the lives of the next generation will be better than those of the current generation, that this young mother can give her child something she never had.[10]

It is teenagers' unwillingness (or inability) to be rational actors that frustrates concerned adults: these young mothers seemingly refuse to think ahead and see how young they are, and how poor, and how dubious a prospect for marriage and fatherhood most of their young men are. Yet the thought of women being self-centered rational actors in the intimate realms of sex, childbearing, family, and home is a rather chilling one.[11] And one that few people really accept, no matter how militant their views in other areas of life. If some Americans are uneasy at the thought of eliminating all welfare for unwed teenage mothers, and if Republican congressmen suggest creating orphanages on a vast scale as a backup remedy, it is because they suspect that even the most draconian changes will have very little effect on what really happens in bedrooms and in abortion clinics, except, as economists say, "at the margin."[12] Even the most militant conservatives would be hard pressed to imagine a scenario in which a passionate midnight embrace is interrupted at the last moment when the young woman insists that her partner don a condom because, after all, their state has just eliminated welfare benefits for mothers under twenty-one.[13] These competing views of family and marketplace, of men and women, of rationality and morality, of rights and obligations are very much front and center in nearly every aspect of American life these days. Teenage mothers and their babies reflect and illuminate these cultural and social wars because they pose so pointedly the contradictions inherent in our ways of thinking about them. To the extent that we view young mothers as young *women,* we want them to be sensitive to the needs of others, altruistic, committed to relationships and to nurturing the next generation. Yet to the extent that we see them as *poor* women, we want them to be careful, forward-thinking, attuned to the market, and prepared to invest in themselves, not in others. We want them to be both more and less selfish, in a society that is constantly redefining what "selfish" means. And because they are women, their lapses from "good" behavior are seen as enormously threatening. Just as women who have abortions call into question the boundaries of self and other, of motherhood and marketplace, so, in a more subtle way, do teenage mothers.[14]

These tensions between self-supporting work in the marketplace and the needs of the family, between self and other, fuel a growing uneasiness over welfare. In a country with a long (though ambiguous) history of attention to vulnerable children, many citizens have come to accept unquestioningly the notion that some amorphous "we"—be it the community, society, voluntary agencies, or the government—have a moral obligation to make sure that children born in less-than-ideal circumstances are not condemned to failure before they can walk. But many of these same citizens are rightly concerned about how difficult and costly it is to help children like David. And some people worry that helping mothers like Michelle will merely produce a great many more babies like David.[15]

The public's apprehensions about poverty and dependency are in turn almost always intertwined with questions of race, given America's complex history on the matter. Many readers, in their mind's eye, will immediately see Michelle and her baby as African American, and this is understandable: the public quite commonly thinks of African Americans as prone to bear children at early ages and out of wedlock. The image is not false—but it's not entirely true, either. African Americans, who make up only about 15 percent of the population of teenage girls, account for more than a third of all teenage mothers. And whereas six out of every ten white teenagers who give birth are unmarried, among black teenagers the ratio is nine out of ten.[16]

But although African Americans do account for a disproportionate share of births to teenagers and unmarried women, unmarried African American teenage mothers are not, statistically speaking, typical unwed teenage mothers. In 1990, for example, 57 percent of all babies born to unmarried teenage mothers were born to whites.[17] And since 1985, birthrates among unmarried white teenagers have been increasing rapidly, while those among unmarried black teens have been largely stable. (Women of all ages—both African Americans and whites, married as well as unmarried—have been having more babies since 1988.)

Some commentators, among them Charles Murray, who has long been a critic of welfare policies and their putative effects on illegitimacy, say that the rising birthrates among white unmarried teenagers presage the growth of a white underclass, which will take its place alongside historically disadvantaged African Americans. In essence, Murray argues that as racial differences become less important in the life of the country, Americans will separate into two new nations—no longer black and white, but married and affluent on the one hand and unmarried and poor on the other.[18]

So Michelle at her algebra exam and David at his bead game have come to represent a tangle of difficult issues—pertaining to sex, marriage, teenagers, race, dependency (as the condition of those who accept means-tested support from the government is conventionally labeled)—that confront the United States on the eve of a new century. If we queried a stranger on the street and a neighbor over coffee, we would not be surprised to find that they, like much of the American public, find early pregnancy a very serious problem. Or that they have concluded that doing something about "babies having babies" is one way of confronting these troubling issues.[19]

As with many issues that arouse a great deal of public worry and passion, that of "teenage pregnancy" is complex in nature and a challenge to conventional wisdom. Not only are Michelle and David more likely to be white than black, but as a high school student Michelle is younger than the statistically typical teenage mother. The majority of teenage mothers—almost six out of ten—are eighteen or nineteen when their babies are born, and they are legal adults in most states.[20] Furthermore, although many people worry that pregnancy among teenagers has attained "epidemic" proportions, teenage women right now are having babies at about the same rate as they have for most of the century. The "epidemic" years were the 1950s, when teenagers were having twice as many babies as they had had in previous decades but few people worried about them.[21] Even the teenage mothers who arouse the most concern—those who are under fifteen, the "babies having babies"—are simply doing what such "babies" did in the 1940s and 1950s, although they are more visible now than their counterparts were then.[22]

Of course, it is true that in the 1950s almost all teenage mothers (in fact, almost all mothers) were married, at least by the time their babies arrived. But within the broader context—the number of babies being born to unmarried women—teenagers account for only a small subset of the problem. Two-thirds of unwed mothers are not teenagers, and in fact about one-fourth of America's unwed mothers are actually "no longer wed" mothers—that is, women who once were married but are not at the time their baby is born.[23]

Out-of-wedlock births are becoming more common around the globe. In Europe, the proportion of babies born out of wedlock has doubled and tripled in the past twenty years. Many people assume that this is because European welfare states support single mothers (and the poor overall) more generously than the U.S. government does. And this belief is prevalent in a more extreme form: some people believe that unwed mothers (especially teens) get pregnant and have a baby just to get a welfare check, and that consequently it's not surprising that European countries have increasing rates. But all industrialized countries, including the United States, are cutting back on welfare provision as a result of the tightening global economy, and out-of-wedlock births have responded by *increasing*. In the United States, the real value of a welfare check has been declining since 1973, even as women of all ages were choosing more often to become single mothers.[24] In fact, the nation with the sharpest increase in the proportion of babies born out of wedlock has been England, which has instituted conservative, anti-welfare policies: in the early 1970s England had a lower proportion of out-of-wedlock births than did the United States, but after twenty years of Thatcherism the figure has quadrupled.[25]

Yet unmarried parents in England have not for the most part been teenagers. Throughout modern Europe, parenthood has historically been limited to older individuals, and teenage mothers have been found only in those countries on the periphery, such as Greece and Portugal. But the United States has always had an anomalous birth pattern. Compared to Europeans, Americans start their families at a younger age, and have done so for a very long time. In the 1950s, for example, there were more married teenagers in the United States, as a proportion of the age group, than in any other first-world country.[26]

Similarly, the rates of abortion among women of all ages are much lower in most European countries than they are in the United States, despite the fact that (according to the limited data available) teenagers in Great Britain, France, Germany, and Scandinavia are about as likely to be sexually active as those in the United States. Although European teenagers have sex—and, like their American counterparts, are increasingly doing so outside marriage—they are much less likely to seek abortions, or to get pregnant in the first place.[27]

Finally, despite what we all think we know about motherhood among teenagers and its effects on later life, having a baby as a teenager does not inevitably lead to abbreviated schooling and economic hardship, either for the mother or for the child. According to some older sources of data, pregnant teenagers *were* very likely to "truncate" their education, as the experts put it—but this curtailment resulted not so much from pregnancy per se as from the strictures that banned pregnant teachers and students from school grounds. Prior to 1975, when such policies were outlawed nationally, pregnant schoolgirls were "throwouts" more often than "dropouts."[28] Now that secondary schools often have daycare facilities like the Sullivan Center, students who become pregnant in high school are increasingly likely to graduate and are beginning to do so at rates approaching those of nonpregnant teens. This is all the more surprising since the kinds of young people who get pregnant (and, in these days of legal abortion, *stay* pregnant) are usually the kinds of young people who are floundering in school long before a pregnancy occurs.

So if the easy assumptions about early pregnancy (that there's an epidemic of early births, that unwed mothers and teenage mothers are one and the same, that being a teenage mother is a short, quick route to poverty) aren't quite tenable, what do we know about pregnancy among teenagers? How did we come to think about it as a social problem? And what can we—should we—do about it?

In most of the public discussion of early pregnancy and motherhood that has taken place to date, the question about what we *should* do has predominated. Since pregnant teenagers in general and teenage mothers in particular raise such troubling questions about sex and gender, poverty and welfare, selfishness and altruism, self-indulgence and self-discipline, there is something approaching a consensus about what they and we should do. For their part, teenagers shouldn't have sex; if they have sex they should use contraception; if they get pregnant despite using contraception, they should have an abortion or give up the child for adoption; and failing all of that, they should marry the fathers of their babies. In terms of that amorphous "we" of the public, our obligation is to use moral suasion, economic incentives, and the whole repertoire of public policy to enable and sometimes coerce teenagers to do the right thing.

The only problem with such a consensus about what teenagers should do is that it seems to be falling on remarkably deaf ears. The picture here is a mixed one: teens are having more sex at the same time that they are using more contraception and using it more effectively. Compared with teenagers of twenty years ago, today's teens are getting pregnant less often but are also more likely, once pregnant, to go ahead and have their babies. Moreover, these days very few teens give up their children for adoption, and relatively few get married in order to make their babies "legal"—the two really notable revolutions in this area of American life.

On the national level it seems that society has recreated a situation familiar to all families with teenagers: adults are expressing strong, even violent opinions about what teenagers should be doing, and teenagers are just not listening. Not surprisingly, U.S. public policy concerning early pregnancy reflects the rather limited set of options that frustrated adults have at their disposal in the face of recalcitrant teenagers. Easygoing, liberal people conclude that the problem is merely lack of information: if adults just tell teenagers more clearly what they should do and why it's good for them, they will do it. More old-fashioned and authority-conscious people conclude that the problem is one of incentives and controls: if adults just cut off teens' allowance and limit their access to those privileges that society has under its control, teenagers will straighten up and do the right thing.

Neither of these strategies is working very well at present, and it is probably a waste of time to expend much more energy in this book or elsewhere debating whether "soft" or "tough" love is more effective in combating early pregnancy. The real question here is why teenagers do what they do, and how the world looks from their vantage point. Clearly, teenagers are not ignorant victims, but neither are they rational actors. The declining value of a welfare check over the last twenty years, and the increasingly tight eligibility requirements for receiving one in the first place, should make it immediately clear that if teenagers are simply "investors" they are exceedingly foolish ones.

Luckily, more than two decades of research on early pregnancy have given us a rich and complex body of information about teenagers and why they do what they do. The short answer to why teenagers get pregnant and especially to why they continue those pregnancies is that a fairly substantial number of them just don't believe what adults tell them, be it about sex, contraception, marriage, or babies. They don't believe in adult conventional wisdom—not because they are defiant or because they are developmentally too immature to process the information (although many are one or the other and some are both), but because the conventional wisdom does not accord with the world they see around them. When adults talk to teenagers, they draw on a lived reality that is now ten, twenty, thirty, forty or more years out of date. But today's teenagers live in a world whose demographic, social, economic, and sexual circumstances are almost unimaginable to older generations. Unless we can begin to understand that world, complete with its radically new circumstances, most of what adults tell teenagers will be just blather.

As we will see, the issue of early pregnancy assumed public importance in the early 1970s, ironically a time of *declining* birthrates among teenagers. Yet many other changes were taking place in American society, some directly and visibly relevant to the problem (such as increasing rates of premarital sex among teenagers) and some less obviously related (such as the way gender roles were changing, partly in response to a changing economy).[29] To many people, pregnancy among teenagers became the concrete symbol of many of those unsettling changes and a focus for anxiety over events occurring in a larger arena. A number of the issues surrounding early pregnancy have been worrisome to Americans since at least the colonial period, but they did not become associated with teenagers until the mid-1970s. How and when *teenagers* came to be seen as the core of the problem are facts that need explaining.

We will also examine the controversial question of long-term effects: To what extent does having a baby while still a teenager compromise the life chances of a mother and her child? Overall, there is no question that teenage mothers and their children will be much worse off in almost all respects than they would have been had the woman given birth later in life. But is this due to what some call "untimely" parenthood, or are other factors at work? As we will see, arriving at Michelle's position is a long and drawn-out process; typically the young woman is disadvantaged in life and discouraged in school long before conception occurs.

And we will consider another major social change: the revolution that has taken place in the lives of wealthy and middle-class women. Whereas in the 1950s and 1960s most American women had their first babies either during or just after their teen years, now affluent women are waiting until their thirties, forties, and—given new advances in reproductive technology—even later to have their first babies. Thus, a sixteen-year-old mother seems much younger today than she did in the fifties and sixties, when she was only a few years younger than most first-time mothers. This revolution has had little effect on the lives of poor women (that is, those who were poor before they ever become pregnant). Such women have held to the traditional pattern of bearing children early in life. So although it is true that young mothers tend to be poor women, it is much more meaningful to say that poor women tend to become young mothers.

Both groups of women—poor teenage mothers, such as seventeen-year-old Michelle, and older, more affluent women seeking a pregnancy for the first time—are trying to come to terms with profound, indeed epochal shifts in American life that involve sexuality, parenthood, marriage, work, and the larger economy. Michelle and David represent only the aspects of these shifts that have attracted the most attention and concern. The affluent unwed older mother is rarely seen as a social problem, and few studies have been conducted to examine her motives. But in order to appreciate Michelle's situation fully, we must see her in a larger social context, one that includes "old" and "young" mothers alike.

In this book we will look at what American society can and should be doing for teenage parents and their children, as well as ways in which teenagers might be persuaded to postpone childbearing. The discussion will be shaped by what is sometimes called the social-construction model of analysis. This model assumes that whatever the "facts" about pregnancy and parenthood among teenagers, the public is nonetheless concerned because teenagers and their pregnancies have come to represent a host of other worrisome changes that are deeply rooted in American society—changes involving race, age, gender, and poverty.

Yet to say that parenthood among teenagers is not the problem we think it is, and that people like Michelle and David are not the people we think they are, is not to say that there is no problem at all or that the problem has been "socially constructed" in all its aspects. After all, there must be reasons for the fact that an increasing number of affluent American women are choosing to postpone childbearing, for the fact that rates of pregnancy among teenagers in advanced European countries are uniformly lower than those in the United States (although the rates in other "frontier" countries— Canada, New Zealand, Australia—come closer), and for the fact that motherhood among young women, especially young unmarried women, is increasingly concentrated in the disadvantaged groups of our society, both white and minority. And what is the effect on children when their parents are very young, especially if these parents come from the poorer communities of America? Why is it that young mothers are especially likely to become single parents, and what does this fact mean?

In short, how can society's concern about teenagers and their babies be mobilized to good effect? How can such anxiety be made less confused and inchoate—be made to reflect real problems? Most centrally, how can society ensure that this anxiety—which relates to sexuality, race, poverty, gender, and a changing world economy—not simply exacerbate the existing problems of young women and their babies? Both the Clinton administration and the Republican-dominated Congress, despite their many differences, agree that efforts to reduce the rates of pregnancy among teenagers should be the cornerstone of any welfare reform plan. But the ambitious schemes that have been proposed will almost surely fail, as their predecessors did, because they are based on a fundamental misunderstanding of the problem; and there is a very real risk that yet another failed program will lead to even more draconian and punitive measures aimed at young women.

Michelle and David represent a challenge to American social attitudes and policies, one whose contours are only now becoming clear. As we consider the young woman at her algebra exam, her baby at play at the Sullivan Center, and the young man who cannot earn enough money to support that woman and child, we owe them our clearest thinking. In trying to find a way to better their lives and the lives of others like them, American society will have to confront some hard choices—choices that it would be easier to avoid facing. But to give these young people anything less than the nation's best effort would be a tragedy. For better or for worse, they are America's future.

2

BASTARDY, FITNESS,

AND THE INVENTION

OF ADOLESCENCE

When Americans today talk about "babies having babies," their thinking is shaped, whether they know it or not, by discussions that have been going on for the better part of three centuries. The Puritans, for example, were keenly aware of the perils of young love, and expended a great deal of energy trying to keep unmarried young people from yielding to temptation. But even with this level of vigilance, Puritan society had its share of premarital sex, out-of-wedlock births, and babies who came along just a little too soon after marriage.[1]

The kinds of concerns that troubled the Puritans—the moral problems posed by sex without marriage and the economic problems posed by babies without fathers—are still rife in the United States, together with a host of more recent worries about such things as who should have children and when, and what kinds of resources are needed to raise a child successfully. So when Americans talk about pregnancy among teenagers, they are talking about something which is both very new and very old. New in the 1970s was the focus on pregnancy, which for Americans of the late twentieth century signals the existence of legal abortion and the realization that not every pregnancy becomes a birth. New, as well, was the focus on teenagers; the Puritans would never have restricted their concerns to people under twenty.

But three major strands in the current discussions about teenagers and pregnancy have deep roots in U.S. history. These have to do with who is "too young" to have a baby, with childbearing by unmarried women, and with the levels of education and income that make women and men "ready" to have a baby—criteria that earlier generations referred to as "fitness" for parenthood. Is the American public primarily concerned with the *age* of the young people involved? If all of the women currently considered pregnant teenagers would just postpone pregnancy until after their twentieth birthday, would the critics be satisfied? Or, in contrast, is the public really worried about what earlier centuries called "bastardy"—children born out of wedlock? If so, and if the approximately 12,000 girls under age fifteen who have children each year all managed to marry before giving birth, would this be considered a satisfactory solution to the problem? These questions touch on the issue that was of greatest concern to the Puritans and that still bothers many Americans today—namely, the question of what kinds of people should have children and what determines when they are "ready" to do so.

As formulated in current American discussions about the matter, the issue of pregnancy among teenagers incorporates elements from all three of these historical debates, often in ways that are at odds with the facts. Since the end of the nineteenth century, Americans have come to take it for granted that adolescents are too young for childbearing, an idea the Puritans would have found astonishing. In fact, two-thirds of all teenage mothers are eighteen or nineteen—adolescents only in the generous sense of the term, and hardly the "babies having babies" of public debate. Even very young mothers, those under fifteen, have been bearing children at about the same rate for most of the past seventy years. Not only do many people underestimate the average age of teenage mothers and imagine them as unmarried and poor, but they also assume that early childbearing leads inevitably to a life of hardship and stress which could be avoided if young women would simply postpone their childbearing. As we saw in Chapter 1, all of these notions are mistaken.[2]

Although the debate over early pregnancy shows a great deal of historical continuity, Americans of the late twentieth century evince some new anxieties that have come to be attached to the problem. If we are to understand present-day attitudes toward early pregnancy and childbearing and understand how, in the past twenty years, those attitudes have come to focus almost exclusively on teenagers, we must trace back the roots of society's thinking about teenagers and their pregnancies.

CHILDREN OF UNMARRIED PARENTS

Perhaps the oldest issue related to pregnancy among teenagers is the dilemma of children born out of wedlock. In colonial America, bastardy was of enormous concern because it resulted from sexual transgression—a sin in the eyes of the Church—and often created an economic burden.[3] A child born out of wedlock was likely to become a public charge, and small, rural, economically pressed communities found it hard enough to support children who had lost a parent, much less children who never had both parents to begin with.[4]

For these reasons, the colonies punished bastardy with great harshness when it was discovered. In the seventeenth century a Maryland court sentenced one Agnes Taylor, an unmarried woman, to be given twelve lashes "in the Publicke Vew of the People" for having borne a child out of wedlock. In Maryland the maximum punishment for this misdeed was thirty-nine lashes; in Connecticut it was ten lashes and a fine of five pounds; in Massachusetts it was a public whipping or a fine of ten pounds. Many of these laws applied in theory to both men and women, but women were more likely to be convicted (their relationship to the child being more visible) and, lacking property that would enable them to pay fines, were more likely to be whipped.[5]

Yet babies born out of wedlock continued to pose a problem for colonial communities. The little historical information that exists suggests that the number of such children may have increased throughout the colonial period, especially toward the end of the seventeenth century, and may have accelerated markedly in the second quarter of the eighteenth century.[6] Despite the severe penalties, the reluctance of communities to support illegitimate children, the stigma imposed on single mothers by public and religious sentiment, and the vigorous surveillance of the young and unmarried, babies conceived out of wedlock were a familiar part of life in the American colonies.

In those days, when a woman was discovered to have conceived a child out of wedlock, the solution was likely to be the one that has been standard throughout much of American history—namely, a hastily arranged marriage. Such marriages were surprisingly common: perhaps as many as one bride in ten in Massachusetts and one in three in the Chesapeake Bay colony were pregnant when they married. The Puritans carefully kept track of pregnancies and births, and fined the parents of babies that came along too soon. In 1652 a certain Nicholas Davis and his wife were fined for having a child "five weakes and four daies before the ordinary time of weemen after marriage."[7]

When a marriage could not be arranged, town officials would try to ascertain the father of the child in order to make him financially liable for its upkeep. Colonial Quakers punished unmarried women who did not name the father by expelling them from the community (thereby, according to one demographer, seriously reducing its size), and the Puritans expected midwives to cross-examine unmarried women in labor so as to learn the father's identity. In those days an accusation of paternity from a woman in labor had much the same force as a deathbed confession: it was assumed to be true.[8] The court records of Puritan communities and other settlements contain numerous documents concerning paternity cases. Needless to say, the courts were usually inclined to protect the financial interests of the towns.[9]

Once the father was identified, he was typically charged a sum for the maintenance of his offspring, at least until the child could be apprenticed or placed in another family to earn his or her keep.[10] Maryland was so intent on preventing births out of wedlock that in 1657–1658 it began implementing a novel penalty: any man who was convicted of fathering an illegitimate child was forbidden to testify in court or to hold office.[11]

During the colonial period some men and women had no choice but to bring bastard children into the world. Slaves and indentured servants, for example, usually had no legal right to marry; and between 1691 and 1741, Virginia, Massachusetts, Maryland, Pennsylvania, and North Carolina passed laws that denied even free African Americans and whites the right to intermarry.[12]

Slaves, of course, were legally considered property, and this status overrode any questions about the legitimacy of their children. A child born to a slave woman was a slave and hence lacked all rights. A child born to indentured servants was born a bastard, and often the mother's period of indentured servitude was extended to cover the time during which she had been pregnant and unable to work. (Some unscrupulous masters impregnated their women servants as a way of extending their servitude. This happened often enough for some communities to decree that when a woman's master was the father of her child, her term of service had to be sold to another.)[13] Offspring of racially mixed marriages (even when both parties were free) were, by legal definition, illegitimate, since no legal marriage could be contracted between partners of different races.[14]

In the eighteenth century the economic burden imposed by dependent and fatherless children became an even greater concern than the immorality of extramarital sex. Penalties for fornication were lightened, while communities made more strenuous efforts to assign financial responsibility for bastardy.[15] As part of this process, public policy for the first time officially confronted a dilemma that is still a policy issue today. On the one hand, reformers wished to protect bastard children, arguing that innocent children should not bear the brunt of their parents' bad behavior. Moralists, on the other hand, warned that this was a false kindness: alleviating the dreary lives of such children would only lead to an increase in their numbers. Eventually, policymakers chose to protect children.[16]

For their part, reformers defended child protection on both moral and practical grounds. Morally, protecting children seemed increasingly right in a society that was coming to value (and at times sentimentalize) childhood. Practically, making it harder for children to be declared bastards (and thus making it easier for them to be legitimated or made legal heirs) ensured that they were less likely to become public charges.

The changes proposed by reformers were consonant with an American temperament that valued and facilitated marriage, recognized the limitations of a mobile society, and distrusted European attempts to protect the "purity" of the marriage contract. American legal treatment of bastard children was quite liberal compared to the treatment they received in England. Courts there, for example, had traditionally sought to preserve the clear boundaries of marriage; any irregularity in procedure meant that the marriage was void and the children illegitimate.[17] In contrast, American courts and lawmakers made every effort to protect children, even going so far as to create, in the nineteenth century, a legal fiction known as "common-law marriage," according to which people who acted as if they were married were, in fact, married.[18] American practice also legitimated children born of annulled marriages (marriages that, retroactively, were found never to have taken place). So committed were Americans to this principle that they even allowed children of polygamous—that is, Mormon—marriages to be recognized as legitimate. And children could be legitimated after the fact if their parents subsequently married. (The one group ignored in this eagerness to legitimate consisted of children born of unions illegal under miscegenation laws.) In English law an out-of-wedlock child was legally *filius nullius,* literally a "child of no one," with no legally recognized relatives. Yet American courts increasingly permitted unmarried parents to forge legally recognized bonds with their children and tended to treat any relationship that resembled a marriage as a legal union.[19] In short, Americans fundamentally transformed family law as it pertained to bastard children, in order to reflect new social needs and values.

In the late 1800s and early 1900s, attitudes toward bastardy changed yet again. What had originally been viewed as a moral problem with financial overtones, then as an economic problem with moral overtones, increasingly came to be seen as a *social* problem, an index of what was wrong with society. Women reformers, mobilizing for the first time *as women,* engineered a new way of talking and thinking about "women in trouble." Whether prostitutes, abandoned mistresses, or unmarried mothers, such "unfortunates" were now defined as victims of social and economic circumstance rather than as moral pariahs. The reformers, who came out of a rich evangelical tradition, were armed with an implicit (and at times explicit) critique of gender relations. Most centrally, they saw themselves as not so different from the women they wished to help: anyone, they argued, could fall prey to sin and to the devil in the person of men. One of the earliest of these crusading groups was the New England Female Reform Society, whose journal, *The Friend of Virtue,* publicized the stereotype of the "ruined" woman that would endure for the better part of a century: a virtuous, innocent woman, often from the country, who had been betrayed by a selfish, wealthy, usually urban "cad."[20]

In the closing days of the nineteenth century, as urbanization and immigration were causing America's social ills to spread, reformers' concern came to focus more narrowly on unmarried mothers. By 1900 the Florence Crittenton Homes, originally founded in 1883 as refuges for "fallen women" (that is, prostitutes), and Salvation Army shelters, opened in the 1880s for "the drunkard, the drug addict, the homeless, the prostitute," had become almost exclusively homes for unwed mothers.[21] The shift from a broad concern with "fallen women" to a concern with "ruined girls" is evident in the rapid proliferation of Crittenton and Salvation Army homes in their new incarnation as homes for unwed mothers.

The United States had fourteen Salvation Army homes by 1904 and seventy-eight Crittenton homes by 1909. One Crittenton home was reserved entirely for African American women, and in 1909 W. E. B. DuBois noted that there were seven other homes of this type, run by various organizations.[22]

During the Progressive Era (conventionally dated 1880–1920), the public's concern with unmarried young women dovetailed with a growing attention to children; unmarried mothers and their children came to be seen as an increasingly appropriate group for social reform. Then, as now, changes in the American family and in the larger social order—changes precipitated by immigration, the rise of cities, and altered sexual and social mores—led many to infer that there was a deep crisis in American society, one most clearly manifested in what was widely seen as a breakdown in the family. Reformers concluded that giving children the "best start in life" would solve, and in many cases prevent, the social problems whose effects seemed so evident.

Reformers and policymakers believed that healthy children in healthy families were an essential ingredient in a long-range reform strategy that would eventually eliminate poverty, delinquency, overcrowded living conditions, and other social ills. They worried that children, especially poor and immigrant children, if left unattended by society, would grow up to create such dire social problems that the republic itself would be imperiled. Progressive reformers focused on children because these innocents were seen as more worthy of attention than "corrupt" adults—a theme that would recur with some regularity in American history and that has particular resonance with the modern theme of "babies having babies."[23]

That the public's views of bastardy were changing is apparent in the evolving terms of the discourse. From the colonial period onward, children born to unmarried parents were known as bastards and the problem they represented was known as bastardy; but by the mid-nineteenth century they were being described less judgmentally as "illegitimate." On the eve of the new century, as a broad-based "childsaving" movement was taking shape, reformers advocated using the still more neutral phrase "out-of-wedlock," because such language would not stigmatize the child.[24] One commentator, writing in a Crittenton publication, made a point that would have seemed distinctly odd a century earlier:

In the whole range of human relations the one example in which injustice may be said to be absolute, and in which it is instantly admitted to be so by every mind, is the fastening of the stigma of illegitimacy on the child of unmarried parents. Slowly the civilized world is working away from this refined cruelty. In its reappraisal of old habits of mind the new spirit of the times need not linger over this a single minute before rejecting it as archaic and absurd. And in this respect it but swings into step with the Florence Crittenton Mission, whose unceasing insistence on fair play for these nameless little ones, so many of whom have been ushered into the world under its auspices, has been of incalculable influence in lightening the bar sinister.[25]

In 1917, in a decision holding that illegitimate children could inherit benefits (a pension) owed to their natural father, a Connecticut court made much the same point: "We are unable to discover how the cause of morality is to be advanced by the treatment of innocent children, although born of illicit relations, as so far outcasts from the social and legal pale that they are to be denied the benefit of those beneficial provisions which our law has adopted for the care, welfare and maintenance of those who, helpless of themselves, are dependent."[26]

As out-of-wedlock children and their mothers were increasingly perceived as social problems in need of communal money and care, they also came to be seen as appropriate targets for governmental investigation and reform. An early sign of this new attitude was the establishment of a federal Children's Bureau in 1912. One of its first surveys, conducted in 1914, concerned illegitimate children in Boston; the study revealed that babies born to unmarried parents had mortality rates three times higher than those of other children. The bureau found similar conditions in New Bedford, Milwaukee, and Baltimore.[27] Clearly, illegitimate children were at high risk and needed government intervention to alleviate their plight. The pressure to assist such children intensified. In 1926 a researcher with the Children's Bureau pointed out a fact that was to become one of America's most urgent social concerns: she noted that fully a third of the illegitimate children born in an unspecified large city were dependent on public or private childcaring or childsaving agencies—that is, were on welfare.[28]

During the Progressive Era, reformers initiated not only new ways of thinking about illegitimacy but new ways of dealing with it. In earlier centuries, the policy had been to make fathers financially responsible for their illegitimate offspring and often to expel unmarried pregnant women from the community. But by the turn of the twentieth century the saving of "unfortunate" women and children had been transformed into a professionalized enterprise run largely by women and had became a legitimate topic of government concern.[29] The plight of women abandoned and abused by men, and the needs of their illegitimate children, evoked for the first time an official language of compassion instead of condemnation and an awareness of society's stake in the future of these children.

All of the apparatus that came to surround illegitimacy—homes for unwed mothers, an emphasis on "understanding" out-of-wedlock births, and a network of social workers charged with looking out for the best interests of the children—were largely products of the Progressive Era. Americans had once shunned community responsibility for children born to the unmarried; now, in response to the urging of Progressive reformers, they were coming to accept that children who lacked family resources had claims to protection by the state and were the appropriate subjects of a newly professionalized concern.

Along with this trend came a subtle shift in the way the public thought about unwed mothers and about the reasons for their situation. As the problem of illegitimacy came under the purview of the "helping professions," researchers, social workers, and administrators, many of them women, began to use their newly acquired scientific expertise to redefine the problem and to differentiate themselves from the nonprofessional, religiously motivated reformers who had preceded them. Whereas the nonprofessionals active prior to World War I had viewed illegitimacy as a result of social forces, by the 1920s experts in the field were drawing on the work of Sigmund Freud, especially his theory of the unconscious. They tended to regard "sex delinquency," a newly defined category of behavior that included premarital and extramarital sex and that was most visibly represented by unwed pregnancy, as the product of psychodynamic forces rather than social ones. According to their notions, the fundamental cause of illegitimacy was the "unadjusted girl"—an individual first described by the psychologist W. I. Thomas in 1923.[30] Rather than the victim of some social ill, the unwed mother was now seen as the active (albeit unconscious) agent in her own downfall.

In 1954 Sara Edlin, who for forty years had been the director of a home for unwed mothers, noted the changes that had taken place in the etiology of the "ruined girl." In the past, she said, she would have ascribed the girl's condition to "poverty and lack of access to sex education," but she had since concluded that "the predominant factor in this difficult problem is an unwholesome child-parent relationship"—that is, a troubled relationship between the pregnant girl and her parents.[31] In the same year Leontine Young, another long-term observer of the problem, noted that the unmarried mother "in the truest sense . . . is a victim, not of a seducer, but of herself."[32]

The grounds of the debate over out-of-wedlock pregnancy had thus undergone a radical shift, from sin to individual psychology; but the movement was in fact circular. For the Puritans, sex outside marriage had been a problem of personal immorality. Over the next two centuries, the perceived causes of illegitimacy came to be located in the social arena (particularly in the relationship between the "seducer" and the "seduced"). After World War I out-of-wedlock births were once again seen as the fault of the individual—but now they were considered a sin of psychological rather than moral origin. As the government's role in social issues increased, the problem assumed importance not just for the individual or for reformers but for society as a whole. The state, with its various legal, educational, and preventive capacities, was now seen as the appropriate agent to limit such births.

By 1890 many of the practices and policies we think of as "modern" were already in place. Young women pregnant out of wedlock were, ideally, to enter an institution staffed by professional social workers and administered by physicians. Once the child was born, it would be adopted by a middle-class couple so that it could be brought up in a "normal" (two-parent) family; and the young woman would likewise resume a "normal" (childless) life. Of course, this "treatment" was typically limited to white, middle-class women; right up through the 1960s, most maternity homes remained unwilling to accept African Americans. And since experts saw illegitimate births as a function of psychological dynamics, the fate of an individual woman was often determined by the way in which a particular official evaluated her history or demeanor. Some women who refused to show penitence or to comply with the restrictions in force at such institutions were denied access to the "rehabilitation" that the homes offered. Even when the young women were recalcitrant, however, society tended to agree that their children, at least, deserved some type of support.[33]

Solving the larger problem of how to prevent illicit intercourse and consequent pregnancies was no easier for the Progressives and their successors than it had been for the Puritans. Progressive reformers understood that illegitimacy was a product as well as a cause of social disorder. At different times they advocated sex education, more playgrounds, safer housing, better wages for women (so that young women would be less susceptible to the attentions of wealthy men), better recreational opportunities for boys and girls, and better parent-child communication. And there the matter stood, with only minor variations, until the late 1960s.

HOW OLD IS OLD ENOUGH?

Surprisingly, teenagers—adolescents—did not become a recognized segment of the U.S. population until the early twentieth century. The very word "adolescent" dates only from 1904, when the American psychologist G. Stanley Hall published his monumental book *Adolescence: Its Psychology and Its Relations to Physiology, Anthropology, Sociology, Sex, Crime, Religion and Education.*[34]

It is extremely difficult for us, living in an era almost fetishistically concerned with people's precise age, to realize how recent a phenomenon this concern is. Until well into the nineteenth century, age-based distinctions were quite broad. Prior to the rise of the common school in the early 1800s, people had learned to read and write in a variety of settings (homes, church schools, public schools, academies) in which students of all ages, from young children to older teens, sat side by side. Age-graded schooling dates only from the 1850s, and minimum ages for attending elementary school and high school were not established until the 1870s.[35] Throughout the first half of the nineteenth century, colleges such as Harvard and Yale had student bodies composed of boys and young men ranging in age from fourteen to twenty-six, and advice books written for "young men" aimed at a readership that ranged between fourteen and twenty-one; one author assumed that "manhood" began at ten.[36]

To social historians who study how societies think about age, this is not surprising. As a general rule, complex, well-differentiated age grades are a product of modern industrial life. Earlier generations of Americans, largely rural and agricultural, recognized changes in age over the life course, but those changes, for the most part, were not socially or functionally meaningful. People were tied together by bonds of kinship or interest, not by age.

The stages of youth, maturity, and old age were, just as they are now, part of the human condition; but the boundaries depended less on people's chronological age than on their economic circumstances. In colonial times, for example, children were often apprenticed at the age of six or seven to learn the trade that would become their life's work. (Laws concerning the financial responsibility for bastards often stipulated support until this age, under the assumption that children would subsequently be earning their keep.) Puritan wills recognized such traditional milestones as eighteen and twenty-one, but they often gave children as young as twelve the right to choose their own guardians should their parents die. And a man could become a "freeman"—that is, a voting, fully participating member of the male community—at any age between twenty and forty, depending on when he reached full economic independence.[37] As Howard Chudacoff notes, in the eighteenth century "the term 'youth' . . . could apply to practically anyone between ages seven and thirty. The word 'boy' had mixed implications, referring as it did to a very young male, an unmarried male, and a male servant of practically any age."[38]

During the 1800s, as the United States became industrialized and urbanized, Americans began to treat children as a special category. By the end of the century, they had come to recognize adolescence as a discrete stage between childhood and adulthood, yet the development of this awareness was slow. The earliest child labor laws, which date from the 1840s, established surprisingly low boundaries for the end of childhood: in 1848 Pennsylvania prohibited individuals younger than twelve from working in mines; in 1855 Connecticut decreed that nine was the age at which people could be employed; and in 1866 Massachusetts defined "child labor" as work performed by those under ten. As late as 1881 the American Federation of Labor, in its campaign against child labor, advocated that the minimum age of employment be fourteen.[39]

If individuals acquired the right to enter the working world at an early age, the same was true for two other important "adult" rights—namely, the right to marry and the right to consent to sex. Immediately after the Revolution, Americans confronted the task of establishing the age at which people were legally too young to comprehend the serious responsibilities of marriage. Americans had high hopes for marriage as the moral and social foundation of the new republic, and thus they were concerned to set ages below which "children could neither physically consummate a marriage nor intellectually understand its significance."[40] But the fledgling states, taking English common law as their basis, established ages that to our minds seem shockingly low: twelve for women and fourteen for men. Though few Americans actually married that early (one study has shown that in Connecticut in 1774, 0.9 percent of males and 3.2 percent of females between the ages of ten and nineteen were married), courts and legislators repeatedly affirmed that they could, suggesting that the common-law ages had not been adopted simply out of habit. For example, a New York law of 1830 that attempted to raise the minimum marriage-age to fourteen for women and seventeen for men was repealed soon after its passage. Similarly, a Massachusetts court in 1854 refused to annul the marriage of a thirteen-year-old girl at her mother's request, on the grounds that the marriage was legally binding.[41]

Another indication of the way in which Americans in earlier times thought of age, particularly in conjunction with the issues of sex and pregnancy, is the history of the campaign to reform (that is, raise) the "age of consent." In common law this was the age at which a woman was deemed old enough to decide to have sex; intercourse with a girl below the age of consent, regardless of her willingness, was and still is statutory rape. According to British common law during the colonial period, the age of consent was seven. Today we are astounded that girls of this age were assumed to know enough about sex (or about sin) to make such a decision competently.

In the eighteenth and nineteenth centuries the age of consent gradually rose. States replaced the common law with their own statutes, and some set the age of consent as high as fourteen.[42] In the late 1800s many of the same women reformers who were devoting their efforts to helping "ruined" girls maintained that the low age of consent was part of the problem. In 1885 the Women's Christian Temperance Union (WCTU), the largest mass movement of American women at that time, began a campaign to persuade legislators to protect young women by raising the age of consent.[43] (In those days, of course, women could not vote and all legislators were male.) A survey conducted by reformers a year later revealed that although only the state of Delaware had retained the common-law age of seven, twenty-five states had set the minimum age at a mere ten. As female reformers noted indignantly, the low age of consent meant that men received harsher sentences for stealing a girl's purse than for stealing her "honor."[44]

In 1887 the WCTU, joined by male allies in the Knights of Labor, petitioned Congress with a list of signatures two hundred feet long and half a yard wide. As a result, Congress passed laws raising the age of consent from ten to sixteen in the District of Columbia and the territories. Subsequent campaigns were mounted in 1886, 1893, and 1895.[45] Repeated efforts were needed because legislators proved extremely reluctant to raise the age of consent. Initial successes were often repealed in later legislative sessions, and, after a decade of activism, the WCTU had managed to raise the age of consent in the United States to an average of only fourteen.[46]

The age-of-consent campaigns were among the first in which women reformers and their male allies initiated a form of sexual politics aimed at modifying male behavior. Legislators who opposed the reformers took it for granted that girls of seven could be competent decisionmakers on the question of whether or not to engage in sex. In fact, the main argument against raising the age of consent was that doing so would create situations ripe for blackmail. Inherent in this claim was a belief that girls whom we have come to think of as preadolescents were not only competent enough to decide to have sexual intercourse, but also sufficiently clever to use that competence to compromise men.

Despite the worries of male legislators, new forces were at work changing public notions about the "appropriate" ages for sex and marriage. The causes taken up during the Progressive Era—the plight of "ruined" girls and their babies, the professionalization of social aid—were part of a broad social shift in ways of thinking about children, particularly adolescents. By the late 1800s and early 1900s, U.S. society had begun to treat children as a distinct group—one with its own medical problems (pediatrics was officially organized as a specialty in 1888), magazines, advice books (including sexual-advice books), protective services (the Society for the Prevention of Cruelty to Children dates from 1875), and special needs.[47]

As the United States grew more urbanized, children became something of a leisure class, kept in school by compulsory-schooling laws and out of the workplace by child labor laws. People began to think of childhood as a time of innocence and vulnerability—an attitude that both resulted from and encouraged the process by which children were being excluded from the nation's economic life. Reformers continually evoked images of youthful minds and bodies that, because they were still developing, could not be subjected to adult pressures.

This process culminated in the early 1900s, when the public came to view adolescence—especially female adolescence—as a time in which the individual was particularly vulnerable. The colonial settlers certainly recognized puberty as a milestone in human life, but only at the end of the nineteenth century was it assumed to have certain psychological and social concomitants. As G. Stanley Hall put it, "The dawn of puberty is soon followed by a stormy period . . . where there is a peculiar proneness to be either very good or very bad."[48] Whereas a century earlier adolescents (and even preadolescents) would have been deemed legally capable of getting married and having sex, psychologists such as Hall were now claiming adolescents were not *developmentally* capable of either.

Social policy both drew on and reinforced the new psychological theories. Adolescents were defined as passing through a crucial stage of development; "burdening" them with adult concerns such as work, marriage, and sex—especially the latter two—would impede this development. The belief that children needed to be protected from the adult world until they were "ready" or "fit" to assume adult responsibilities led to a slow rise in the minimum legal age for marriage. By the 1850s the legislatures of many states had begun to raise the marriage-age to sixteen for women and eighteen for men. Yet even as late as 1906, seventeen states and territories still adhered to the old common-law standards of twelve and fourteen.[49]

Since adolescents were considered physically and developmentally unsuited for sex, marriage, and childbearing (physicians began to assert, for example, that until a woman was twenty her pelvis was not fully formed), public policy sought to "protect" young women. In 1899, under the vigorous leadership of Judge Ben Lindsay, Jane Addams, and other Progressives, the states began to establish juvenile courts that would dispense "sympathetic" treatment to young people in trouble with the law, rehabilitating them rather than punishing them. Being a juvenile had come to mean being vulnerable and not fully mature. By 1917 virtually every state had created a juvenile justice system and was no longer incarcerating children alongside adults.[50]

According to the Freudian theories espoused by experts such as Hall, young women who were sexually active in inappropriate ways and at inappropriate ages—who were unable to govern their impulses—needed to be protected from themselves and others; likewise, society had to be protected from them. Such young women ended up in the new juvenile justice system. Whereas young men typically entered this system because they had committed crimes against property or persons, an increasing number of young women were incarcerated for sexual "crimes"—that is, for being sexually active. In the early 1900s reformatories for young women began to spring up all over the United States. Between 1910 and 1920 twenty-three new facilities were opened—as many as had been established in the preceding sixty years. In addition, older reformatories were expanded, and a number of private reformatories were transferred to state control.[51] Although the majority of the young people who came before the courts were male, those young women who did enter the juvenile justice system were more likely than their presumably more violent brothers to be put on supervised probation, to be consigned to reformatories, and to be incarcerated for longer periods—a pattern that has persisted to the present.[52]

DETERMINING FITNESS

When the American colonists pondered the issue of who was fit to assume adult responsibilities, especially the adult responsibility of becoming a parent, they were primarily concerned with fitness to *marry,* since childbearing outside marriage was unacceptable. Suitable spouses were people "such as may be fitt . . . both in reference to their spiritual and outward estate"—that is, people who were both morally worthy and financially secure.[53] The early laws of the colony of New Plymouth contained admonitory clauses concerning "diverse persons unfitt for marriage both in regard to their young years as also in regard theire weak estate": those who were considered too young (a label that, as we have seen, was largely assigned according to their financial means) or too poor were clearly unlikely to make either good mates or good parents. But whereas today society's concern focuses on young women, in colonial times it centered on young men. In the text just quoted, the "unfitt persons" referred to are charged with "practising the enveagling" of "daughters and mayde servants."[54]

Until the mid-nineteenth century, however, courts were generally reluctant to interfere with the right to marry and hence to have children. For much of this period, family influence and economic circumstances served to minimize the number of "inappropriate" marriages. Even when one or both of the prospective spouses suffered from mental illness or retardation, judges were disinclined to use this fact as the sole reason for preventing the marriage. Rather, judges would simply make a subjective determination as to whether the couple could understand the meaning of matrimony and could manage their common affairs.[55]

Prior to the 1880s, there were only two exceptions to this generally laissez-faire attitude toward marriage and childbearing. First, U.S. law forbade relatives to marry each other—a ban that had its roots in medieval canon law. Still, in the United States the statutes governing prohibited degrees of kinship for marriage were much less strict than those in Great Britain, where the legal definition of incest was very broad. The well-known interdiction against marrying one's first cousin gained much of its force during the eugenics movement of the late nineteenth and early twentieth centuries, when popular theory held that first-cousin marriages produced "degenerate" children.[56]

Second, attitudes about who could marry were often influenced by racism—what Michael Grossberg calls the "fault line" that runs through the history of American marriage law. Prior to the Civil War, slaves were not allowed to marry and interracial marriages were prohibited in most states. After the war, when slaves became citizens, the courts recognized their right to marry and recognized as legal marriages the unions that slave couples had established. But in 1864 a new word—"miscegenation"—entered the ·English language, and in subsequent years many states and territories (twenty-eight by the year 1916) ratified laws that forbade people of different races to marry.[57]

Nevertheless, throughout most of the nation's history, the right to marry was subject to only a few limitations—those based on race and consanguinity. American law and public policy tended to protect marriage, to define it broadly, and to see it as playing a fundamental role in shaping the national identity. In the late 1800s and early 1900s, when many people proposed restrictions on this right, it represented a shift in public policy. Those wishing to restrict the right to marry were alarmed by the large-scale social changes then taking place: new waves of immigration, visible signs of spreading poverty, public demands for welfare, and an increase in violent crime. Americans in colonial and pre–Civil War times had tacitly assumed that a restriction on marriage was de facto a restriction on childbearing. Now, however, late-nineteenth-century reformers who advocated limiting the right to marry did so *explicitly* because they believed it was the most direct way of reducing the number of "unfit" children. Elizabeth Cady Stanton expressed this view as early as 1869: only those "who can give the world children with splendid physique, strong intellect, and high moral sentiment, may conscientiously take on themselves the responsibility of marriage and maternity."[58] Stanton, it should be noted, was an ardent supporter of the movement on behalf of "voluntary motherhood"—that is, women's right to make choices about marriage and childbearing.[59] Yet others were less sanguine about the efficacy of voluntary choices. As it became clear that education and social reform would not soon alleviate the problems facing American cities—that social ills could not be eliminated by simply altering the environment—public discussions acquired a more pessimistic tone, one that focused on eugenic and authoritarian solutions.[60]

In the face of what seemed to be rampant social disorder during this period, Americans formed certain assumptions about the nature and consequences of human behavior. Under the influence of the eugenics movement, which preached that an individual was "superior" or "inferior" to others based on his or her genetic makeup, they came to believe that social maladies—crime, drunkenness, prostitution, poverty—resulted not from the environment or bad influences but from inborn characteristics. Furthermore, they were convinced that these problems were beginning to pose an intolerable social and economic burden on the country.

In 1912 Dr. John N. Hurty of the Indiana State Board of Health gave a strongly worded speech advocating that the "feebleminded" (the word was new in those days) be denied the right to have children:

> If the businessman who is in the saddle and who runs things, could realize the vice, crime, misery, suffering, and the heavy burden of taxation caused by feeblemindedness, and then could realize that hygiene knew how to prevent it, all false sentiment and prudery would depart in a hurry, and practical science would have its beneficial say.
>
> The criminally inclined and the feebleminded regard marriage vows very lightly, frequently paying no attention at all to them, not caring or not understanding the situation. Their increasing number is apparent in our statistics, and the expense of maintenance grows annually. Each criminally inclined and each feebleminded person who lives will almost certainly produce his kind and may bring blight and disease into blood of normal character.[61]

Concerns over genetic defects led quite naturally to attempts to keep the "unfit" from reproducing—attempts that led in turn to restrictions on marriage. By 1930 forty-one states had passed laws that denied "lunatics," "idiots," "imbeciles," and the "feebleminded" the right to marry. But whereas previous generations had used common sense to determine who was or was not mentally impaired, experts were now armed with a "scientific" tool: the intelligence test.

Developed by Alfred Binet in the early part of the twentieth century, the test was used to identify the so-called feebleminded. Unfortunately, however, it could not effectively distinguish people who were mentally impaired from those who did not speak English well, could not read, lacked formal schooling, or simply didn't feel like cooperating with the examiners. The situation was complicated by the fact that those eventually labeled feebleminded were often tested initially because they were the types of people who were deemed a burden or a threat to the social body. It was a self-fulfilling cycle: paupers, alcoholics, prostitutes, and immigrants were subjected to testing on the assumption that they were likely to be feebleminded, yet these were precisely the people who tended to have little formal education, to be native speakers of languages other than English, and to lack motivation to comply with the testing procedures. Their scores on the Binet test could hardly be anything but low. Armed with this "evidence," reformers urged legislators to implement social policies based on the premise that such people were mentally deficient to a disproportionate extent.

The conflation of poverty, social deviance, and feeblemindedness became clear in 1907, when the state of Washington passed one of the first laws denying the feebleminded—as well as imbeciles, lunatics, and idiots—the right to marry. The law included in its purview any man who had been in the county workhouse during the preceding five years; it thereby extended the label "unfit" even to the poor or unproductive.[62]

As the unfit came to be seen as a source of widespread social dysfunction, pressure to reduce their ranks intensified. Specifically, the assumption that forbidding the unfit to marry would also stop them from having children began to seem increasingly problematic. After all, "scientific" evidence showed not only that the unfit were genetically and intellectually subnormal, but that they were responsible for a disproportionate share of criminal behavior as well. As the category of "unfitness" became a staple of public discourse, there was considerable confusion about whether people in this category were inherently incapable of making the right choice when it came to having children, or were merely unwilling to do so. Either way, laws forbidding the unfit to marry seemed inadequate to the task, since the unfit—whether from incapacity or criminality—were unlikely to respect such laws in the first place.

Accordingly, the next logical step was to deprive the unfit of the capacity (rather than just the right) to reproduce, and "eugenic" sterilization became a tool of public policy. In 1907 Indiana became the first state to permit forced sterilization of the unfit, including "criminals, idiots, imbeciles, and rapists," as well as the feebleminded. Two years later Dr. H. C. Sharpe, medical director of the Indiana State Reformatory, reported in the *Journal of the American Medical Association* that he had performed more than 400 vasectomies on prisoners, with no "untoward results," and that in all cases the patients were happier and more tractable.[63]

In the following decade sixteen states passed statutes similar to Indiana's, and by 1931 the number had reached twenty-seven. Sterilization laws were controversial, and evoked objections especially from conservative religious groups; in Indiana and New York such laws were eventually declared unconstitutional. Elsewhere, however, courts tended to uphold them provided that due-process rules were met and that the laws did not apply solely to the institutionalized.[64]

Indeed, forced sterilization became a favored remedy of those trying to reverse what they saw as a precipitous decline in Americans' intelligence and vigor. In 1927 the policy was affirmed at the highest judicial level when opponents of sterilization brought the case of Carrie Buck before the U.S. Supreme Court. An inmate in the Virginia Colony for Epileptics and Feeble-Minded, Carrie was scheduled for sterilization on the grounds that she, her mother, and her infant daughter were all feebleminded. To the dismay of the policy's opponents, Justice Oliver Wendell Holmes upheld the Virginia statute providing for eugenic sterilization, and voiced his support for the underlying principles by declaring that "three generations of imbeciles are enough." Sterilization, he maintained, was good public policy: "It is better for all the world, if instead of waiting to execute degenerate offspring for crimes, or to let them starve for their imbecility, society can prevent those who are manifestly unfit from continuing their kind."[65] By 1932 Virginia alone had sterilized 658 people, 446 of them women, and more than 12,000 eugenic sterilizations had been performed nationwide.[66]

Amid the reformist zeal to rid society of undesirable and unproductive elements, the concept of fitness easily became linked with the desire to promote social control and eliminate poverty. In the case of Carrie Buck, there is little hard evidence that any members of her family were mentally impaired. What was incontrovertible, however, was that the Bucks were poor and that both Carrie and her daughter, Vivien, had been born out of wedlock. (In all likelihood, Carrie had originally been institutionalized not because she was feebleminded but because she was the mother of an illegitimate child.) In 1938 experts conducted a review of the sterilization policies at the Virginia institution where Carrie Buck had been confined, and found that "sexual license" had characterized the behavior of all of the women who had been recommended for sterilization. A similar review in California noted that three out of four women sterilized under eugenic sterilization laws had been "sexually delinquent." Clearly, society regarded illegitimacy, poverty, and women's sexual "delinquency" as both a product and cause of feeble-mindedness and as natural indicators of the need for sterilization.[67]

In part because of what some saw as burdensome due-process requirements and in part because of changing attitudes, sterilization laws gradually disappeared from the books. But some states, such as California, made frequent use of them while they were in force (7,000 people were sterilized in that state alone in less than a decade), and even after they fell into disuse the debate about fitness continued.[68] As the courts once again extended the right to marry and limited the scope of sterilization laws, social workers and private physicians took up where state laws had left off, recommending the sterilization of certain individuals and thus continuing to sever the right to marry from the right to procreate. Through the 1960s, doctors and social workers urged disproportionate numbers of poor women—particularly African Americans and recipients of public assistance—to be sterilized, and they seemed to be doing so out of concern over the women's fitness rather than concern for their welfare. The Carrie Bucks of the 1960s were women like the Relf sisters of Mississippi, who were sterilized at the ages of twelve and fourteen for allegedly being feebleminded. Whereas Carrie had been white, they were African American; but they, too, were poor.[69]

Decades later, having become more cynical, Americans realize how tempting it is to see the poor and vulnerable as being that way because of some defect in the individual rather than in the environment, or because of some complex interaction between the two. Yet the debate over fitness continues in various forms, and the kinds of social problems that evoked concern in the early 1900s are now more pressing than ever.

OLD PROBLEMS, NEW PERSPECTIVES

By the end of the Progressive Era, the debates over bastardy, fitness, and the appropriate minimum ages for marriage and parenthood had produced a self-reinforcing definition of the problem of young unwed mothers. Americans now considered adolescence a special developmental stage between childhood and adulthood, and perceived young people in ways that would have seemed astonishing only fifty years earlier. They no longer believed that young women (and to a lesser extent young men) were psychologically, emotionally, or physically prepared for adult responsibilities such as childrearing, and they took it for granted that women who embarked too soon on an adult path were jeopardizing both their future and that of their children. Moreover, such women would contribute to a progressive decline in the vigor of the American "race" and, ultimately, of the republic itself. Once adults came to believe that adolescents were unfit to assume adult responsibilities, they became critical of those who did try to work, marry, have sex, or bear children. These teenagers posed a moral and practical problem—one of particular significance in the case of childbearing because it had implications for a whole new generation.

Young women who were sexually active, particularly if their activity resulted in out-of-wedlock births, continued to represent an economic threat. But the events of the Progressive Era put this traditional issue in a slightly different light. If, as the experts claimed, teenage women were naturally unsuited for adult sexuality, it followed that those who were sexually active could be characterized only as passive victims or deliberate wrongdoers. The notion that "ruined" women had been the victims of unscrupulous men persisted, but nearly a century's worth of reform efforts aimed at controlling male behavior had proved unsuccessful, so policymakers focused their attention on young women instead. In what amounted to preventive detention, young unmarried women thought to be at risk of becoming pregnant because they were sexually active were placed under the supervision of the courts and the probation system—a process facilitated legally by the fact that sexual activity itself was thought to be prima facie evidence of feeble-mindedness or delinquency. Especially disturbing to prevailing mores were the "brazen" girls, those whose sexual behavior and values were at odds with middle-class expectations of purity, modesty, and innocent girlishness. Since existing ideologies had no place for young unmarried women who actively chose to have sex, the logical conclusion was that these women were incapable of making appropriate choices. And since they also tended to score poorly on the Binet test (because they were uneducated working-class girls, or immigrants, or unwilling to cooperate with the examiners), their sexual assertiveness was seen as blurring into delinquency and their delinquency into feeblemindedness. All routes led to the same end: these were women who needed protection, and society needed protection from them.

Whether passive victim or willing participant, the young woman who was sexually active, particularly outside marriage, and particularly when intercourse led to an out-of-wedlock birth, was perceived as deviant, unfit. And the problem did not end with her: her child represented the antithesis of reformers' hopes for societal improvement, by becoming yet another link in a chain of unfitness. Born to an immature and presumably unfit woman, the illegitimate child evoked reformers' worst fears for future generations.

In 1920 Paul Popenoe, a noted eugenicist, wrote that unwed mothers tended to be young, poor, and unemployed; they were of "inferior mentality" (one study conducted in Boston concluded that, out of 468 such women, 100 were "subnormal") and came from homes of "bad character." He concisely summarized the conventional wisdom: "The typical illegitimate child, then, may be said to be the offspring of a young mother of inferior status mentally, morally and economically; and of a father who is probably a little superior to the mother in age, mentality, and economic status, if not in morals."[70]

A number of shifts are thus apparent in the way Americans have historically viewed young, unfit, or unwed parents and the degree to which the individuals involved are responsible for their actions. Americans of colonial times were clear on this point: each individual had the capacity to choose between good and evil and was responsible for his or her choice; the circumstances were irrelevant. But since all mortals were at risk of sin, transgressors could be rehabilitated. Sinners who confessed and took responsibility for their actions were reintegrated as full members of the community.[71] Over the course of time, however, departing from the straight and narrow, whether sexually or otherwise, came to be seen not as something all mortal flesh was heir to but rather as a product of innate badness or incapacity, or perhaps of exposure to a bad environment. Though the shift was profound, it left few clear directions for policy. Should deviants (in this case young unwed parents, usually thought of as young unwed mothers) be condemned and punished, or cared for and rehabilitated?[72]

Echoes of this dilemma can still be heard. Are young unwed mothers rational actors, responding to a welfare system replete with what the economists call "perverse" incentives—incentives that encourage behavior at odds with the common good? Or are pregnant teenagers simply too young to make realistic decisions—simply babies having babies? Young mothers often are all of these things, and more. But the important point here is that three centuries of discussion on these matters have left us with a set of taken-for-granted categories, usually polarized, which shape how we think about these issues—categories which impoverish our thinking and serve to obscure complexity and variety in the lives of young parents. Young mothers are viewed as *either* rational actors *or* victims of adult male lust. Likewise, they are *either* babies having babies *or* cunning women wise beyond their years who exploit a morally bankrupt welfare system.

Deeply woven within these questions of responsibility and treatment is the matter of gender. Again the Puritans had unambiguous beliefs on this issue: men and women were *equally* at risk of sexual sin, although women, being the daughters of Eve, were considered more vulnerable to temptation. But by the early nineteenth century new notions of female character and behavior were making it harder to think of women as active agents in their own downfall, except in special cases. Increasingly, women were seen as the helpless victims of male lust, and the reformist discourse of the period included a powerful stereotype which persisted until the eve of World War I: that of the innocent working-class or country girl seduced and abandoned by a middle-class city man who is heedless of the costs to her. The rhetoric of this discourse, which placed "girls" in opposition to "men," both illustrated and strengthened the prevailing asymmetry of gender roles.

But the movement on behalf of gender equality—which began in the mid-nineteenth century and culminated in 1920, when women won the right to vote—brought new images of womanhood into the public arena. The image of the passive female victim was now increasingly at odds with more active images of women. As women began to participate more fully in civic life and gain more control over their personal and professional lives, reformers turned to psychological theories to explain why young unmarried women were continuing to become pregnant.

Ironically, the focus on the psychological was created at least in part by women newly admitted to the profession of social work, eager to practice the new, "scientific" management of the "unadjusted girl." Although images of "girls in trouble" brought a measure of compassion and institutionalized care, they also meant that women (or, more commonly, girls) were now defined as responsible for the fate that had befallen them, whether this responsibility was rooted in unconscious dynamics or, as it became fashionable to think in the 1970s, in ignorance (about contraception, sex, and other matters).

None of these images of teenage mothers has been able to command the public imagination entirely. In recent years, even as young women have come to be seen as active but ignorant decisionmakers, the public has simultaneously harbored the Victorian image of young mothers as victims of male lust, innocent bystanders amid the drama that surrounds them.

Teenage women, it is argued, are simply the unwitting victims of male stratagems and coercion, and find themselves pregnant because they are forced or misled to their unhappy fate.[73]

As feminist theorists remind us, coerced sexual activity is often a part of the sexual lives of women, regardless of their age. But the important point here is that once again a rather threadbare set of categories is shaping our views of early pregnancy. These categories induce us to label one sex or the other as the main participant in early pregnancy and childbearing, and we forget that pregnancy results from a dynamic that includes two people. Likewise, whichever model we select as *the* paradigm for early pregnancy— that young women are coerced or are psychologically mixed up or are just plain ignorant—we again fail to note the effects of the interaction between individuals and their context.

Finally, in the area of public policy, Americans have debated whether the ultimate goal was to protect the family as a corporate entity or to protect the interests of children born outside that entity. The childsaving movement that arose at the turn of the century showed that Americans were unwilling to penalize children for the actions of their parents, and as the government took on a broader role in solving social problems, citizens came to feel that the state should step in when parents were absent or inadequate. But by the mid-1920s legislators were already expressing concern that the cost of maintaining illegitimate children was placing an undue burden on public coffers.

All of these debates have left their imprint on our thinking about early pregnancy and childbearing. For example, as a residue of nineteenth-century beliefs about the physical limits of young people, many adults have come to take it as an article of faith that teenagers are biologically incapable of giving birth to healthy children. Yet generations of Americans, even as recently as the 1950s, came into the world as the children of teenage mothers and fathers. Many if not most of the physical problems associated with early childbearing stem from the fact that young mothers are poor mothers (about 80 percent of teenagers who had a baby in 1988 were poor or very poor before they gave birth), and poverty, not youth, is responsible for a large proportion of the medical problems they face.[74] In fact, some experts argue that when good medical care, good nutrition, and good prenatal care are available to all women, rich and poor, the teen years might be the ideal time to have a child, at least from the standpoint of physical health.

Likewise, Americans—with their long history of moral and social worries about children born out of wedlock—immediately assume that a child born to an unwed parent is destined for a limited and dreary fate. Often there is considerable truth in this assumption. Children born to unwed parents are more likely to grow up in a single-parent home than are children whose parents are married, and social-science research confirms what most people intuit: that children who grow up with a single parent have, on average, fewer of every kind of resource than do children who grow up in two-parent families.[75] Moreover, out-of-wedlock childbearing, although becoming more common in all ranks of society, still occurs most often among the poor, so that unwed parents are disproportionately likely to be poor and disadvantaged. Consequently, when we look at the children of unwed parents, we are looking at children who risk having only one parent's love, attention, and income to draw on, and also at children who, because they come from poor families, face independent risks of hardship, whatever their parents' marital status.[76]

This is where it becomes important to sort out the historical residue in America's attitudes toward out-of-wedlock childbearing, so that we can think about it clearly when it occurs among teenagers, or among people of any age. (Remember that although a very high proportion of babies born to teens are born out of wedlock, two out of every three children born to an unmarried parent are born to a person who is *not* a teenager.) Fresh ways of thinking about the issue are particularly necessary in view of the significant changes that have occurred in American marriage patterns and family life. For example, it is increasingly true that not all unwed parents are single parents. As with most Europeans, Americans are now much more likely than ever before to bear children in reasonably stable partnerships which nonetheless lack a formal, official marriage tie. By the same token, given that the rate of divorce in the United States is so high, children have no guarantee of growing up with two parents even if they are born to a married couple. And it is a sad fact of American life that the children of divorced couples rarely see their fathers. Contrary to prevailing notions, unwed fathers see their children more often than do divorced fathers who have remarried.[77]

But Americans, with their long-standing concern about out-of-wedlock childbearing, have only two categories for people—"married" and "unmarried"—and overlook all the questions that today are so urgent, occasioned by the profound changes of recent years. Does it really matter whether a mother and father are legally married, so long as their partnership is more or less stable? True, such couples are more likely to break up than are legally married couples, but a quick look at the divorce rates reveals that this is only a matter of degree, not a fundamental difference between the two kinds of couples. And should we focus all of our collective worry on children who are growing up with unwed mothers, when they seem to be seeing their fathers more regularly than the affluent children of suburbia whose fathers are preoccupied with a new wife and family? To put this another way, the children of unwed parents do face some daunting problems growing up, but these problems are now shared by more and more American children. Though in the United States the public habitually categorizes children and their problems according to the legal status of their parents' relationship, we must ask whether this tradition might not have outlived its usefulness, now obscuring more than it illuminates.

The debates we have looked at in this chapter raise a troubling question that nineteenth-century reformers were willing to confront directly: Which is better—to be born to a disadvantaged (poor, young, unmarried) parent, or never to be born at all? Framing the issue as one of early pregnancy has permitted us to evade this question. One of America's national myths has been that if teenage mothers simply postponed childbearing until they were more mature, their lives would improve substantially and the costs to society of early childbearing would decline dramatically. Such mothers would be more affluent, more likely to be married (and stably married), and more likely to bear healthy babies—babies who as adults would be well prepared to compete in the new global economy. But this myth is exactly that—a myth.

Although the evidence is not yet conclusive (we will examine it later in this book), it is clear that persuading young people to postpone their childbearing would result, at best, in only modest changes. Perhaps they would be a little better off financially, perhaps a little more likely to marry, perhaps a little less likely to rely on welfare; but overall, the effects would be small. As reformers in the nineteenth century appreciated (but those in the twentieth century have not), the same social conditions that encourage teenagers to have babies also work to prevent them from ever being "ready" to be parents in the way that a white, middle-class public might prefer. Preexisting poverty, failure in school, a dearth of opportunities for personal and professional fulfillment, persistent divisions between the races, and traditional gender-role expectations all lead both to early pregnancy and to impoverished lives. Since there is a chance that early childbearing may slightly worsen the already compromised lives of the sorts of teenagers who are most at risk of becoming pregnant, any public policy that encouraged people to postpone parenthood would probably be worthwhile. But this would speak very little to the larger problem of how compromised and limited their lives are in the first place. And because it neglects the larger problem, such a policy would surely be hard to sell to teenagers. Teens, unlike reformers, know that the timing of a first birth doesn't make much difference in the grand scheme of things. With respect to the troubles that confront young and poor Americans, early pregnancy—specifically early motherhood—is a symptom, not a cause.

Almost everyone in America has come to believe otherwise, and this is a story in itself, the unintended consequence of a new wave of reform aimed at improving the lives of teenagers. That such a noble aim was transformed over time into a conviction that poor teenagers were bringing most of their troubles on themselves by becoming "premature parents" is one of the ironies of history.

3

POVERTY,

FERTILITY,

AND THE STATE

Although Americans have been worrying since colonial times about the health and fitness of coming generations, only in the nineteenth century did the United States institute formal, legal policies ensuring that some people would never contribute to those coming generations. Limiting the right to marry, incarcerating "wayward" girls, and passing laws to sterilize the poor, the criminal, or the "feebleminded" were different routes to the same end—namely, preventing the "unfit" from reproducing.

But this was only half the story. Influenced by Darwinian thought and its domestic variants, Americans realized that policies to keep the unfit from reproducing needed to be matched with policies encouraging childbearing among the fit. If the first set of policies shapes people's image of teenagers as unfit parents, the second set of policies—and their unintended consequences—explain why almost all of the public's concerns about "unfitness" have come to rest on the shoulders of teenagers alone.

THE BANNING OF CONTRACEPTION AND ABORTION

In the mid-nineteenth century, American observers of social patterns, like observers in Europe, began to notice a curious fact: different groups of people reproduce at different rates, a phenomenon that demographers today call "differential fertility." Of particular concern at that time was the inverse relationship between fertility and social status. The "best" people (those who most closely resembled the observers, usually native-born Protestant whites who considered themselves the highest stratum of society) had far fewer children than people deemed to be of "lesser stock"—immigrants, the poor, Catholics, and blacks. In 1887, for example, the Reverend S. W. Dike noted that the families of foreign-born women were 50 percent larger than those of native-born women. Worse, he warned, "many of the families which are best fitted so far as pecuniary means and social opportunity, are deliberately choosing to be unfruitful."[1] In 1902 Charles Eliot, the president of Harvard, fueled national alarm by noting that Harvard alumni were failing to replace themselves: as a group, they were having children at only 70 percent of the rate needed to replenish their ranks. And in 1907 a much-discussed article described the results of a survey that claimed to have found only fifteen children among the residents of the sixteen most affluent blocks in New York City. The differences in fertility between immigrants and the native-born, between blacks and whites, and between the well-off and the poor were so striking that in 1903 Theodore Roosevelt coined a term—"race suicide"—to describe this long-standing and worrisome phenomenon. Why wasn't the intellectual and social elite of the nation perpetuating itself?[2]

Clearly, the government had to ensure that the "fit" bore their fair share of children, and it did so by limiting access to contraceptives and abortions—both of which, surprisingly, became widely available and technologically sophisticated in the nineteenth century. At the beginning of the century, Americans were using the same contraceptive techniques that humans had used for three hundred years—withdrawal *(coitus interruptus)* and expensive, difficult-to-obtain condoms made from sheep intestines. In 1839, however, Charles Goodyear discovered how to vulcanize rubber, rendering it stronger, more flexible, and less likely to turn brittle in cold weather. This new substance was quickly adapted for making devices to prevent pregnancy. By 1850 Americans had access to relatively inexpensive and increasingly available condoms, vaginal diaphragms (then called "pessaries"), and bulb syringes used for contraceptive douching after intercourse. Abortion technology changed substantially during this period as well. In the early years of the century, women and doctors alike primarily used herbal remedies to end a pregnancy. Modern pharmacological research suggests that some of these treatments could end pregnancy at least some of the time; but as medical accounts of the era show, the remedies were both unpredictable and quite capable of killing the woman. After the Civil War, as physicians became bolder at invading the human body, instrument abortions became more common, and women soon learned how to imitate medical practice and end their own pregnancies. By the 1880s the surgical abortion as we know it was common medical practice, and the hook used for fastening high- buttoned shoes had already become what the coat hanger would be in later decades—a homely tool with which desperate women ended pregnancies they did not want.[3]

Consequently, in the latter half of the nineteenth century the government began to establish policies limiting the ability of native-born white and affluent women to use these more effective contraceptives and abortions for the purposes of "selfishly" evading their "womanly" duties, an evasion that seemed to increase the threat of race suicide.[4] The Comstock Act (1873), which outlawed the mailing of supplies or information pertaining to contraception and abortion, effectively ended the burgeoning trade in rubber contraceptives and abortifacient pills.[5] Many states, as well, passed laws restricting access to abortion. By the mid-1850s, American physicians had begun to decry what they saw as a disturbing trend. Abortion, once thought to be the province of the seduced and abandoned single woman, was becoming common among respectable—even affluent—matrons. In 1864 Dr. Hugh Hodge, a passionate opponent of abortion, wrote:

> Married women, from the fear of labor, from indisposition to have the care, expense, or the trouble of children, or some other motive equally trifling and degrading, have solicited that the embryo be destroyed by their medical attendant . . . This low estimate of the importance of fetal life is by no means restricted to the ignorant, or the lower classes of society. Educated, refined, and fashionable women—yea, in many instances, women whose moral character is in other respects, without reproach; mothers who are devoted, with an ardent and self-denying affection, to the children who already constitute their family—are perfectly indifferent regarding the foetus in utero.[6]

In 1870 a physician in Philadelphia made much the same complaint: "I have been shocked beyond measure by having proposals made to me to procure abortion by women of education and respectable position in society, and who were even professors [adherents] of religion in some cases. They were in all instances married women."[7] Although such partisan statements must be interpreted with caution, late-nineteenth-century physicians did report rates of abortion very similar to those that have obtained in the United States since the legalization of abortion: between a fourth and a third of all pregnancies, they thought, were being terminated.[8]

Physicians led the crusade to make abortion illegal and were remarkably successful. By 1900 virtually every state in the Union had a law that forbade abortion. But despite the fact that contraception and abortion had been banned at both the state and federal levels, the fertility of American women—in particular, that of the "better classes"—showed no signs of rebounding. Whereas in 1800 the average American woman had borne about seven children, a century later this number had been reduced by half.[9]

That American fertility continued to decline is due to an irony undercutting the original logic of the laws banning abortion and contraception. Although state and federal laws limited the rights of *women* to control their fertility, the ban on contraception and abortion was never total. Under the so-called therapeutic exemption, *physicians* retained the right to prescribe contraceptives and perform abortions when, in their professional opinion, such measures were necessary to preserve a woman's life or health. Thus, women of the "better classes"—the original targets of the antiabortion and anticontraceptive laws—were the ones who evaded the strictures: in contrast to poorer women, they could more easily afford the services of a physician and had greater access to contraception and abortion. The courts repeatedly vindicated the right of doctors in good standing to perform abortions whenever they saw fit, and in 1915 a federal Court of Appeals went so far as to hold that the therapeutic exemption applied even to *information* about abortion sent through the mail. Medical journals reported that doctors were performing abortions for a very wide range of reasons: alcoholism in the family, hereditary mental illness—even a family's economic difficulties, which could worsen if the wife had another child.[10]

The medical profession gradually extended its "ownership" of contraceptive practice as well. When Margaret Sanger, America's most prominent birth control advocate, opened a clinic in Brownsville, New York, in 1916, she was arrested under that state's little Comstock Law, which forbade the giving, loaning, or selling of "any recipe, drug or medicine for the prevention of conception." The law did, however, contain an exemption for physicians who prescribed materials for the prevention of disease.[11]

Mrs. Sanger was duly convicted. Though a trained nurse and an expert in birth control, she was not a physician and thus could not claim protection under the exemption. But her legal defeat heralded a greater victory: in the process of upholding her conviction, the New York Court of Appeals affirmed that physicians could prescribe contraceptive devices to protect patients from any disease, not just—as many physicians had thought—venereal ones.

Legal protection under the therapeutic exemption henceforth extended to contraceptives not only for men (condoms) but for women (diaphragms and vaginal spermicides), and a de facto therapeutic exemption for contraception was established, at least in New York State.[12]

Two federal cases further expanded the rights of doctors to prescribe contraceptives. In 1930, in a case known as *Youngs Rubber,* the Second Circuit Court of Appeals declared that the Comstock Law prohibited only "illegal contraception," thus creating by default a new category of "legal contraception."[13] Six years later the same court ratified its reasoning in a landmark case known rather comically as *United States v. One Package of Japanese Pessaries.* The pessaries (diaphragms) in question, addressed to Dr. Hannah Stone (an early advocate for birth control), had been sent through the mail and were therefore in clear violation of the Comstock Law. Yet Judge Augustus Hand, writing for the majority, concluded that the Comstock Law was not designed: "to prevent the importation, sale or carriage by mail of things which might intelligently be employed by conscientious and competent physicians for the purpose of saving life or promoting the well-being of their patients."[14] Although *One Package* was ambiguous on some issues, and although at least two states, Massachusetts and Connecticut, declined to apply the reasoning of the New York and federal courts to their own state laws, the general principle was clear: physicians could prescribe contraception when, in their judgment, it was "medically necessary."[15] The right to use contraception and to have a safe, legal abortion was de facto limited to those who had a personal physician—that is, to those who were well off.

The Comstock Law and state abortion laws strove to maintain public morality by keeping medically dispensed contraception and abortion out of the hands of the poor. Women who could not afford a private physician simply had no options. As a way out of this situation, Margaret Sanger and her followers opened low-cost contraceptive clinics in a number of states; by the end of World War II, there were almost 800 such clinics.[16]

But the Comstock Law and its state adjuncts forced these clinics to keep a low profile, limiting their ability to make their services known, and women had to present clear medical reasons for requesting birth control. Massachusetts and Connecticut summarily closed their few birth control clinics, and—despite the rulings in *Youngs Rubber* and *One Package*—their state courts denied the existence of any exemption allowing physicians to prescribe contraception, even for the protection of a woman's health or life.[17]

Although Connecticut and Massachusetts represented an extreme, many other states limited access to birth control by prohibiting state funding, intimidating those who wished to open privately supported clinics, and restricting access to information about the clinics that did exist.[18] Society's desire to uphold morality, foster proper roles for women, and encourage the "best" people to "reproduce their kind" meant that contraceptive clinics, when they existed, were often unknown to those who needed them most.

Medically performed abortions were also the province of the wealthy. Every published survey of "therapeutic" abortion shows that affluent women were substantially overrepresented.[19] Private hospitals serving the wealthy routinely performed many more legal abortions than did public hospitals serving the poor; within public hospitals, wards for private patients reported more abortions than did public wards, where women depended on charity for their medical care. In addition, poor women and women of color were overrepresented in the ranks of those who came to medical attention because of the consequences (sometimes fatal) of illegal and self-administered abortions.[20]

In sum, a policy originally intended to keep wealthy women from shirking their duty, both to their class and to their gender, had exactly the opposite effect. Public morality demanded that abortion and contraception be outlawed, but practical considerations made a total ban unrealistic. Consequently, physicians assumed the role of intermediaries; it was they who decided when the general ban on contraception and abortion could be breached on the grounds of individual "medical necessity." In other words, there was a working compromise on this delicate issue: the public sector officially defined fertility control as illegal and policed it as such; yet the private sector (the medical profession) was permitted to make exceptions to the rule. So despite the fact that these policies had originated in worries about "race suicide," they succeeded only in ensuring that wealthy women could legally obtain birth control and abortions whereas poor women could not. That old adage—"The rich get richer and the poor get children"—was de facto public policy.

On occasion, of course, the rules were eased, especially during the Depression. A few southern states did permit county health departments to distribute publicly funded family planning information. But such programs were few and far between; on the eve of World War II they existed in only eight states. (The fact that rural poverty, particularly among blacks, was considered a severe problem in the South may have forestalled objections to these efforts.)[21] So powerful was the public perception that birth control was immoral, illegal, and wrong, that even the programs that did exist were very small and very quiet. In 1935 a survey of local federal relief offices revealed that there were some contraceptive programs for people "on the dole," but not one administrator would admit for the record that birth control advice was being disseminated.[22]

Similarly, although birth control advocates persuaded the Roosevelt administration to ensure that the Social Security Act of 1935 included authorization for modest contraceptive programs, the Children's Bureau (later a division of the U.S. Department of Health, Education, and Welfare, or HEW)—which would have been called upon to implement the programs, within a larger set of maternal and child welfare initiatives—completely refused to do anything until the 1940s, when women workers became vital to the war effort and denying them birth control advice would have seemed unpatriotic. As late as 1963 only thirteen states had any tax-supported birth control programs whatsoever, and these were typically small, cautious, and unpublicized.[23]

Since birth control was considered immoral and obscene (immoral because it permitted people to have sex without consequences, and obscene because it related to sexuality), enormous controversy arose whenever birth control supporters tried to change the status quo. Opponents could do nothing to curtail private services provided by physicians to fee-paying patients, but they could and did resist all moves that would have made birth control legal and hence eligible for public funding. The most visible players in these controversies usually were officials of the Catholic Church. In New York, after the ruling in *People v. Sanger* (1918), which permitted doctors to prescribe contraceptives, Catholic spokespersons actively opposed any further liberalization of the state law. When advocates in Connecticut lobbied for a legal exemption so that physicians in that state could prescribe contraceptives to protect maternal life and health (as physicians in other states could), the Church preached sermons against birth control, identified candidates opposed to the legislation, and began vigorous voter-registration drives to oppose the measure. And in 1936, when Ernest Gruening, a physician and an administrator of relief programs in Puerto Rico (where Depression-era poverty was even more severe than on the mainland), suggested that birth control be provided as part of maternal and child health programs, the proposal so enraged Cardinal Spellman that the cardinal took the matter directly to the chairman of the Democratic National Committee.[24]

49

Consequently, until well into the 1960s birth control was unavailable to poor women who had to rely on public hospitals for their medical care. In New York in 1958, Louis Hellman, an obstetrician and gynecologist (who would later become head of HEW in the Nixon administration), created a furor by prescribing a diaphragm for a diabetic patient because he believed that another pregnancy would be injurious to her health. Such an action, well within the federal guidelines established in *One Package* and the state guidelines laid down in *People v. Sanger,* would have been thoroughly uncontroversial had the woman been one of Dr. Hellman's private patients. What made the case problematic was the fact that the woman was a patient at Kings County Hospital, a municipally supported facility, and thus public moneys had paid for her diaphragm.[25]

This opposition to public provision of contraception tended to be the rule rather than the exception. Cook County Hospital, the largest public hospital serving the poor in Chicago, for many years simply refused to prescribe any birth control whatsoever to poor women. In 1963, when the governor of Illinois, Otto Kerner, proposed changing this policy as a way of reducing the numbers of people receiving Aid to Families with Dependent Children (AFDC), he evoked a storm of protest. In Pennsylvania, attempts to make birth control available in public hospitals led to similar results: sixty newspapers ran full-page advertisements signed by all of the Catholic bishops in the state.[26]

People who did not live through that era can get some idea of the fervor of its controversies by looking at the passions surrounding the issue of abortion today. Although Catholics and evangelical Protestants are the most active opponents of abortion, they claim a moral rather than a religious basis for their opposition and hence the right to speak for what they see as the common good. In much the same way, during the first half of the twentieth century Catholic officials were just the most visible supporters of a position that few were willing to challenge: because birth control was immoral, the state had no business providing—or permitting others to provide—poor women with contraception.

Thus, there was a working compromise on the delicate issue of fertility control. Abortion and contraception were illegal, but physicians had the right to modify the nominally strict laws in individual cases. Controversy arose only when the state in its fiscal or legal capacity was required to admit that some women could and did control their fertility. Clearly, what was at issue was women's right to control their fertility. By a curious legal fiction, contraceptives for men—that is, condoms—were legal in almost every state, so long as the purchaser declared that they were intended to prevent venereal disease rather than pregnancy.[27]

Even the knowledge that there was a considerable distance between the laws and everyday practice, as well as major discrepancies between the intent and the effect of these laws, was irrelevant. Sporadic attempts to make the contraceptive laws more realistic were routinely defeated as immoral and dangerous to the public weal; any legislator who supported such efforts would have been committing political suicide.[28] Again, there are parallels with today's debate over abortion: the fact that only poor women are denied reproductive freedom when abortions are illegal is unpersuasive to those who oppose abortion on moral grounds. Many of the arguments being voiced by such opponents—that abortion is fundamentally wrong in terms of the Creator's plan, that it will lead to a devaluation of human life, that it will permit women to be "casual" and "selfish" at the expense of future generations—were the very ones that motivated opponents of birth control. So powerful were these sentiments that they controlled public policy for almost a century.

In retrospect, it is astonishing how quickly these sentiments—and the laws that embodied them—changed. As they did so, poor women and eventually teenagers became the focus of a very different public policy, one that linked contraception and issues of fitness in totally new ways.

THE WAR ON POVERTY

Many events came together in the 1960s to alter the climate of opinion surrounding birth control and, later, abortion. Perhaps most important was the development of the birth control pill (by a Catholic researcher, no less) and, a few years later, of the intrauterine device (IUD). The effect of "the Pill" on American life was enormous. (It is the only pharmaceutical that one can refer to unambiguously with this completely generic term.) Americans now had the ability to control their fertility almost completely; for the first time in history, sex and procreation were truly separate. As a corollary, unwanted or untimely pregnancies came to be viewed as technological failures rather than inescapable realities.[29] The Pill was the first method of birth control for women that was reversible and entirely independent of intercourse; if used properly, it was nearly 100 percent effective and made traditional methods such as the diaphragm and condom seem risky. Introduced in 1960, within five years it had become the most popular contraceptive among married women in the United States.[30]

But the Pill was also the most clearly medical of birth control devices. Since it prevented pregnancy by releasing high levels of powerful hormones into the body, it was considered a safe method only if used under a doctor's supervision and it thus widened the gap between women who could afford medical care and those who could not. Now, however, this disparity caused concern not because it reactivated old fears that birthrates among the affluent would decline but because experts feared it would sustain high birthrates among those deemed unfit.

This time the issue of fitness was concerned specifically with people who depended on what had come to be called "welfare"; the focus had shifted from poor immigrants to African Americans. When Governor Kerner suggested instituting a more humane and logical contraceptive policy as a possible remedy for various social ills, particularly for the high rate of welfare dependency in Chicago, he was simply the first of many to advocate this course. After World War II, Chicago had become noteworthy as a major destination for one of the most massive peacetime migrations in history—thousands of African Americans moving from the South. As these migrants settled in urban neighborhoods throughout the country, their problems assumed national importance.[31]

The poverty of America's inner cities has become one of the central concerns of the latter half of the twentieth century. In trying to explain the persistence and growth of urban poverty, particularly among blacks, sociologists and historians have begun to reexamine the role of the Social Security Act of 1935. This legislation, which laid the basis for the first national welfare system, incorporated racial and gender assumptions that led millions of women to become dependent on the most stigmatized and limited forms of public aid.[32] The original Social Security Act contained several parts, each aimed at a specific segment of the poor: the elderly (who were provided with pensions), the disabled, the infirm, and single mothers. The last group was the target of the section concerning Aid to Dependent Children (ADC), which sought to improve the lot of women trying to raise children without the help of a male wage earner.[33]

Aid to Dependent Children (which in 1961 was renamed Aid to Families with Dependent Children, or AFDC) built on and institutionalized a particular view of women's claims to government assistance: the only women who were regarded as having claims on this assistance were mothers, and "respectable" mothers at that. Between 1910 and 1920, forty states had passed legislation providing pensions specifically for mothers; this aid, a precursor of ADC, had originally been designed to protect an ideal of motherhood rather than real mothers. Only the "deserving" poor woman, a widowed mother leading an exemplary life, was entitled to a pension, and many reformers had envisioned these pensions as a seal of approval for outstanding motherly behavior under difficult circumstances; giving aid to the undeserving, in their opinion, would have diminished the carefully constructed social esteem associated with such pensions.[34]

When ADC became a part of the safety net created by the Social Security Act, women activists insisted that its purview—unlike that of earlier pensions for mothers—extend to unmarried, divorced, and deserted mothers (that is, "unworthy" and "unsuccessful" mothers). But the working assumption behind ADC was that most of the mothers receiving assistance would be widows who had fallen on hard times through no fault of their own. And since in the 1930s and 1940s most single women with children were in fact widows, there was no reason to examine this assumption too closely.[35]

The earlier distinction that many states had made between worthy and unworthy mothers had left an indelible imprint on ADC and AFDC, however. Whereas the original Social Security Act had envisioned a broad range of programs to keep people from need, the actual programs established under the act created a two-tiered, gender-based system. Except for what we now call welfare (that is, AFDC), most forms of aid provided by the original Social Security Act eventually came to be seen as entitlements: people expect them simply by virtue of being citizens. Old-age pensions for all Americans, both those who need them and those who do not, have come to represent "Social Security" in its entirety. They are regarded as rights, and no one regulates how recipients spend their pension money or whether it can be supplemented by additional income.[36] Any legislator who proposes modifying this system does so at the risk of his or her political career. Such pensions—which are actually welfare in disguise, since most workers pay into the system less than they take out in benefits—have become synonymous with the whole notion of Social Security. Yet the "welfare" provisions of the Social Security Act have come to mean something else entirely, namely benefits to single mothers. AFDC benefits have a great deal in common with old-age pensions, in that both are income transfers from one segment of the population to another. But in contrast to old-age pensions (and in contrast to such programs in most European countries), AFDC

53

payments are *not* viewed as entitlements due fellow citizens simply because they are in need. In several fundamental ways, aid to poor mothers is a special kind of safety net and differs from other parts of the Social Security Act of 1935: the levels of AFDC grants were and still are determined by the states rather than the federal government; AFDC was and still is means-tested, such that only those who can demonstrate need are eligible; it was and still is implemented in a highly bureaucratic way. Out of all the programs envisioned in the Social Security Act, only payments to poor single mothers are seen as charity, as having negligible social effect, and as being vulnerable to constant abuse by the recipients.[37]

Reformers originally conceived ADC as a stopgap—a temporary measure that would support needy widows and their children until sufficient numbers of working fathers were covered by other insurance plans designed to protect their families when they died. In the event, however, large social and economic forces conspired to change both the numbers and types of women and children on AFDC. These changes became particularly visible in the sixties. In 1960 only 800,000 families were receiving assistance; a mere five years later, the figure had swelled to one million—a 25 percent increase; and by the end of the decade 2.2 million families were enrolled in AFDC.[38] Also by that time, the typical recipient was no longer the poor but honest widow (whom reformers had usually imagined as white) but the sort of mother—unwed, divorced, deserted—who had historically been seen as unworthy. Exactly as the original framers of the Social Security Act had envisioned, widows came to be covered by other forms of social insurance and thus moved out of the pool of single mothers in need of help from AFDC. In 1939, for example, Congress passed legislation creating Survivors' Insurance, which protected the children of deceased and disabled workers in specific occupations. Survivors' Insurance is funded and administered by the federal government, not the states; it is not means-tested; and its payments are substantially more generous than those of AFDC, so that fewer and fewer widows needed to turn to AFDC.

At the same time, since life expectancy among men was increasing, fewer women were becoming widows, especially at ages when they were likely to have young children. Furthermore, increases in divorce, desertion (often known as the "poor person's divorce"), and out-of-wedlock births meant that "worthy" widows were gradually being outnumbered by "unworthy" single women. In 1947 about half of all single mothers in the United States were widows, another third were married women whose husbands had deserted

54

them, and most of the remaining 20 percent were divorcées; only one-half of one percent of them had never been married. By 1970, however, the population of single mothers had changed greatly: 20 percent were widows, more than half were divorced or separated, and approximately 7 percent had never been married. And by 1990, a mere 7 percent were widows, almost 60 percent were separated or divorced, and one-third had never been married.[39] In four decades the demographic profile of single mothers had almost totally reversed.

This shift intersected with new economic forces that had an especially noticeable effect on African Americans. During and after World War II African Americans began to move out of the rural South in large numbers, fleeing the strictures of legal segregation and new federal policies that had made traditional sharecropping much less profitable for white landowners. In the South they had been largely ineligible for Social Security, since they often worked in domestic and agricultural jobs, both of which were specifically excluded from the original 1935 act.[40] In the North they were more often eligible for Social Security but were rarely covered in full; the range of occupations open to them was still fairly narrow. Consequently, poor African Americans, especially poor mothers with children, tended to be outside the safety net that white Americans increasingly took for granted (programs such as Survivor's Insurance). They were thus overrepresented in the one remaining social insurance program open to them, namely AFDC.[41]

The overrepresentation of African American women in the welfare population was exacerbated by changes in marital and childbearing patterns that would soon characterize all Americans but that became apparent first among African Americans. Until World War II, African Americans were almost as likely to be living in two-parent families as whites, but out-of-wedlock births began to increase sooner in the black community. By 1970, when about 7 percent of all single mothers had never been married, the figure was 3 percent for whites and 16 percent for blacks.[42]

Thus, over time, AFDC became something quite different from the program its framers had envisioned. Political bargains had shaped the very core of the Social Security Act: categories of workers in which southern African Americans were overrepresented had been excluded, social protection schemes had been designed for men rather than for citizens of both genders, and entitlement to benefits such as unemployment coverage, workers' compensation, health care, and Social Security was closely tied to the individual's previous experience in the labor market. As a result of these conditions, people who drew on AFDC tended to be not the "deserving" widows of hardworking men, but women at the edges of the labor market—never-married, divorced, and deserted women who were, moreover, disproportionately African American. AFDC came to be perceived as the last resort of "failures": women who had failed at marriage and whose partners had failed at work. Thus, in the 1960s the idea of parental fitness and concern over birthrates were once again back on the public agenda, but this time the issue was framed in terms of the "excess" fertility of the poor (specifically the "undeserving" poor) rather than the fertility "deficits" of the rich.[43]

At this point in the public discussion, poverty was not yet linked to the problem of births among teenagers. In the eyes of the experts, the most salient fact about single mothers was that they tended to be poor (usually defined as being, or likely to be, dependent on AFDC), not that they tended to be young. Reformers devoted their attention to the fertility of poor women rather than of young women.

In the context of these new attitudes toward excess fertility among the poor, the political relationship between fertility and poverty began to change in the 1960s; nineteenth-century laws on contraception and abortion—laws based on fears of race suicide—were soon to vanish from the books. In the decade after World War II, Americans had begun to take notice of the way in which population was burgeoning in the poorer parts of the world, places where improvements in public health had reduced mortality but not fertility.[44] This unease about world overpopulation (and its alleged effects on global peace and political stability) had its own domestic counterpart: increased worries about the fertility of the American poor, worries exacerbated by the first signs of economic decline among U.S. cities and by rising numbers of AFDC recipients. One commentator claimed that poor residents of inner-city Chicago (that is, Chicago blacks eligible for welfare) had birthrates on a par with those of the people of India.[45] Experts recognized the fact that most middle- and upper-class Americans were controlling their fertility and that increasing numbers of them were doing so with virtually foolproof methods available only from physicians. Yet the poor continued to have far more limited access to birth control.

Discussions about poverty in America had now taken on a distinctly racial cast. They acquired special urgency from some surveys of American contraceptive and fertility patterns undertaken in the early 1960s—surveys whose findings greatly alarmed public officials. For example, a survey on the growth of American Families, conducted in 1960, revealed that 17 percent of white couples and 31 percent of nonwhite couples had wanted no more children at the time their most recent child had been born. Worse, of those families in which the wife had never attended high school (an indirect measure of low income), 31 percent of the whites and 43 percent of the nonwhites said their most recent child had been unwanted.[46] The National Fertility Survey of 1965 yielded similar findings: 34 percent of the poor reported unwanted births, compared with only 15 percent of the nonpoor. Since these same survey data had suggested that nonwhite and poor families actually wanted *smaller* families than did well-to-do people and whites, it seemed clear that poor people had been left out of the contraceptive revolution. More troubling still (given that AFDC rates had gone up by 25 percent in just five years) was the fact that in 1965 only 2 percent of births among the nonpoor were to unmarried people but 16 percent of all births to poor women were out of wedlock, resulting in many babies and mothers likely to need AFDC.[47]

In a much-cited article published in 1968, the eminent demographer Arthur Campbell argued that there were at least 5 million poor women in need of publicly subsidized family planning services; if poor and nonpoor women had had equal fertility, he noted, there would have been about 3.5 million fewer births in the country. In other words, if poor women had had access to the contraception that well-to-do women now took for granted, one out of every three births to poor women would have been (as demographers liked to say) "averted." When poor women were having unwanted, out-of-wedlock births in such large numbers (out-of-wedlock births were assumed to be unwanted births), and when unwanted babies seemed to be swelling AFDC rolls, an archaic birth control policy that kept contraceptives out of the hands of the poor seemed ludicrous, if not tragic.[48] Americans once had worried about declining birthrates among the wealthy; now they worried about "excess" fertility among the poor, specifically the poor who were dependent upon AFDC. The troublesome solutions (such as involuntary sterilization) that, in an earlier era, had been associated with a zealous pursuit of fitness seemed much less relevant when it became clear that poor women were having children they themselves did not want.

The War on Poverty, officially inaugurated in 1964, led to a vast expansion of the welfare state and has been the subject of much recent scholarship. Debated in this literature are questions about the motives behind the War on Poverty, the degree to which it was haphazard or planned, and the identity of its intended beneficiaries (that is, whether it was aimed at urban African

Americans or Appalachian whites).[49] One thing certain is that its architects were deeply convinced that preventing pregnancy was a logical first step in preventing poverty. Under the aegis of the Office of Economic Opportunity (OEO), which administered the War on Poverty, the federal government in 1964 initiated one of its earliest antipoverty efforts: a cautious move into funding birth control for poor women. The first programs were small and very circumspect, limiting their services to married women living with their husbands. Fearful of arousing the kind of noisy opposition that had surrounded Governor Kerner's attempts to initiate a contraceptive program at Chicago's Cook County Hospital only a year earlier, OEO demanded that its early birth control programs eschew all publicity; in its efforts to reverse a century's worth of official public policy on birth control, OEO moved quietly and slowly. Its small pilot program cost a mere $8,000, and in the ensuing four years it spent a total of only $16.5 million (slightly more than one-half of one percent of its budget) on family planning.

The political and legal climate surrounding the issue of contraception was changing rapidly, however. In 1965, in *Griswold v. Connecticut,* the U.S. Supreme Court held that Connecticut's little Comstock Law was unconstitutional and concluded that married couples, at least, had a legal right to contraception. Perhaps in part because the Pill had already become the most widely used contraceptive in America, the decision was accepted with little public protest, even by traditional opponents of birth control. In this new climate, the connection between poverty and "excess" fertility seemed compelling enough to permit various branches of the government not only to sanction the use of birth control but to fund it as well. After 1964 Congress passed a number of far-reaching laws granting more people the right to free or low-cost birth control services, increasing the amount of money spent on such programs, and eventually moving them out of the Office of Economic Opportunity and into the mainstream of the government. For example, in 1966 a bipartisan congressional committee decided that publicly funded birth control would be made available to any woman on AFDC who was older than fifteen, whether married or not.[50] A year later, Congress named family planning as a program of "special emphasis" in the War on Poverty. In fiscal year 1968 alone, OEO spent 10 million dollars on various programs for contraception.[51] Also in 1968, amendments to the Social Security Act mandated that henceforth 6 percent of all Maternal and Child Health moneys be dedicated to family planning and that such services be offered to all past, present, and future AFDC recipients; every dollar of state money used in family planning was matched by three dollars of federal money (increased in 1972 to nine dollars). The amendments also permitted states to purchase family planning services from nongovernmental organizations—often, ironically, from Planned Parenthood clinics, an outgrowth of Margaret Sanger's activism of a half-century earlier. By 1973, federal contributions to family planning had amounted to an estimated $180 million.[52]

In 1970 Congress extended its commitment to publicly subsidized birth control, passing the Family Planning Services and Population Research Act. This legislation established two new agencies within HEW—the Office of Population Affairs and the National Center for Family Planning Services; allocated $382 million for services, research, and training in family planning; and, most important, instituted Title X of the Public Health Services Act, which for most of the next two decades would be the largest source of federal funds for contraception.[53] Congress, obviously persuaded that poor women should not be forced to have children they did not want, children who moreover ran the risk of ending up on welfare, passed this legislation easily: the vote was unanimous in the Senate and overwhelming (298 to 32) in the House.[54]

Even the Nixon administration, not usually considered a strong supporter of either poor people or contraception, continued the commitment to reducing "excess" fertility among poor women—commitment that had been strongly manifest in the Kennedy and Johnson administrations. Nixon passed legislation requiring that Medicaid (a federal program created in 1965 for the provision of health care to the poor) offer contraception as a "mandatory service" after 1972. This meant that any hospital, clinic, or other organization that wanted to accept Medicaid funds could do so only if it included contraception in its menu of services. Congress further decreed that the federal government would reimburse 90 percent of the cost of contraceptive services—a rate far higher than the 50–80 percent it paid for other Medicaid services.[55]

The logic behind this federal enthusiasm for birth control was articulated by Joseph Kershaw, OEO's first assistant director for research and planning. "We looked into family planning with some care," he said, "and were amazed to discover that it is probably the single most cost-effective anti-poverty measure."[56] The use of federal funds for birth control services thus had enthusiastic and sustained bipartisan support. Liberals favored the policy because it enabled poor women to take advantage of facilities and services that well-to-do and middle-class women took for granted; traditional conservatives liked it because it promised to reduce AFDC rolls. Birth control—which in earlier decades had been, at best, precariously legal when practiced by wealthy people on the advice of private physicians—had become so central to antipoverty policy that Republican as well as Democratic administrations were willing to bear the cost. In just under a decade, birth control funding had assumed the status of a natural government function. As one historian phrased it, family planning had been transformed "from private vice to public virtue."[57]

TEENAGERS: A NEW POPULATION AT RISK

Within this nationwide effort to "fight poverty with a pill," teenagers were at first included only peripherally. They were able to take advantage of the government's initial family planning programs, but only as poor women and not as teenagers per se. The Title X program, during its first year of operation, provided contraceptive services to about a quarter of a million teenagers, but adolescents were not specifically mentioned as an eligible category.[58] Such casual inclusion was not to last. Over the course of the 1970s, both Congress and the courts took steps to make sure that teenagers were explicitly designated as a group that could and should have access to contraception, and later abortion.

Most Americans have become so accustomed to the notion that teenagers have both a right to and a need for contraceptive services that they forget how unusual a claim this once was. Teenagers, though no longer utterly dependent like small children, live in a legal world which is very different from that of adults. Depending on their age, they cannot sign contracts (the sine qua non of citizenship in this most contractarian of countries), cannot get married without parental consent, and cannot even consent to their own medical care. The fact that public policy has given them a right (however qualified) to contraception and abortion is therefore something that needs explaining. Key to this is understanding the political process that made teenagers legitimate recipients of publicly funded birth control and that, in so doing, inevitably shaped the public's image of unwed pregnant teenagers.[59]

Federal provision of family planning to poor women has been one of the most significant, and least heralded, public-policy successes of the past half-century. By 1972, less than a decade after the first programs had begun, an estimated 3.5 million women were obtaining services annually in 3,000 government or publicly funded nongovernmental clinics; women in two-thirds of the nation's counties had access to low-cost, publicly subsidized birth control.[60] Such access greatly changed the way in which American women—particularly those from poor and minority communities—lived their lives. In an astonishingly short time, poor women acquired the sort of control over their fertility that had long been available to the wealthy. According to just about any measure, birth patterns among the poor changed tremendously in the late sixties and early seventies, in large part as a result of more readily accessible birth control.

In 1965, the year the U.S. Supreme Court declared Connecticut's little Comstock Law unconstitutional, African American wives were twice as likely as white wives to be using no contraception at all, and four times as likely to be using traditional homemade methods such as douching.[61] They were also twice as likely as white wives to say that their most recent babies had been unwanted (fully 41 percent of recent African American births were described this way). Similarly, wives with only a grade school education (a rough indicator of low socioeconomic status) were substantially more likely to have had recent unwanted births than were more highly educated women.[62]

During the following seven years, the number of American women reporting unwanted births declined by about a third. And by 1982, only one in ten African American wives and about one in twenty white wives had births they described as unwanted. In this period, the proportion of unwanted children born to women with the lowest level of education began to approach the proportion born to the most highly educated women: the difference in the figures reported shrank from sixteen percentage points to six.[63]

This decline in "excess" fertility, among both rich and poor, had a particular social and demographic meaning. For the most part, those using the new contraceptive services were older women who had already completed their families and wanted no additional children.[64] But just as these older women were moving out of the population "at risk" (that is, at risk of unwanted fertility and hence, supposedly, also of poverty), younger women were moving in. In the early 1970s surveys showed an increasing likelihood that unmarried people in general and adolescents in particular would be sexually active outside marriage. One of the earliest and most-cited surveys revealed that toward the middle of the decade about 40 percent of unmarried urban teenagers were sexually active.[65] Almost all the available evidence suggests that a revolution was indeed occurring in the sexual lives of teenagers, though the precise magnitude of the change is still being debated.

The very fact that such evidence was gathered in the 1970s but not earlier is itself significant, suggesting that something previously considered private had emerged into the public realm.[66]

It was not fully understood at the time that the boundaries of the problem of excess fertility were shifting in subtle ways. By the mid-1970s, people who had traditionally suffered from excess fertility, mainly poor and minority couples with more children than they had intended, were beginning to control their childbearing either by surgical sterilization or by highly effective contraception, helped in no small part by public subsidization of these services. But with the spread of sexual activity among teenagers and the first indications that out-of-wedlock births were on the rise, demographers and family planners began to devote less attention to older women who were having unplanned children at the end of their family-building years and greater attention to teenagers who were having babies in an "untimely" fashion. If in the early 1960s the image of the typical woman needing family planning was that of a woman on welfare surrounded by a gaggle of unkempt children, by the mid-1970s it had become the image of a bewildered adolescent who, incongruously, was both visibly pregnant and carrying an armload of schoolbooks.

Two sorts of organizations played a major role in persuading decision-makers to consider teenagers as being among the people who were at risk of unwanted fertility and hence of poverty. The first consisted of small advocacy groups that emerged within the public and private nonprofit sectors in the 1960s and that represented Americans concerned about the way in which early childbearing limited a young woman's education—a limitation with clear implications for the future of both the young woman and her children. Such concerns were well founded. According to traditional notions of age- and gender-appropriate behavior, education and female sexuality were inherently incompatible. Any young woman who was obviously sexually active (that is, either married or pregnant) was usually dismissed from school. A survey conducted by the Children's Bureau in 1968 found that more than two-thirds of the nation's school systems had a policy of expelling pregnant students immediately, whether they were married or not. The remaining one-third let them stay on only until their families had made "appropriate arrangements" for alternative instruction (usually tutoring at home). Only one school permitted such students to continue their education on the premises.[67] Young men were rarely if ever expelled from school after getting married or after impregnating a young woman, though at least one school advocated that fathers of illegitimate children be denied "leadership roles" (such as membership on the football team), lest the school appear to condone the students' behavior. Such attention to the young men seems to have been the exception rather than the rule.[68]

That society took note of the plight of pregnant or married female students only in the late sixties seems a little odd, when we consider that in the 1950s the United States had a higher rate of marriage among teenagers than any other major industrialized country. A program designed to keep such young women in school should logically have emerged a decade earlier.[69] But in the 1950s, the cultural ethos placed great emphasis on female domesticity. A young woman who dropped out of high school to get married (perhaps because she was pregnant) was simply conforming to expected social roles, albeit somewhat prematurely.

The far-reaching ideological and demographic changes of the sixties and early seventies challenged these assumptions about women's roles, and did so in fundamental ways. The women's movement, for example, sharply questioned the notion that marriage and the family constituted the entirety of the proper female sphere; the assumption that women didn't really need an education if they were getting married or having babies seemed increasingly misguided. Public perceptions that more and more children were being born out of wedlock, particularly to urban African American women, and the reality that early marriages were quite fragile led people to worry about how young women would support themselves and their children. When marriage was thought to be a lifetime proposition and most childbearing occurred within marriage, the fact that women who became wives or mothers as teens would later be disadvantaged in the labor market was interesting but not particularly relevant. But when marriage seemed less secure (and when divorced and never-married women seemed ever more likely to turn to AFDC as a way of supporting their families), the "human capital" that women represented became more important. Finally, in the context of the sexual revolution and feminists' demands for equality, the practice of expelling a young woman from school because she was sexually active seemed increasingly arbitrary and discriminatory, especially since young men rarely faced any public consequences whatsoever. Thus, advocacy groups, fueled by liberal, conservative, and feminist concerns, worked to place the problem of school-age mothers on the public-policy agenda.

The important point here is that in its early days this was a low-key issue, of interest primarily to professionals but scarcely at all to the general public.

It was limited to the educational establishment and a few scattered youth-serving groups, and was the subject of tentative, small-scale studies and pilot projects. An interagency task force within the Department of Health and Human Services, for example, first addressed the issue of school-age mothers in the early 1960s, and in 1965 funded a demonstration school aimed at helping young mothers finish their education. Subsequently the commissioner of education, Sidney Marland, publicly announced that every girl, pregnant or not, was entitled to an education.[70] In some ways, the campaign on behalf of student mothers was a dress rehearsal for the one on behalf of teenage mothers more broadly construed. Advocates gathered data, wrote memos, and in the early seventies gained a very modest level of public attention.[71]

The problem of student mothers would probably have remained of concern only to strategic professionals—on a par, perhaps, with the problem of lead poisoning among children—had it not attracted the interest of a larger and ultimately more successful group of advocates that had emerged during the War on Poverty. These people were dedicated to the proposition that all women should have ready access to low-cost contraception, and they became the natural allies of those who were defending pregnant students' right to an education. Together these advocates began to make new and historically unprecedented claims on behalf of teenagers. They noted that teens were increasingly likely to be sexually active outside marriage and argued that, as sexually active people, teens had a right not only to contraception but to programs specifically tailored to their needs.[72] In their campaign, advocates were facing a legal reality that differentiated teens from the older women who had so successfully used federally funded contraceptive programs to change their fertility patterns, and this led them to make their claims with particular urgency.

TEENAGERS AND CONTRACEPTION

Providing sexually active teenagers with contraception raised unique moral issues. It was easy to claim that poor married women, or even poor divorced women, needed publicly funded contraception. One could even advocate that such services be offered to unmarried women of any age who had already had children out of wedlock. But to provide publicly funded contraceptives—with all the symbolic acceptance that implied—to young women in general, married and unmarried, mothers and not-yet-mothers, rich and poor, black and white, not only questioned the relationship between sexuality and procreation but raised the thornier issue of sexual activity outside marriage. In 1972 Dr. Paul Cornely, a professor at Howard University Medical School and a member of the Commission on Population Growth and the American Future, voiced strong reservations when the commission endorsed the idea of giving all teenagers access to contraceptives:

> The recommendation that contraceptive information and services be made available to minors is indeed objectionable when applied to all minors. There is no question that this should be so in reference to . . . emancipated minors, such as married teenagers or self-supported ones who may be living within or outside their parents' home . . . On the other hand when we as a society accept the responsibility of giving contraceptive advice and services to those who are minors living in the family unit, we are striking at the foundation and roots of family life, which are already weakened by our misuse of affluence and technology.[73]

The issues at stake were sufficiently troubling that another member of the commission, Senator Alan Cranston, a liberal from California, agreed with Dr. Cornely. He doubted the wisdom of "medical authorities' providing contraceptive services to unemancipated teenagers without parental consent or knowledge."[74]

Offering contraception to teenagers raised not only moral questions but legal ones as well. The Supreme Court had affirmed that married adolescents had the right to use contraceptives (*Griswold*, 1964), as did unmarried adults (*Eisenstadt v. Baird*, 1972). But in the mid-1970s this right was still very ambiguous in the case of unmarried teenagers, particularly unmarried minors; here the legal landscape was a patchwork of local practices, common law, and evolving policy. To make matters more complex, the age of majority (the age at which a young person legally becomes an adult), which in the early 1960s had been twenty-one throughout most of the country, now varied as states moved to bring local legislation into line with the Twenty-Sixth Amendment. That amendment, ratified in 1971, had given eighteen-year-olds the right to vote, and state governments were in the process of modifying a wide range of laws lowering the age of majority from twenty-one to eighteen, on the grounds that if eighteen-year-olds could vote, then they were surely due other adult rights and obligations. Moreover, adulthood was already viewed through the prism of gender: in some jurisdictions young women, if married or pregnant, were deemed adults, whatever their chronological age.[75]

Traditionally under common law, young people who had not reached the age of majority needed their parents' consent for any medical or surgical treatment, and in many parts of the country in the 1970s this was interpreted to include contraception and abortion. But common law exempted two broad classes of minors: those who were "emancipated" and those who were mature. Emancipated minors were defined as those having a substantial degree of independence from their parents; they usually lived "separate and apart" from the family home and managed their own financial affairs. Subsequent court cases established the category of the "mature" minor—a young person who, although not living apart from the family home, was reasonably able to appreciate the implications of medical "treatments" such as contraception.[76] Yet the very fact that a young woman was living in her parents' home raised vexing questions about how mature she was, how mature she should be, and how far public policy should go in supporting her sexual autonomy. As a result, many states, localities, and clinics had de facto or de jure policies that prevented doctors and pharmacists from providing contraceptives to those under a certain age—an age that was by no means standard from community to community, or even from clinic to clinic within the same community. Furthermore, despite the fact that no physician or clinic had ever been brought to court for providing minors with contraceptives, the moral issues were so sensitive that some medical professionals tried to forestall any controversy by requiring all young people to supply tangible evidence of parental consent. This usually meant that the young person had to arrive at the clinic either with a parent in tow or with written parental approval, a situation that advocates for teens rightly concluded had a tendency to discourage young people from using contraceptive clinics. "Ironically," a congressional committee noted in 1978, "the effect of such provisions may be that an adolescent who already has a child can obtain contraceptives without parental involvement, while an adolescent who is attempting to prevent an unwanted first pregnancy may not be allowed such access."[77]

In short, family planning advocates could not assume that teenagers had a clear legal right to contraception, or that physicians and clinics would not add extralegal requirements to protect themselves. Using language that had been successful and widely accepted in the fight to make contraceptives legally available and financially accessible to all women, advocates made the case that teenagers needed contraceptive services (and, later, abortion services) as a way of avoiding poverty. They had compelling data that seemed to support their claims. Overall, women who became mothers as adolescents were poorer than women who had their children after the age of twenty; they were also more likely to be school dropouts, to wind up on welfare, and to be poor later in life. Moreover, partly because there were relatively few married teens, a very large proportion of all babies born to teenagers were illegitimate, and this proportion was increasing. In 1960, 15 percent of all teenagers who gave birth did so out of wedlock; ten years later, the figure had doubled to about one in three, whereas among women aged twenty to twenty-four it was only one in ten.

Alarming as these data were for teens in general, they were even more alarming for African Americans. In comparison to whites, African Americans—traditionally more economically and socially disadvantaged—were more likely to have children as teenagers and were far more likely to have them at very young ages, such as fourteen and fifteen. In addition, rates of out-of-wedlock births were substantially higher among nonwhites, although between 1960 and 1970 the rates for whites had virtually doubled (going from 6.6 per 1,000 to 11.1) while those for nonwhites had increased only about 15 percent (from 76.5 per 1,000 to 88.8).[78]

Thus, advocates were able to present teenagers as simply the final frontier, the last of the poor women who were kept from controlling their fertility by the vestiges of the Comstock Law. But in so doing they inverted the arguments made in the 1960s on behalf of older women: whereas formerly advocates had argued that older women lacked access to contraception and abortion because they were poor, advocates now claimed that teenagers were poor *because they lacked access to contraception and abortion.*

This argument was compelling to a wide variety of audiences, particularly at a time when affluent women were postponing childbearing and often using abortion to do so. American society was coming to accept the idea that teenagers could legitimately use contraceptives and have abortions—a change in thinking that is evident in federal court cases and legislation. In 1964, for example, when the U.S. Supreme Court handed down its decision in *Griswold* and thereby struck down Connecticut's restrictive contraception law, it explicitly noted that the right to use contraception belonged only to *married* couples. Justice William O. Douglas, writing for the majority, declared that although the states had the right to regulate certain aspects of human behavior, they could not control the intimate reaches of married life:

"We do not sit as a super-legislature to determine the wisdom, need and propriety of laws that touch economic problems, business affairs, or social conditions. This law, however (e.g., the Connecticut law forbidding the use of contraception), operates directly on intimate relations of husband and wife and their physician's role in one aspect of that relation."[79] In *Eisenstadt v. Baird* (1972) the Court extended this principle, holding that the right to control one's fertility was not limited to married people but included the unmarried as well. The Massachusetts law under review forbade the dispensing of contraceptives by anyone other than a physician or a pharmacist and to anyone but a married person, but the Court argued that forcing young women to bear children (and thus placing an economic burden on the public) did not seem a rational way to prevent premarital sex, particularly in a state that permitted the sale of condoms to married and unmarried people alike. (The Court also noted that the punishment for "fornication"—sex outside marriage—was a thirty-dollar fine or ninety days in jail, whereas the penalty for illegally dispensing a contraceptive was five years in prison.) In a much-cited paragraph that made the Court's concession of a state right to regulate the sexual behavior of the unmarried seem something of a fig leaf, Justice Brennan wrote:

> If under *Griswold* the distribution of contraceptives to married persons cannot be prohibited, a ban on distribution to unmarried persons would be equally impermissible. It is true that in *Griswold* the right of privacy in question inhered in the marital relationship. Yet the marital couple is not an independent entity with a mind and heart of its own, but an association of two individuals each with a separate intellectual and emotional makeup. If the right of privacy means anything, it is the right of the *individual,* married or single, to be free from unwarranted governmental intrusion into matters so fundamentally affecting a person as the decision whether to bear or beget a child.[80]

Finally, in *Carey v. Population Services International* (1977), the Court found unconstitutional a New York State law that forbade the sale of all over-the-counter contraceptives to those younger than sixteen, holding that even unmarried minors could not be arbitrarily denied contraceptive services.[81] Thus, the Court had gradually expanded an important legal boundary: decisions to control fertility were grounded in the right to privacy—a fundamental right that may be abridged only for the most compelling reasons. The right to privacy was not restricted to adults in the marital bedroom but was an individual right. Finally, any person, regardless of age or marital status, was entitled to use contraception to avoid an unwanted and unintended pregnancy, because such a pregnancy might create burdens for the individual and society.

Congress acted in much the same way when advocates presented evidence that the sexual behavior of the young was changing markedly and that childbearing among teenagers showed a clear correlation with poverty. Legislators tried to ensure that sexually active teenagers had access to birth control, particularly in view of the fact that unplanned and unwanted children were thought likely to end up on welfare. Beginning in 1972, Congress required state welfare departments to offer birth control services to "minors who can be considered to be sexually active."[82] In 1974 and 1975 it stressed that the population served by federally funded family planning clinics had to include adolescents. And in 1977, when it reauthorized Title X (the legislation providing most of the money for public contraceptive services), it singled out teenagers as a group whose contraceptive needs had not been met.[83]

Since there was strong political support for providing birth control to poor women, and since advocates had been successful in their arguments that childbearing among teenagers was linked to future poverty, Congress classified virtually all teenagers as poor, whatever the financial status of the families from which they came. It accomplished this by specifying that eligibility for low-cost family planning (a means-tested program) would henceforth be determined on the basis of the young person's own financial status, rather than on the financial status of her (or, more rarely, his) parents. Since most teenagers had not fully entered the paid labor force or were in the early stages of such entry, most of them were, by definition, poor. In 1979 HEW policy specified that the eligibility of even unemancipated minors be calculated on the basis of their own resources and not those of their families.[84] And in 1978, when Title X came up for reauthorization again, Congress specifically mentioned adolescents in the statutes and showed that it had given serious attention to reports of an "epidemic" of childbearing among teenagers.[85]

Teenagers also made their way into the ranks of those thought to have a right to an abortion, although this right was more modulated than the right to contraception. In *Roe v. Wade* (1973), the Supreme Court extended the principle it had established in *Griswold*, holding that decisions about whether to "beget" and "bear" children were also within the "zone of privacy." Although the main plaintiff in *Roe* was not a married couple but a single woman, the Supreme Court followed the pattern it had laid out in the *Griswold* line of cases and soon extended this zone of privacy to include adolescents.[86]

For example, in *Planned Parenthood of Central Missouri v. Danforth* (1976) the Court struck down a number of restrictions on abortion, among them the laws requiring that minors obtain their parents' consent. Drawing on the logic of earlier cases, the justices reasoned that the right to privacy, which now covered both abortion and contraception, was both fundamental enough and broad enough to extend to people under eighteen. This right outweighed the State of Missouri's claim that written consent of at least one parent was necessary "to safeguard the authority of the family relationship." Justice Harry Blackmun stressed that young people had a certain degree of legal autonomy: "Constitutional rights do not mature and come into being magically only when one attains the state-defined age of majority. Minors, as well as adults, are protected by the Constitution and possess Constitutional rights."[87] Yet he cautioned that the adolescent's rights were not absolute. A blanket parental-consent law may have been unconstitutional, but "our holding . . . does not suggest that every minor, regardless of age or maturity, may give effective consent for termination of her pregnancy."[88] In *Belotti v. Baird* (1979), however, the Court went so far as to require state governments to facilitate a young woman's abortion even in the face of her parents' disapproval. The states were directed to set up a speedy and confidential alternative process (for example, a court hearing) by which the young woman could plead her case to a third party—a system known as a "judicial bypass."[89]

Both Congress and the Supreme Court gradually embraced the idea that young people, like their elders, were experiencing a sexual revolution and that the government, as a protector of public health and a provider of welfare, was responsible for mitigating the effects of this revolution. Within two decades, federally funded family planning had become an accepted part of American life, and teenagers were included as legitimate—indeed targeted—users of such services. Between the early 1960s and the late 1970s, the government instituted four major programs—Title X of the Public Health Act and Titles V, XIX, and XX of the Social Security Act—which provided contraception to people who could not afford it, including virtually all teenagers.[90]

PREGNANT TEENAGERS: A SPECIAL CASE

Pregnancy among adolescents emerged officially as a social problem only in 1975, when Congress held its first hearings on "teenage pregnancy" and Senator Edward Kennedy proposed his National School-Age Mother and Child Health Act. Kennedy had many ties to the various segments of the public that had historically shown a concern for teenagers and their sexual behavior. His sister, Eunice Kennedy Shriver, was president of a family foundation devoted to furthering the education and welfare of young people, including "school-age mothers"; her husband, Sargent Shriver, had been the director of the Office of Economic Opportunity when it began sponsoring federally subsidized birth control for poor women. Kennedy's legislation established the parameters of the issue—parameters that would influence debate and policy for the next twenty years.

In its "Findings and Declaration of Purpose," the National School-Age Mother and Child Health Act stated that "(1) pregnancy among adolescents is a serious and growing problem; (2) such pregnancies are a leading cause of school dropout, familial disruption and increasing dependency on welfare and other community resources."[91] Hearings on the bill elaborated on this statement: "All of the experts agree that the birth of a child to a school-age parent has tremendous consequences to the mother, the father and the child itself. Pregnancy among school-age girls is the leading cause of high-school dropout among girls, and imposes a terrible burden on the girl, as well as a social burden on society. And for about 60 percent of these girls, the birth of a child begins a cycle of dependency upon public welfare."[92] Although the hearings were formally limited to the issue of "school-age mothers" (a phrase that implies only women under eighteen rather than women under twenty), it was during these hearings that the concept of "teenage pregnancy" as we know it was first formulated publicly. Neither Senator Kennedy nor the many witnesses who came before his committee tried to restrict the discussion to women of school age, and the testimony ranged over all aspects of the problem of pregnancy among teens.

The National School-Age Mother and Child Health Act did not pass. Though advocacy groups argued vigorously that teenagers were a special population, the Ford administration, as evidenced by testimony from HEW officials, was not yet ready to classify teenagers as a group apart. Rather, they defended the traditional view—that "teenagers in need" were a subcategory of other populations, such as the poor, or unwed mothers, or women seeking an abortion.[93] But the hearings, which made extensive use of demographic data compiled by the Alan Guttmacher Institute, brought teenagers to the public's attention. Moreover, the fact that abortion had been legalized in 1973 made teenagers more visible and enlarged the focus from young women who had babies to young women who were pregnant. Teenagers, like older women, were seeking abortions, and the idea of teenagers having abortions is particularly troublesome to many people. Whatever ambivalence Americans might feel when an adult terminates her pregnancy is magnified when the woman involved is a teenager, and even greater when she is living in her parents' home.

As the topic of abortion began to reshape electoral politics, candidates searched for a middle ground that would satisfy all parties to the debate. This type of strategy was tried in 1976 by Jimmy Carter, who promised that, if elected to the presidency, he would take steps to lower the rate of pregnancy among teenagers and provide an "alternative to abortion."[94] Such a campaign promise would have been unimaginable only a decade earlier. Even if teenagers as a group had been perceived as a problem and if their pregnancies rather than their births had been the focus of attention, the average American in the 1960s would scarcely have thought that the federal government should help resolve an issue touching so intimately on sexuality and private life.

In the context of the heated debate over abortion, teenagers and their sexuality seemed a legitimate object of congressional intervention. In 1978 Senator Kennedy held a second set of hearings on the issue of pregnancy among teenagers. This time, his proposed legislation—the Adolescent Health, Services, and Pregnancy Prevention and Care Act—won the approval of Congress, with the support of a White House that had made pregnancy among teenagers a campaign issue.[95] Maris Vinovskis, a historical demographer who served as a congressional staff member at the time, has pointed out an interesting feature of the bill. It seems to have had everything stacked against it: it was, as Vinovskis puts it, "remarkably hasty and ill-conceived"; it was a relatively expensive undertaking for a Congress nervous about taxpayer discontent (California's Proposition 13, an antitax measure, had very recently been passed); and Congress handled the bill in a highly imprecise and inept way.[96] Yet the bill passed even before the hearings began. There was considerable support for it. Senator Alan Cranston, who just six years earlier had doubted the wisdom of making contraceptives available to adolescents, now declared that pregnancy was "the major social and health problem affecting adolescents," and his words set the tone for the rest of the hearings.[97] Whereas in 1975 the Ford administration (specifically its HEW bureaucracy) had been extremely reluctant to define teenagers as a special population needing special programs, the new director of HEW, Joseph Califano, vigorously supported the opposite view, basing his argument on recently compiled data:

Teenage pregnancy—the entry into parenthood of individuals who barely are beyond childhood themselves—is one of the most serious and complex problems facing the nation today . . . The birth of a child can usher in a dismal future of unemployment, poverty, family breakdown, emotional stress, dependency on public agencies and health problems of mother and child . . . Scarcely anyone—liberal or conservative, permissive or restrictive—can read these figures about teenage pregnancy without a sense of shock and melancholy. Whatever our opinions about adult sexuality and morality, it is sad to contemplate the specter of children becoming suddenly and prematurely faced with the responsibilities of adults—of children becoming parents while they are still children.[98]

This quote illustrates how successful advocates had been in their efforts to characterize pregnancy among teenagers as a fundamental cause of poverty. It is not surprising that the Adolescent Health, Services, and Pregnancy Prevention and Care Act was successful, despite the many factors working against it.

Again and again senators and witnesses stressed the relationship between early pregnancy and poverty. According to Harrison Williams, who presided over the hearings, "Teenage pregnancy is a problem of many dimensions, cutting across social and economic boundaries and occurring in every community—urban, suburban, and rural—across the country . . . The social, moral, and economic implications of teenage pregnancy are great. But, more important, it inflicts serious consequences not only on their immediate future but on their entire lives. The young mother . . . faces a bleak future—limited employment prospects, poor chances of developing a meaningful career, and lifelong difficulties in providing financial support for herself and her child."[99] Secretary Califano noted that "in 1975 about half of all mothers in AFDC families were women who had had their first child during adolescence, and of children born out of wedlock, almost 60 percent end up on welfare."[100] Senator Riegle of Michigan, while supporting the Adolescent

Health, Services, and Pregnancy Prevention and Care Act, warned that the House just the previous day had slashed HEW's budget dramatically in response to California's Proposition 13, and noted that the public wanted to shrink public spending. Riegle was nonetheless confident that a case could be made for the costly programs that would be initiated by the act: "I think . . . we have the basis for making a rational argument, because in the end it is going to save us money. This is an investment that will pay off and will save us vastly more money in social and welfare programs of various kinds."[101] Califano enthusiastically agreed: "I believe we can and we will . . . make the case for the fact that in cold economic terms this is a program that will pay enormous dividends and will, in the long run, save this country lots of money, just the way that immunizing children saves this country a lot of money."[102]

Unfortunately, several assumptions embedded in this way of thinking about teenagers proved to be highly problematic. Noting that older poor women had taken advantage of federally funded birth control to make dramatic changes in their fertility, advocates assumed that young women would do much the same thing. And in fact, many of them did: legions of teenagers and young adults took advantage of publicly funded birth control programs to keep from getting pregnant. In the 1970s more teenagers than ever used contraceptives, which they mostly obtained from public clinics.[103] Yet the young women and the few young men who used these contraceptive programs were disproportionately affluent and white—people who had never presented much of a threat to the public purse to begin with. Moreover, because advocates who once claimed that poverty caused a lack of contraception were now claiming that a lack of contraception led to poverty, almost everyone concerned assumed that publicly funded contraceptive programs aimed at teenagers would bring about steady declines in the rates of pregnancy and out-of-wedlock childbearing among teens, and, over the long run, a decline in AFDC dependency. If pregnancy made people poor, then it was obvious that teens should use these new resources to help themselves do better in life.

People who held these views, however, overlooked several important points. Since most teenage mothers were poor to begin with, there were serious problems in assuming that providing them with birth control would suddenly make them resemble their more affluent peers who postponed pregnancy. In this respect, teenagers were probably more astute than the advocates when it came to assessing the likely effect of a pregnancy on their already limited futures. Also overlooked were dramatic demographic changes that in the end counterbalanced even the very real successes of public contraceptive programs for teenagers. More teens were engaging in sexual activity (although there is no evidence that the provision of contraception itself encouraged this activity).[104] In addition, there was a rapid and dramatic decline in marriage among the young, along with a greater willingness among people from all segments of society to have children without being married.[105]

In the new rhetoric that emerged in the 1975 and 1978 hearings, young women who became pregnant in an "untimely" fashion were seen as an important cause of poverty.[106] Furthermore, emerging discussions of early pregnancy tied age, fitness, and legitimacy together by seeming to promise that intervening in the actions of young people could eliminate, or at least attenuate, social pathology and poverty and largely do away with the troubling issue of abortion. In contrast to complicated, expensive, and structural changes that would improve the distribution of advantage in American society—a distribution that leaves the kinds of people statistically likely to become pregnant, especially parents, at the end of the queue—doing something about early pregnancy seemed very attractive. And to the extent that doing something about early pregnancy seemed to promise a reduction in abortions, all the better.

Thus, by the end of the 1970s the parameters of public discussion had been set: the target group was teenagers, the issue was pregnancy (which subsumed both childbearing and abortion), and the remedy was to make sure teenagers had the same access to contraception and abortion that older women did. The overarching logic was that teenagers, like older women, would use this access to low-cost and easily available contraception and thereby alleviate two social problems at once: abortion and "untimely" childbearing, which in turn led to poverty (or so it was thought). Yet public policy concerning teenagers failed to provide the kinds of visible change in behavior that had accompanied the provision of contraception to older women. Pregnancy rates among teens did not come down (although they did not increase as much as they should have, given the increase in the numbers of young people who were sexually active).[107] Early childbearing, though on the decline, continued to be concentrated among poor and minority women. And out-of-wedlock births became even more common. A public policy that had been a dramatic—albeit unheralded—success among older women was, at least at first glance, a failure among teenagers.

This failure eventually undermined the fragile consensus uniting Congress and the Supreme Court. Prior to 1980, people from all parts of the political spectrum had tended to agree on the optimum approach. They had defined the problem as an epidemic of pregnancy among teenagers; they had advocated more contraception and sex education; and they had believed that teenagers should be the focus of attention, since teens seemed to be the one group of poor women that the contraceptive revolution had not yet reached.

ENTER THE CONSERVATIVES

In 1980 a new kind of conservative rose to power, particularly in Congress, espousing a world view that challenged all of these assumptions. Such conservatives sought not merely to cope with the social trends that had taken place in the past decades, but actually to reverse them. With respect to early pregnancy and childbearing, for example, the problem was not teenagers' pregnancies but their sexual activity; the remedy was not contraception but chastity; and thus attention should be devoted not to the young woman but to her family, who needed help in regaining its control over her. Indeed, in some post-1980 hearings the teenager herself seemed to disappear; she was characterized as either a daughter or a mother, and ceased to be an individual in her own right.

Though political scientists still debate the meaning of the "Reagan Revolution," all parties agree that Ronald Reagan won the presidency in 1980 with the considerable support of evangelical Christians and other conservatives, who were in large part energized by "hot-button issues" such as abortion.[108] These people evidently found the sexual and reproductive behavior of many young women objectionable (they rarely, if ever, mentioned the behavior of young men). Young women became the focus of much congressional attention after 1980, when control of the Senate passed from the Democrats to the Republicans and when prominent conservatives assumed the leadership of many strategic congressional committees.

To be sure, conservative activists had already sought to limit government support for abortion. Between 1973 and 1976, for example, Medicaid had paid for almost a fourth of all the abortions performed each year, a policy entirely consistent with earlier concerns about excess fertility among the poor. But in 1976 Representative Henry Hyde proposed amending the Medicaid bill so that public funds could not be used for abortions unless the life of the woman was at stake. After eleven weeks of what has been described as "raucous" debate, Congress passed the Hyde Amendment, which was reauthorized in every subsequent Congress.[109] Henceforth, only a tiny number of abortions—fewer than a hundred a year—were paid for by the government. The Supreme Court, mindful of the increasing political volatility of the abortion issue, deferred to congressional wishes. In three different cases it upheld the constitutionality of the Hyde Amendment, declaring that the state had a right to use public money to encourage and support childbearing but not abortion.[110]

After 1980 the Supreme Court also acknowledged that teenagers had become a symbolically important group within the context of abortion politics and strengthened the rights of parents, permitting states more leeway in passing laws requiring either parental consent to an adolescent's abortion or (a milder measure) parental notification of an impending abortion. By the end of the decade, at least ten states required parental consent and seven others required parental notification. Most of these laws withstood judicial challenge.[111]

Buoyed by these victories, conservatives strove to eliminate public funding not just for abortion but for contraception as well, again directing their efforts primarily at young women. When Title X had come up for reauthorization in 1978, Harold Volkmer, a representative from Missouri, had proposed amending the bill so as to require parental notification whenever anyone under the age of sixteen obtained contraceptives at a publicly funded clinic. The amendment had been defeated by supporters of the Carter administration, who had argued that teenagers needed confidentiality if they were to use contraception, but both the House and the Senate had amended the bill so as to *encourage* parental consultation. Congress had also defeated an amendment to the Medicaid bill that would have required minors to obtain parental consent before receiving federally funded contraception.[112] The situation changed radically after 1980, as the "New Right" consolidated its power. First, the Reagan administration proposed that federal funds for contraceptive services be dispensed in the form of block grants to the states. The federal government, which had been defraying 90 percent of the cost, now proposed to pay only 80 percent in 1981 and 60 percent in 1982. Each state could then decide whether or not it would make up the difference, and states that were strongly conservative could choose to eliminate public funding of contraceptive services altogether. Congress, however, declined to approve the plan.[113]

In 1981 the Reagan administration began a new assault on contraceptive services for teens: the Omnibus Budget Reconciliation Act contained language encouraging parental involvement in federally funded contraceptive services for teenagers. A year later the administration proposed a rule (popularly known as the "squeal rule") requiring that all clinics receiving Title X funds notify the parents of any woman under eighteen who received such services. Moreover, eligibility for services would henceforth be determined not on the basis of the adolescent's own financial resources but on those of her parents.[114]

The squeal rule was enjoined by the Federal District Court in the District of Columbia and eventually turned back as inconsistent with congressional intent.[115] But in 1981 the Adolescent Health, Services, and Pregnancy Prevention and Care Act of 1978 (Senator Kennedy's "teenage pregnancy" bill) was superseded by the Adolescent Family Life Act, sponsored by Senator Orrin Hatch of Utah and popularly known as the "chastity bill."[116] The 1978 act had been designed to "prevent unwanted early and repeat pregnancies and to help adolescents become *productive, independent contributors to family and community life*" (emphasis added). Like earlier acts, it had encouraged but not required unemancipated minors to discuss birth control services with their parents.[117] New Right conservatives, though, had had strong reservations about the wisdom of such policies and, consistent with their definition of the issue, threw their support behind the "chastity bill," which set up services that specifically aimed "to discourage adolescent premarital sexual relations and the consequences of such relations." The services, which targeted both teenagers and their parents, strove "to find effective means, *within the context of the family,* of reaching adolescents before they become sexually active in order to maximize the *guidance and support available to parents and other family members,* and to promote self-discipline and other prudent approaches to the problem of adolescent premarital sexual relations, including adolescent pregnancy" (emphasis added).[118] Sexual activity among teenagers was no longer merely an "antecedent" to untimely pregnancy; now it was the central problem.

Perhaps most important, though largely unnoticed, was the fact that the very definition of "family" was being questioned. In 1978 Eunice Kennedy Shriver could argue that services to a pregnant teenager were cost effective because they were services to a family—namely, the woman and her child, and often the man involved. The new conservatives, in contrast, thought it wrong that the young woman's parents should be left out of the issue. The point of public policy, as they saw it, was to strengthen the "parental family" (the unit that included the teenager and her parents) and to discourage measures that increased the autonomy of daughters. The Adolescent Family Life Act did not, however, give unlimited control to parents: it specifically provides for government intervention in those cases where the parents want their daughter to have an abortion.[119]

The Supreme Court (as the old saw has it) follows the election returns. During the 1980s the Court, now containing Reagan appointees, tried six times to craft a public policy that would enable teenagers to have abortions while allowing parents to play a substantial role in the decision.[120] The process culminated in 1990 with two cases that clearly illustrated the tensions between these two imperatives. In *Hodgson v. Minnesota,* the Court declared unacceptable a Minnesota statute requiring that the pregnant teenager or her doctor notify both parents, even in cases where the father had never married or even lived with the adolescent's mother. Yet the Court permitted the law to stand if the state could provide a judicial bypass whereby a pregnant teenager who could not find or did not wish to notify this parent could plead her case. Likewise, in *Ohio v. Akron Center for Reproductive Health,* the Court said that states could make pregnant teenagers wait forty-eight hours before obtaining an abortion, though it conceded that such a policy could lead to significantly greater delays.[121]

The issue of "teenage pregnancy" thus entered public-policy debates at a critical historical moment. Eventually it became a focal point for conflicting views about the autonomy of young women and the role of the family. In the 1960s and early 1970s, unmarried women had acquired greater rights to control their fertility by means of contraception and abortion. At the same time the government, by expanding federal funding for birth control services and contraceptive supplies, had made it easier for women to exercise these rights. Extending such rights to young women meant that minors still living in the family home could, with the tacit support of the state, engage in behavior that their parents might be ambivalent about or might disapprove of completely.

Constance Nathanson has made the interesting point that conceptualizing the problem as being pregnancy among teenagers, rather than abortion or premarital sex or out-of-wedlock births, combined two sets of public concerns: those relating to the reproductive behavior of poor and black teenagers and those relating to the sexual behavior of affluent and white ones.[122] There is considerable truth in this. Such a blend of concerns—over whites and blacks on the one hand and sex and reproduction on the other—had indeed created the fragile consensus among liberals and traditional conservatives. But official rhetoric was always more complex than this neat distinction would suggest, and divisions *within* the conservative camp undermined the consensus. In the 1970s both liberals and conservatives (the latter including politicians such as George Bush, who prior to 1980 had been an active supporter of public funding for contraception) had regarded teenagers as simply the last group to be included in the contraceptive revolution. Like the poor women who had gained support during the War on Poverty, teenagers had been the only women who, because of their status (young, unmarried, often minority), their poverty, and the public's outmoded standards, were still unable to control their fertility. And this lack of control had been considered a source of social problems. Most important, poor women with unwanted pregnancies had been candidates either for abortion or for AFDC. Liberals and traditional conservatives, though using different arguments, had agreed that neither of these was a desirable outcome.

For supporters of the New Right, however, teenagers at risk of pregnancy represented the epitome of what had gone wrong with American society. Such conservatives thought it logical that public policy should target young people in an effort to undo the rights revolution of the sixties—a revolution that, as they saw it, had gone out of control. Such a view proved to be extremely popular, extending well beyond the ranks of the New Right.

That new conservatives could make the case that there was something terribly wrong with teenagers and their pregnancies was in part a product—an unintended one, to be sure—of the very success of earlier conservative, liberal, and feminist advocates in making contraception available to America's teenagers. By portraying teens as simply the last group of women whose fertility was held hostage to the antiquated laws of the nineteenth century, advocates fostered a belief that teens were fundamentally implicated in poverty and that they were likely to change their behavior as dramatically as had earlier groups of poor women, once contraception was made available. By the 1980s contraceptives were readily available to most American teenagers, but behavior among adolescents did not change in the way that advocates had hoped. When teens continued to get pregnant, large parts of the American public began to worry about them, and these worries were exacerbated by social changes newly visible on the horizon.

4

CONSTRUCTING

AN

EPIDEMIC

By the early 1980s Americans had come to believe that teenagers were becoming pregnant in epidemic numbers, and the issue occupied a prominent place on the national agenda. "Teenage pregnancy," along with crack-addicted mothers, drive-by shootings, and the failing educational system, was beginning to be used as a form of shorthand for the country's social ills.[1] Everyone now agreed that it was a serious problem, and solutions were proposed across the ideological spectrum. Conservatives (members of the New Right, in particular) wanted to give parents more control over their daughters, including the right to determine whether they should have access to sex education and contraception.[2] Liberals, doubting that a "just say no" strategy would do much to curtail sexual activity among teenagers, continued to urge that young men and women be granted the same legal access to abortion and contraception that their elders had. Scholars debated the exact costs of early pregnancy to the individuals involved and to society, foundations targeted it for funding and investigation, government at all levels instituted programs to reduce it, and the media gave it a great deal of scrutiny.[3] In the early 1970s the phrase "teenage pregnancy" was just not part of the public lexicon. By 1978, however, a dozen articles per year were being published on the topic; by the mid-1980s the number had increased to two dozen; and by 1990 there were more than two hundred, including cover stories in both *Time* and *Newsweek*.[4]

Ironically (in view of all this media attention), births to teenagers actually *declined* in the 1970s and 1980s. During the baby boom years (1946–1964), teenagers, like older women, increased their childbearing dramatically: their birthrates almost doubled, reaching a peak in 1957. Subsequently, the rates drifted back to their earlier levels, where they have pretty much stayed since 1975.[5] The real "epidemic" occurred when Dwight Eisenhower was in the White House and poodle skirts were the height of fashion.[6] But although birthrates among teenagers were declining, other aspects of their behavior were changing in ways that many people saw as disturbing. From the vantage point of the 1970s, the relevant statistics could have been used to tell any one of a number of stories. For example, when abortion was legalized in 1973, experts began to refer to a new demographic measure, the "pregnancy rate," which combined the rate of abortion and the rate of live births. In the case of teenagers an increasing abortion rate meant that, despite a declining birthrate, the pregnancy rate was going up, and dramatically so.[7]

Since the rise in the pregnancy rate among teenagers (and among older women as well) was entirely due to the increase in abortions, it is curious that professionals and the public identified pregnancy, rather than abortion, as the problem. It is likewise curious that although the abortion rate increased for all women, most observers limited their attention to teenagers, who have always accounted for fewer than a third of the abortions performed. Teenagers *are* proportionately overrepresented in the ranks of women having abortions. But to pay attention almost exclusively to them, while neglecting the other groups that account for 70 percent of all abortions, does not make sense.

A similar misdirection characterized the issue of illegitimacy. In the 1970s teenagers were having fewer babies overall than in previous decades, but they—like older women—were having more babies out of wedlock. Compared to other women, teenagers have relatively few babies, and a very high proportion of these are born to unmarried parents (about 30 percent in 1970, 50 percent in 1980, and 70 percent in 1995). But although most babies born to teenagers are born out of wedlock, most babies born out of wedlock are *not* born to teens. In 1975 teens accounted for just under a half of all babies born out of wedlock; in 1980 they accounted for 40 percent; and in 1990 they accounted for fewer than a third.[8] Obviously, teens should hardly be the only population of interest.

Thus, in the 1970s and early 1980s the data revealed a number of disquieting trends, and teenagers became the focus of the public's worry about these trends. More single women were having sex, more women were having abortions, more women were having babies out of wedlock, and—contrary to prevailing stereotypes—older women and white women were slowly replacing African Americans and teens as the largest groups within the population of unwed mothers. These trends bespeak a number of social changes worth looking at closely. Sex and pregnancy had been decoupled by the contraception revolution of the 1960s; pregnancy and birth had been decoupled by the legalization of abortion in the 1970s; and more and more children were growing up in "postmodern" families—that is, without their biological mother and father—in part because divorce rates were rising and in part because more children were being born out of wedlock. But these broad demographic changes, which impinged on women and men of all ages, were seen as problems that primarily concerned *teenagers*. The teenage mother—in particular, the black teenage mother—came to personify the social, economic, and sexual trends that in one way or another affected almost everyone in America.

A number of different responses might have been devised to meet the challenge of these new trends. It would have been logical, for example, to focus on the problem of abortion, since more than a million abortions were performed each year despite the fact that people presumably had access to effective contraception. Or the problem might have been defined as the increase in out-of-wedlock births, since more and more couples were starting families without being married.[9] Or policymakers could have responded to the way in which sexual activity and childbearing were, to an ever greater extent, taking place outside marriage (in 1975 about three-fourths of all abortions were performed on single women).[10] Yet American society has never framed the problem in any of these broader terms. The widest perspective was perhaps that of the antiabortion activists, who saw the problem as abortion in general. A careful reading of the specialist and nonspecialist media suggests that, with a few exceptions, professionals and the general public paid scant attention to abortion and out-of-wedlock childbearing among older women, while agreeing that abortion and illegitimate births among teenagers constituted a major social and public-health problem. Why did Americans narrow their vision to such an extent? How did professionals, Congress, and the public come to agree that there was an "epidemic" of pregnancy among teenagers and that teenagers were the main (if not the only) population worth worrying about?[11]

A STORY THAT FITS THE DATA

As we saw in Chapter 3, advocates for young people had used Congress and the media to publicize an account of teenagers and their circumstances that seemed to make sense of the emerging demographic data and that was extremely persuasive. In essence, they claimed that teenagers, like older women, were increasingly likely to have sex and that their sexual activity was increasingly likely to take place outside marriage. Teens, however, like poor women of earlier generations, had been left out of the contraceptive revolution that had so changed the lives of other American women. They were having babies they did not want and could not support. Many of them were too inexperienced to know how to avoid conception, to appreciate the difficulties of childrearing, or to obtain an abortion (besides, abortion was expensive). And most gave birth without the support of the partner who had impregnated them. Unless they were granted access to affordable contraception and abortion, they would continue to have babies out of wedlock and would be mired in a life of poverty. Advocates noted that most babies born to teenagers were born out of wedlock, and that babies who lived with one parent were obviously less well off than those who lived with two. Moreover, black teenagers, who have always been disadvantaged in American society, had much higher rates of childbearing and illegitimacy than whites, although the reproductive behavior of white teenagers was beginning to resemble that of blacks. And in this account, teens who gave birth were much more likely to drop out of school than those who did not, so that as adults they were less well educated and hence poorer than women who postponed their childbearing.

Taken together, the data added up to a story that made sense to many people. It convinced Americans that young mothers like Michelle Brown— those who gave birth while still in high school and who were not married— were a serious social problem that brought a host of other problems in its wake. It explained why babies like David were born prematurely, why infant mortality rates in the United States were so high compared to those in other countries, why so many American students were dropping out of high school, and why AFDC costs were skyrocketing. Some people even believed that if teenagers in the United States maintained their high birthrates, the nation would not be able to compete internationally in the coming century. Others argued that distressing racial inequalities in education, income, and social standing were in large part due to the marked difference in the birthrates of white and black teenagers.

Yet this story, which fed both on itself and on diffuse social anxiety, was incomplete; the data it was based on were true, but only partial. Evidence that did not fit the argument was left out, or mentioned only in passing. Largely ignored, for example, was the fact that a substantial and growing proportion of all unmarried mothers were not teenagers. And on those rare occasions when older unwed mothers were discussed, they were not seen as a cause for concern.[12] Likewise, although the substantially higher rates of out-of-wedlock childbearing among African Americans were often remarked upon, few observers pointed out that illegitimacy rates among blacks were falling or stable while rates among whites were increasing. Few noted that most of the teenagers giving birth were eighteen- and nineteen-year-olds, or that teens under fifteen had been having babies throughout much of the century.[13]

This story, as it emerged in the media and in policy circles in the 1970s and 1980s, fulfilled the public's need to identify the cause of a spreading social malaise. It led Americans to think that teenagers were the only ones being buffeted by social changes, whereas these changes were in fact pervasive; it led them to think that heedless, promiscuous teenagers were responsible for a great many disturbing social trends; and it led them to think that teenagers were doing these things unwittingly and despite themselves. When people spoke of "children having children" or of "babies having babies," their very choice of words revealed their belief that teenage mothers, because of their youth, should not be held morally responsible for their actions. "Babies" who had babies were themselves victims; they needed protection from their own ungovernable impulses.

In another sense, limiting the issue to teenagers gave it a deceptive air of universality; after all, everyone has been or will be a teenager. Yet the large-scale changes that were taking place in American life did not affect all teenagers equally. The types of behavior that led teenagers to get pregnant and become unwed mothers (engaging in premarital sex, and bearing and keeping illegitimate children) were traditionally much more common among African Americans than among whites, and more common among the poor than among the privileged.

For average Americans in the 1970s, life had undergone profound changes in just a few short years. Unmarried couples were engaging more readily in sex, and doing so much more openly. Many of them were even living together, instead of settling for furtive sex in the back seats of cars. When an unmarried woman got pregnant, she no longer made a sudden marriage or a hasty visit to a distant aunt; now she either terminated her pregnancy or openly—even proudly—had her baby. Often she chose to live as a single parent or to set up housekeeping with her partner, rather than allowing her child to be adopted by a proper, married middle-class couple. In the 1970s people of all ages began to follow this way of life, but the inchoate fears of the public coalesced in large part exclusively around teenagers. The new patterns of sexual behavior and new family structures were simply more visible among younger people, who had not committed themselves to the older set of choices. At the same time, teenagers, especially those who had children, were defined as people who were embarking on a lifetime of poverty. The debate, in centering on teenagers in general, thus combined two contrasting features of American society: it permitted people to talk about African Americans and poor women (categories that often overlapped) without mentioning race or class; but it also reflected the fact that the sexual behavior and reproductive patterns of white teenagers were beginning to resemble those of African Americans and poor women— that is, more and more whites were postponing marriage and having babies out of wedlock.

The myriad congressional hearings, newspaper stories, and technical reports on the "epidemic" of pregnancy among teenagers could not have convinced the public to subscribe to this view if other factors in American life had not made the story plausible. The social sciences abound with theories suggesting that the public is subject to "moral panics" which are in large part irrational, but in this case people were responding to a particular account because it helped them make sense of some very real and rapidly changing conditions in their world.[14] It appeared to explain a number of dismaying social phenomena, such as spreading signs of poverty, persistent racial inequalities, illegitimacy, freer sexual mores, and new family structures.[15] It was and continues to be a resonant issue because of the profound changes that have taken place in the meanings and practices associated with sexuality and reproduction, in the relations among sex, marriage, and childbearing, and in the national and global economies. Through the story of "teenage pregnancy," these revolutionary changes acquired a logic and a human face.[16]

THE SEXUAL REVOLUTION

In the 1950s and 1960s (as those who long for the good old days are fond of telling us) sex was a very private matter.[17] Like childbearing, it was sanctioned only within marriage. Respectable women were careful lest their behavior earn them a reputation for being "loose," which would limit their ability to marry a "nice" man. True, in 1958 about four out of ten unmarried women were sexually active before their twentieth birthday, but in those days premarital sex was in a strict sense *premarital,* for the most part occurring within a committed relationship that soon led to marriage.[18] Though the data collected by Alfred Kinsey and his colleagues in the 1940s and 1950s are not nationally representative, they do show that for earlier generations of American women, most premarital sex was in large part "engagement" sex—sex with the man the woman was planning to marry, and then for only a relatively short period before the wedding. In the Kinsey report, almost half of the married women who had engaged in premarital sex had done so only with their fiancés, and for less than two years prior to their marriage.[19] More recent and more representative data suggest that this pattern continued for some time: in the 1960s half of all women who engaged in premarital sex did so with their fiancés. By the mid-1980s, this proportion had fallen to less than a fourth.[20]

Many people recall the transformation in sexual behavior that took place in the 1970s, but they may well have forgotten the rapidity of that change. In 1969 the overwhelming majority of Americans—almost 70 percent— agreed that having sex before marriage was wrong; three out of four agreed that magazine photos of nudes were objectionable; and more than four out of five agreed that nudity in a Broadway show (for example, "Hair" or "Oh! Calcutta") was unacceptable.[21] A mere four years later, only traces of these values remained: the percentages of Americans who objected to premarital sex and to nudes in magazines had both dropped an astonishing twenty points, and the percentage of those who objected to nudity on the stage had dropped eighteen points.[22] Similarly, a Roper poll conducted in 1969 found that only 20 percent of the public approved of premarital sex; four years later, the respondents were equally divided on the issue. The General Social Survey conducted by researchers at the University of Chicago asked the question in a slightly different way: in 1972 it found that only 26 percent of the public thought premarital sex was "not wrong at all"; but a decade later this figure had jumped to 40 percent, while the percentage of those who said it was "almost always wrong" had correspondingly declined.[23]

Not surprisingly, as more and more people engaged in premarital sex or extramarital sex (after being divorced, separated, or widowed), it became increasingly difficult to claim that sexual activity should be limited to adults. By what logic could sex be declared taboo for the young? And how young was too young? This created a genuine dilemma. In 1969 the rules about sex were clear, even if they were often ignored in practice. Sex was for married people, and if society sometimes turned a blind eye to sex between unmarried partners, it did so only for those who had attained or were close to attaining legal adulthood. Minors, unless they were deemed mature or emancipated, could not obtain contraception, and in most states "minors" included everyone under twenty-one. Moreover, under the age-of-consent laws that were in force in many states, young women could not legally consent to have sex.[24] In challenging these rules in the courts and in Congress, advocates had been successful in claiming that teenagers had a right to contraception, and therefore a right to have sex. But the new concept of rights for teenagers created a "bright-line" problem. Once adults accepted that unmarried people could have sex and that teenagers had a right to contraception, by what logic was an unmarried thirteen-year-old too young to have sex? What bright line separated the too young from the old enough? The category "teenagers" or "adolescents" included people who were barely out of childhood as well as people who were legal adults. And if teenagers had rights, why not even younger people?

Ever since the late nineteenth century, Americans have assumed that individuals in this amorphous category are not emotionally or physically mature enough to have sex. Furthermore, nowadays few teenagers have the financial resources or the educational preparation necessary to raise a family. The public thus evinces received worries about the *emotional* capacities of teenagers, combined with realistic concern about their *social* capacities— capacities to deal with marriage and children, both of which often follow sexual activity. Many people take it for granted that teenagers are capable only of infatuation or puppy love. And in most cases teenage couples today, unlike their counterparts in the 1940s and 1950s, are not engaged and ready to settle down in a year or two. In short, adults tend to think that teenagers are unprepared for the serious business of building a family and are capable only of careless premarital sex that is rooted in pure pleasure. And the very fact that the category "teenagers" is so broad, ranging from seventh-graders to legal adults, exacerbates the problem.

The few data available tend to confirm the commonsense notion that American adults consider premarital sex acceptable for themselves but not for teenagers. In 1977, for example, 63 percent of respondents to a public-opinion poll said that they believed sex between unmarried teenagers was morally wrong; in 1994, in answer to a slightly different question, 50 percent said it was wrong. Polls conducted between 1986 and 1994 found that a consistent 85 percent of respondents considered premarital sex unacceptable for people aged fourteen to sixteen: nearly 70 percent thought it was "always wrong," and nearly 20 percent thought it was "almost always wrong."[25]

But in the late 1960s and early 1970s, whatever adults may have preferred, patterns of sexual behavior were changing for everyone, and that included teenagers. Although it is debatable whether these changes constituted a "revolution" among adults, they unquestionably did among teenagers. Current statistics show that in a typical group of forty teenagers (with an equal number of each sex), five of the women and ten of the men will have had intercourse by the time they enter the tenth grade; twelve of the women and fourteen of the men will have done so by the time they are seniors; and fully fifteen of the women and seventeen of the men will have done so before they are twenty.[26] Virtually all studies confirm that the young people of today are more likely to have premarital sex than were those of earlier generations. In 1970 it was estimated that slightly more than a fourth of all unmarried women aged fifteen to nineteen were sexually active; by 1984 the proportion had risen to just under a half.[27] In 1982 the National Survey of Family Growth found that whereas in the 1950s 40 percent of teenagers had reported engaging in premarital sex, among women who had turned twenty between 1979 and 1981 the figure had jumped to 70 percent. There was a substantial increase in sexual activity among younger women as well: in the mid-1950s only three out of a hundred engaged in premarital sex before the age of fifteen; in the mid-1970s one in ten did so. Among more recent groups of teens, the increase in activity is even more striking.[28]

These changes in the statistics, dramatic though they are, do not begin to capture the extent of the transformation that has actually taken place in teenagers' sexual behavior. For example, we tend to speak of their involvement in "premarital sex," and this is technically correct: today 96 percent of American teenagers have sex before they get married. But this is not the "engagement sex" that young women allowed themselves in the 1950s. Now teenagers are sexually active whether or not they have immediate plans to marry. And for reasons that no one fully understands, Americans of all ages are retreating from marriage. As a result, many of the teenagers who are engaging in sex and having babies are doing exactly what teenagers did in the 1950s, but the nontrivial change is that they are doing so without the benefit of wedlock.

On the one hand, the median age at first marriage has been rising throughout the century and today is virtually the highest it has ever been since the United States began keeping accurate records: twenty-four for women and twenty-six for men. On the other hand, age at first menstruation has slowly been going down, probably because of better nutrition. Thus, young people are becoming fertile a bit earlier than they used to but getting married much later, and hence face very long periods of time during which they are physically capable of sex and childbearing but unable or unwilling to marry. Furthermore, public attitudes toward out-of-wedlock sex have become increasingly liberal. As a result of all these factors, young white Americans in general face about a decade in which they are sexually active but not married. For blacks, who have very low marriage rates, the period is even longer: twelve years for women and nineteen for men.[29] So today's teenagers, in contrast to those of earlier generations, face a whole new set of issues and dilemmas not easily resolved by slogans such as "just say no" to sex or childbearing. It probably isn't realistic to ask today's teens to abstain from sex for a decade or two, but we have no clear guidelines on when young people are "ready" for sex. At the same time, longer periods of sexual activity outside marriage surely change the nature and meaning of sex for the people involved. To take just one example, teenage women face real dilemmas negotiating sex, intimacy, and plans for babies over a number of partners. In 1971 approximately six out of ten sexually active teenage women in metropolitan areas had had only a single partner; by 1979 this figure had declined to only one in two. In the early 1990s more than 70 percent of such women had had more than one partner, and one in five had had six or more partners. Counter to the stereotype, however, most of these teens, like most adults, engaged in serial monogamy.[30]

These broad demographic data hint at the dismay that many Americans feel in response to such radical social change, especially when teenagers are involved. Sexual behavior, like any other behavior, is situated within a complex web of social ties based on factors such as race, class, gender, and ethnicity. When women in the 1950s engaged in premarital sex, it was thought of simply as marital sex beginning a little before the wedding. Today, however, teenagers become sexually active not when they move out of the parental home and into a family of their own making but while they are still defined primarily as children. Since they are under the control (however nominal) of their parents, their sexual activity raises troubling questions about the purposes and meaning of sex, particularly in the case of young women. Many Americans object to the idea of "casual" sex, meaning sex that is not closely linked to the process by which people form couples and settle down. Yet teenagers, especially young teenagers, are almost universally regarded as too young to "get serious" and contemplate marriage. The kinds of sex that *are* appropriate for them (short-term relationships for the purpose of pleasure, not procreation) run counter to the basic values espoused by many adults. This double bind, according to which serious commitments are premature but casual sex is immoral, makes sexual activity among teens inherently troubling for many adults and, as we will see, can make it very difficult for teens to manage their sexual lives.

In addition, sexual behavior in the United States has long been governed by notions of propriety that depend on gender and racial distinctions, and teenagers' sexual activity has altered some of these traditional notions. For example, the statistics show that young women are almost as likely as young men to be sexually active before marriage. And the patterns of sexual activity among blacks and whites are converging to a remarkable extent. In 1988 the rate of premarital sexual activity among young white women was only three points lower than the rate for young black women. Never before had the margin been so narrow—an indication that such activity was increasing among whites, and perhaps decreasing among blacks.[31] Furthermore, scattered data suggest that as sexual activity among teenagers becomes more widespread, differences in the sexual experiences of people from various classes are diminishing. Many studies, beginning with the Kinsey report, have demonstrated that the likelihood of engaging in premarital sex and the age at first occurrence are both linked to class: the higher an individual's class background, the older he or she will be when first engaging in premarital sex, and the more likely it is that he or she will never engage in such sex at all. Since more and more people are postponing marriage and since teens of all classes are becoming sexually active, the relationship between sexual activity and class has greatly diminished among the young.[32]

To the extent that choices about sexual behavior (like choices about any other form of social behavior) both reflect and constitute social roles, these developments are bound to be troubling. Sociologists from Max Weber to Pierre Bourdieu have noted how groups of individuals use behavior patterns as "markers" to distinguish themselves from others. Behavior that people may have no objection to when they observe it in a young working-class man (particularly a young working-class man of color) will affect them very differently when they observe it in a young white upper-middle-class woman.[33] Whereas sex outside marriage was once appropriate only for "unruly" types (adult men, and young people from working-class or minority backgrounds) or for "nice" girls in love with their fiancés, the boundaries are no longer clear. Although adults now tend to think that premarital sex is acceptable when it is accompanied by emotional commitment, society seems to want young people—young middle-class white women in particular—to sustain this kind of sex throughout almost a decade without "getting too serious" or "being cheap." A difficult task, indeed.[34]

Public-opinion polls, when read carefully, suggest that adults have complex preferences about the best way to deal with sexual activity among teenagers. Most adults don't want teens to be sexually active, but for a surprisingly long time they have agreed that teenagers who *are* sexually active should have access to birth control information and contraceptives. Most have also long favored providing sex education in the schools, but they are remarkably skeptical about its ability to curtail sexual activity or pregnancy among teenagers. They disapprove of unmarried teenage mothers and consider them a source of social problems, but a majority are strongly in favor of laws that require parental approval before a teenager can have an abortion. In fact, about 40 percent of Americans think that a young woman should not be permitted to have an abortion even if pregnancy would cause her to drop out of school.[35] In short, most adults seem to have a clear first choice—namely, that teens should not have sex. At the same time, a large majority of them support contraceptive and sex education programs for teens, a fact that suggests they doubt they will get their first choice. In general, adults want teens to have access to services and programs that will reduce the problems associated with sexual activity, but they do not wish this access to be unrestricted. Thirty to 40 percent believe that contraceptives should be made available to teenagers only if they have their parents' approval, and 70 to 80 percent believe that such approval is needed if a teen wants an abortion.[36]

In general, when it comes to teenagers Americans are much more liberal than they used to be on issues such as the availability of birth control information, the provision of contraceptive services, access to abortion, and openness on matters of sexuality and reproduction. A small, fairly constant number of people still long for the old sexual order; most Americans do not. What parents *do* seem to want is some measure of control over how their children behave in the world of sexual freedom that opened in the 1970s. Many Americans, however, think that their authority over their children is precarious at best. A Harris poll undertaken for Planned Parenthood in 1985 found that almost half of the parents surveyed felt they didn't have much control over their teenagers' sexuality, and an additional 18 percent felt they had no control at all. The data also suggest that *daughters'* decisions are of particular concern to parents. In 1986 a poll of fathers found that 26 percent were "very worried" about their teenage daughters' sexual activity, and an additional 32 percent were "somewhat worried." The figures for teenage sons were, respectively, 10 percent and 36 percent.[37] In addition, people are alarmed about the prevalence of sexually transmitted diseases, including AIDS. To put the matter simply: the rules of the game have changed, and they have done so in ways that are particularly troubling for parents. In the 1970s, as the current generation of parents was coming of age, the old order ended. Premarital sex became more common, and public opinion on the issue shifted dramatically.

Today's parents want to protect their children from the myriad dangers— seen and unseen, life-threatening and emotionally bruising—that sex entails these days. And they want to set their own timetable, so that they themselves can decide when their children are old enough to have sex. Often parents find it difficult to allow a child to be sexually active while he or she is still living as a dependent under their roof. Yet the point at which many parents consider a child old enough to be sexually active—whether they define it as when the child marries, or moves out of the parental home, or becomes self-supporting—is occurring ever later in American life, due to societal and economic changes over which individuals have minimal control. Except for the relatively few people who think that sex outside marriage is always wrong (and whose problem is chiefly one of finding a way to promulgate their values in an unsympathetic society), Americans have numerous questions relating to teenagers' sexual behavior. Should teens be sexually active? At what age? With whom? How are parents to encourage the use of contraception without seeming to push a teenager into having sex before he or she is ready? How can individuals reconcile their antipathy toward abortion with their desire to see fewer children born out of wedlock? In short, the contradictions inherent in teenagers' sexual activity make it hard for adults to give a clear, precise, and unambiguous message to today's young people.

Teenagers, however, are simply the most visible aspect of a far larger problem. Nowhere has public or private life caught up with the sexual revolution of the 1970s, and most Americans do not yet fully appreciate how far-reaching the changes really were. Now that sex seems to have been permanently disconnected from marriage (or as permanently as anything ever is in social life), private citizens as well as policymakers must grapple with a host of legal, ethical, medical, and social issues. Teenagers are a focus of anxiety because so many of them are participating in the new world of sexual freedom and because most adults are (often rightly) doubtful about the skills and resources these young people possess. The challenge facing parents is to find a way to protect their children and their children's children without making unrealistic or impractical demands, yet still maintain some authority over them. As a consequence, public attitudes toward teenagers' sexual activity are an awkward amalgam of attempts to come to terms with vague fears and a sense that young people are out of control. The American public supports sex education because it has long thought that providing knowledge and skills can modify behavior. At the same time, people are skeptical about the ability of education alone to change patterns of sexual behavior, which are so strongly motivated. They believe that early pregnancy can best be prevented if parents readily communicate with their offspring, but they are confused and ambivalent about what sort of information parents should provide and how they should go about conveying it, as evidenced by the relatively small number of parents who actually talk to their children about sex.[38] Adults disapprove of sexual activity and childbearing among unmarried teenagers, but are generally resigned to the fact that such activity takes place. Many adults prefer the lesser of two evils—contraception as opposed to pregnancy—even to the point of allowing schools to dispense contraceptives. But a substantial minority strive to maintain some degree of control in this area and continue to favor parental-consent laws for teenagers who wish to obtain contraception.[39]

THE REPRODUCTIVE REVOLUTION

Teenagers are not only the most visible exponents of new patterns of sexual behavior but are participating in innovative family structures whose long-term effects are still uncertain. These structures—which have received less attention than the changing sexual mores but which may have even more significance for American society—call into question the relationship between childbearing and marriage. For an increasing number of Americans (and Europeans, for that matter), having and raising a child no longer takes place exclusively within marriage. Demographers have estimated that if present trends continue, an astonishing 50 percent of all American children will spend at least part of their childhood in a single-parent family. In the early 1990s, slightly more than half of these children were being raised by one parent as a result of divorce, but the rest had been born to unmarried mothers.[40]

This change is apparent not only in the United States but throughout the industrialized world. There was a time when only women living in liberal Sweden had babies without benefit of marriage, but today unwed parents are common in every country in Europe. Exactly why this should be the case is still a mystery. Out-of-wedlock births increased just as all industrialized societies were cutting welfare spending, so the assumption that welfare promotes such births is not borne out by the facts.

That women of all ages are more willing to bear children out of wedlock is usually attributed to the fact that illegitimacy has lost its stigma. This explanation is certainly true. Public attitudes toward what colonial Americans called bastardy have changed dramatically in a relatively short time. In 1970 only about one American in ten thought that childbearing outside marriage should be legal, but four years later that percentage had more than doubled, to 25 percent. By 1985 the figure had risen to 40 percent. Although a majority of Americans still oppose out-of-wedlock childbearing, opinion shifts of this magnitude can truly be called revolutionary.[41]

But these data tell only half the story. It used to be that, for an unmarried woman, becoming pregnant was "a fate worse than death." We can get some idea of what the old days were like, and of how radically society has changed, if we look at media reports from the late 1960s and early 1970s. Neither those who wrote about unmarried mothers nor the unmarried women themselves questioned the belief that having a baby out of wedlock was very wrong. In 1965 *Time* magazine ran a story revealing just how stigmatizing illegitimacy was: a New York Court of Claims had permitted a child to sue for damages resulting from "the mental anguish of being born a bastard."[42] In 1966 a journalist writing in *Ebony,* a magazine aimed at black readers, noted: "In the pecking order of America, unwed mothers are perhaps the most despised minority. They are the targets of abuse from legislators bent on punishing them. They are the scapegoats of moralists decrying an alleged lapse in public morality. They are the butt of jokes by school children and adults."[43] In 1968 a young woman wrote: "I'm a teenager who has made a big mistake. I am pregnant. I'm not proud of what I've done and I hope and pray other teenagers will read my letter, wake up, and start to lead a good, clean life."[44] That same year *Good Housekeeping* ran an article about an unwed mother (a "superior girl" who had been at the head of her class throughout high school) who was grateful that her attending physician did not make her feel "dirty or cheap" when he found she was pregnant and unmarried.[45] Another unwed mother, the subject of a *Life* magazine profile on adoption, described how she had pretended to gain weight and even to have menstrual periods, in order to hide her real condition.[46] A sixteen-year-old unwed mother, writing in the November 1968 issue of *Seventeen,* described how she had felt after she'd discovered she was pregnant: "In the next few days, I tried to slit my wrists with a razor blade, but just scratching it hurt so much I gave up the attempt. I walked into the streets several times hoping a truck would run over me, but the trucks in my town appeared to have amazingly good brakes."[47] In 1970 *Reader's Digest,* a conservative publication, even argued that the hardship and unhappiness suffered by unwed mothers were so severe they could serve a pedagogical function:

> Traditionally U.S. public schools have felt that a pregnant girl should be expelled (1) to keep her from "contaminating" the rest of the girls and (2) as an object lesson in the wages of sin. But the logic of this policy is poor. When did a pregnant girl ever get another girl pregnant? Most youth psychologists feel that expulsion destroys a chance to make a compelling point. A single pregnant schoolgirl in study hall—ungainly, unhappy, she

and the boy facing responsibilities or hard decisions affecting the rest of their lives—is more eloquent than six sex education lectures.[48]

Social scientists may eventually understand fully why attitudes toward sex and marriage changed so profoundly. Whatever the mechanisms, in less than a decade a shameful condition was transformed into a personal choice. The rise of the women's movement, the sexual revolution, the greater availability of abortion (which made out-of-wedlock childbearing truly a choice), and the increasing fragility of marriage all no doubt contributed to the astonishing shift in the social meaning of illegitimacy.[49]

In March 1970 a twenty-seven-year-old journalist told a revealing story in the *Atlantic* magazine. She had informed her employer that she was pregnant and had been summarily fired for "gross personal misconduct"— that is, simply for being pregnant and unmarried. Others had reacted similarly when she revealed her condition: subsequent employers had treated her "like scum," and a diaper company—in the liberal town of Cambridge, Massachusetts—had refused to deliver diapers to her home because of her shameful status. When she had tried to run a small advertisement in the personals section of the newspaper, in an effort to contact other unwed mothers and form a support group, no legitimate newspaper would print the ad. As a hint of things to come, however, she had finally discovered a women's liberation group and, with the new language of the women's movement, had been able to make the unprecedented claim that she was not a woman "in trouble" and hence beneath contempt but a woman making an active and praiseworthy choice.[50]

Likewise, in 1971 a young woman succeeded in changing forever the way schools dealt with pregnant students. Fay Ordway—honors student, editor of the yearbook, and student chair of the scholarship committee—was expelled from her high school in East Pepperell, Massachusetts, because she was pregnant and unmarried. She was offered home tutoring, the traditional option for pregnant students. Since such programs were typically grudging at best, she soon found tutoring inadequate. She was forbidden to enter the school grounds during class time (lest she "contaminate" the other students, as *Reader's Digest* had put it), although she was allowed to speak with the teachers after everyone else had left. Alas for her education, she soon discovered that the teachers, too, left the school when instruction was over. So Ordway sued, arguing that she had a right to attend regular classes. She had carefully considered and rejected the options that were available to pregnant unmarried women. She was reluctant to marry too young, and she objected to having an abortion. When she found that if she entered the local Florence Crittenton home she would be assigned a social worker, her response was, "My social worker! Like I was a criminal or something! I thanked them, but I wasn't going to go there."[51] So she decided to go to court. "I couldn't see that my being married or not being married had anything to do with my education. Everyone should be entitled to an education—everyone needs an education. So I decided to fight for mine."[52] Commonplace as these sentiments were to become just a few years later, they were nothing short of astonishing at the time.

Yet when an old cultural order is challenged, one is often amazed to see how shallow its foundations really are and how much it depends on people's unquestioning acceptance of their values. The very boldness of Fay Ordway's attack undercut the idea that "everybody agreed" unwed pregnant students were young women who had "gone bad" and who should be kept away from their classmates. Consequently, the school chose to argue that the prohibition was not moral but practical, designed to protect the health of the pregnant woman. Testimony by Ordway's obstetrician eventually demolished that argument and she was permitted to return to school, but the issues involved were so potent that the case worked its way to the Supreme Court. Her challenges to the reigning orthodoxy did not leave her unscathed, however. She was excluded from the Honor Society, despite her high grades; she was denied a college scholarship that she had been promised; and she eventually gave her daughter up for adoption.[53] Fay Ordway was a pioneer, but a pioneer on a opening frontier. The old order did not fall apart because one unwed pregnant teenager from East Pepperell, Massachusetts, sued for the right to stay in school. But the fact that she was *willing* to sue and thereby draw public attention to her situation, the fact that the school felt compelled to mount a defense based on pragmatic rather than moral grounds, and the fact that her obstetrician was willing to testify on her behalf all showed that public attitudes were changing.

So were the mothers themselves. In 1970 half of all unmarried mothers were teenagers, though older women received more attention and did more to undermine the stereotypes. In that year, *Time* magazine noted that Mia Farrow, Vanessa Redgrave, and the Irish politician Bernadette Devlin had all recently had babies out of wedlock "openly and happily"; maternity homes were closing because women no longer felt that they had anything to hide; and Blue Cross had begun to pay medical benefits to single women.[54] The increasing willingness of women to bear and raise children out of wedlock occasioned spirited debate in the media, including publications aimed at young women.[55] Public school teachers, who had always served as role models for the young, eventually earned the right to keep teaching while pregnant and unwed, but they had to fight for it. Prior to the 1970s, schools often forced pregnant *married* teachers to leave their jobs. In the early 1980s, therefore, when unmarried pregnant teachers in two different cities decided to carry their babies to term while continuing to teach, they ignited considerable public controversy.[56] The women hired lawyers and were eventually permitted to keep their jobs. Unwed mothers were no longer wrongdoers—at least if they were affluent, employed, and older. Of course, unwed mothers had a much harder time gaining acceptance if they were young, poor, and African American. The final, ironic stage in the breakdown of long-standing mores came in 1985, when the Girls' Clubs fired a young black woman for being pregnant out of wedlock. They argued that it was not the issue of illegitimacy per se that concerned them, but the fact that she would be a poor role model for young black women, who were now considered to be at high risk of "teenage pregnancy."[57]

Some people argue that American society should turn back the clock, should restore the stigma to out-of-wedlock births. But this solution presents a number of practical problems and would be unlikely to succeed. For one thing, no one really understands how or why out-of-wedlock childbearing lost its stigma, so that making it shameful again is probably not something that can be done by exhortation alone. (This is especially true since it has lost a great deal of its stigma in almost all modern, industrialized societies.) Moreover, although abortion may be a practical alternative to out-of-wedlock childbearing, public-policy advocates will find it difficult to argue that more abortion is a good thing. Finally, stigmatizing out-of-wedlock childbearing presents some of the bright-line problems that afflict the issue of sexual activity among teenagers. Is it realistic to argue that no one should have children unless he or she is legally married? (This was, after all, what Vice-President Dan Quayle implied when he criticized a television character who gave birth to an illegitimate child.) This might be the fairest solution, but opinion polls suggest that the public is not troubled if the unwed mother is old enough and affluent enough. Yet how old and how affluent does she have to be? Even if society could reach a consensus that the United States should have a policy discouraging out-of-wedlock births, the fact that women all over the world are having children outside marriage suggests that rhetorical urging is not likely to be very successful.

THE ECONOMIC TRANSFORMATION
OF AMERICAN LIFE

The fact that the public accepts out-of-wedlock births among older, affluent, white women but deplores them among young, poor, minority women is intimately tied to a third profound change in the lives of Americans—namely, the decline of American economic power and of middle-class affluence.

Today's young Americans are the first generation in living memory who face the prospect of doing less well economically over their lifetimes than did their parents. In recent years the gap between the well-to-do and the poor has grown: the rich are getting richer and the poor are getting poorer. Economists use various measures to estimate the distribution of income, and virtually all of them show that income distribution is "hollowing out," meaning that individuals are more likely to find themselves at the top or bottom of the income distribution and less likely to find themselves in the middle.[58] And inequality among *families* is growing even faster. Poor families are not only getting poorer, but they now tend to be poorer in the United States than elsewhere. When we compare the income of the poorest 20 percent of households in the United States to that of the poorest 20 percent in other industrialized countries, it is clear that Americans are faring very badly. In the late 1960s and early 1970s, in the United States the poorest households were receiving about 3.8 percent of all taxable income; in the United Kingdom, 4.4 percent; in Germany, 5.4 percent; and in Japan, 7.6 percent. More recent data show that the poorest families in the United States receive a smaller part of their nation's income than do the poorest families in ten comparable European countries.[59] All of these figures suggest that the middle class is shrinking and that its members are rising or falling on the income scale. As a result, economists have begun to talk about a "declining middle class."[60]

But growing disparities in income are not the whole story. As international comparisons reveal, such inequalities have long existed in the United States, and the increases in the 1980s were well within historical trends.[61]

In 1969 the richest one-fifth of families earned about $7.25 for each dollar the poorest fifth earned; by the late 1980s the richest fifth were earning $9.60 for each dollar the poorest earned—an increase, to be sure, but one that occurred in the context of an income distribution that was already fairly polarized.[62]

Much more significant than income disparity is the decline in real wages that took place in the 1970s and 1980s, meaning that individual income lost purchasing power as measured in constant dollars. Between the end of World War II and the first oil embargo of 1973, real wages grew rapidly; then came nearly twenty years of very slow growth or stagnation. In the first period the median annual income of a man at the peak of his earning capacity (forty-five to fifty-four) who worked full time year-round more than doubled, going from $15,529 in 1946 to $32,752 in 1976 (in constant 1987 dollars). This represented an increase of 20 to 30 percent per decade. Between 1976 and 1986, however, real wages increased much more slowly, on the order of 1 percent a year.[63] The increase in real wages after World War II meant that the middle class was expanding, not because it was receiving a larger share of national income (although, to a modest extent, it was) but because overall wages were rising so rapidly. Median income for families (as opposed to median income for men) went from $15,000 in 1947 to $29,000 in 1969, measured in constant 1987 dollars. But after 1973, as real wages declined, family income increased only marginally—to $30,600 in 1986. To put this most dramatically, in the 1950s and 1960s a young man could expect, by age thirty, to be earning 15 percent more than his father had at the same age. By 1986, in contrast, he could expect to be earning 15 percent *less*.[64]

The causes of this decline are complex and much debated. Economists have pointed to a number of factors: jobs for skilled blue-collar workers have declined, particularly in manufacturing (and there are fewer unionized and hence high-wage jobs among the ones that remain); productivity has fallen; international competition has intensified; new immigrants have changed the composition of the work force. The upshot is that for the first time the American middle class is confronting the prospect of "declining fortunes," not only in relative terms but in absolute terms—something that has occurred only rarely in American history.[65] After 1973 young people coming onto the labor market faced both declining wages and a dearth of well-paying jobs. Consequently, many people began to fear the loss of key elements of the American dream—the dream of owning their own home, earning a good and increasing wage over the life cycle, sending their children to college, and seeing their children attain a higher standard of living than they themselves had, in a constant pattern of generational upward mobility.

In the 1970s there were also dramatic changes in the nature of poverty and the structure of families. Once, the poor had been elderly and the elderly had been poor: in 1959 more than a third of all elderly people had been poor. But the programs instituted under Lyndon Johnson's Great Society, in particular the indexing of Social Security to inflation, altered the makeup of the poor population. The poverty rates for older people fell by half between 1959 and the mid-1970s, and have continued to decline. Today the poverty rate among the elderly is lower than the national average.

Children, in contrast, are moving in the opposite direction. Although their poverty rates likewise declined as a result of Great Society legislation, during the past fifteen years the risk that an American child will grow up in poverty has increased by about a third. Children, in comparison to adults and the elderly, are now twice as likely to be poor: 20 percent of all children are poor, accounting for fully 40 percent of the poor people in the United States.[66] The fact that poverty among children is growing and that poverty in general is becoming more apparent all across the United States is one cause of the public's concern about pregnancy among teenagers. Looked at from a broad perspective, American families seem to have followed two trajectories. The pattern of traditional families has hollowed out, just like the income distribution.

One large group of Americans has responded to declining real wages by making its family structure more *concentrated*. These people are postponing marriage and childbearing to an ever greater extent, having fewer and fewer children, and forming a growing number of two-career marriages. This trajectory, which we might call the yuppie pattern (after the Young Urban Professionals who adopt it), is the new middle-class norm. Women in particular are investing more time in their education, are training for careers rather than jobs, and are continuing to work even after they have children. This pattern has become so prevalent among the middle class that we often forget what a major shift in behavior it represented when it first appeared. For much of U.S. history, American women married fairly young, had their children fairly early, and retired from the work force until their children were grown. But the new yuppie pattern is available only to the affluent, people who can realistically expect that the market will reward their sacrifices. For people who have fewer resources, there is another shift in the American family: these people *rearrange* the traditional family. They either never get married or start a family at all, or they have children without being married.[67]

The traditional family of the forties and fifties thus was transformed in the seventies and even more in the eighties. The "Ozzie and Harriet" family (in which the husband worked but the wife did not) gave way to two new and distinct configurations. America's "households" (to use the Census Bureau's term for groups of people living together) ceased to consist mostly of traditional families and began to comprise married working couples on the one hand or single-parent families on the other. (Eighty-seven percent of single parents are in fact single mothers.)[68] In 1970, out of all families with children, almost nine out of ten included both spouses, whereas only one in ten was a single-parent family. Furthermore, of the single-parent families, fewer than ten percent (or about 1 percent of all families with children) were families in which the parents were unmarried. In 1992, in contrast, six out of ten American families were single-parent families, and only four in ten were two-parent families. Among single-parent families in 1992, the largest group consisted of those headed by never-married mothers. Overall, today about one out of every three families with children is headed by a woman who has never been married.[69]

We've already noted that throughout the 1970s and 1980s many individuals got richer while many others got poorer. The same thing happened to families: the income distribution for them was hollowing out as well. More and more families, headed by single women who on average earned less than men, lived in poverty, while other families, comprising a mother and father who were *both* wage earners, lived in financial comfort. And people appeared to select the family pattern that would perpetuate the status they had prior to the birth of their first child. Those who were affluent tended to postpone childbearing and to have children only after they were married; those who were poor tended to have their first child at an early age and out of wedlock.

These trends were visible at all levels of society and in every racial and ethnic group. But contrary to stereotype, in the seventies and eighties married blacks were *more* likely to be two-earner couples than were married whites. In 1989, for example, 64 percent of black married couples were two-earner couples, compared to only 57 percent of white couples. Yet married couples as a proportion of all households declined much more rapidly among blacks than among whites. In 1969 married couples accounted for almost 60 percent of all black households, but twenty years later the figure was only 36 percent. There was a slower but similar decline among white married couples, from 73 percent of all households in 1969 to 59 percent in 1989. Thus, relatively affluent two-income families tended to be white, and relatively poor single-mother households tended to be black. In 1969 two-earner couples accounted for about the same proportion of households among blacks and whites (29 percent and 28 percent, respectively); by 1989 such families comprised a third (34 percent) of all white households, but only a quarter (23 percent) of all black households.[70] Furthermore, while single mothers were becoming more numerous among all racial groups, whites and blacks became single mothers in different ways. Whites tended to do so as a result of divorce (although, as we have seen, rates of childbearing among white never-married women have doubled since the 1970s); most black single mothers have never been married.[71]

As common sense suggests, single-mother households are poorer than two-parent households. If in 1989 the ratio of married couples to all households had been the same as it had been in 1970, income for blacks in 1989 would have been 15 percent higher than it actually was, and income for whites would have been 10 percent higher. To put this another way, if in 1989 black households had comprised the same percentage of single parents that white households did, income for blacks would have been 22 percent higher than it actually was. The effects of changes in family structure should be seen in context, however. Although overall family income in 1989 would have been higher if families then had been structured as they had been in 1970, rates of poverty would have been only slightly different: about 4 percent lower for blacks and about 1.5 percent lower for whites.[72]

Taken together, these figures indicate that in the face of new economic and social conditions, Americans seem to have hollowed out the family structure just as the economy was hollowing out the income distribution. Traditional married couples in which only the husband worked were becoming scarcer, while two-income families and single-parent families were proliferating. In many cases changes in family structure were closely related to—in fact, an adaptation to—changing economic circumstances, and differed according to race. In the 1950s and 1960s virtually all American women married at an early age (especially in comparison to European women), had their first child soon afterward, and completed their childbearing within a few years. But this pattern became less common as fortunes declined and the middle class shrank. The lucky and prosperous were able to invest more in education, obtain a greater return on their investment, and move into the professional upper-middle class. (College-educated people began to receive more of a return on their educational investment than they had in earlier years.)[73] And when men and women invested more in education, they tended to postpone marriage and childbearing, to form two-income families, and to have fewer children. Among people with less money and less cultural capital, this pattern seems to have been less attractive.[74] They may have postponed or forgone marriage, or entered into a partnership that was not a legal marriage, but they did not give up bearing children: poor women continued to do what all American women had done in the postwar era—namely, have babies at an early age—but more and more of them had children out of wedlock. Affluent and successful men and women tended to forsake this older pattern, leaving it mainly to poor women. The new, bifurcated economy, in which good jobs got better and bad jobs got worse, was paralleled by a bifurcated family pattern, in which the affluent postponed their childbearing and had their babies in wedlock while the poor did not.

Consequently, just as the issue of pregnancy among teenagers was being debated in Congress and in the media, many Americans were viewing it from the vantage point of their own restructured lives. People who were affluent and well educated, who had delayed marriage in order to further their schooling, who were members of two-earner couples, and who were postponing and limiting their childbearing had little sympathy for teenage mothers (who were often conflated in the public mind with unwed mothers). The behavior of these young women seemed not only unwise and self-destructive, but unwise and self-destructive in ways that hit particularly close to home. They seemed to be having babies before they were ready, and, worse, to be doing so without a legal husband, at a time when many Americans were becoming keenly aware that it took two or more workers in a family to maintain a middle-class lifestyle. People who had scrimped and saved until they could marry and set up a household, who lived with all of the burdens of the "second shift" (the burdens incurred when wives enter the labor force but are still expected to fulfill their traditional nurturant role), and who were postponing childbearing until they could afford it were particularly unsympathetic: teenagers who had babies seemed to be heedless, irresponsible, and heading for trouble.[75] And those in the middle, the ones whose highly paid blue- and white-collar jobs were becoming scarce and who were having difficulty passing on these middle-class jobs to their children, were no more understanding: young people who had sex and babies too soon seemed to be bringing their troubles on themselves.[76]

In short, pregnant teenagers made a convenient lightning rod for the anxieties and tensions in Americans' lives. Economic fortunes were unstable, a postindustrial economic order was evolving, sexual and reproductive patterns were mutating. Representing such teenagers as the epitome of society's ills seemed one quick way of making sense of these enormous changes. This was particularly true as poverty was becoming ever more visible and being poor appeared to be the direct result of immoral or unwise behavior. Pregnant teenagers seemed to embody the very essence of such behavior. Indeed, the phrase "teenage pregnancy" continues to be a powerful shorthand way of referring to the problem of poverty.

The rhetoric of the 1970s, generated in good faith by advocates who wanted to ensure that young women had access to contraception, created a comforting but unrealistic fantasy to explain the fact that some people were getting poorer in an uncertain economy. By noting that young mothers were poor mothers, advocates persuaded the public that young mothers are poor *because* they had untimely pregnancies and births. This in turn led to the conclusion that if young poor women simply did what young affluent women do, then they, too, would be affluent. It is not surprising that when affluent people dramatically change their attitudes and behavior toward marriage and childbearing but poor people do not, the well-to-do would try to explain the existence of poverty by saying the poor have failed to adapt. In recent years, both liberals and conservatives have tended to ascribe poverty to the sexual and reproductive decisions that poor women make. What gives this argument resonance is the fact that the affluent are postponing their childbearing and early motherhood is increasingly the province of the "left behind"—poor women who realistically know that postponing their first birth is unlikely to lead to a partnership in a good law firm. But the deep cultural belief that it *might* continues to attract people of every ideological persuasion. Commentators as diverse as Charles Murray and David Ellwood, one a conservative bent on undoing the welfare system and the other a liberal bent on saving it, agree on the foolishness of early pregnancy.[77]

There is no arguing the case that teenagers who bring a child into the world put a strain on public patience, values, and funds. The public assumes that teenagers are unable to support a child financially, and in the overwhelming majority of cases this is true. Moreover, poor mothers tend to have children who will themselves grow up to be poor. Not surprisingly, teenagers and their babies have come to be perceived (to use the words of a *Time* essayist) as "the very hub of the U.S. poverty cycle," often creating up to three generations of poor people who will depend on the public purse. Congress, the media, reports by the National Academy of Sciences, and statements by private voluntary groups all associate poverty with childbearing among teenagers. But this linkage depends on an assumption that reducing pregnancy among teenagers, specifically among unmarried teenagers, can reduce poverty.[78]

In the opinion of many well-meaning middle-class people, the trouble with poor and pregnant teenagers is that they do not do what middle-class people do: invest in an education, establish themselves in a job, marry a sensible and hardworking person, and only then begin to think about having a baby. Many poor people do these things, of course, and so do many poor teenagers. But the deck is stacked against people at the lower levels of a world in which the job distribution has been hollowed out. People who lack an education are less well off than ever before, and thus find it ever harder to maintain a marriage and support a family. Even if they work at one or more of the "lousy jobs" at the bottom of the wage structure, full-time year-round employment is insufficient to keep a family out of poverty, as the father of Michelle Brown's baby found out in his job at McDonald's.[79] The idea that young people would be better off if they worked harder, were more patient, and postponed their childbearing is simply not true—and is unlikely to become true in the foreseeable future—for a great many people at the bottom of the income scale. Even when poor people obtain more education, for example, they only displace other people at the end of the queue, and the problem of poverty and childbearing among young people continues.

A compelling body of scholarship now shows that although people who become parents as teenagers will eventually be poorer than those who do not, a very large proportion of that difference is explained by preexisting factors. Well over half of all women who give birth as teenagers come from profoundly poor families, and more than one-fourth come from families who are slightly better off but still struggling economically. Taken together, more than 80 percent of teenage mothers were living in poverty or near-poverty long before they became pregnant.[80] Teenage parents are not middle-class people who have become poor simply because they have had a baby; rather, they have become teenage parents because they were poor to begin with. More than two decades of research, summarized in the National Academy of Sciences' report *Risking the Future* (1987), make clear a point not highlighted in the report itself: at every step of the process that leads to early childbearing, social and economic disadvantage plays a powerful role. Poor kids, not rich ones, have babies as teenagers, and their poverty long predates their pregnancy. By the same token, poor kids, not rich ones, have babies without being married. In part this is also a product of the hollowing out of the income structure. Low-wage jobs rarely pay enough to support a family if only the father works; and if both parents work, they are likely to face daunting childcare problems—problems exacerbated by the fact that such jobs are often episodic, with unpredictable hours and swing shifts.

In addition, conservatives are right: AFDC as it is structured in most states exacts a subtle, and in some cases not so subtle, marriage penalty. Only about half the states permit AFDC funds to go to families in which the father lives in the home, and these programs (known as AFDC-UP) are open only to unemployed men who have an employment record—a difficult criterion to satisfy in communities where unemployment can run to more than 50 percent and where many of the low-wage jobs do not meet the eligibility criteria for AFDC-UP. As a result, two-parent families make up only 7 percent of AFDC cases. Still, states that permit poor fathers married to poor mothers to obtain AFDC seem to have higher rates of marriage than do states without AFDC-UP, suggesting that AFDC itself penalizes people for getting married.[81]

But if teenage mothers are poor before they ever become mothers, if in many cases they would be poor and in need of welfare at whatever age they had their first child, and if marriage brings its own set of problems to poor people, much of the easy equation that identifies early pregnancy as a cause of poverty breaks down. If the real problem is poverty, not the age or marital status of young women when they give birth, then it is not surprising that poor women tend to have children and even grandchildren who grow up to be poor. Preventing teenagers from getting pregnant and persuading them to delay their childbearing would merely postpone the problem of poor women and their dependence on welfare. Childbearing among teenagers has relatively little effect on the levels of poverty in the United States. But income disparities have become a pervasive fact of American life, and it is scarcely surprising that when experts in the 1970s labeled "teenage pregnancy" a fundamental cause of poverty, Americans were willing to listen.

5

CHOICE

AND

CONSEQUENCE

In the late 1970s a government official, speaking with political scientist John Kingdon, blamed America's distressingly high infant mortality rate on the fact that so many teenagers are getting pregnant. "If you take only women over nineteen, we have the best rate in the world. The reason that the infant mortality rate is so bad is that young women are getting pregnant long before they should."[1] Many people would agree with the logic of this statement. It implies that America's dismal infant mortality rate—like a number of the nation's other social ills—can be traced to the fact that teenagers in the United States are getting pregnant and having babies at a higher rate than teens in other countries. At the same time, by using the word "should" it also implies that the young women involved are responsible for their situation and its consequences—that pregnancy is an option they could reject if only they chose to do so.

This official might just as easily have said that the trouble with the U.S. infant mortality statistics is that they include so many poor people—that if we considered only the affluent, the United States has one of the lowest infant mortality rates in the world. Or that they are skewed by the high rate among African Americans—that if we looked only at whites, the statistics are much more reassuring. Both of these statements are incontrovertibly true; in fact, they are truer than the statement about pregnant teenagers. If we consider the infant mortality rate for all ages, races, and classes, the United States ranks twenty-ninth in the world. For women older than nineteen, it moves up two places, to twenty-seventh. For whites, it ranks twenty-second in the world, on a par with the Netherlands Antilles. And for the affluent, it ranks fourteenth, just above Canada.[2]

Yet one would have to be heartless to say that infant mortality rates among whites and the affluent are fine, and to blame poor people and African Americans for making the level of infant mortality in the United States an international scandal. Although one might think of poverty or minority-group status as a determinant of negative outcomes such as infant mortality, one cannot hold individual poor people or African Americans *responsible* for being either poor or black. In fact, the reason it seems wrong to boast of the lower infant mortality rates among whites and the well-to-do is that society has failed poor and minority people, not that they have failed society.

Even though 80 percent of teenage mothers come from poor backgrounds and approximately 40 percent are African American, the public perceives teenagers as a separate entity, responsible for their fate in ways that poor mothers or black mothers are not. Since most adults think that teenagers choose to become pregnant and that the negative outcomes associated with early pregnancy result from these choices, they assume that if teenagers could just discipline themselves to wait a few years before having babies, then all would be well, or at least better. They thus combine two different issues into one. They assume that teenage mothers lead difficult lives simply as a consequence of having had a baby, and as a result they assume that young women can avoid difficult lives just by choosing to postpone child-bearing.

No one questions that teen mothers have a much harder lot in life than those who wait until they are older to have a child. Research from more than two decades has shown that teen mothers are in poorer health, have more medical problems during pregnancy, and give birth to more stillborn, short-lived, low-birthweight, and medically compromised babies.[3] Teen mothers are also less likely to have finished high school and are thus more likely to wind up in routine, precarious, unsatisfying, dead-end jobs later in life.[4] They are more likely to be single parents (either because they never married or because many of them divorce) and more likely to depend on welfare.[5] In short, their lives tend to be "lives on the edge."[6] Most Americans know that poverty and other social ills are linked with early pregnancy because in the 1970s advocates for teenagers told them so. As the dire statistics made their way from research journals to Congress to the media and then acquired the status of conventional wisdom, the association between early childbearing and poverty (asserting that where we find one, we find the other) moved from a correlation to a causative relationship. Since teenage parents were more often poorer, less educated, and more liable to problematic pregnancies than older women, the public soon found it logical to assume that early childbearing *caused* these conditions. From the outset, however, the people who get pregnant as teenagers and who carry their babies to term are substantially different from people who do not. Many of these young mothers would be poor (and would have children who grew up to be poor) no matter how old they were when they gave birth.

The precise extent to which early childbearing compromises a young woman's chances in life, if at all, is one of the most vigorously debated questions in the field of public policy right now. Despite the arcane statistical techniques that are sometimes used, the issue is far from academic. If teen parents would be in much the same plight even if they did postpone their childbearing, then a full-fledged effort to prevent them from getting pregnant and having babies would at best only push the problem back a few years. If we knew for a fact that childbearing per se had little or no effect on the life chances of those who become teen mothers or on the future of their children, we could get on with devising interventions that might really make a difference in their lives. But if teens really do bring about some of their own misfortunes by choosing to become pregnant, then current policies need to become more vigorous and imaginative.

The question of the timing and consequences of early pregnancy dovetails with a question that lies at the heart of much of the ongoing debate about poverty: To what extent does poverty result from the social and economic structure that an individual confronts, and to what extent does it result from the individual's own actions? Liberals stress the structure; conservatives, the choices. In the case of teenage parents, the issue is complicated by the type of person who becomes a teenage mother in the first place, and by the need to sort out the effects of social and economic forces from the additional effect that early childbearing may have on her life chances and those of her children.[7] Some people argue that virtually all of the observable differences between teen mothers and other mothers can be explained largely by what economists call "selection effects"—that is, preexisting differences between the kinds of young women who become mothers as teenagers and those who do not. Others argue that whatever troubles a poor young woman faces are compounded if she chooses to have a baby. To put this in human terms, those on one side of the argument believe that a woman like Michelle Brown, long before she ever gets pregnant, is not only poorer but also less ambitious, less committed to getting ahead, and more bruised by life than her peers who do not have babies. If, later on, her circumstances are very different from theirs, then the differences are due to these preexisting conditions rather than to the fact that she was a young mother. Adherents of the other position hold that although women who become teen mothers do in fact come from especially disadvantaged backgrounds, early childbearing makes a bad situation even worse. Whatever problems Michelle may have as a poor woman from a troubled family in a poor neighborhood (the situation of many young women who become teenage mothers), the fact that she has borne a child while still in high school adds one more obstacle to her life—an obstacle that her childless friends who come from similar backgrounds, attend the same school, and live in the same neighborhood do not have to contend with.

Whether early childbearing makes much difference in a teenager's life is not only a technical question but a moral one. Many Americans believe that teenagers are making a bad choice when they have a baby, and that they must be encouraged or in some cases coerced to make a different decision. But if young parents would face essentially the same circumstances no matter when they had a baby (and if the baby would have the same limited range of future opportunities no matter when its parents brought it into the world), then there is no point in blaming teens for making choices that, although they may seem like bad ones from a middle-class point of view, have little in the way of real consequences for the young people involved.

Many Americans feel that there is not much to debate between the liberal and conservative positions. In part because of the efforts of those activists who put early pregnancy on the national agenda in the 1970s, the media and much of the public simply take it for granted that early pregnancy is one of the basic mechanisms sustaining poverty and that teens who have babies are doing the wrong thing. It is commonly assumed, though not often explicitly stated, that the high birthrate among African American teens is a major reason for the fact that, although some thirty years have passed since the inception of the Civil Rights Movement, blacks and whites continue to face very different life chances. In 1994 *People* magazine (in an article tellingly entitled "The Baby Trap") concluded that "on average, only 5 percent of teen mothers get college degrees, compared with 47 percent of those who have children at twenty-five or older. And one-third of the daughters of teenage mothers will go on to become teen mothers themselves—perpetuating what is usually a cycle of hardship and deprivation."[8]

For the media, at least, the relationship is clear: early childbearing leads women to curtail their education, to be poor, and to have daughters who, learning by example, have babies as teenagers and thus keep the cycle of poverty going. Is this true? In the light of what we know, does early childbearing make women poorer than they would otherwise be? What effect *does* it have on them? On their children? On society as a whole?

WHO BECOMES A TEENAGE MOTHER?

Sorting out cause and effect would be easy if pregnant teens and teenage mothers (especially unmarried ones) were as common in Grosse Pointe as in Harlem and as much a feature of life in Beverly Hills as in East Los Angeles. If this were true, we could assume that the disadvantages we see in the lives of teen mothers and their children are due to the fact that these women chose to become mothers early in life. But such mothers are not randomly dotted across the social landscape. At every step of the process, people who are already poor are more at risk of early pregnancy and childbearing. Worse yet, the risk goes up for young people who are in the process of being pushed to the margins of society, whatever their social class. Although poverty alone is a strong predictor of early childbearing, teenage parents, compared with people who don't become parents as teens, are much more likely to have many other problems in their lives even before they get pregnant: they are more likely to come from a single-parent family, to have trouble in school, to have been held back a grade, to come from a home that has been broken by divorce or separation, and to live in bad neighborhoods.[9]

Historically, these "precursors" of early pregnancy and childbearing were more common among young people from minority backgrounds; and, not surprisingly, such young people were far more likely to become teenage parents, especially out of wedlock. In recent years, however, as these precursors have become more common among whites, so has early child-bearing. In 1970, for example, young women from minority backgrounds were nine times more likely than whites to bear a child out of wedlock, but by the early 1990s they were only three times more likely.[10] Overall, women who already have limited chances in life are much more likely to bear children while still in their teens. Thus, the real question is to what extent their lives are worsened by their decision to have a baby, if "decision" is indeed the right word.

Some two decades ago, demographer Jane Menken examined the traditional association between early childbearing and poor maternal and infant health, and questioned some long-standing assumptions about the nature of that association. She recognized, as had others before her, that in comparison to older mothers teenage mothers are significantly less likely to receive medical care during their pregnancies, more likely to have more complications during pregnancy and childbirth, more likely to be ill during pregnancy, and more likely to have premature and low-birthweight babies. There is even some evidence that they are more likely to have children who are injured or hospitalized during the first five years of life.[11] Yet Menken concluded that the negative outcomes associated with early pregnancy had more to do with *the kinds of people who become pregnant as teenagers* than they had to do with the age at which women become pregnant. A great many of the conditions usually ascribed to "teenage pregnancy" are actually a function of poverty and the insidious effects of being both black and poor, she argued. Few of them can be blamed on the fact that a woman is a young mother, as opposed to being simply a poor mother or a minority-group mother.[12] "Even if childbearing is postponed beyond age twenty," Menken wrote, "unless social and economic conditions change for these young people, they may encounter the same difficulties at a later age."[13] Today there is a very large body of data to support her assertion. Typically a young person ends up as a teenage parent only after going through a series of steps, and at each step the successful and affluent are screened out.

For example, although premarital sex is becoming more common among all American teenagers, those who come from poor and minority backgrounds have historically begun to have intercourse at a slightly earlier age than their white and affluent peers. They also tend to delay using effective contraception more than their affluent peers, and to use it less consistently when they do start. Moreover, because they started sex earlier, they have a longer period of time during which this less consistent, less effective contraceptive use can take its toll.[14] In addition, both early sex and ineffective contraceptive use are more common among young people who have lower educational aspirations and who do poorly in school. About 40 percent of pregnant teens seek an abortion; those who seek abortions tend to be affluent and white, to have more ambitious educational and career goals, and to have higher grade point averages.[15] All these factors taken together mean that affluent teens, a bit more than 60 percent of the age group, account for fewer than a fifth of all early births.[16] Furthermore, middle-class and affluent teens who do get pregnant and who do not seek an abortion are much more likely to marry than are poor ones.[17]

A number of scholars have noted that even in low-income minority communities, where a great many people are disadvantaged, those who become teen mothers are often the more discouraged of the disadvantaged.[18] Among one group of pregnant teenagers who were all low-income urban blacks, those who sought abortions had higher aspirations than those who decided to carry their babies to term.[19] Young black women who perform well in school are often dissuaded from becoming pregnant by parents and others who urge them not to get involved with young men.[20] Daughters who seem most likely to succeed are cautioned that they will be "throwing their lives away" if they get pregnant and have a child too soon.[21] This is so much the commonsense view within the communities themselves that a group of black high school students, when presented with a vignette describing a young black couple with high ambition and the opportunity to succeed, agreed unanimously that the woman would not get pregnant. Their comments ranged from "She's a hard worker so I doubt a pregnancy occurs" to "They don't want to get serious." Confronted with a vignette about a young couple whose families were poor, who didn't like school, and who were already two years behind, students were equally unanimous in believing that the woman would get pregnant. "If she's two years behind in school there is . . . no hope for her. She ain't never going to be nothing."[22]

Other data suggest that these patterns hold true across racial lines. In 1980 a large national survey of young women aged fifteen and sixteen found that about 5 percent of the whites, 13 percent of the blacks, and 9 percent of the Hispanics said they "definitely" would consider having a child out of wedlock. For each group an additional 20 percent or so said that they "might" consider this option. Two years after the survey, a significant number of those who said they would consider having a child out of wedlock had indeed done so. Of particular interest is that those who thought they might have a child out of wedlock, and especially those who did, fit the profile of people we have been describing as both disadvantaged and discouraged. They were young women of all races who, in comparison to their peers, came from less affluent backgrounds, performed less well in school, had lower scores on ability tests, and were more likely to be living in a female-headed household. They were also more likely to have developed a pattern of disciplinary problems in school and to have had records of truancy and absenteeism.[23] Thus, they were young people who were already experiencing difficulties in life on several fronts and who had little optimism about their futures.

Poor and minority teens are also at greater risk of early childbearing because they live in poor neighborhoods where few people have much hope of improving their lot. A teen who lives in a neighborhood in which virtually all the people are poor and members of minorities, and in which she can see few if any successful role models, faces an increased risk of getting pregnant and having a baby. A young black or white woman who is poor, having trouble academically, and becoming convinced that she is unlikely to get ahead is better off—whatever her individual risk factors—if she is in a good suburban school where a majority of her peers view pregnancy as an obstacle to achievement. If she is living or attending school in a ghetto neighborhood, especially one in which a great many of her peers are having sex, she is more likely to have sex, less likely to use contraception, and more likely to get pregnant than she would be in the suburban school.[24]

All along the way, it is more likely to be the poor woman and the minority woman who will have sex early, who will fail to use enough contraception to keep from getting pregnant, who will not have an abortion, and who will not get married if she becomes pregnant. The process by which young women become teenage mothers (especially unmarried ones) acts like a sieve, filtering out the rich and successful, letting mostly the poor and discouraged through. Consequently, although pregnant teenagers are found in all communities, they are much more prevalent in poor neighborhoods; when teenagers from rich communities get pregnant, they deal with the situation differently. In comparison to their peers, women who have a child while they are teenagers, especially while still unmarried, are far more likely to be poor, more likely to be rural, more likely to be black, and more likely to be southern if they are white.[25] They are much more likely to have accumulated educational deficits and to hold lower aspirations for themselves. Thus, even before she bears a child, a teenager who becomes a mother is already subject to significant limits that will affect her in many ways no matter when she has her first baby.

This "selection effect" should make us cautious when we try to assess the effects of early childbearing. According to the conventional wisdom, for example, teenagers are at great risk during pregnancy because their bodies are too immature for motherhood; teen mothers, faced with the demands of a baby and schoolwork, tend to drop out of high school; and teen mothers who have dropped out lose any educational chances they may have had, condemning themselves and their children to lives of disadvantage. But since the teens who become pregnant are discouraged and disadvantaged to begin with, and since the fact that they are living in bleak circumstances increases the likelihood that they will get pregnant, the real question is whether early childbearing has additional effects on their lives. We must try to study it apart from these background factors that are implicated in the process by which young women become teenage mothers and that presage a grim future for a young woman no matter when she has her first child.

HEALTH, SCHOOLING, ECONOMIC WELL-BEING

Many Americans still believe the old nineteenth-century maxim which claims that teenagers are simply too immature physiologically to give birth without great risk to themselves and their children. This belief has been partly reinforced by studies showing that early pregnancy *is* associated with greater risk of maternal illness, miscarriage, stillbirth, and neonatal death. We now know, however—as Jane Menken warned us twenty years ago—that a very large proportion of these outcomes are a function of the fact that young mothers are poor, rather than that they are young. Poor women generally have more trouble obtaining routine medical and prenatal care, live in more stressful circumstances, and often have more limited diets—all factors that can substantially alter a woman's health during pregnancy, independent of her age. Exacerbating the problem is the fact that Medicaid, the medical-care system for poor people in the United States, has such complex and cumbersome criteria for eligibility that in some states poor women are well along in pregnancy before they can receive medical care. In most states Medicaid eligibility is also closely tied to AFDC status, and as welfare provisions become more and more restricted, a poor pregnant woman can find herself ineligible for both AFDC and health care until late in her pregnancy and sometimes until after her baby is born. Furthermore, Medicaid reimbursements are so low that many physicians refuse to accept Medicaid patients at all.[26] For all these reasons, teenagers are less likely than older women to get medical care during pregnancy. In 1992 it was estimated that 40 percent of all pregnant teenagers lacked medical care during the first, critical trimester of pregnancy. The younger and the poorer the teen, the less likely she is to get such care.[27]

An accumulating body of data strongly suggests that when young mothers *do* get access to routine health care (in particular, routine prenatal care), a very large proportion of the health risks associated with early pregnancy disappears. If teenage mothers were randomly distributed across the population as a whole, rather than being concentrated among the disadvantaged and the discouraged, they might even do better on a range of outcomes during pregnancy than older mothers. In countries with national health care systems (although these countries tend to have extensive welfare provisions and few teenage mothers), teenagers who give birth generally face lower physical risks than do older women. Even in the United States, young mothers face lower risks on some outcomes of pregnancy than older mothers: they are less likely to miscarry or to have babies that die, and some studies suggest that their children have better growth patterns early in life. Indeed, it may be that in terms of physiology alone, if a woman is given access to good health care, the later teen years may be the ideal time to have a baby. One should keep in mind, of course, that about two-thirds of teenage mothers in the United States are in fact eighteen or nineteen.[28]

All of this suggests that the obstacles separating young mothers from healthier pregnancies and births are largely social rather than physical. Teenagers, because of their youth, inexperience, and lack of confidence, have great difficulty navigating a health care system that is inadequate for Americans of any age. But according to this reasoning, one is really arguing that teenagers should postpone their pregnancies a few years in order to become more skillful at coping with inadequate and confusing medical systems—that individuals should adapt to an inadequate system, rather than that medical bureaucracies and crowded city clinics should be seen as problems in and of themselves. This argument also overlooks the fact that postponing pregnancy may have its own costs. Older women face a greater risk of infertility, and postponing pregnancy only a few years may weaken a poor woman's claim on her kinfolk when she needs help with childrearing.

Thus, one can argue against early childbearing on health grounds only if one has unambiguous data showing that the mother's age in itself causes additional and unacceptable health risks to her and her child. Yet the data indicate that a very large proportion of the health risks associated with early childbearing are the product of a fragmented and inadequate medical-care system and not of physiological immaturity. The only exceptions to this pattern seem to be the very young mothers, those under fifteen, who account for fewer than 2 percent of all teenage mothers and who do seem to show some health effects associated with age. But these very young mothers are also likely to be quite poor, even compared to teen mothers in general, and their pregnancies are more likely than the pregnancies of older teens to be a result of involuntary sexual activity. These factors may compound the effects of very early childbearing.[29]

The health effects of early childbearing are of concern to professionals, primarily health care professionals. For the average American, the most salient concern is probably the fact that such childbearing, especially among unmarried teens, is often associated with poverty in later life. Teen mothers are poor mothers; affluent teens become pregnant less often, have more abortions, and get married more often. And these differences are exacerbated by race: poor black teens are three times more likely to become unwed mothers than poor white ones, and there are many more poor black teens to begin with. But partly as a legacy of the 1970s, when feminists and family planning advocates linked early childbearing with poverty, many Americans have come to believe that there is a causative connection.

One key element in their logic is the fact that teenage mothers tend to drop out of school. Most people intuit (and the available data agree) that once a student drops out, he or she will find it very difficult to go back and complete the degree, and that nowadays dropping out of high school is a surer route to poverty than ever before. In 1977 family planning activist Frederick Jaffe said, "Pregnancy is the most common cause of school dropout among adolescent girls in the United States," and his observation has become an article of faith.[30] There is no arguing the fact that the age of a teen mother at the birth of her first child, especially if the mother is a high school student, is strongly associated with truncated schooling, and this association is perhaps the most thoroughly documented of all in connection with early childbearing.[31] Effects on schooling are easy to measure (several large-scale, nationally representative longitudinal studies have revealed a great deal about educational attainment among different groups of people) and are extremely important. Americans have always viewed schooling as a ladder upward; they see failure to graduate from high school as the first, insidious step toward low-wage jobs, poverty, and welfare dependency. Thus, if there is a considerable body of evidence showing that early childbearing causes high school dropout, then it will be easier to prove that such childbearing has a negative effect over the life span.[32]

Although at first glance such evidence does seem to be compelling and although early studies appeared to bear out Jaffe's claim, it turns out that the cause-and-effect relation becomes much murkier once certain caveats are taken into account. Over the last twenty years most of the relevant research has been based on the analysis of large-scale longitudinal data—that is, surveys of many young people over a number of years. These surveys yield broad measures of patterns (Did the mother give birth to a child while in her teen years? Did she graduate from high school? Was she dependent on welfare at any point? Did she have any experience in the labor market?), but rarely give any precise sense of how these patterns interact in the individual's life or whether they are causally related.[33] In some of these data bases it is often impossible to sort out whether a young woman got pregnant and then dropped out of school or dropped out of school and then got pregnant—sequences that have very different implications for public policy. Some estimates suggest that as many as one-fourth to one-third of teenage mothers drop out before they get pregnant. In one recent study a *majority* of the dropouts had a baby more than nine months after they left school, a fact clearly indicating that pregnancy could not have "caused" the dropping out.[34] Other studies suggest that young women may already be drifting away from school long before pregnancy gives them an official excuse to do so.[35]

Interpretation of the data is further clouded by another statistical and theoretical problem: in many earlier studies of the effect of pregnancy on education, teen mothers were compared not with women who waited until their twenties to have a baby (which would have been the appropriate comparison) but with *all* women who did not have a baby during their teen years, including those who never had a child at all. Very highly educated women are likely to be childless, and this fact will inflate the statistical differences between the two groups unless the comparison is limited only to those who have had children.[36] Moreover, longitudinal data easily become dated. By the time enough years have elapsed so that researchers can draw some conclusions from a particular investigation, broad social shifts may have made those conclusions obsolete, especially with regard to newer generations. This is a particular problem when one is investigating the issue of early pregnancy, which has been greatly affected in recent years by social and demographic changes. For example, teenage mothers in earlier studies (conducted in the 1950s and 1960s) were much more likely to be married than such mothers are now.[37] Although marriage can have some very favorable effects on teen mothers, in this context it tends to have an independent negative effect on the likelihood that a pregnant student will graduate. Women who are married often have a socially acceptable reason to drop out of school and assume the role of wife, and many feel social pressure to do so. Teenage mothers in earlier eras were also likely to have larger families than women who gave birth at a later age, and additional children can in themselves be an impediment to attending school. Although teenage mothers, unlike older ones, tend to have a second child soon after the first, their propensity to have more children overall than older mothers has declined considerably. It is no longer the case that a woman who becomes a teenage mother will have a number of babies in close succession and wind up with a large family.[38]

Most important, political and legislative events have affected the relationship between school attendance and early childbearing. As we saw in Chapter 4, *Ordway v. Hargraves* (1971) made it illegal for schools to expel students who were known to be pregnant. Congress added force to this decision by passing Title IX legislation: beginning in 1975, schools who did not comply with the law would be denied federal funds.[39] By the late 1970s, accordingly, most school districts had adopted policies to keep students in regular classes throughout their pregnancies, and many provided pregnancy and parenting programs designed especially for teenagers. Surveys prior to the 1970s, when pregnant teens were forced to leave school, and after the 1970s, when Congress and the Supreme Court gave them a choice, show substantial differences. Whereas in 1958 only 18.6 percent of school-age mothers received their diplomas or the equivalent, 29.2 percent graduated in 1975, and 55 percent graduated in 1986. Moreover, the graduation rate of teen mothers increased much more quickly than the graduation rate for all women, suggesting that special policies for them did have a substantial impact.[40]

Still another problem is that teenagers are a remarkably heterogeneous lot, and large-scale studies do not always distinguish between different groups. With respect to education, young teen mothers appear to be somewhat different from older teen mothers. Surprisingly, some studies suggest that younger teens are more likely to graduate than older ones, perhaps because younger mothers tend to be living at home with parents who encourage and facilitate school attendance. Or, conversely, older teen mothers may think of themselves and may be perceived by others as readier to start an independent life, one that is incompatible with staying in school.[41] Racial differences are also clearly apparent: for example, black teenage mothers are more likely to graduate from high school than white teenage mothers, although why this should be is still not clear.[42] And class is likewise a factor. It is well known that family advantage diminishes many of the effects of early childbearing. In 1985 about 87 percent of all women aged twenty-five to twenty-nine, and 55 percent of the ones who had been teenage mothers, had a high school diploma or its equivalent; but among the teenage mothers who came from middle-class backgrounds, the proportion rose to 71.5 percent. These figures, too, showed racial differences: 70.8 percent of the middle-class whites and 75.6 percent of the middle-class blacks had a diploma. The many variations associated with factors such as age, race, and class indicate that the relationship between having a baby and dropping out of school is fairly complex.[43]

When all of the problems inherent in the data are taken into account, the impact of early childbearing on education diminishes considerably. Still, there is a substantial difference between the level of education attained by those women who give birth while in junior high or high school and the level attained by those who do not. Is this difference meaningful? Does having a baby truly change a teenager's life in significant ways?

Here, as in earlier parts of this discussion, it is important to keep in mind that women who become pregnant as teens and who carry their babies to term differ from other women even before they conceive. As far back as 1950, ninth-grade students who subsequently became teenage mothers came from poorer families, displayed lower academic ability, and had lower educational goals than did their peers who had no children. (So did the students who subsequently became teenage fathers.)[44] Such differences, both in background and in what is loosely thought of as "motivation," between the kinds of people who become teen parents and those who do not have been confirmed by many studies. In the more recent ones, where researchers have been able to control more effectively for these differences, the disparity in the educational levels of teenage mothers and older mothers has diminished considerably, although there remains a small but significant difference in later-life educational attainments.[45] Taking all these factors into account, can one say with certainty that early childbearing leads a woman to curtail her education?

This question is currently the subject of vigorous debate in public-policy circles. Although virtually all researchers concede that a great deal of the difference between teen mothers and older mothers disappears once background factors are considered, young mothers may possibly differ from older ones in subtle ways not easily measured in the data bases available. In a particularly ingenious experiment, Arline Geronimus and Sanders Korenman examined a number of pairs of sisters, each of which comprised a woman who was a teenage mother and a woman who was not. They reasoned that if women who became teenage mothers shared certain subtle or "unmeasured" differences, then sisters would tend to have these differences in common whether or not they became teenage mothers. Indeed, Geronimus and Korenman found that depending on the data set used, the sisters in each pair displayed a roughly equal likelihood of graduating from high school.[46] Saul Hoffman and his colleagues have questioned these findings, noting that when other data bases are used, teen mothers are still slightly more likely to drop out of high school than their sisters who postponed childbearing, but Hoffman's results are just barely statistically significant.[47] Of course, emotional and psychological discouragement contributes to dropout rates and pregnancy rates, and none of the data bases used here incorporated measures of discouragement. Women who are on an upward trajectory, even those who come from poor backgrounds, are less likely to become pregnant than their less motivated peers. If they are enrolled in a college preparatory curriculum (and such enrollment indicates not only that they have high educational goals but that the school is in some measure fostering those goals), they are less likely to become teen mothers—an effect that is even more observable among blacks than among whites.[48] In comparison to other students, a young woman who is enrolled in a college preparatory curriculum is only half as likely to have a child while still a teen.[49] Similarly, using data from the National Longitudinal Survey, researchers have assessed the likelihood of early childbearing by looking at the scores obtained by young women on a test of basic skills. (Such a test measures literacy at so basic a level that any deficiencies almost certainly predated the pregnancy.) Compared with women in the top 5 percent, women in the lowest 5 percent were thirty-eight times more likely to have had a child out of wedlock while they were a teenager. *None* of those in the top 5 percent had had a baby when they were young.[50]

A more general problem is that few studies have examined the effects of being *both* disadvantaged and discouraged, in order to sort out the way in which each influences the likelihood that a young woman will get pregnant and drop out of school.[51] Programs that encourage pregnant teens to stay in school have been proved effective, and nowadays such women are increasingly likely to graduate. Researchers know much about the racial and class differences that influence how discouraged and disadvantaged a woman has to be to get pregnant in the first place, and what decisions she will make with regard to her pregnancy and her education. But the assumption that early pregnancy and childbearing *cause* many students to drop out of school is wrong. Poverty and all its concomitants play a significant and powerful role in determining who obtains an education. The available research suggests that when a young woman not only comes from a poor family but receives low grades in school and loses faith in her own abilities, she is much more likely to get pregnant. Poverty and loss of self-confidence play more of a role in determining her decision to drop out of school than does the pregnancy itself, although a young high school dropout with a child has a very small chance of returning to school. Studies that evaluate the social effects of poverty (disadvantage) and the cognitive-psychological effects of poverty (discouragement) should yield a better understanding of why young people lose motivation in school and how early pregnancy affects the lives of young men and women who are trying to make decisions on a host of issues—sexual activity, contraception, abortion, dropping out of school, taking college preparatory classes.[52] Until we have more sophisticated data on the determinants of early pregnancy and its impact on educational achievement, we can say only that if a teenager has a baby, her schooling will be affected much less than previously thought, if at all, once it has been assessed in conjunction with her ability, motivation, and family background. That early pregnancy has such slight effects may be partly due to the many special programs aimed at keeping teenage mothers in school—programs that are often vulnerable in today's financially strapped school districts.

School dropout is only one of the putative consequences of early pregnancy. Another is the likelihood that teenage mothers will wind up on welfare. According to widely cited estimates, half of all families on welfare at any given time are families that began with a teenage mother.[53] Dramatic as this statement is, it must be understood within the context of the lives and experiences of poor teenage girls. Early childbearing is a reproductive pattern that is becoming increasingly characteristic of the poor, as affluent people focus on social mobility and professional advancement. Thus, it should not be surprising that AFDC, a program earmarked for poor families, would be dominated by people adhering to the reproductive patterns typical of the poor. Yet at any given time, teenagers account for fewer than 10 percent of the people on welfare. Moreover, like most women on welfare, teenagers tend to remain on welfare for short periods of time: almost three-fourths of those who have collected AFDC payments did so for less than three years.[54] Like most poor women, young mothers cycle on and off AFDC, using it as a stopgap to sustain them when they or their children are ill, to help them weather times of unemployment, and to see them through sudden changes in their family arrangements.

Under the provisions of AFDC legislation, the program is jointly administered by the states and the federal government; each state can set eligibility requirements and determine the size of the payments that each family receives. In 1994 monthly welfare payments for a mother and two children ranged from $680 in Connecticut to $120 in Mississippi.[55] Such discrepancies can be explained by differences in the cost of living in various states, and, more important, by the political and economic pressures predominant at any particular time.[56]

The number of families on AFDC grew from about 800,000 in 1960 to about 4 million in 1985. The increase resulted from a number of factors, including a decline in low-wage jobs that could support a family, a rise in the number of single mothers that was due to divorce and out-of-wedlock births, and a civil rights revolution that challenged many of the informal practices which prevented eligible women from applying for aid. These families comprised a total of about 11 million people, or a bit less than 4 percent of the U.S. population.[57] Families on welfare are usually eligible for, and for the most part receive, other forms of subsidy, notably food stamps and Medicaid; these two programs have different eligibility standards which allow them to serve about twice as many people as AFDC. This is important, because medical care has become steadily more expensive and is now the single largest factor in the escalating cost of welfare. Even when this fact is taken into account, the actual cost of AFDC comes to little more than 3 percent of the annual federal budget.[58]

Surprisingly, since 1973 the participation rate—that is, the number of people eligible for AFDC who actually use it—has fallen, although the number of people on welfare has grown. This is largely a result of the fact that the eligible population—mostly poor single mothers—has increased enormously: in 1970 only 11 percent of all families with children under eighteen were eligible; in 1992 the figure was 20 percent. (In about half the states, a poor two-parent family with children and an unemployed parent can obtain AFDC-UP, where "UP" stands for "unemployed parent"; but such families account for only about 7 percent of all people on welfare.)[59] This irony—that a smaller proportion of eligible people are using welfare although the number of people on welfare has increased—is a function of the startling increase in the number of single parents, virtually all of whom are mothers. It contains the essence of the conservative charge against welfare and explains why people from all segments of the political spectrum have focused on teenage mothers. Although the benefits paid to individual families are so low that families can't actually live on them (imagine raising two children, even in Mississippi, on $120 a month) and although the overall cost of AFDC is a negligible fraction of the federal budget, people worry that the welfare system perpetuates the very problem it was set up to solve—that it leads to an increase in the number of single mothers and hence of poor families. In blaming the welfare system, many people blend pragmatic concerns with moral ones. All other things being equal, most Americans would prefer that children be born into a stable family with at least two mature adults to care for them; they believe that those adults should do what they reasonably can to keep themselves and their children in comfort. According to the popular stereotype, welfare encourages people, specifically teenage women, to have babies that they would not otherwise have had. A poor young woman brings into the world a poor baby who would not otherwise have been born, thus keeping the cycle of poverty going. But does this image accord with what we know about the effects of welfare on early childbearing? Does the mere prospect of receiving a welfare check change the behavior of teenage women such that they do things they would not otherwise do? And does having a baby as a teenager make a poor woman poorer than she would otherwise be?[60]

If welfare encouraged early childbearing, then more generous welfare benefits should coincide with an increase in the number of teenage mothers, especially unmarried ones. But the facts disprove this hypothesis. The United States provides less support for single mothers than any other industrialized country, yet it has one of the highest proportions of teenage mothers, married and unmarried. Sweden, which maintains one of the most generous social welfare systems for single mothers, has much lower birthrates among married and unmarried teens; and the actual rates are probably lower than official ones, since many of the unmarried mothers are in stable though not legally recognized relationships. Teenagers in other European countries show much the same pattern.[61]

Moreover, welfare benefits vary widely across the United States. If welfare encouraged early and out-of-wedlock childbearing, we would expect states with more generous benefits (such as California) to have more such childbearing, and stingy states (such as Mississippi) to have less. But a number of comparative studies have demonstrated that there is no correlation between the level of benefits and the level of out-of-wedlock births.[62] In addition, welfare benefits have not kept pace with inflation. The actual dollar value of welfare has declined every year since 1973, so the welfare check that an individual receives is effectively shrinking. Yet although the birthrate among teenagers has remained stable, the proportion of babies born to unwed teenagers has increased substantially. Logically, if welfare were encouraging early childbearing, especially among unmarried teens, then the plummeting value of welfare checks should have led to much lower rates of out-of-wedlock childbearing among teens.[63] Some researchers have included the value of food stamps and Medicaid in their assessments of the effects of welfare on the reproductive and marital behavior of poor women, but the value of these benefits, too, has been dropping. Such logic assumes that food stamps and Medicaid are equivalent to money in the bank; the equivalence might hold true for food stamps but is dubious in the case of Medicaid, since this benefit goes directly to the provider of the medical services.[64]

The few studies that have found a relationship between welfare policies and out-of-wedlock childbearing among teenagers typically discover only very weak effects that tend to vary by ethnic group. Among black teens, for instance, rates of out-of-wedlock childbearing are weakly affected, according to some studies, by the stringency of AFDC eligibility requirements and by the availability of AFDC to two-parent families. Among white teens, rates are affected by the size of the benefit and the absence of "workfare" requirements (the stipulation that an individual must work in order to receive payments). Among Hispanics, none of these policy variables had an effect on out-of-wedlock births.[65] Thus, the data suggest that if there is a relationship between welfare in the form of AFDC and the rate at which young women get pregnant and have babies, it is not what economists would call a robust one. If it exists at all, it probably varies by racial and ethnic group.

But this is only half of the question. AFDC may not encourage early out-of-wedlock childbearing; but does such childbearing make a young woman poorer than she would otherwise be, given that it does not lead directly to truncated schooling as people once thought? Does it make a mother and her child poorer than they would be if she postponed her childbearing? Many of the researchers who have examined the effects of early childbearing on education have also looked at the effects on socioeconomic status—and this makes sense, since truncated education is usually thought of as the first step toward poverty in later life. The data indeed show that teenage mothers wind up much poorer than other mothers. One estimate suggests that about 28 percent of all teenage mothers will be poor in their twenties and thirties, compared to only 7 percent of those who postponed their childbearing. The figures show an even higher risk for unmarried teenage mothers.[66] But since about 80 percent of all teenage mothers were already poor before they got pregnant, this suggests that a substantial number of poor teenage parents become not-so-poor adults.

The process by which a teenage mother becomes a poor adult is extremely complex. Let's take the case of Michelle Brown. She probably grew up in poverty, and poor children are likely to become poor adults. Moreover, women who give birth as unmarried teenagers may find it harder to marry later in life (although the data on this point are scanty and inconsistent), and marriage, since it often combines two incomes, is associated with a lower risk of poverty.[67] Those teenagers who do marry are more likely to divorce or separate than older people, but whether this is due to early marriage or early marriage-and-childbearing is uncertain. In other words, a teen mother becomes poor later in life for a great variety of reasons, only some of which are related to early childbearing. Once we take background variables into account, the differences between young mothers and older mothers are greatly reduced. Since teen mothers today are likely to have much smaller families than was the case in earlier decades, the effects of family size are probably waning. And relatively few of the schooling deficits that a woman displays later in life are actually due to the fact that she had a baby when she was a teenager.

HOW DO THE CHILDREN FARE?

Virtually everyone is concerned about the effects of early childbearing on the next generation—the children a teenage mother will raise. The debate in the nineteenth century over "inappropriate" childbearing set the stage for today's discussions, since it was based on the assumption that women who are not fit for motherhood will bring disadvantaged children into the world. "Readiness" is the modern, more ambiguous term referring to fitness for parenthood. The phrase "teenage pregnancy" was particularly attractive as a shorthand way of talking about poor and minority mothers because it seemed universal (emphasizing age, rather than race or class) and because it implied that unready teens would sooner or later become adults ready for parenthood.

Early childbearing, now in large part limited to the discouraged and disadvantaged, does mean that teenagers are giving birth to children who, being the offspring of poor parents, are themselves likely to be poor in later life. The rhetoric of "teenage pregnancy" as it emerged in the late 1970s suggested that if teenagers waited to give birth, they would be wealthier and so would their children. American society is now confronting the question that preoccupied the nineteenth century: Which is better—to have been born to a poor mother who happens to be young, or to have never been born at all? Phrasing the question this way highlights how it has become muddled in the past two decades. Many of those who oppose early childbearing do so in the honest belief that if teenage women would just wait until their twenties or later to give birth, they and their children would be better off financially. But as we have seen in our discussion of teenage mothers, schooling, and poverty, this belief is misguided, since teenage mothers differ from older ones long before they conceive. Though no one would deny that the more financial resources a parent can bring to a child the better, there are scant grounds for thinking that postponing a birth will help the average teen mother accumulate a lot more of those resources. The kinds of discouraged and disadvantaged women most at risk of having a baby in their teens are unlikely to become encouraged and advantaged simply by postponing their first birth for a few years. Thus, one must ask the question: Do children who are born to teenage mothers suffer other, concomitant effects?

In general, the children of young mothers are more likely to be born prematurely or at low birthweight, both of which are factors associated with later health problems. (Black mothers of all ages are more likely to have low-birthweight babies, even when the socioeconomic status of the mother is taken into account.) In addition, the babies of teenagers are more likely to have impairments in their cognitive development, to perform less well in school, and to exhibit behavioral problems; and some studies suggest they may be more likely to be abused and neglected by their mothers.[68]

Among the most frequently cited studies on this issue is the one in which Frank Furstenberg and his colleagues looked at the situations of a number of teenage mothers and their children five years and seventeen years after the birth of the mother's first child. The study, conducted between 1966 and 1984, has a number of limitations: in those days, young women were far more likely to be married than they are today, abortion was not a realistic option for most of them, and American society was very different. But the data that resulted are still the best we have on the long-term effects of early childbearing on the children themselves. At the seventeen-year mark, Furstenberg compared the children of teen mothers to the children of older mothers studied in the National Survey of Children and found that the children of teen mothers were doing less well, on average, once other factors were taken into account. A significant number of the children of teen mothers had dropped out of school or had been involved with the criminal-justice system. On the other hand, almost two out of three had graduated from high school, and another 10 percent had obtained a General Equivalency Degree. The children of younger mothers, when asked about their activities during the previous year, were more likely to report having gotten drunk, having smoked marijuana, having had sexual intercourse, and having gotten pregnant.[69] Since the teenage mothers as a group were poor before they got pregnant and poor afterward, many of the data in the Furstenberg study measure the effects of growing up in poverty. When socioeconomic background prior to the pregnancy is taken into account, much of the difference between the children of young mothers and those of older mothers disappears.[70]

It is more difficult to assess, especially at the same time, the cognitive-psychological factors and the unobserved differences that may subtly separate the kinds of people who become teen mothers from those who do not, as well as to assess the effects on children. But if teenage mothers are women who had a difficult life long before they got pregnant, we would expect that constellation of psychological, emotional, and cognitive traits to affect their children. In a variation of their work on schooling, Geronimus and Korenman looked at the children of pairs of sisters in which one sister was a teenage mother and the other was not, reasoning again that all the sisters had grown up in roughly similar social and material circumstances. As was the case in the study of schooling, on a variety of outcomes the children whose mothers had given birth as teenagers did just as well as, and sometimes better than, children whose mothers had given birth later in life.[71]

So the jury is still out on whether teenage parents make bad parents, since the situation becomes very complex when we take into account all the precursors that lead a person to become a teenage parent in the first place—poverty, despair about the future, problems in numerous areas of life. True, Americans of the late twentieth century subscribe to many of the views that emerged in the late nineteenth century: that teenagers are self-centered, immature, egoistic, and emotionally and psychologically unprepared to raise a child. And these views prevail despite the fact that teenagers have been raising emotionally and psychologically healthy children all over the world throughout human history. The reality is we know alarmingly little about the psychological skills and about the types of parent-child matches that lead to healthy children. It is probably safe to say that the more life experience and wisdom a parent has accumulated, the better off the child will be. Yet there is no evidence clearly identifying one particular stage of life as the ideal time to have a child; indeed, folk wisdom claims that parents who are "too old" may tend to spoil children and may be reluctant to set healthy boundaries. Although most people agree that prospective parents should be mature and ready for parenthood, there is much less consensus on the nature of this maturity and readiness. We need more research on the effects of age per se on childrearing before we can state categorically that teenagers make inept parents.

We do have a fair amount of evidence showing that teenage parents tend to have children who themselves become teenage parents. Many people believe that teen mothers thus perpetuate the cycle of hardship and deprivation. In both the National Survey of Children and the Furstenberg study, about one in ten children (male and female) of teen mothers reported a pregnancy by age sixteen. Yet almost two-thirds of the children did *not* become teen parents themselves.[72] Again, given the powerful roles that disadvantage and discouragement play in the making of a teenage parent, we should not be surprised that these factors have an independent effect on the way children turn out. The kinds of people who become teen parents are people who are having a hard time in life, both socially and psychologically, long before they get pregnant. They are likely to be poor and discouraged parents, and their children will suffer accordingly. It is difficult, especially when the sample being studied is small, to sort out the effects of maternal age per se, as opposed to the effects of precursors such as school failure and poverty. If early childbearing in itself has any particular effect, it is a subtle and marginal one.

When we take into account all of the voluminous evidence on the effects of early childbearing on parents, children, and society as a whole, we must conclude that it pays to be cautious. More than a decade ago, Frank Furstenberg, who had been studying these effects for more than twenty years, sounded a warning: "The evidence that early childbearing increases the risk of social and economic disadvantage is compelling. However, it is less clear whether this risk is sufficiently high to justify the social stereotype of the teenage mother that has emerged from social science research and its portrayal in the mass media. The popular picture of the teenage mother is that of an unemployed woman with many ill-cared-for children who is living on the dole . . . Such interpretations seem to go well beyond the available evidence."[73]

In the years since Furstenberg wrote these words, new research has raised even more doubts about the extent to which early childbearing causes disadvantage. But we face a major limitation: what we really want to know—the extent to which early childbearing affects mothers' lives, once we take into account that it occurs mostly among the discouraged and disadvantaged—is not clearly revealed in the available data. The data sets let us compare teenage mothers with women who postponed childbearing, but, as Geronimus' work has shown, they do not provide information about unmeasured factors that differentiate teenage mothers from other mothers. Worse, few of them allow us to gauge the combined effects of material disadvantage and psychosocial disadvantage—what we have been calling "discouragement." We need a data set that covers women only after 1975, when pregnancy was no longer a cause of involuntary school dropout. It should include a wide range of measures of material advantage and disadvantage (family income, family structure, socioeconomic class and educational level of each teenage mother's parents) and should reveal how these circumstances changed as the women were growing up. It should incorporate data linked to specific neighborhoods, because we know that an individual's life decisions may be affected just by the fact that he or she grew up in a bad neighborhood rather than a good one. Furthermore, we need measures of the way in which young women view their own lives, and of the kinds of personal resources they bring to their assessments. We need measures of the women's tested ability, of their educational aspirations, of their progress through school, of their confidence and faith in the future.

Ideally, the data set should contain large numbers of sister pairs, each comprising one teen mother and one nonteen mother. Of course, it would also have to be longitudinal so that we could track people over time, taking into account that some married and some did not, some went on welfare and some did not, and some had larger families than others. Such a data set is unlikely to be available anytime soon; meanwhile, we will have to try to tease out the effects of early childbearing from the inadequate measures that currently exist.

Americans must ask themselves what, realistically, they want teenagers to do. Should young women postpone childbearing until society deems them fit for parenthood? Should they simply get married, and run the risk of winding up financially worse off if they divorce? Or should early childbearing be seen as a young woman's response, limited and at times self-defeating, to the racial, class, and gender barriers in her life? Americans have every right to be concerned about early childbearing and to place the issue high on the national agenda. But they should think of it as a *measure,* not a cause, of poverty and other social ills. A teenager who has a baby usually adds but a slight burden to her life, which is already profoundly disadvantaged. Tempting as it may be to imagine that poverty is largely a result of teenagers' "untimely" choices, the data simply do not bear this out. Early childbearing may make a bad situation worse, but the real causes of poverty lie elsewhere.

6

WHY DO

THEY

DO IT?

It's difficult to be the mother of a very young child. It's more difficult still when the mother is a teenager. And if she's not only a teen but unmarried, her life can be even grimmer than the most outspoken opponents of early childbearing can imagine. Many young mothers, when asked about their situation, readily describe how hard it is to raise a child. For some of them, having a baby was a serious mistake.[1]

> I'm not living with my family. I'm living with a friend. It's really bleak and confusing. I miss everything I left behind. (Christina, seventeen, white, Colorado)[2]

> If I thought I didn't have freedom before the baby, I didn't know what freedom was. My parents watch every step I take. After all, they are paying for me and my baby. (Holly, sixteen, white, Colorado)[3]

> After they cut Marquis's umbilical cord, they just put him up on me and I told 'em, "Get that ugly baby off of me!" He was all covered with blood. It upset me. They took him, washed him off, put him back in my arms. I was just so tired. All I could say was, "He look just like William." And I turned my head to the other side. It took me a long time to get use to Marquis. I didn't want to accept at fifteen I have a baby. It took me about two months to get use, to get really use to Marquis. (Sherita, fifteen, black, Washington, D.C.)[4]

> I was going to have an abortion since I was only fifteen, but my family talked me out of it because of their religion, I love my baby now, but I'm

only sixteen. I feel like I'm still a child—and here I have a child. It's completely changed my life. I look at other sixteen-year-olds and know that I can never be like them again. I sometimes wonder if an abortion wouldn't have been better. (Angela, sixteen, white, Colorado)[5]

It's hard to be a parent by yourself. If I had it to do over again, I'd do things really different. When people tell you it's going to be difficult, believe them. My child is with me all the time . . . shopping, school, wherever I go. It's even harder than they say it is. I knew it would be hard, but not this hard.[6]

Why is it that young people have babies, despite these depressing stories in which teens frankly admit how difficult it is for them to be mothers, and despite the national consensus that it's a very bad idea? No one in the United States is in favor of early childbearing: elected officials campaign against it, the public disapproves of it, and professionals warn that it is costly for everyone concerned. Even the group thought to be most accepting of unwed teenage mothers—the African American community—is far more disapproving than most people think. Acceptance of a teenage mother or father is not the same as approval: young mothers, both black and white, often report widespread censure from those around them. Their own mothers, many of whom were once teenage mothers themselves and were hoping for a better life for their daughters, sometimes express a disappointment bordering on rage.[7]

So why do they do it? Why do approximately one million young women get pregnant each year? More than half a million carry their babies to term, and about two-thirds of them will be unmarried when they give birth. Certainly, adolescents live in a world very different from that of adults, but the evidence suggests that age is not the only factor leading teenagers to reject the path those older and wiser would choose for them. Through their actions, teens are trying to come to terms, sometimes ineptly, with the immense social and economic challenges they face in today's world: a shrinking job market, an indifferent community network, and public skepticism about the worth of minorities. Early pregnancy and childbearing are not an isolated problem restricted to a small but growing number of poor, young, and minority women; they are the result of an array of problems in American society—problems that have no easy solutions. Unwed teenage mothers are pioneers on a frontier where increasing numbers of Americans are now settling.

DREAMS AND REALITIES

Today, half of all marriages end in divorce, only half of divorced fathers make their full court-ordered child support payments, and unwed fathers visit their children more often than divorced fathers who have remarried. Even as the cultural meanings of "husband" and "wife" are shifting, men and women are expected to work in the paid labor force for much of their adult lives.[8] Although there are still "men's jobs" and "women's jobs," one can no longer automatically assume that the former are better paid and more secure than the latter.[9] In the tidy world of the 1950s, society expected that women would be virgins when they married (or at least when they got engaged); would remain married throughout their lives to the same man; would stay home, take care of the housework, and raise the children while their husband worked at a stable, well-paid job that he would keep until he decided to retire. This predictable scenario no longer exists for today's teenagers, although many of its cultural ideals live on in their dreams.

What it means to be an adult man or woman is now in constant flux, and we do not yet live in a world of perfect gender equality. Indeed, the sexual revolution seems to have stalled: women have taken on many of the responsibilities of men, but men have yet to assume their fair share of the nurturing and caretaking roles traditionally assigned to women. On the one hand, a young woman can no longer expect that she will have a husband on whom she can be totally dependent, both economically and emotionally. On the other hand, she can't expect a husband to share the burdens of childrearing and homemaking equally.[10] Such changes in gender roles intersect with new uncertainties surrounding the meanings of race and class in American society. Between World War II and 1973, when wages were steadily rising, minorities and blue-collar workers could hope for the same job mobility and financial stability that white professionals enjoyed. But today's young people must compete intensely for jobs that are increasingly scarce, and must strive to meet meritocratic criteria that punish the less advantaged. They confront the future with far less assurance.

Young women in particular are finding life extremely complex. The rules that applied in their mothers' day were simple, at least in theory: do what it takes to get a good man, and keep him happy. Now women are aware of what this formula can lead to: displaced homemakers, divorcees and widows who are unprepared to support themselves, women who think they have no value unless they have a male partner. But dreams die hard. Today's young women say that they want a career in addition to, not instead of, a family life.[11] No teenager hopes to end up as an unmarried mother on welfare. Although many disadvantaged teens do dream of motherhood, they dream of white-picket-fence motherhood, or at least the version of it to which girls from poor neighborhoods can realistically aspire.

I want to have an average American life, not the average Puerto Rican life with a break-up here and a fight there. (Diane, Hispanic, New Jersey)[12]

[I see myself] mainly being a housewife, a mother, and probably going to school, trying to get my trade or something like that. I want me a job too, but jobs is so hard to find. I want one through the University. My sister told me, she said, "You can't be picky and choosy." So I told her, "Okay, I guess I just want me a job so bad." (Roberta, eighteen, black, Florida)[13]

I don't want to be dependent on my parents for the rest of my life. I want to help out, even though my parents aren't putting any pressure on me. (Woman from rural New England, eighteen, white)[14]

I want to live in a two-bedroom apartment with a TV and carpeting. Nice and clean. If I'm older I have a car. I'd rather work at night and have somebody be there or early in the morning and come home by two or three. Other than that I be satisfied. Once I do what I want to do, I don't go back, I keep going. That's what I want to do. Get on my own with my baby and get situated. You know, I be having a good job. (Young woman living in an East Coast city)[15]

I want to be a good mother, givin' my kid all, everythin', and makin' my kid go to school, college, somethin' that I can't get.[16]

Unfortunately, the odds against achieving even these modest dreams are getting longer. Young women with limited educational and labor market skills face many more obstacles to a stable relationship and a secure job than they used to, especially when they are members of minority groups and come from poor homes. And the young men in their lives have bleaker employment prospects than ever, making them a slender reed for young women to rely upon. Roberta's sister is right: when it comes to men and jobs, these young women can't be "picky and choosy." But even their willingness to be adaptable may not ensure that they get what they want.

It is hard for young people who have grown up in poverty to figure out how to make their dreams come true, how to negotiate the small steps that get them from one point to another. Moreover, young women of all classes must find a way to balance investments in their own future with commitment to a partner. Women have always had to decide whether and when to make such "selfish" investments, as opposed to devoting their energies to meeting the needs of a partner and children. Today they have to make decisions whose outcomes cannot be known. And teens of both sexes are on radically new terrain when it comes to making choices about sexual activity, marriage, family, and work. The sexual revolution has transformed Americans' values, attitudes, and behavior in ways that are unlikely to be reversed. How do teens—should teens—think and act in this new world, and reconcile its alluring promises with its hard realities? How can they manage the consequences of their sexual freedom?

Many people of all political persuasions think that teenagers should simply stop having sex. Liberals argue that public campaigns have induced teenagers to curtail their drug use and that such campaigns could likewise induce them to abstain from sex; conservatives plead for "a little virginity."[17] Unfortunately, both groups are working against the historical tide. Premarital sexual activity has become steadily more common in the twentieth century, throughout the industrialized world. But the sexual revolution has not been fully integrated into people's lives, especially the lives of teenagers. The American public is still unsure whether the tide can or should be turned back. Given society's deep ambivalence about sexual activity among teenagers, young women often find themselves in a state of confusion—a state that is often apparent in the ethnographic accounts. They tell researchers about their decisions concerning sex, contraception, and pregnancy. But when we say that teens "decide" on a course of action in such matters, we may be using much too active a verb. On the one hand, young people are told to "just say no"; on the other, their friends, the media, and society at large foster the idea that sexual activity among teenagers is widespread and increasingly commonplace. If a young woman doesn't want to have sex, she has little in the way of support, since sexual activity has come to be expected.

They looked at a virgin as being something shameful. They were the type of people who would always tell what happened if they made out with a boy or a boy made out with them. I was the only one they never heard from. They would say, "You don't know what you're missing." The more they talked, the more curious I got. (Theresa, eighteen, black, Washington, D.C.)[18]

All of my friends were having sex and I was curious to see what it was all about. I didn't even know the guy very well and I don't even want to know him. It wasn't like it is shown on TV or in the movies. I didn't even enjoy it. (Young woman from Colorado)[19]

All my friends were doing it and they dared me. After all, I was seventeen and had never had sex. I thought maybe I really was missing something. (I wasn't.)[20]

Some girls will have sex to get guys to like them. Some girls do it thinking, "Well, I'm going to keep this boyfriend." If I could, I would tell them, "Don't, until you feel they respect and love you. You're too good to be chasing and trying to make someone stay with you." (Robyn, black, Colorado)[21]

The sexuality that young women express in such ethnographic accounts is often curiously passive. Although a few young women brag about their sexual conquests and skills, many simply make themselves available, in part because it seems that everyone else is doing it.

Even as they feel pressure to be sexually active, teens are urged to abstain, or at least to "be careful" and use contraceptives. Thus, in their accounts they describe their first sexual intercourse as an experience remarkably devoid of pleasure. They are anxious, in a hurry to get it over with, eager to cross the Rubicon in a leap before courage fails; or they see it as something that "just happened," without anyone's having made an active decision.

Then he asked me to have sex. I was scared and everything, and it was like, "What am I gonna do?" The first time I told him no and he understood. We watched some TV. And he brought me home. Then a couple of days after that he asked me again, I said okay. I guess I said so because I just wanted to show him I wasn't scared to have sex. I was scared. And he kinda knew I was scared. But I guess I was playing a role. I wanted to show him that I'm not scared. So we had sex . . . and now it's like we don't get along. (Young black woman from Oakland, California)[22]

We was going together for two years and we didn't do anything. I was like "no" and he was scared also. Finally we just—hurry up and get it over with. We just took off our clothes real quick. Just hurry up and get it over with and we both shaking and crying. (High school student in a midwestern city)[23]

I didn't talk to my boyfriend about sex, and he didn't talk to me. One day we were together and started hugging and kissing, then we just did it. (Latisha, fifteen, black, Chicago)[24]

And I used to go home and he would call me on the phone and then we were like that for about a month or so and then we just started to get involved. I don't know, he just asked me and I said sure, if that was what you want to do . . . We just did it to do it and then I just got pregnant. (Sally, fifteen, white)[25]

He was someone to lean on. When I was depressed, I figured, I'll lean on him. Next thing you know, I figured I started to listen to him. Then I saw him as more of a friend. Then why not kiss him? Why not touch him? It seemed that one thing led to another. Afterward we never made a big deal out of it like, "Wow, wasn't that great last night." We never even talked much about it . . . We said we shouldn't have let that happen. It won't happen again. And then it did happen again. (Ivy, seventeen, black, Boston)[26]

Not only are many young women confused and indecisive when it comes to their first sexual encounters, but they often know few adults whom they can comfortably ask for guidance. According to their own accounts, even their mothers offer little or no help:

Only thing she said was, "Don't be out here messing with no boys." And that was it. (Sherita, twelve, black, Washington, D.C.)[27]

I love my mother, but she never really talked to me, and I don't feel like I can talk to her about private matters. She acts like we shouldn't talk about sex. She only told me after my period, that I shouldn't go with boys. (Latisha, fifteen, black, Chicago)[28]

She didn't want me to know nothing about sex but "just don't do it." But I was like—I was like, gosh, but everybody is doing this and I wanted to try it, too. (Fourteen-year-old, attending high school in a midwestern city)[29]

The little information available on young men shows that they, too, see themselves as failures if they have not had sex. For them, sexual activity is an indication of maturity and masculinity.

If they haven't [had intercourse] then they are like outcasts. Like, "Man, you never made love to a girl!" Some of them get teased a lot. It's like on the baseball team and they start talking about that and you have got the younger guys out there and you could tell because they are all quiet and stuff and they won't talk. Some of the other people start laughing at them and start getting on them and get them kind of upset. (Male high school student in a midwestern city)[30]

Premarital sexual activity has become increasingly common in the twentieth century. This is partly due to the fact that people are getting married later, but it is also a function of America's transition from a rural, kinship-based society to a modern, industrial one that tends to disconnect sex from marriage.[31] Some experts argue that the real sexual revolution in the United States occurred in the 1880s and was largely over by 1915. Others maintain that there were two sexual revolutions, one between 1915 and 1925 and the other between 1965 and 1975.[32] All agree, however, that sexual activity among teenagers is not peculiar to the late twentieth century; rather, it is the result of long-term trends shaped by social and economic forces that are probably irreversible. Furthermore, whatever it is about modernity that makes sex independent from marriage, it is present in most of the industrialized nations. Teens all over the developed world are engaging in sex before marriage.[33] When in 1984 the United Nations undertook a survey of adolescent sexual and reproductive behavior, it concluded that "without doubt, the proportion of teenagers who have experienced sex by age nineteen has been increasing steadily over the years among all adolescents."[34] Even conservative Japan—a communitarian society with strongly internalized social controls—has reported increases in sexual activity among its teenagers, as well as a rise in out-of-wedlock childbearing. Surveys conducted by the Japanese government in 1981 found that in Japan about 28 percent of young women and 37 percent of young men were sexually active by the end of their teenage years—figures that were less than half of those for the United States but that, compared with the proportions in 1974, represented an increase of 40 percent for young men and an amazing 150 percent for young women.[35]

According to conservatives, the fact that contraception was made available to teenagers in the late 1960s was the fuel that ignited the explosion of early sex. Prior to 1964 contraceptives were nominally illegal in many jurisdictions, were never mentioned in public (much less advertised), and were difficult to obtain. In pharmacies, condoms were typically kept behind the counter, and some pharmacists in small towns refused to sell them to young men they knew to be unmarried. Since out-of-wedlock pregnancy was stigmatized and likely to lead to a clandestine abortion or a hasty marriage, there is a certain logic to the notion that the stunning reversal in the status of contraception—from illegal and unmentionable to widely available at public expense—fostered the spectacular increase in sexual activity among teenagers. And since this increase in activity and the proliferation of low-cost birth control clinics both occurred in the late 1960s and early 1970s, there is at least a temporal connection between the two.

This commonsensical and comforting notion (comforting because it implies that one way to curtail sexual activity among teens is to limit the availability of contraception) has several things wrong with it. First, a great many aspects of American society were changing in the sixties and seventies. Public attitudes shifted radically on issues such as contraception, premarital sex, abortion, and illegitimacy; family planning clinics were only one part of the context surrounding teenagers' behavior. Second, as we have seen, young people throughout the industrialized world have increased their premarital sexual activity, despite the fact that policies regarding contraception vary widely from country to country. Finally, and perhaps most tellingly, in the 1980s federal funding of family planning services dropped sharply—from $400 million in 1980 to $250 million in 1990—but sexual activity among teens continued to increase. The states compensated in some measure for the cutbacks, but they by no means filled the gap entirely.[36] Though it is disappointing not to be able to pinpoint a cause for the increase in sexual activity among the young, historical and international evidence suggests that it is probably the result of a blend of factors. What *is* extremely clear is that the welter of societal changes and conflicting messages surrounding sexual activity has left many young people confused, misinformed, and adrift.

THE PATH TO PREGNANCY

Some teenagers get pregnant for exactly the same reason that older women do: they are married and they want a child. It is true that in the United States marriage rates among teens have declined dramatically and the median age at first marriage is higher than it has ever been. Still, in 1990 about 7 percent of all American teens (about 10 percent of all eighteen- and nineteen-year-olds) were married, and about one out of every three babies born to a teen was born to a married mother.[37] It is important to keep in mind that discussions of early pregnancy and childbearing include these married teenagers, whom the public usually does not think of as part of the constellation of problems associated with "teenage pregnancy."[38]

Other teens are unmarried but are using contraception to avoid pregnancy. Stereotypes to the contrary, teenagers are using more contraception, and using it more effectively, than ever before. In 1982 about half of all American teenagers used a contraceptive method the first time they had sex; in 1988 about 70 percent of them did.[39] Of all the sexually active teenage women surveyed in the 1988 National Survey of Family Growth who were currently having sex, who were neither pregnant nor seeking pregnancy, and who had not been sterilized, about 80 percent were using some method of contraception. Among poor teens, those whose family income was less than twice the poverty level, the rate was a little lower (72.5 percent), and among affluent teens it was a little higher.[40] But if teens are using contraception to such an extent, why aren't their pregnancy rates plummeting?

One major reason is statistical. Teens today actually do have a lower risk of getting pregnant: in 1972 the odds that a sexually involved teen would become pregnant were about one in four; by 1990 they had decreased to one in five. (These figures include married teens, who accounted for approximately 26 percent of all sexually experienced teens in 1972, but only about 15 percent in 1984.)[41] Unfortunately, however, the decline in the odds that an individual teen would get pregnant did not lead to a decline in the pregnancy rate for all teenagers: the increase in effective contraceptive use was offset by the fact that so many more unmarried teenagers became sexually involved during this period. In 1972, in a population of approximately 10 million teenage women, about 2.5 million were sexually active—a rate of roughly 25 percent. By 1984 the total number of teenagers had decreased slightly to 9 million, but the number of sexually active teens had grown to 4 million—a rate of about 50 percent.[42] Thus, although an individual teen had a smaller chance of getting pregnant, the fact that there were twice as many teens at risk meant that there were more pregnancies. Still, the two trends balanced each other so that the pregnancy rate among all teenage women remained roughly stable: in 1972 it was 95 per thousand; in 1984 it was 108 per thousand; and in 1988 it was 117 per thousand.[43] This may be even better news than it seems: some observers think that teenagers' rates of premarital sexual activity are leveling off, and since there is no evidence that the propensity to use contraception is declining, some of the incidence of pregnancy among teens may be a lag effect that will persist only while they are learning how to use contraception well. But the pregnancy rates among American teenagers are worrisome, especially when about half of the pregnancies end in abortion. Despite more than two decades' worth of research on the matter, there are no clear answers as to why the rates remain so high in the United States, compared to those in other countries.

Within a general pattern of increased contraceptive use, there are a number of factors that enable one to predict which teenagers will use contraception more consistently and effectively than others. For example, the higher a teen's socioeconomic status and educational aspirations, the more likely he or she is to use contraception. Older teens are more consistent users than younger ones, for two reasons: sexually active teens get better at it over time; and teens who are older when they have their first sexual experience are more careful than those who start at an earlier age.[44] Contraceptive use also tends to be relationship specific. That is, young men and women are not users or nonusers, but change their practice with individual partners. We know that older women (that is, women whose teen years are behind them) are likely to get pregnant after the breakup of a relationship: about one-fourth of all babies born out of wedlock are born to women who have left one marriage but have not entered into another. This suggests that when experienced users move out of a stable relationship, the meaning and practice of contraception change.[45] Thus, young women are even more at risk, since their sexual relationships tend to be more short-lived and sporadic. Studies have shown that sexually active teens in fact go through long periods during which they have no sex at all because they are not involved in a relationship, and often have relatively low rates of sex even when they are. And when sexual activity is unpredictable, using contraceptives becomes more difficult.[46]

Contraceptive use may also change over the course of a relationship. When young people have sex for the first time, they tend to rely on male protection methods, notably condoms. In 1982, 23 percent of teenage women reported using condoms the first time they had intercourse, and an additional 13 percent said they used withdrawal; in 1988 about 65 percent used condoms and virtually none used withdrawal.[47] After their first sexual encounter, unmarried adolescents tend increasingly to use female contraceptives (diaphragms and the Pill) instead of male methods. In 1982 about 43 percent of sexually active teenage women were on the Pill, 15 percent were using condoms, and almost 30 percent were using no contraception at all. Similarly, in 1988 about 47 percent were on the Pill, 27 percent were using condoms, and 20 percent were using no contraception.[48] Contrary to stereotype, young black women are *more* likely than young white women to use highly effective contraception, mostly because they are much more likely to be Pill users; but they also tend to begin using contraception at a later age, so their overall risk of pregnancy is higher. Poor teens and affluent teens are almost equally likely to be Pill users.[49]

So why do teens get pregnant if so many of them are using contraception? The short answer is that some get pregnant the first time they have sex, because they use no contraception, use relatively ineffective methods, or use methods inadequately. Others get pregnant during transitions—either within a relationship, as they move from male methods to female methods, or between relationships, when they stop using a certain method. (About 70 percent of all sexually active teenage women have had more than one partner by the time they reach their twenties.)[50] Still others get pregnant because they use no contraception: either they have never used it, or they are not presently using a method they used earlier. Finally, a small number get pregnant even though they are using contraception faithfully.[51]

One troubling and rarely acknowledged fact is that teenagers' sexual involvements are not always consensual, particularly in the case of young women. The younger the woman, the more likely this is to be a problem. In one national survey of American teens, about 7 percent answered yes when they were asked, "Was there ever a time when you were forced to have sex against your will, or were raped?" Thirteen percent of the white women and 8 percent of the black women reported having coercive sex before they were twenty; among young men, the figures were 1.9 percent for whites and 6.1 percent for blacks. An astonishing 74 percent of all women who had had sex before the age of fourteen reported that they had had coerced sex; among those who had had sex before the age of fifteen, the figure was 60 percent. Since most experts think that the respondents in such interviews underreport coercive sex, these numbers are probably conservative.[52] And the question used in the survey defined coercive sex rather narrowly: as the national debate on rape and date rape makes clear, it is difficult to draw the exact boundaries of sexual consent.[53]

In the days when premarital sex was considered wrong, young men and women typically negotiated the meaning of each step (the first kiss, the first caress, "petting") and where it fit into the relationship; the woman permitted increasing sexual intimacy in return for greater commitment from the man.[54] Young women today have no such clear-cut rules. Society has become more tolerant of the notion that an unmarried couple may be sexually involved if they are emotionally committed to each other, but the emotional and social context within which sexual encounters take place has become quite fluid.[55]

When sexual activity is coerced, as it is for a small but important subset of American teens, it is extremely unlikely that the victim will have planned ahead to use contraception. But even in consensual situations, young people—especially young women—still face obstacles to effective contraception use. Social pressures concerning gender roles and sexual activity exert some real constraints on the ability to use contraception effectively—constraints that are similar in effect, if not in degree or kind, to those of coercive sex.

During the past thirty years, for example, contraceptive use has become increasingly feminized: both men and women tend to think that contraception is the responsibility of the woman and that it's the woman's fault when something goes wrong. This represents a revolution—one so subtle that most Americans have scarcely noticed it. Until 1965 condoms were the most frequently used form of contraception in America, at least among married couples. There was a time when a young man would carry a lone, crumbling condom with him wherever he went, and carry it so long that it would wear its outlines into his wallet. But with the development of the Pill and the IUD, contraception came to be considered something for which women were responsible and accountable. Interestingly, concerns about sexually transmitted diseases (especially AIDS) and the health effects of the Pill have made condoms popular once again, only today they are marketed to both men and women. What this means in practice is that couples often must negotiate which contraceptives to use and when to use them, with little in the way of clear social rules.

In such negotiations, women tend to be culturally handicapped by society's expectations of appropriate female sexual behavior. The first time a woman has intercourse, she is considered to be "giving away" something valuable: her virginity. If she is young and unmarried, she is culturally enjoined from looking too "ready." (This may explain the increasing popularity of the condom, which the man usually provides and which became popular among teens prior to the recent concern with AIDS and other sexually transmitted diseases.)[56] An unmarried woman who is in the early stages of getting involved in a relationship and who must not look too "ready" for sex is therefore forced to rely on the goodwill and motivation of her partner, who may not be as committed to the relationship as she is and who will suffer fewer consequences if something goes wrong. The first time the couple has sex, he is the one who typically takes the contraceptive precautions, yet he has a very different set of incentives and faces a very different set of risks. Many of these pressures at first intercourse recur every time a woman has a new sexual partner. (Most adolescent women are still having sex in serially monogamous relationships.)[57]

The prevalence of premarital sex means that a "nice girl" is no longer defined as a young woman who has never had sex. Rather, it means a young woman who has had sex but not too much of it, or who is sexually active but not promiscuous. Alas, one simple way of showing that one is a "nice girl" is to be unprepared for sex—to have given no prior thought to contraception. Both at first sex and with each new partner, a young woman is thus subject to powerful cultural pressures that penalize her for taking responsibility. To use contraception, a woman has to anticipate sexual activity by locating the impetus within herself, rather than in the man who has overcome her hesitancy. She must plan for sex, must be prepared to speak about contraception frankly with someone she may not know very well (at a time when, according to cultural expectations, her emotions rather than her intellect are supposed to hold sway), and must put her own long-term welfare before the short-term pleasure of the couple, especially of the man.

When young women talk about the obstacles to using contraception, they frequently describe the way in which conflicting social pressures intersect with their own ambivalent and contradictory feelings:

> I went to Planned Parenthood and I had my aunt help me get the diaphragm. I didn't like it, it didn't feel comfortable and I was embarrassed. You know, jump up [during sex] and say, "Um, wait a minute."[58]

Many American teenagers receive at least some information about contraception (often in sex education classes), but this information must be assessed in terms of a complex set of parameters concerning the way in which a teenager views sexual activity and why he or she is using contraception. Young people often report misunderstandings about contraception—misunderstandings that are shared by those around them.

> I think I was thirteen when I first started having sex. My best friend thought I was crazy 'cause I went to my mother and said, "Well, Mom, I like this boy and I might be doing something with him and would you

take me to get birth control?" And she said, "No, because once you start taking these pills, you'll become sterile." See, I love kids, I love 'em and I want 'em. So it scared me . . . but she knew I was going to do something. (Sixteen-year-old)[59]

I wish I had taken the pill. I waited too long. I just kept telling myself, "Well, I can wait a little bit longer." And then I found out it was too late. I wasn't afraid to take it—I just kept putting it off and putting it off, and I put it off too long. (Kimberly, white, Colorado)[60]

In short, the skills a young woman needs in order to use contraception effectively are precisely the skills that society discourages in "nice girls," who are expected to be passive, modest, shy, sexually inexperienced (or at least less experienced than their partners), and dedicated to the comfort of others. A woman who obtains contraception in anticipation of sexual activity is thought to be "looking for sex" (as teens say) and is culturally devalued. More to the point, she risks being devalued within the relationship. When it comes to contraception, she is caught in a net of double binds. She is the one who is supposed to "take care of it," the one at whom most contraceptive programs are aimed, and the one for whose body the most effective methods have been developed. Yet she is expected to be diffident about sex, and interested in it only because love and erotic arousal have spontaneously led her to be "carried away." And if she seems too interested in sex for its own sake, as evidenced by her use of contraception, she is in a weak position to trade sex for commitment and intimacy from the man involved.[61] These pressures are often exacerbated because the woman's partner is older than she is, and presumably more experienced and sophisticated. Scattered data suggest that the partners of teenage mothers are typically older, sometimes significantly older: in 1988, although about 80 percent of teenage mothers had a partner who was within a few years of their own age, 20 percent had a partner who was six or more years older than they were; for very young mothers (fifteen-year-olds), the figure climbed to 30 percent.[62]

A couple may go through a period in which they use no contraception, while they try to work out the meaning of the relationship and how contraception fits into it. Young women who seek contraceptive services sometimes say that they are doing so because their relationship is becoming more serious—meaning they have used no contraception up to that point.[63] Of course, their statistical risk of getting pregnant is just as high in the early months of their relationship as it is later, and may in fact be higher: one study showed that most young women who got pregnant did so in the early, perilous part of their relationship.[64] This suggests that what has changed are not the statistical odds of getting pregnant, but the social cost. Once a relationship is defined as getting serious, it's easier for the young woman to make the commitment to contraception without risking her commitment to her boyfriend. And it may be easier for him to argue for contraception without seeming as if he's "leading her on."

So commitment to and by a partner may counteract some of the pressures that serve as obstacles to contraception. Some young women say that they put off seeking contraceptive services because they are afraid of being found out, particularly by their parents. Yet once their relationship is defined as serious and the young man has demonstrated his commitment, the young woman's sexual desire is transformed from potentially promiscuous into true love, and she is equipped to take the public step of obtaining contraception. Young women whose significant others (parents, partners, and best friends) urge them to get contraception are more likely to obtain it before becoming sexually active and more likely to use it effectively.[65]

Teenagers from different classes and racial groups tend to have different patterns of contraceptive use, both at first intercourse and subsequently.[66] Although there are few studies of the way in which class and race affect the meanings attached to specific contraceptives and to contraception in general, one can make two broad observations. First, when sexual partners come from different social or ethnic groups (as they increasingly do these days), they may have additional problems communicating about contraception. Second, researchers who study sexual and contraceptive decisions in contexts where AIDS is a factor tell us that young women who have a sense of power and efficacy in their lives are more able to protect themselves in their sexual relationships than women who feel weak. Since many poor and minority women lack sources of esteem and power in their lives, they may be more vulnerable in their relationships.[67]

Of course, the desire or lack of desire for a baby plays an important role in the decisions that people make about contraception. The American public often assumes that teenagers have babies simply because they know little about, or ignore, birth control practices. But in many cases this is untrue. In 1984 a sixteen-year-old urban black woman named Tauscha Vaughan made the following comment to *Washington Post* reporter Leon Dash: "Will you please stop asking me about birth control? Girls out here know all about birth control. There's too much birth control out here. All of them know about it. Even when they twelve, they know what birth control is. Girls out here get pregnant because they want to have babies!"[68] This young woman highlights an important fact: that decisions about contraception are intimately related to whether or not one wants a child. But the situation is more complex than this simple statement would make it appear.

When young women talk about their lives, it is clear that their feelings about childbearing exist in a context of numerous shifting assessments. For example, they often describe a partner who does not use contraception or who stops using a contraceptive.

> It [the condom] didn't feel comfortable, and I didn't enjoy it either, so I kept taking my chances on withdrawal. (Reggie, black, Washington, D.C.; father of Tauscha Vaughan's baby)[69]

> We had sex for about a year before I got pregnant. I wasn't using birth control, not at first. Then he said, we'll use something. We didn't really talk about it. The condoms he used hurt him and they irritated me, you know, real bad. I didn't enjoy it and I said, "No, I don't think we'll have it, if it's gonna bother me so bad."[70]

> I knew that it could happen; I just thought I would be lucky and not get caught. We used condoms sometimes, but he said it feels better without them. But when I knew I was pregnant I kept acting like it wasn't real. (Young woman in a Teen Parenting program with black, white, and Hispanic participants)[71]

For many adults, quotes such as these are just one more example of teenagers' fecklessness, of their inability to plan ahead or to see the consequences of their own actions. But when such accounts are read more carefully, many of them reveal that behind the seeming aimlessness are some serious, complex, and often hidden negotiations about the meaning of the relationship—negotiations that teens, like adults, are often reluctant to conduct straightforwardly. In many cases, for example, a young woman thinks that if she and her boyfriend use no contraception, there is a tacit assumption that they are sharing the risk: he must love her so much that he wants to have a child with her and is willing to stand by her if she does:

> I expected the father to be helpful; to take care of the baby. All three of us to go places and have fun. Live together as a family. (Shana, black, Oakland, California)[72]

I expected commitment of just being a father. Of being there saying, "I'm going to help you. I'll be there to take care of Jimmy when you want, when you need to do other things." I expected his support emotionally, financially, as much as he could. I expected him to be there for me . . . I expected him to love me because I was the woman who had his baby. But he loves everyone else who didn't. (Diane, black, Oakland, California)[73]

Cynics may ascribe such expectations to wishful thinking; but caught up in a relationship, boys sometimes do make promises—promises that are difficult to keep.

We were going to be married in April. We didn't want to have a baby right away, but neither of us wanted to use birth control, so when I asked J. if he was ready for the consequences he said yes. He said if I got pregnant he'd want to be with me and the baby always, which is what he said when he found out I was pregnant. Then he changed his mind and split. (Seventeen-year-old, white, rural New England)[74]

I dated John for about a year. He always told me that if anything happened he would take care of me. When I told him I was pregnant he said that it wasn't his baby. He dropped me and started dating my best friend. It was hard for me to accept that he didn't care as much as he said he did before I got pregnant. (Robyn, black, Colorado)[75]

Although some teenagers try to prevent pregnancy and fail, others get pregnant because they believe pregnancy is not such a bad thing. Young unmarried women, like young married ones, may become pregnant because they want to, or at least because they are not sufficiently motivated to avoid it. Experts have long debated whether teenagers want their pregnancies and births. A recent study by the Alan Guttmacher Institute estimated that only 7 percent of all such pregnancies were intended.[76] Does this fully capture what we know about teens and their plans?

It seems at first glance that most young women would prefer not to have a baby. About half of all pregnant teens have abortions, and about 87 percent of those who carried their babies to term in 1988 described their pregnancies as unintended. These findings come from the National Survey of Family Growth (conducted in four cycles: 1973, 1976, 1982, and 1988), which asked a national sample of women the following question:[77] "Was the reason you (had stopped / were not) using any contraceptive method because you yourself wanted to become pregnant?" If a woman answered no, she was asked another question: "It is sometimes difficult to recall these things; but just before that pregnancy began, would you say you probably wanted a(nother) baby at some time, or probably not?"[78] This is a rather inflexible way to investigate a fluid, complex, and constantly reexamined decision. The National Center for Health Statistics is revising its methods for the next round of the survey, but we must keep in mind the questions as they were posed if we are to understand the responses fully. Until the 1970s, the typical woman in need of family planning was a woman who had already had all the children she wanted and who was at risk of having additional children she did not want, and the language of the questions reflected the situation of such women. Teens fit into this group awkwardly, if at all. Since teens are just starting to build their families, the questions posed by the survey do not reveal their plans or preferences very well. Few teens have babies that are unwanted in this traditional sense; mostly they say that their babies came earlier than planned. Thus far, the wording of survey questions has not allowed researchers to assess the effects (if any) that early childbearing may have on women's life plans.

The concept of wantedness has been subject to a good deal of criticism. A woman may find it very difficult to tell interviewers that she did not want her baby. Moreover, an unwanted pregnancy may well result in a wanted child. And there is a deeper and more philosophical problem with efforts to measure wantedness by means of questionnaires, particularly in the case of teenagers. Surveys assume that people perceive clear choices and that they feel empowered to act on them. Such certainty and confidence can, of course, be deduced in some instances. If a woman and her partner say that they consistently and effectively used birth control up to the date of conception, and then terminate the pregnancy, we can be fairly confident that they did not want the child. Likewise, if a woman tells an interviewer that she deliberately stopped using contraception because she wanted to become pregnant, we can be reasonably certain that she wanted her baby. But for most teenage mothers, these two extremes rarely capture the lived experience. Contraception, particularly among unmarried people and particularly among the young, may be a casualty of unspoken dynamics in the relationship. Say, for instance, a young man complains about using condoms and finally decides not to use one, and his girlfriend interprets this to mean that he will marry her if she gets pregnant. Is her subsequent pregnancy a wanted pregnancy? What complicated negotiations between a woman and a man determine whether a baby is wanted or unwanted?

Still, the information that interviewers glean from women is interesting, especially when it changes over time. In 1973 the National Survey of Family Growth revealed that of all the children that had been born to American wives in the previous five years, 14 percent had been unwanted at the time of conception. In 1982, when the survey included both married and unmarried mothers, it found that only 7.7 percent of the children born in the previous five years had been unwanted. By 1988, the figure had risen again, to 10.3 percent. And the survey revealed significant differences according to age, race, and socioeconomic status: black women, poor women, and older women were all more likely (again, because of the way the question was worded) to tell interviewers that their children had been unwanted.

But the data are most troubling and most opaque in the case of teenagers. Since the survey asked women if they wanted a baby or another baby at some time, it presumably succeeded in reaching teenagers who had definitely not wanted a baby. Prior to 1982 unmarried women were not interviewed unless they had a child living with them, so we have comparative data only from 1982 and 1988. But in 1988 about 15 percent of white teens and about 30 percent of black teens said that they had not wanted their baby at the time of conception.[79] Thus, although many young mothers did find themselves with babies they had not wanted, 85 percent of white teens and 70 percent of black teens told researchers that they had indeed wanted their children. Most, however, were unhappy about the timing of the birth: more than eight out of ten teenagers who said that they had wanted their babies also asserted that they had become pregnant sooner than planned.[80]

In 1988 analysts took a new approach to the data. Previously the survey had made a distinction only between babies that had been wanted at the time of conception and those that had not; and this made sense, given that the women of interest were older and had nearly completed building their families. Wanted babies were then subdivided into those wanted at the time of conception and those wanted later. In 1988, however, the number of unwanted children was combined with the number of wanted children who had arrived sooner than expected. The resulting new category of "unintended" births was probably designed to accommodate the new demographic reality that teens represented. But the concept of unintendedness is just as slippery as the notion of wantedness. From the available data, we just cannot tell when a young woman would have preferred to have the baby that came too soon. In view of the way the survey questions were worded, a teen who was eager to be a mother but who would have preferred to wait a few months cannot be distinguished from a teen who planned eventually to become a mother but who viewed her recent pregnancy as a serious disruption in her life plans.

According to other studies, poor teenagers are more likely than affluent ones to report that a pregnancy was intended, and are more likely to continue their pregnancies to term. Furthermore, those who deliberately become pregnant and who do not seek abortions tend to be less advantaged teenagers. The entire issue of wantedness must thus be considered in the context of teenagers' available choices, which are often highly constrained.[81]

ABORTION, MARRIAGE, ADOPTION

The decision whether to terminate a pregnancy is powerfully affected by class, race, and socioeconomic status. The more successful a young woman is—and, more important, expects to be—the more likely she is to obtain an abortion. Women from affluent, white, and two-parent homes are far more likely to end their pregnancies than are women from poor, minority, and single-parent homes. Young women from families who are on AFDC are less likely to seek an abortion, because such families are already so disadvantaged. Even among young women from disadvantaged backgrounds, those who are doing well in school, who are getting better grades, and who aspire to higher education for themselves are more likely to seek an abortion than their more discouraged peers.[82] Among well-to-do teens who get pregnant accidentally, about three-fourths seek an abortion; among poor teens, the proportion is less than one-half. Likewise, about 60 percent of white teens terminate their pregnancies, whereas the figure for blacks and Hispanics is about 50 percent.[83]

Not surprisingly, the opinions of people around a young woman, particularly her significant others, will influence whether she carries her baby to term. Her boyfriend, female friends, and mother will all have an important effect on her decision. Teenagers whose boyfriends are younger—and presumably less well situated for parenthood—are also more likely to seek an abortion.[84] Even in African American and white ethnic families, where in principle there is strong opposition to abortion, parents and friends will sometimes urge an abortion when the man and woman are seen as too young to have a child or when the man is considered completely unreliable:

Mark and I have been going together since I was fourteen. When I got pregnant the first time, he said, "No way, no way you can have a baby at your age. You're too young and you will ruin your health." So I got an abortion—but I still have some scars left. When I got pregnant this time, we got married because neither of us wanted another abortion. (Kimberly, seventeen, white, Colorado)[85]

At first he really didn't say anything—just sat there. And then he asked what did I plan on doing and I said I planned on having it. He said he didn't think it was a good idea and that I was still young and I should have an abortion. (Black adolescent, California)[86]

Several neighborhood studies suggest that young women who are acquainted with single teenage mothers—who have visible role models—are also more likely to decide against having an abortion. This may be an example of social learning, of the fact that friends may exert good or bad influences. It may also be a more complicated process having to do with the way people choose friends. "High-trajectory" teens, meaning those with dreams for the future, may seek friendships with other high-trajectory teens who will support their goals and who are unlikely to be single mothers.[87]

The fact that abortion selects out the more successful and ambitious from the pool of potential teen parents raises the important question of whether such selection is an effect (a perverse effect, to be sure) of public policy, or whether it is the result of individual choice. In 1972, before abortion was legalized nationwide, an estimated 75 percent of pregnant teenagers gave birth. After *Roe v. Wade,* the rate dropped to approximately 50 percent. In recent years, however, the proportion of pregnant teens giving birth has risen again, to 60 percent. Does this mean that antiabortion policies (many of which are directed at teenagers) have had an effect, or does it simply mean that teenagers are choosing more often to carry their babies to term? Public policies may indeed be part of the cause. Since the liberalization of abortion in 1973, an increasing number of barriers have been placed in the way of those who would seek an abortion, and there is some evidence that these barriers fall disproportionately on young people. The fact that federal funding for abortion was withdrawn in 1977, the fact that about 82 percent of American counties do not have anyone within their borders who performs abortions, and the fact that women must often travel long distances to have an abortion all ensure that teenagers, who are less likely than older women to have private resources or private physicians, will find it more difficult to obtain an abortion.[88] According to the limited data, funding restrictions do seem to bring about a modest reduction in the proportion of pregnant women who terminate their pregnancies, and the effect is more visible among young women and ethnic minorities. (Sorting out these effects is complicated by the fact that after the withdrawal of federal funding for abortion, several states used state money to provide funding for abortions, and some—for example, North Carolina—explicitly included minors among those eligible for subsidized abortions.)[89] In addition, a number of states have passed legislation mandating that teenagers obtain either parental consent or notify their parents—legislation that is extremely popular with the public. Do these policies, taken together, force or encourage young women to give birth who would otherwise seek abortion?

Although this is surely one of the most central questions surrounding early pregnancy and childbearing, there are no clear data to resolve it. According to the National Survey of Family Growth, between 1982 and 1988 virtually all women of all ages and ethnic groups reported having more unwanted children: the hard-won control that women gained over their fertility in the 1960s and 1970s may be imperiled by changing attitudes and policies. Despite the many reasons to believe that restrictive government policies affect mainly teenagers, it seems that all women are having more trouble achieving their fertility preferences.

Thus, policies that try to limit access to abortion seem to have effects that are small and subtle. They can delay abortions—but the later the abortion the riskier it is for the woman's health and the more troubling it is for people who believe that the fetus gains moral rights as it develops. And they can ensure that a greater number of women from all age groups carry their babies to term. Among teens, they may cause a modest increase in illegitimate births—an ironic effect of antiabortion policies. Most married teenagers who are pregnant—about 75 percent—carry their babies to term anyway.[90]

Advocates of such laws have several hopes. They say that they wish to encourage parent-child communication. In fact, most young women discuss abortion with their parents (usually their mother), and the younger the teen the more likely she is to do so.[91] Furthermore, advocates hope that by making abortions harder to obtain they will encourage young parents to think about giving up their child for adoption. From the point of view of people who oppose abortion (and welfare), this would be a desirable result.

Young parents would have a second chance to pursue their education or training, and the many infertile couples in the United States would have a child to raise. The available evidence, however, suggests that this is probably wishful thinking. Adoption is not an easy, uncomplicated alternative.

Many adults may understand how events can lead to an unwanted pregnancy and may even understand why some teens do not have abortions, but they still may find the whole issue of adoption mysterious. Why don't more pregnant teens give up their child for adoption, since there are so many infertile couples who want one? Or, if they're so committed to raising a child, why don't they get married? Public rhetoric and popular stereotypes notwithstanding, a substantial portion of teenage mothers *are* married: in 1990, about a third of all babies born to teenagers were born to married women. In addition, the available data (now more than a decade old) suggest that some pregnant teens get married in the months after they give birth. In 1980–1981, among the teenagers who had their first out-of-wedlock child (approximately 50 percent of all pregnant teenagers), about 20 percent got married within a year of the birth, and 40 percent were married three years later. Whether they married the father of the baby or someone else is not clear from the data.[92] There were, to be sure, striking racial differences in the patterns. Although in 1980–1981 about 30 percent of all teenage first-time mothers were married at the time of conception, for white women the figure was closer to 40 percent and for blacks it was only about 5 percent. In other words, by the early 1980s six out of ten white babies and nine out of ten black babies were being conceived out of wedlock.[93] Likewise, about a quarter of the white teens but only one-tenth of the black teens got married before their baby arrived. White teens and more affluent teens were also more likely than blacks to marry after the birth of their child.[94] Aside from teens who are married when their child is born and those who marry soon after, some teens are in stable couples. One survey found that 40 percent of the young men who admitted fathering a child out of wedlock reported that they had lived with that child during the first year of the child's life.[95] And data from the National Survey of Families and Households indicate that about 22 percent of the children born to unmarried teens had mothers who were living in stable relationships, some of which would become legal marriages.[96]

Thus, a substantial proportion of all babies born to teenagers live with both a mother and a father for at least some years of their childhood (in the early 1980s the fraction was two-thirds), although the figure is higher for whites than for blacks. It is true that a baby born to teenagers who are living together, whether they are married or unmarried, has a higher-than-average risk of spending part of his or her childhood in a single-parent family; but this is a difference of degree, not of kind, when such a child is compared with children born to older parents.

In short, pregnant teenagers get married or settle down with a partner more often than people think, and are not dramatically different from a great many other American parents who are raising children alone. They are part of the much larger transformation of society that we have already discussed: Americans of all ages are less likely to get married than ever before, more likely to live together without being married, and more likely to be divorced. Thus, explaining why teenagers seem to be having and raising children outside marriage does not (as some might think) entail explaining why teenagers are so different. Rather, it means explaining why their behavior is so similar to that of everyone else, despite the fact that public attention has singled them out for worry and scorn.

Theories that attempt to explain the declining marriage rates of recent years and the rising rates of out-of-wedlock births have focused on women's increasing economic independence, on the increasing inability of men (particularly minority men) to obtain well-paying jobs that could support a family, and on the many cultural factors we have examined that, for many women, can make marriage undesirable and out-of-wedlock childbearing more attractive.[97]

The young woman who is considering whether or not to marry confronts a world in which many of the women around her are single parents, with or without the benefits of having being married previously. As divorced mothers have told us, the simple fact that a man and woman have been a married couple does not guarantee that the man will continue to provide support, either financial or emotional, once the marriage is over. More subtly, young women see that marriage often comes with a price tag: marriage brings with it certain entitlements, especially for men, and not all of these are welcome to both partners. As young women describe it, the marriages they see around them give them pause.

I don't want to get married, 'cause I've seen what my mother went through with her marriage and I'm not ready for that at all. (Dee, black, Boston)[98]

She split with him because he was beating on her and tried to strangle her when he was drunk. She said he never tried to do that before they was married. That's what they do is wait 'till after they're married. (White teenager, living in the rural Northeast)[99]

It will be a lot easier for me if I'm a single parent, because the father is one pain in the rear end. (Holly, white, Colorado)[100]

He's a child. He whines. He expects people to do things for him. He's nasty to me. He doesn't like to wash dishes and he thinks I'm supposed to do them for him. He likes people to cook for him, and he irritates me. He likes to sleep and watch TV. He works down the street, so I see him every day. The first time I met his father, who just moved up here, he asked, "Do you want to marry him?" I looked at him and I said, "Why would I want to marry your son?" He said, "He might grow up after you marry him." I said, "I can't take that chance." No, I would not marry him. He acts like a baby and I have two of my own. I don't need him plus the kids. His mother can keep him. (Corrie, black, Boston)[101]

My boyfriend wanted to get married from the beginning. But I didn't know whether I wanted to or not . . . I'm glad I'm single, because all I have to think about is feeding the baby, feeding myself, and doing homework, and that's it. There's nobody else to feed, nobody else to keep company. Your husband is going to want to have a conversation and tell about the hassles at work and you've got to listen. (Maria, Hispanic, Colorado)[102]

Obviously, conservatives are onto something: there has been a civil-rights revolution in the home. For whatever reasons, women are much less willing to put up with the unequal power relations and division of labor that came with the traditional marriage. They have also become much less tolerant of the violence and selfishness that many husbands inflict on their wives, and it is not at all clear that this intolerance is a bad thing, unless one values hierarchy for its own sake. If this revolution of rising expectations is not taken into account, getting women back into marriage (or keeping them there once they've been disillusioned) may be much more difficult than those who advocate "family values" anticipate. At the same time that women have started expecting more from marriage, men have been able to do less, at least when it comes to the one thing traditionally expected of a husband—namely, bringing home a reliable and adequate paycheck. During the past two decades, men on average have been contributing less to the family income. Since 1973 their real incomes have fallen, and high-wage jobs, particularly for semiskilled workers, have become scarcer. A woman these days is increasingly likely to be at least partly supporting her household, and in some cases her husband as well. Concurrently, the women's movement has fostered the realistic expectation that wives will receive fair treatment in exchange for assuming more of the financial burdens of the family.

In their own accounts of their lives, women make remarks suggesting that this fair treatment isn't always in the cards. Young mothers and pregnant women feel that, for the sake of their children, they must be very careful about making commitments to a man who may or may not stick around.

Marriage wouldn't solve my problem. I have to think of my baby now. How would it be for him to have me break up with my boyfriend after just getting to know him? (White teen living in the rural Northeast)[103]

I'm really scared about getting married. My boyfriend has a lot going for him, like getting scholarships and going to college. If we get married, and something goes wrong, he can say it's all the baby's fault. I don't want him to feel closed in and feel like he had to give up everything he's always wanted. I know we both made a mistake, but it's different for me. I didn't plan to go to college after I graduated. I wouldn't want for us to get a divorce and hate each other. I would rather have us not get married at all and both have the baby. I don't want to feel guilty and I don't want the baby feeling guilty. (Tammy, sixteen, white, Colorado)[104]

I could picture him as my boyfriend, even as the father of my child, but not as a husband. (Charmaine, sixteen, black, Washington, D.C.)[105]

Blacks in general have lower marriage rates than whites, but it is unclear whether this disparity is a result of some factors specific to the African American community, or a function of blacks' greater economic disadvantage, or an effect of earlier shifts in the gender relations between men and women.[106] Whatever may be causing such major changes in the American demographic profile—declines in marriage rates, increases in premarital sex and out-of-wedlock births—they are observable throughout the industrialized world. The sexual and reproductive behavior of American teens is part of the larger national context, and this national context is in turn linked to patterns characteristic of all developed countries.[107]

In order to think vigorously and carefully about the plight of teenagers, we need a great deal of information that we do not at present have. Among other things, we need more data on the extent to which teens who are unmarried are actually living in stable relationships. According to the latest available data, approximately two-thirds of all teenage mothers have a partner at the time they give birth or when their child is still young. Still, this means that about a third have no stable partner in the early years of their children's lives. Who are these young women? How do they differ from other teenage parents who have at least temporarily stable partnerships in which to raise their children? And how do they differ from older women who are having children on their own? How do they differ from women who are married or partnered at the time of the child's birth, but who end up raising children as a single parent?

Truly single young women who give birth (in contrast to unmarried women living in a de facto marriage who do so) raise yet another set of issues in the public mind concerning the choices they face. If many of these women are having babies they did not "intend" (and if some of their babies are actually unwanted in the terms the surveys specify), why aren't more of these women willing to consider giving up their babies for adoption, assuming that for whatever reasons they are committed to continuing the pregnancy? Advocates for adoption as a solution to childbearing among unwed teens ignore a number of inconvenient facts. For example, most infertile couples seeking to adopt are white, and most of them wish to adopt only healthy white newborns. (An estimated half-million children are living in foster care, but there is little political pressure to make these children available for adoption, because they are the wrong color, the wrong age, and the wrong class.)[108] But white teenage mothers—who in 1992 accounted for about 60 percent of teens giving birth out of wedlock—are more likely than black teenage mothers to marry after the birth of a child and to be living with the father of their baby at the time of the birth, making them unlikely candidates to relinquish their children. Thus, if more women gave up their children for adoption, there would simply be more children in foster care, since many of them would be black and the adoption market for such children is limited.

Throughout the past half-century, unwed pregnant women were encouraged to enter a maternity home, have their baby, give the baby up, and return to life as unmarried women.[109] At least, this was the preferred option for white women. As early as 1935, observers were confident that black extended families would be able and willing to accept out-of-wedlock children, although it is not clear whether such families would be acting out of preference or making a virtue of necessity; until the mid-1960s, most homes for unwed mothers refused to accept blacks.[110] Today it is much less common for an out-of-wedlock child, of any race, to be given up for adoption. Whereas just thirty years ago the single, never-married mother was something of an oddity, now women of all ages are choosing to live as single mothers. In the 1965–1972 period, about 20 percent of white babies and 2 percent of black babies were relinquished for adoption; in 1973–1988, the proportions fell to 8 percent and .2 percent, respectively; and in 1982–1988, the figures were 3 percent and 1 percent.[111] Even among unmarried mothers younger than seventeen, only about 8 percent of infants are given up for adoption.

These figures are only estimates because nowadays a substantial number of adoptions are arranged privately between the birth mother and the adopting couple, without the intervention of any state or federal agency. Often a lawyer assists in the process, but he or she is a private agent working for individual clients. The national adoption tracking system was disbanded in 1975,[112] but Christine Bachrach has estimated that in 1982 more than 90 percent of all unmarried teenage mothers kept their children, and that even in 1971, before abortion was legalized nationally, more than 70 percent of white teenage mothers and 90 percent of black teenage mothers kept their children. Here, as in so many areas of sexual and reproductive behavior, the patterns among white and black teens are becoming increasingly similar.[113]

The limited data we have also suggest that those young women who do give their children up for adoption resemble young women who have abortions more than they resemble young women who choose to rear their children. They are more affluent, have higher aspirations for themselves, and are performing better in school. Early motherhood is still not the first choice of young women who see themselves as having options.[114] Since abortion is now legal and single mothers are no longer stigmatized, young women must actively choose whether or not to become mothers. Thus, although there are still young women who become pregnant out of wedlock and who do not wish to get an abortion or to be a mother (that is, women who are candidates for giving a child up for adoption), their numbers are relatively small, and dwindling. For many young women, choosing to continue a pregnancy means choosing to raise a child.[115] Today the decision to keep a child is one that tends to be made before the baby is born, and unless abortion is recriminalized this situation is unlikely to change.

Still another barrier to using adoption as a way of solving the problem of early childbearing is the fact that the moral landscape has changed in the past three decades. People now think about adoption and its meaning in very different ways. Regardless of their opinions and decisions on the adoption issue, young mothers can be heard using moral language to talk about their choices:

> I know I can't keep my baby. I can't give it all the things a baby needs and I sure can't dump it on my parents because they can't afford to take care of their own family. I've decided to give it up for adoption. I think it's better for the baby to give it up to parents who can't have a baby themselves. I think that I'm really doing a favor to my baby, although I'm always going to wonder what it looks like and what it's doing. (Christina, seventeen, white, Colorado)[116]

This traditional position is becoming rarer these days, and was never very common among minority mothers, who knew that their children would have a difficult time finding adoptive homes. More common is the view of adoption expressed by this young mother:

> Sure I thought about it, but I never could do it. I know a lot of people could do a better job than me of being a mother and they can't get pregnant, but that's not my fault. I'm not going to go through nine months and then give someone else the benefit. (White sixteen-year-old, living in rural New England)[117]

This skepticism is enhanced by the fact that since single mothers are no longer vilified by society, giving up a baby has come to seem dictated only by material considerations, as the young mother above suggests. Young women believe they can love their children and can gauge the depth and commitment of their love, whereas the love of adoptive parents is an unknown quantity (and in recent years media reports of adoptive parents who abuse or even kill their children have given a special edge to this concern). So for many young women the only argument in favor of adoption is that their baby will have a better material life. In its starkest aspect, adoption means placing more value on cold hard cash than on a young woman's capacity to love.

Recent discussions focusing on adopted children who have sought reunions with their biological mothers raise another question—namely, the ways in which adoption may be harmful to children:

> I think as the kids got older it might be harder on them, because they would think, "Well, why didn't my mom want me? Was it because she just didn't want me, or because she couldn't support me, or . . .?" There's always going to be that time of depression. (Kimberly, white, Colorado)[118]

In view of the new options that have come to characterize pregnancy and parenting in recent years, asking an unmarried teenage mother to consider giving up her child for adoption is no longer as simple and morally correct as it once was. Whereas for earlier generations (especially white teens) giving up a child for adoption was thought to be in the best interests of the child and something that every mother who really loved her child would seriously consider, today the moral discourse surrounding adoption has shifted. For many young women these days, both white and black, the sentiments that traditionally surrounded adoption in the black community have more resonance: adoption is giving away your own flesh and blood; it breaks the ties between generations; and there is no guarantee that some stranger can and will love your child as much as you will, or at least as much as you imagine you will. Also, adoption means placing more value on money than on love, while deprecating the one thing that poor and discouraged teens can value in themselves: a capacity for maternal love. Oddly enough, the conservative dream of "family values" plays itself out in perhaps its purest form among unwed teenage mothers in poor communities. These young mothers express a commitment to moral values over material advancement, a passionate attachment to children, and a willingness to try to sustain a family (albeit a nontraditional one) whatever the social and financial cost. As a result, policies aimed at facilitating adoption may be praiseworthy and valuable in their own right, but are largely beside the point as strategies to reduce the rates of pregnancy and childbearing among teenagers. Since they will do little to alter the options confronting young women, they will have correspondingly little effect on teenagers' behavior.

WHAT'S GOING ON?

As we have seen, when it comes to the common outcomes of unwanted pregnancy—abortion and out-of-wedlock childbearing—teenagers are just a small part of a very large problem.[119] In the United States, women over twenty account for most abortions, 70 percent of unmarried mothers are not teenagers, and teens make up a declining proportion of all unwed mothers.[120] If we look at the statistics for a number of industrialized countries, we get yet another perspective: the real question is not why teenagers have so much trouble managing their fertility in terms of the public's apparent aversion to abortion and preference for in-wedlock childbearing; the question is why so many Americans in general have trouble doing this.

Abortion rates are very high in the United States among women of all ages, and with respect to out-of-wedlock births the question is even broader. Why are women in the developed world choosing to separate children and marriage? And why are American teenagers having so many more children than their European peers? The birthrate among teenagers in the United States (53 per thousand) is comparable to that of Spain or Greece or the eastern European countries, rather than that of Canada (18 per thousand), Scandinavia (9 to 18 per thousand), France, Germany, or Great Britain. What's going on?

We don't know very much about why women in the United States—a country with modern, accessible, publicly funded contraception—should have so many abortions. In 1988, American women gave birth to about 4 million children and had an estimated 1.5 million abortions, which means that a bit more than one-fourth of all pregnancies were terminated.[121] The available data are incomplete, but such a ratio seems to put the United States on a par with eastern European countries or Japan (where contraceptives are difficult to obtain and abortion is the primary form of fertility control) rather than with other countries in the developed world.[122] At this point, it is impossible to tell why American women of every age find it so hard to use contraception effectively, but the key point here is that this is a national problem confronting all women, rather than a problem confined to teenagers.

Perhaps America's Puritan heritage makes contraceptive use difficult (though no one has yet shown how practices and beliefs that prevailed three centuries ago can impinge on current behavior). Perhaps Americans' individualism or heterogeneity puts special barriers in the way of those who would use contraception. Whatever the cultural, structural, or moral pressures that impede such use, they affect Americans of all ages. If we wish to understand why teens don't use contraception, then we must investigate the issue as part of the examination of a much larger problem.

Regarding the rates of out-of-wedlock births, the real question is what is happening to families—to the relation between men and women, and between parents and their children—in postindustrial society. These changes, whatever their cause, are global in nature rather than uniquely American: out-of-wedlock childbearing is on the rise throughout the developed world, with the exception of parts of Scandinavia, which already had very high rates. In Europe, the ratio of illegitimate births to legitimate births has doubled, tripled, or (in Margaret Thatcher's England) quadrupled in recent years, even in the face of striking reductions in welfare systems—reductions that by conservative logic should have lessened the propensity to bear children out of wedlock.[123]

If rates of out-of-wedlock childbearing are rising, there must be corresponding shifts in people's tendency to marry and in their willingness to have a child even though they may be single. The first pattern is particularly visible in the United States: more and more Americans are avoiding or postponing marriage; moreover, they are choosing not to marry during the prime family-building years. Between 1980 and 1991, the number of never-married men aged thirty-five to thirty-nine more than doubled, from about 8 percent to about 20 percent. Never-married women in this age group also increased, from about 6 percent to about 12 percent.[124] The trend was even more striking among blacks: in 1991 almost one-third of all black men aged thirty-five to thirty-nine had never been married, compared to only 18 percent in 1980 and 15 percent in 1970. The increasing unwillingness or inability to marry is apparent among men and women from all age groups and ethnic backgrounds.[125] And whereas divorced Americans were once very likely to remarry, this pattern is changing as well.[126]

The unwillingness to marry or remarry does not, however, translate into an unwillingness to have children. Childbearing and childrearing have become increasingly disconnected from marriage. If present trends continue, almost one out of every six white women and seven out of ten black women will have given birth to a child without being married. And the rates for whites may turn out to be even higher than these estimates suggest, since unmarried whites seem to be increasing their childbearing more rapidly than unmarried blacks.[127]

In terms of the forces that are profoundly reshaping the way in which Americans make reproductive, marital, and life decisions, teenagers, especially young women of color, differ from the rest of society only in the extent and timing of the changes. They began out-of-wedlock childbearing earlier and more enthusiastically than did older, white women, but the latter seem to be closing the gap. Precisely why this is happening is unclear. William J. Wilson has devised a "male marriageability index," a measure of the percentage of men in a particular age group who are employed. He has shown that since the 1960s the number of employed nonwhite males per hundred women in each age group has declined; hence black men have become less marriageable, and this may be why the number of black single mothers has increased.[128] But it has not been as widely remarked that in the late 1970s and early 1980s the marriageability index for white men began to decline as well. The decline in the marriageability index for men of all races is almost surely linked to the loss of well-paid, unionized blue-collar jobs; the bifurcation of the labor market into high-skill, well-paid jobs (open to those with advanced education) and low-skill, poorly paid jobs (open to those with a minimum of education); and the proliferation of service jobs, which typically pay less than manufacturing jobs. All these factors reduce the marriageability index for blacks and whites alike.[129] And if these trends continue, as they are expected to, patterns of family formation among poor whites will probably begin to resemble those that historically have been prevalent among blacks.

One ethnographic study, by the anthropologist Mercer Sullivan, looked at a group of poor and working-class young men—Hispanic, black, and white—all living in the same section of New York City. In the early years of his study, Sullivan found that when one of these teenagers got a girlfriend pregnant, he was more likely to marry her if he was white than if he was black or Hispanic. Among whites, an unintended pregnancy simply precipitated a process of family building that was going to happen sooner or later. Blacks and Hispanics, however, tended to replicate the national patterns of out-of-wedlock childbearing for these groups. Sullivan traced the ways in which the young men's expectations of the future affected their attitudes toward pregnancy. The whites expected to work in skilled, well-paid, unionized jobs in the manufacturing sector (where their fathers and other male relatives already worked), while blacks and Hispanics had more modest hopes. Over the five years of the study, as the Northeast lost more of its industry and skilled blue-collar jobs left the area, the behavior of the young white men increasingly came to resemble that of the blacks and Hispanics: they became less likely to marry their pregnant girlfriends as their future came to seem more uncertain, and they began to encounter more problems with drugs and alcohol, which surely made them less attractive mates.[130] This does not mean, of course, that such decisions to marry are reducible solely to economic factors. At virtually all levels of income, blacks are less likely to marry than are whites (data on Hispanics are not available). But if decisions regarding marriage cannot be reduced to economics, neither can they be reduced to some mysterious force in black or Hispanic culture. Here, as in so many parts of social life, culture and economics intersect.

Decisions about whether to marry are complicated by the stalled revolution in gender roles. Although many men are earning less money than previously and although wives are much more likely to be working full time, few men truly share the household labor and childcare tasks. In fact, husbands seem to create more labor in the household by their mere presence—as much as eight hours more labor per week—despite the work that they do perform in the home. In other words, even when a man's labor in the household has been taken into account, he causes eight additional hours of labor.[131] This extra labor in the household, at a time when more and more women are employed outside the home, is what social scientists call the second shift, and is described as a persistent source of pain and unhappiness even among affluent men and women. When men are increasingly less able to contribute financially to the household and when they show little willingness to do more work around the house, women will inevitably revise their thinking about marriage, work, and the raising of children.[132]

The way in which both men and women think about marriage and its desirability must surely also be shaped by the ubiquitous evidence of what happens when a marriage ends. A marriage certificate is no guarantee, for example, that a father will continue to support his children financially or even come to visit them. In the United States, only 70 percent of divorced fathers make *any* court-ordered child support payments, and only half make them regularly and in full.[133] In comparison to the children of divorced and remarried parents, children of unmarried parents are more likely to see their father at least once a week, although one-third never see their father at all.[134] Evidently, marriage is no bulwark for children: about half of all marriages in the United States dissolve.

At the same time that society has become more accepting of unwed mothers, other incentives have made their lot more attractive. Until about 1965, middle-class women worked in the labor force before they married and after their children had left home, but not in the interim. And substantial numbers of women never worked outside the home at all.[135] Today the typical family has two wage earners, instead of a wage earner and a homemaker. But little else in family life has changed to accommodate this fact. It is extremely difficult for most working women to find adequate childcare—and astonishingly, most working wives pay for childcare out of their own pay. In addition, most of them continue to shoulder the main burdens of caring for the household. A 1983 survey found that a married man whose wife works outside the home and who has small children spends only three-quarters of an hour more a week on housework than a childless married man whose wife does not work.[136] As a consequence of these conditions, many young women who expect to work throughout their lifetimes and who expect to have children are ambivalent about having a husband. And if young women who have considerable social, educational, and economic assets are confused, it is not surprising that less privileged women find the decision even more difficult.[137]

Changes in family life and expectations are often subtle, gradual, and shaped by the existing structures of power and privilege in a society. The historian Lawrence Stone has argued that in the early modern period (1600–1700) the family was an emotionally neutral, even chilly entity: its main tasks were to bear and raise children, and to conserve inheritances. Emotional intimacy was not one of the things people expected from families. In more recent times, however, the family was slowly transformed into the intimate, emotionally intense, "companionate" marriage-with-children that today we regard as the ideal. Now it seems that the postindustrial era is transforming families just as radically as the dawning of the industrial era did some three centuries ago.[138]

Despite the fact that all Americans have trouble managing their fertility and all industrialized countries are experiencing a severing of marriage and childbearing, the fact remains that teenagers in the United States have higher rates of childbearing than teens in any other industrialized country. American women have traditionally had children young, although typically they were married when they did so. Early childbearing has always been part of American "exceptionalism."[139] But today these babies are more likely to be born to mothers who are unmarried and poor. In the years since the baby boom, when teenagers of all classes had babies, middle-class women have begun to postpone their childbearing, whereas poor women have held to the traditional American pattern of having children young. How are we to understand this?

Americans, in contrast to Europeans, think of having children as a private enterprise, one that will receive little support from the larger society. Even the much-vaunted Family and Medical Leave Act, hailed by its supporters as a landmark piece of family-friendly legislation, grants only *unpaid* leave for parents of newborn or seriously ill children, and then for only about half of all working women.[140] This approach contrasts with that of almost every other modern democracy, where childbearing and childrearing are considered directly relevant to the larger society. Accordingly, most European countries make sure that anyone having a child can rely on a range of social policies that make childrearing easier. Although countries differ in the scope and generosity of such programs, virtually all Europeans can count on a national health care system that subsidizes the cost of bearing a child; paid maternity leave (and in some cases paternity leave) after the birth of the child; family allowances that partially cover some of the costs of having children; and free or low-cost childcare.

In the United States these policies have historically been outside the scope of government intervention, and this situation is unlikely to change in the current parsimonious political and social climate. As a result, it is uniquely difficult to combine work and family in America—a problem, since most people's childbearing and childrearing years coincide with their prime working years. When the United States was sufficiently affluent that few women needed to work in the paid labor market, the absence of policies that let women combine work and motherhood was not so striking. But in the new global economy (and in the face of a declining middle class) the absence of a social structure that supports both work and motherhood has created a situation in which there is never a "good" time to have a baby.

Thus, the birth patterns of poor and affluent women in the United States have begun to bifurcate, as each group tries to come to terms with the difficulties of having children in a country that provides so little support. Poor women continue the traditional American pattern of early childbearing, because in this way they can become mothers before they enter the paid labor force and while they can make moral claims on kinfolk who will help with the childrearing. Affluent women, on the other hand, tend to wait until they are well established in the labor force before having a child.

Almost all middle- and upper-class people have friends or acquaintances who have postponed childbearing until their thirties or forties. They may realize that it is a way of combining education, work, self-realization, and a relationship with a partner; and they may be aware that behavior patterns would have been very different twenty years ago. But the actions of poorer and younger women are often thought of as accidents, rather than as efforts to cope with the same pressures using different resources. Arline Geronimus has argued that poor women are simply trying to "beat the clock" by having a child before rather than after the prime working years. She sees this happening in the black community in at least two ways. First, older black women tend to accumulate health conditions that can impair fertility; thus, a teenager who has a baby may be catching her fertility at its highest point. Second, early childbearing lets young women take advantage of the good health of their own mothers. There is a greater chance that the mothers will be able to help their daughters raise their babies—an important concern in view of the fact that poor communities have high rates of illness and early death.[141]

Given the peculiarities of the American situation, it makes sense for poor women, both black and white, to have babies at an early age. Since the United States is the only industrialized country without a national health care system, poor women run real risks if they try to postpone pregnancy as affluent women do: expensive fertility treatments are certain to be beyond their reach, and births to older women often entail more medical treatment for mother and child than births to younger women.[142] In addition, a sixteen-year-old has a much larger claim on the attention and resources of her extended family, especially of her mother, than does a twenty-four-year-old. A young woman from a poor community may see few acquaintances becoming affluent professionals who can afford to postpone childbearing, but her kin may give her an advantage that wealthier women have to wait to acquire—namely, help with the tasks of childrearing.

What is not immediately apparent is that both of these strategies entail costs, although to date only the costs of early childbearing have been the occasion of public handwringing. People often speak of the costs of being a teenage mother, but very few mention the costs of pregnancy among older women. No one has ever referred to an epidemic of pregnancy among forty-somethings, but there is one, and the costs of pregnancy among older women are socially subsidized just as surely as are the costs of births to younger women, though the former are more hidden. Fertility declines among older women, so that increasing numbers of them turn to high-technology forms of assisted reproduction. The *New England Journal of Medicine* estimates that each child conceived through *in vitro* fertilization in cases where the woman is over forty costs between $160,000 and $800,000.[143] And when older women do become pregnant, they run special risks. In comparison to younger women, first-time mothers over forty, whose birthrates tripled between 1985 and 1992, are more likely to have babies that are premature, short-lived, and of low birthweight.[144] The National Center for Health Statistics recently pointed out that the medical costs of older mothers are creating their own crisis in the medical system. Since so many of these mothers have fertility problems, they are more likely to seek technically sophisticated solutions and as a consequence are more likely to have multiple pregnancies—twins, triplets, and the like. But their babies, precisely because they are multiples, are likely to weigh very little at birth and to require immense social and medical resources in their first months of life.

Much like the babies of very young mothers, these multiples tend to suffer from a range of medical and developmental handicaps; it has been estimated that treatment amounts to an average of $70,000 per child, apart from normal delivery costs.

It is true that older women have fewer babies than teenagers do, although the numbers will vary depending on how one defines "older." In 1992 about 350,000 women had their first baby while they were teenagers; roughly the same number had their first baby after they turned thirty; and about 100,000 did so after the age of thirty-five. Many of the problems characteristic of early childbearing can be alleviated by relatively simple and inexpensive interventions that bring young mothers into the health care system. But there is no easy remedy for the problems of late childbearing, because many of these problems are iatrogenic—that is, a result of infertility treatments. The costs are not generally considered worthy of note. Once again, the way in which a problem is framed distracts attention from the underlying social and economic forces that are compelling women to have children either very early in life or very late in life.[145]

Some people will object that this comparison of very young mothers and very old mothers is inappropriate. Teenagers needn't wait until they're in their thirties to have their first child; they merely need to postpone their childbearing a few years—until they're twenty-four, say. This strategy has two problems: it assumes that young women have control over their choices, whereas their actual options may be contingent and limited; and it assumes that postponing childbearing is an unqualifiedly good thing. As we have seen, the notion that young women freely make the decisions by which many of them become unwed mothers—whether to have sex, whether to use contraception, whether to have an abortion—ignores the fact that men and women often engage in complex negotiations over these issues. Young women, especially those who do not expect to have a successful career and satisfying life work, tend to see their future in terms of a relationship with a man; such a relationship seems to promise them a better life than they already have. But if they postpone childbearing, thus risking infertility and the loss of their mother's help, they must be reasonably sure that the risk is worth it.

The basic difficulty is still there. People who are in their twenties and thirties are in their prime working years as well as their prime reproductive years, but American society provides virtually no assistance to women who wish to combine childrearing with paid employment. It thus forces them to devise individual solutions for a massive social problem. Furthermore, since teenage mothers are already seriously disadvantaged before they get pregnant, it may well make little difference in their lives if they postpone their childbearing for five or six years. Such postponement may increase their labor market skills, may help them accrue human capital, but they will still be at the end of the queue. It may also reduce their chances of becoming pregnant and of getting help from their kin in raising their children.[146]

Gender roles have changed enormously since the 1970s, and these changes are refracted in different ways by the lenses of class and ethnicity. American society has come to expect that women will work for some significant part of their lifetimes, but girls are still educated in the belief that a woman's primary function is to be a mother. Young women have few role models or institutional services to help them think about and manage the complex tradeoffs involved in investing in themselves and their children. This is a dilemma for even the most privileged women, but teenagers from poor, disadvantaged, and minority backgrounds may see few options open to them and no reason to postpone having a child. Although professionals focus on the costs of early childbearing and the benefits of postponement, teenagers may see the other side of the equation: the extent to which postponement may mean losing a relationship, compromising fertility, and losing kin support. They are involved in what decision theorists call a "risky shift"—a gamble that entails high loss and high gain. Young women who are already disadvantaged by their age, gender, race, and socioeconomic status, who are struggling in school, and who have been given short shrift by the health care and social systems may find themselves in no mood to be gamblers. They may hope that having a baby and building a loving relationship with a man will provide them with a better life than other women have, and thus they may not feel that they are taking such a big risk in the limited lottery they are forced to play. And for many of them, a baby, however much it may curtail certain parts of their lives, is a very satisfactory consolation prize.

These factors may perhaps explain the historical differences in the rates of out-of-wedlock childbearing among blacks and whites, as well as the fact that teenagers have tended to adhere to this model of childbearing more often than older women. Probably as a result of racial discrimination, the ratio of women's wages to men's wages is higher among blacks than it is among whites. And the wages of men and women diverge over time, for complex reasons. At age eighteen, women who are employed full time and year round earn almost as much as men; by age thirty, their income streams have diverged. Thus, ironically, wage discrimination among young people and minorities makes the wages of young women and minority women more equal to those of men than to those of older women and white women. And as the job market becomes tighter for older workers and for whites, the wages of white men are declining. A situation formerly common among young women and black women is now becoming prevalent among whites and among men and women of all ages.

Of course, the path to pregnancy is far from direct; there is no simple connection between the job market, marriage, and out-of-wedlock childbearing. The social context in which today's teenagers make life decisions is a product of three decades' worth of changes in public attitudes toward gender roles, marriage, sexual and reproductive behavior, family structures, and single mothers.

7

TEENAGE PARENTS

AND THE

FUTURE

In the 1970s advocates of a public policy aimed at curbing early childbearing promised a cure for many of America's social ills. They argued that everything from dropout rates to infant mortality to poverty could be reduced if teens just had fewer babies. Back then, reducing early pregnancy and childbearing had political appeal for both conservatives and liberals. Conservatives wanted teens to be less active sexually, to have fewer abortions, and to wind up less often as single mothers on AFDC. Liberals wished to help young women gain control over their reproductive and sexual destinies, thereby ensuring that untimely births would not limit young women's opportunities and chain them to a lifetime of poverty. In achieving these goals, liberals preferred to use a carrot; conservatives, a stick. By the 1970s traditional conservatives, who were worried primarily about the economic dimensions of early childbearing, had been joined by members of the New Right, who were concerned primarily about its moral implications. But in those days, the public did not yet perceive the issue as being an extremely urgent social problem.

Now, some two decades later, the debate over early childbearing has become more heated and widespread. As the economy has slowed and Americans have begun to have a harder time finding and keeping jobs, resentment against certain entitlements has escalated; unwed teenage mothers have been a target of particular scorn. The economy is showing even more of a tendency to bifurcate into an upper, affluent tier and a lower, poorer one—a situation in which workers with high-level skills are reaping more and more rewards. Middle-class people have developed ways of adapting to these pressures: they postpone childbearing until they have gotten enough education to compete for dwindling white-collar jobs, and they form two-earner households so that they can afford a home, live in a safe neighborhood, and send their children to good schools.

Teenagers who have babies don't conform with these middle-class assumptions and expectations. Looked at through middle-class eyes, such teens seem to be closing themselves off from the education that could make them self-supporting and take them off the public dole. They also appear to be limiting their ability to find a husband who could support them, thus making it likely that they will remain unwed and on welfare. As the average incomes of most Americans diminish in real value, the public becomes more restive about welfare and the taxes that support it. All women with dependent children who receive benefits are the targets of public anger these days, but young mothers, who account for a tiny portion (about 8 percent) of the women on welfare, provoke special rage.[1] To Americans who are increasingly postponing marriage and childbearing and are limiting the number of children they have, "babies having babies" looks like a recipe for trouble. Worse yet, it's a trouble that young people seem to bring on themselves but that everyone else seems to have to pay for. Not surprisingly, the major political parties have tapped into the public's resentment and now devote special attention to pregnant teenagers.[2]

For most conservatives, early childbearing, especially out of wedlock, is the result of bad values and unwise choices. They see young mothers as inner-city teens who lack stability and guidance, engage in irresponsible behavior, and then expect to be supported by the state. They believe that the welfare system offers what economists call "perverse" incentives—that its mere existence incites young women to get pregnant and live off its bounty. Their remedy: restrict access to welfare, particularly in the case of teenagers. The Republicans' Contract with America, for example, proposes eliminating all welfare payments to children whose mothers were unwed teenagers when they were born, as well as denying them access to food stamps and public housing. The Speaker of the House, Republican Newt Gingrich, has proposed that orphanages be established for children whose mothers cannot take care of them. According to the conservative view, young unwed mothers are rational actors who pursue a course that they see as being in their self-interest; denying teenagers welfare and limiting benefits to older women will reduce the rate of out-of-wedlock births.

Despite a great deal of evidence to the contrary, many people still believe that welfare benefits cause early and out-of-wedlock childbearing. As the Contract with America notes:

> Republicans understand one important thing ignored by most Democrats—incentives affect behavior. Currently, the federal government provides young girls the following deal: Have an illegitimate baby and the taxpayers will guarantee you cash, food stamps, and medical care, plus a host of other benefits. As long as you stay single and don't work, we'll continue giving you benefits worth a minimum of $12,000 a year ($3,000 more than a full-time job paying minimum wage). It's time to change the incentives and make responsible parenthood the norm and not the exception.[3]

But although incentives certainly affect behavior, they do so in a moral and social context that shapes how people interpret those incentives. For all women—rich and poor, teenage and older—decisions regarding childbearing and marriage have a great deal to do with feelings, values, beliefs, and commitments. They are rarely governed solely by the availability of a welfare check.

When speaking about their decision to have and raise a child, young mothers use terms that in other contexts would seem praiseworthy. They stress that they are attempting to take responsibility for their actions, sexual and otherwise. They have difficulty accepting abortion and adoption—the ways in which young women have traditionally hidden their shame from society—precisely because these alternatives do permit women to act as if nothing had happened. To be sure, the moral calculus here includes a measure of self-interest: for young women to whom few good things happen, childbearing offers at least the possibility of making a change in life. But the decision to bear and raise a child is not only a selfish one. Many young women describe how morally complex the choice is:

> Because his [the baby's] father, he didn't believe in abortion, he said I'm here, you're here, so why can't he come in as well? Don't kill the baby, he's going, we already made it. So we discussed that, too, before I got pregnant, if I got pregnant, that I should keep it because it ain't right to just throw away a life, so I said OK. (Lynn, teenager, black)[4]

> I wasn't ready . . . and I thought I should wait a little longer and finish finding pleasure, but my mother didn't want that and she made sure I kept the baby. And afterwards I, like, hey, why not? I started feeling the same,

I wanted it, too. It wasn't just like I had it because she wanted me to and stuff. My mother said she wants all her grandchildren. (Liz, sixteen, black, Boston)[5]

You make your bed, you lie in it. (White teenager, living in the rural Northeast)[6]

If I'm responsible enough to be goin' out and doin' these things getting pregnant, then I should be responsible enough to handle what I got myself into. (Sally, seventeen, white, rural Northeast)[7]

A variety of incentives blend together here. Young African American women know that few families want to adopt a minority child. Some young white and black women, like some of their elders, have moral scruples about abortion; and they believe that raising a child gives a young woman an opportunity to be good at something even if she must make sacrifices. In a poor neighborhood squeezed by a declining economy, there are often few opportunities to be responsible. But motherhood provides that opportunity, as well a spur for a young woman to try make something of herself:

I know I have to go to school because of the responsibility of the baby. It [having the baby] gave me a better outlook on life. I have to be concerned about the baby's future. (Black teenager, Los Angeles area)[8]

Mrs. J. talks about this all the time. She makes us responsible for everything. She says we have two lives to consider now, and she's right.[9]

I think it [having a baby] will press me on to do better and to do more, 'cause I want my child to have, you know, basically everything. And it will help me to do better in school and achieving the goals that I want to. I feel I can handle it. I feel that this baby will push me to strive for what I'm looking for, for a better life. I want my child to have a better life. I'm not sayin' my life is bad, I'm sayin' so it will have what it wants. I think that when you have somethin' right there before you, you have a real goal. You see, when I have that baby there, I say, you got to buckle down, you got to get good grades, you got to get the best.[10]

In fact, some young women outright reject the notion that economic considerations should be the primary motive in the decision to have a child:

I know it's hard to try and bring somebody into the world when you're not rich. But that's it, that's just it, everybody around not rich and people who are rich are doin' worse by their kids than the people who don't have . . . It don't matter if you don't have the money or the know-how, 'cause stuff like that come . . . Experience, it come with havin' a baby. I know I will never have a lot of money, but what I do have will be for the baby.[11]

The moral reasoning that undergirds the decision to have and raise a child is of course shaped by the larger world, the "incentives" that conservatives like to talk about. But the most visible incentive—welfare—has been declining in real value at precisely the time that more teenagers are deciding not to marry, and birthrates among teens have been stable or declining for most of the past two decades. Welfare benefits may appear generous ($12,000 a year, according to the Contract with America), but teenagers are likely to receive most of the payments indirectly, as food stamps or, more important, as reimbursed medical care. If one discounts Medicaid, the real value of the average AFDC check is about $7,200 a year, which at $600 a month (or $150 a week) leaves a family below the poverty level.[12]

The problem that confronts poor young people in the 1990s is the dearth of real alternatives to welfare. In the 1950s and 1960s, a young man could support a family on a low-wage job. There are fewer such jobs now, and they pay less: a minimum-wage job no longer allows a man to support a family or a single mother to support a child, even if they work full time and year round. If a woman has to pay for childcare, she earns less working than she would get on welfare.[13] This poses a dilemma for the American public: poor people can't earn enough to support a family, but no one wants to support them on welfare. One solution is the course advocated by policymakers in the nineteenth century: people who cannot afford to have children should simply stay childless. More humane, but ultimately deceptive, is the notion that poor teens should postpone their childbearing until they are emotionally and financially ready. People who identify early childbearing as the core of the poverty problem believe that teenagers are only temporarily unfit for parenthood and that they will mature into it. Alas, many of these young people will never be ready, at least if we define "ready" as having enough money to support themselves and their children. Given the scarcity of decent jobs, a substantial minority of Americans simply cannot afford to have children without some form of social transfer. A child born to married parents who can fully support it is, like safe neighborhoods and good schools, becoming a luxury accessible only to the wealthy.

Liberal critics of early pregnancy have their own form of myopia about the problem. They realize that the fundamental problem is poverty, but they argue that society should make a greater investment in teenage mothers—

that it should create training programs to increase the human capital that young mothers possess and hence increase their long-term self-sufficiency. From the liberal point of view, teenage mothers are disadvantaged people who would be much less likely to stay poor if they did a few simple things: finished their education, postponed childbearing, found a husband, and acquired marketable skills. Although this prescription sounds straightforward and commonsensical, it ignores the fact that most young mothers inherit multiple problems. They were born poor and grew up in poor neighborhoods. Their early lives were often scarred by violence and disorder, including sexual abuse. They attended rundown, underequipped schools in which teachers struggled to discipline and motivate the students, and they were typically not among the lucky and clever few who managed to obtain a little extra attention from their teachers, coaches, or adult neighbors. They were born into families that were at the end of the social and economic queue, and their life experiences rarely moved them any closer to the front. By having babies, such women are manifesting an almost poignant hope—the hope that a better future lies ahead, for their children if not for themselves.

Thus, training programs have very real limits. Even the good ones can only reshuffle people who are standing at the end of the line, not fundamentally transform the nature of the line. If young mothers acquire more training and skills, at best they simply displace others a step or two ahead of them. Most training programs for young women on welfare have a high rate of success, but this success is very specific: such programs raise the income of participants by amounts that exceed the cost of the program. Unfortunately, these women are so poor that this higher income typically raises their financial status only slightly—from desperately poor to miserably poor.[14] If teenagers and their babies represented only poverty in its traditional form—if they were members of poor two-parent families or were worthy widows, as in earlier decades—the public might be more willing to spend resources to bring them and their children into the mainstream. But poverty today brings with it new family structures that many Americans find troubling.

Poor people are more likely to become parents as teenagers than are affluent people, and they are also more likely to have babies out of wedlock. So when conservatives claim, despite all findings to the contrary, that welfare causes early and out-of-wedlock childbearing, they speak to a public worried about two different things—the cost of welfare and changing family structures—in a way that knits these two concerns together. Liberals have been slow to make this distinction: they constantly remind conservatives that AFDC accounts for only a small fraction of federal spending, especially when compared to other federal programs such as the military. They are correct on this point: even the cost of middle-class welfare programs (Social Security, Medicare, deductions for home-mortgage interest) dwarfs the amount spent on AFDC. Social Security in particular, because it is indexed to inflation, has become a significant income-transfer program for middle-class people: most individuals take out far more in benefits than either they or their employers made in contributions.[15] But liberals have been slow to realize that the public is extremely uneasy about the way family structures have changed, and that this unease has settled on the heads of teenagers and women on welfare. Americans find welfare troubling when it seems to encourage early and out-of-wedlock childbearing, especially among the poor and minorities.

Since the signs of poverty and these new family structures have become more widespread simultaneously, conservatives make a seemingly logical argument when they relate the two. People who believe that welfare is wrong if it creates more single and teenage parents are drawing on a valid intuition: that the more adults there are who are committed to the well-being of a child, the better off that child is. Likewise, they are almost certainly right to suspect that the ties uniting parents with children and husbands with wives have frayed in the last twenty years. They are also right to think that children benefit when their parents have more resources—emotional, spiritual, psychological, financial—to devote to them, and that such resources are becoming ever scarcer.[16] They are wrong, however, in assuming that welfare has had much to do with these unfortunate social trends.

The troubles that teenage parents face today are the same ones that all Americans face: changes in the nature of marriage, in the relations between men and women, in the relations between parents and children. Everyone is having difficulty mustering the emotional, psychological, and financial resources that children need, and many people long for the days when life seemed easier. But Americans are wrong when they assume that teenage parents suffer disproportionately from these problems because they are young; rather, teenage parents are vulnerable parents because they are poor. Society runs the moral risk of scapegoating teenage mothers—symbolically punishing them for trying to solve the problems everyone faces and solve them with more limited resources than most Americans.

Does this mean that people should shrug their shoulders and say that early childbearing is just a fact of modern life? No. The increase in the number of teenage and unwed mothers is an indirect measure of the toll that a bifurcating economy is taking on Americans, especially women of poor and minority backgrounds. It would be better to see early childbearing as a symptom, like infant mortality—not a cause but a marker of events, an indicator of the extent to which many young people have been excluded from the American dream. It is distressing and alarming that early child-bearing—like infant mortality—is more common among minorities, the poor, and those who have been failed by the nation's major institutions. In addition, the plight of teenage mothers reveals not only how hard it is to be poor in America, but the special pressures that confront young, poor women. One of the tragedies of early childbearing is that it is one of the few ways in which such women feel they can make a change in their lives, however illusory that change may prove to be. Having a baby can give a young woman permission to be assertive and motivated on her baby's behalf when she has trouble mustering these qualities for herself. For example, a woman disillusioned with education may decide to stay in high school because she doesn't want her baby to have a dropout for a mother. The fact that birthrates among teens have stayed at high levels indicates how discouraged and disadvantaged many young women are—that they have to take the extraor-dinary step of bearing a child in order to feel they have a meaningful role and mission in society and can make claims on themselves and others.

Having a baby is a lottery ticket for many teenagers: it brings with it at least the dream of something better, and if the dream fails, not much is lost. Some young women say it was the best thing they ever did. In a few cases it leads to marriage or a stable relationship; in many others it motivates a woman to push herself for her baby's sake; and in still other cases it enhances the woman's self-esteem, since it enables her to do something productive, something nurturing and socially responsible. Yet lotteries are by definition unpredictable. To the extent that babies can be ill or impaired, mothers can be unhelpful or unavailable, and boyfriends can be unreliable or punitive, childbearing can be just another risk gone wrong in a life that is filled with failures and losses. Although early childbearing rarely causes a young woman to be poor and discouraged, once she is responsible for a baby a woman may find that she has a harder time taking advantage of lucky breaks and fewer opportunities to make positive changes in her life. What should trouble us when we worry about teenage parents is the fact that poor and minority women feel they risk losing so little by having a child at an early age. American society places great value on individual success, and is remarkably stingy in its support of those who "fail." It is no accident that in the United States—where the penalties for failure are so severe—the birthrate among teenagers is higher than in any other industrialized nation, and 80 percent of babies born to teens are born to poor women. If young men and women felt they had an array of opportunities in life and still chose to become parents as teenagers, their decision would evoke comparatively little concern. But in fact early childbearing is a very constrained choice for poor people who have few other options; for them, being a teenage parent can be much more rewarding and much less costly than is generally supposed. If America cares about its young people, it must make them feel that they have a rich array of choices, so that having a baby is not the only or most attractive one on the horizon.

In the past twenty years we have acquired a great deal of knowledge about preventing involuntary pregnancy and childbearing among teenagers. But it's the young people who voluntarily get pregnant (although we've seen how passive this "voluntary" choice can be) who elicit the most concern and whom we know the least about helping. And many of the current public-policy proposals seem likely to reverse the gains of the recent past.

This is a dispiriting time to be thinking about teenagers and their pregnancies. We know more than ever about how to help young people avoid getting pregnant and having babies they don't want. We can point with pride to effective public policies that since the 1970s have helped keep early childbearing from reaching truly epidemic proportions, though the numbers of sexually active teens have increased enormously in the United States, as they have in most industrialized countries. Despite their success, these policies have never really addressed the plight of young women who want a baby or of those who don't much care whether they have one or not. Yet here, too, accumulating research has begun to suggest ways of encouraging even these teens to postpone pregnancy, while other research (discussed in Chapter 5) shows that the reasons for postponement are much less urgent than once thought. Each new round of the debate on early childbearing and poverty has served to reduce the weight that researchers place on the former as a cause of the latter.

But the dismay and anxiety of the American public in an era of rapid shifts in the economy, in family structures, and in social well-being have led the public discourse about teenagers to become more mean-spirited and irrational than ever. To take one example, government programs have in fact reduced pregnancy rates among teenagers. The political consensus in the 1960s among traditional liberals and traditional conservatives on public funding of contraception has paid off handsomely: today, poor and minority women have the sort of control over their fertility that only middle-class women used to enjoy. And young women have benefited from such programs to a greater extent than most people realize. More and more teenagers have begun using contraception, and using it effectively. Teens can now obtain low-cost or free birth control from a variety of sources (including hospitals, local health departments, and Planned Parenthood clinics), and they make good use of this access: according to one study, about 53 percent of all teenagers—and 72 percent of black teenagers—obtain their first contraceptive from a clinic, whereas about 40 percent of all teens obtain it from a private physician.[17] Between 1969 and 1983 the number of teenagers using family planning clinics increased more than sixfold. By 1988 the figure had doubled again, to approximately 3 million;[18] two-thirds of all teens using contraception identified a family planning clinic as the most recent source of their contraception.[19] During the 1980s, as the economy worsened and medical care became more expensive, clinics became an ever more important source of contraception for teenagers, especially poor ones.[20] In 1983 more than 80 percent of teenage users of clinics came from families living below the poverty level and 13 percent from families on public assistance. Overall, clinic users are likely to be poor and black, and they are younger at first intercourse than people who go to a private physician.[21]

Since the number of sexually active teenagers doubled between 1970 and 1990, it is unlikely that any sort of contraceptive services would have effected a substantial decline in pregnancy rates among teenagers, given that the population at risk doubled. Yet a doubling of the population of sexually active teens did not lead to a doubling of the pregnancy rate, and public funding of contraception is the reason. This enormously successful program—one that has made teens *less* likely to get pregnant than ever before and one whose effects are most visible in poor and minority communities—has been rewarded by having its funding cut almost in half.[22] In part this is due to a resurgence in political opposition to publicly funded contraception, opposition based to some extent on the fact that federal programs have slowed but not reversed the acceleration in the pregnancy rates among teenagers, leading people to see these programs as a failure rather than the considerable success that they are.

If one public policy—public funding of contraception—has been successful in reducing the risk of pregnancy among sexually active teenagers, another public policy—the legalization of abortion—has effected a substantial decline in early childbearing. In 1972, when abortion was legal in only about a third of all states, three-fourths of all pregnant teenagers gave birth. In the years after *Roe v. Wade,* when abortion became available in every state, about half of all pregnant teens gave birth—a proportion that remained stable for about a decade. But recent controversy over abortion has led to more restrictive policies primarily affecting teenagers and poor women. During the 1980s the federal and state governments cut funding for abortion, imposed waiting periods, and implemented parental-consent or parental-notification policies for teens. It is not yet known if such measures are the cause, but since 1988 the percentage of pregnant teenagers who give birth has risen to about 60 percent.[23] If abortion is morally wrong, as some think it is, then it must be wrong for all concerned, and not merely the young and the poor.

A third public policy—sex education—seems to be making some progress in preventing teenagers from getting pregnant in the first place. Although sex education has been a feature of American public schools since the Progressive Era, we are just beginning to understand what makes a successful program.[24] In 1938 Benjamin Gruenberg, a noted Progressive reformer, found that a majority of the nation's high schools had instituted sex education programs, and most of the rest were considering doing so.[25] In his day "sex education" meant everything from brief lectures about menstrual hygiene to complex discussions of the social, ethical, and moral dimensions of relationships between the sexes—and things are not very different now. At least thirty-one states and the District of Columbia have policies that mandate or encourage sex education, but curricula vary widely in their length and their content, and relatively few have been systematically and rigorously evaluated.[26] We do know from surveys that a great many students receive sex education in school and that the number is increasing over time. One study from the 1970s found that 36 percent of public high schools offered a sex education course; another found that 80 percent of large school districts with junior or senior high schools offered such courses, either separately or as part of another course (say, health or biology).[27]

Surveys in the early 1980s found that about 60 percent of young women and 52 percent of young men had taken a course on sex education, and longitudinal surveys suggest that this number is growing—that junior high and high school students today are more likely to have received some sex education than their older brothers and sisters were when they were in school. An analysis of the 1988 National Survey of Family Growth, for example, found that almost 90 percent of teenage girls reported having had sex education by the time they graduated.[28] When asked, even more young people than this report having had sex education, since they include information they have received in nonschool programs such as scout troops, Girls' Clubs and Boys' Clubs, church groups, family planning services, and health clinics, as well as in conversations about sexuality and contraception with their parents.[29]

Some people think that sex education is part of the problem—that by addressing and "normalizing" sexual activity among teenagers, sex education encourages it. This belief has a certain logic, but if sex education does have such an effect at all, it is very weak. One study suggested that taking a sex education course would increase by 2 percent the odds that a teenager, especially a very young teenager, would be sexually active.[30] Another study found that young men who received some instruction in contraception had their first intercourse slightly earlier than other students, whereas those taking courses that covered AIDS education and "resistance skills" (how to say no) tended to have first intercourse at later ages.[31] Still another study found that students taking sex education courses were less likely to have sex than those who did not take such courses.[32] But careful and rigorous review of all the various studies on the matter suggests that, in general, taking sex education courses has virtually no effect on an individual's propensity to become sexually active.[33]

This is good news, because it is becoming apparent that some sex education programs can reduce pregnancy under certain circumstances. Today, as in Benjamin Gruenberg's time, sex education (or "family life" education, as it is often called) covers a wide range of topics in a variety of formats, and most sex education courses in the United States are less than comprehensive in their approach and substance. Some are extremely short, lasting only five to twenty hours, and they often limit themselves to the safer topics, such as anatomy and physiology; in one family life program offered in New Jersey, students were taught how to fill out the state's income tax form.[34] Teachers may be wary of or feel uncomfortable about discussing contraception, and may do so abstractly and euphemistically rather than directly and concretely. Information about reproductive anatomy is certainly educational, but in the absence of other information it is unlikely to prevent pregnancy.

Another factor limiting the potential effectiveness of sex education courses is the fact that many school districts postpone sex education until the later years of high school, when students are thought to be more developmentally mature. But about one-fourth of Americans do not finish high school, and in some urban areas the figure approaches one-half. This means that a substantial number of young people, and disproportionately high-risk ones at that, may never reach the grade level at which sex education courses are offered. Furthermore, many students become sexually active prior to the grades in which sex education is offered: one study in the 1980s found that about 50 percent of young women and 65 percent of young men received their primary sex education from a partner, not from a course. Among young black men, 81 percent had had intercourse before ever receiving any sex education; among white men the figure was 61 percent; and among Hispanics it was 73 percent.[35] Delaying sex education until the later years of high school, therefore, can seriously compromise whatever effectiveness it may have, because some students never get the information at all and others get it after they have already become sexually active. Not surprisingly, when sex education is given to young people who are already sexually active, it seems to have little effect on their contraceptive and risk-taking behavior.

Increasing worries about early pregnancy and AIDS have led many school districts in recent years to offer sex education courses to younger students and to make such courses mandatory rather than elective. Consequently, many more people are receiving sex education these days, and many more of them are receiving it prior to their first sexual experience. One study found that among women who turned twenty between 1983 and 1985, only 56 percent had had sex education prior to first intercourse; among those who turned twenty between 1991 and 1992, the figure was 81 percent.[36]

After the Adolescent Family Life Act was passed in 1984, the federal government established about two dozen projects based on a new concept— that of preventing sexual activity rather than providing contraception. One fairly typical example is the Sex Respect curriculum, developed in Illinois and now used in many school districts throughout the country. It is much more prescriptive than other sex education programs, advising that students abstain from sex if they wish to avoid pregnancy. As a group, such "abstinence-based" programs encourage young people to abstain from sex, warn them of the dangers of sexual activity, and, through discussion and role playing, try to give them the communication skills they need in order to implement their decisions. Proponents of this approach believe that providing information about contraception would undermine the goals of these programs.[37] Some of the techniques used, particularly the resistance skills that help teens say no, have been incorporated into other sex education curricula, and some school districts have adopted abstinence-based sex education while also teaching about contraception. The purely abstinence-based curricula (those that give no contraceptive advice or education) are fairly new and have not yet been rigorously evaluated. Like other sex education programs, they can improve students' knowledge and attitudes, but their effects on behavior are less clear.[38] Early research suggests that some parts of the abstinence-based programs can be quite effective. More conventional programs that have incorporated the teaching of resistance skills, for example, do seem to have some success in encouraging young people to postpone their first sexual involvement, but often the postponement is not very great—on the order of six months or so. Other research suggests that conventional programs which are clearly directive in their teaching (as are the abstinence-based programs) rather than neutral in their approach are more likely to change students' behavior. Preliminary data, however, suggest that all of these programs may entail something of a tradeoff: the ones that focus on helping young people say no have little effect on subsequent contraceptive use, and the ones that impart contraceptive skills do not teach young people how to avoid sex.[39] Since American teenagers face one to two decades during which they are sexually mature but not married, programs that urge postponing sex but that have no effect on contraceptive use may worsen the situation.

According to new research, effective sex education programs *can* change adolescents' behavior. Such programs typically begin before students have become sexually active and they are usually strongly prescriptive in nature. Effective programs focus clearly on goals and carefully evaluate what works. Not only do some programs delay the onset of sexual activity, but others lead to greater use of contraception. In comparison to people who have had no sex education, those who have attended a good sex-ed program are more likely to use contraception the first time they have sex, to obtain effective contraception sooner, and to use contraception more reliably in general.[40]

Thus, in view of all the evidence that public policies have done a reasonably good job of containing early pregnancy despite a vast increase in sexual activity among teens, the current conservative initiatives seem paradoxical at best and self-defeating at worst. There are powerful pressures to cut public funding for contraceptive programs, even as these programs are becoming recognized for the success story they are. Similarly, people who oppose abortions, much like people in the nineteenth century who opposed contraception, have been stymied in their attempts to make abortion either illegal or unpopular for the affluent. They have instead contented themselves with policies that make abortion more difficult for young people and poor people to obtain. Finally, just as we have begun to sort out which sex education techniques work and which ones don't, the very notion of sex education is more contested than it has ever been. In the face of accumulating evidence which suggests that more students than ever are receiving sex education and that well-designed programs can indeed modify adolescents' risk-taking behavior, politically mobilized activists all over the United States are pushing for hasty adoption of abstinence-based programs before rigorous evaluation has been able to show whether they are capable of doing anything other than making adults feel better.

To put this in the bluntest terms, society seems to have become committed to *increasing* the rates of pregnancy among teens, especially among those who are poor and those who are most at risk. Affluent and successful young women see real costs to early pregnancy and thus have strong incentives to avoid it;[41] but poor young women face greater obstacles, both internal and external. Cutting funding for public contraceptive clinics, imposing parental-consent requirements, and limiting access to abortion all increase the likelihood that a young woman will get pregnant and have a baby. Conversely, providing widespread contraceptive services (perhaps even making the Pill available over the counter), extending clinic hours, and affording greater access to abortion will give at least some poor young women an alternative to early childbearing.

The news is even grimmer when it comes to preventing or postponing childbearing among teenagers who are not highly motivated in the first place. Even as we amass evidence showing that early childbearing is not a root cause of poverty in the United States, we are also realizing more clearly that the high rate of early childbearing is a measure of how bleak life is for young people who are living in poor communities and who have no obvious arenas for success. Here, too, just as we are developing a better sense of what it would take to offer these young women and men more choice in life, the political temper of the times makes even modest investments in young people seem like utopian dreams. Far from making lives easier for actual and potential teenage parents, society seems committed to making things harder.

A quarter-century of research on poverty and early childbearing has yielded some solid leads on ways to reduce early pregnancy and childbearing. But because the young people involved have multiple problems, the solutions aren't cheap. In order to reduce the number of teenagers who want babies, society would have to be restructured so that poor people in the United States would no longer be the poorest poor people in the developed world. Early childbearing would decrease if poor teenagers had better schools and safer neighborhoods, and if their mothers and fathers had decent jobs so that teens could afford the luxury of being children for a while longer. If in 1994 the United States had finally succeeded in creating a national health care system (becoming the last industrialized country to do so), this change alone would have had a dramatic impact on poor people generally and poor women specifically. Providing wider access to health care, for example, would have eliminated some obstacles to contraception and possibly even to abortion. More fundamentally, it would have meant that young women and men, even if they did have babies and even if they did have them out of wedlock, could have afforded to raise them without going on welfare.

This is no time to be advocating expensive social programs, however. These days, policymakers seem inclined to shred what remains of the safety net, so the best that teenage mothers and potential teenage mothers can hope for is that programs which make life easier will not be totally eliminated in the drive to reduce the federal deficit. If the few employment programs that exist in the United States survive the budget cutting and if they can increase their outreach to young women, greater employment opportunities may reduce pregnancy rates. A 1978 evaluation of the federally funded Job Corps, for example, revealed that young men and women who were enrolled in the program tended to postpone childbearing and had fewer out-of-wedlock babies.[42] And women who found jobs through other federally funded programs seemed to have lower birthrates than women living in similar communities that had no such programs.[43] Some evidence also shows that macroeconomic forces can affect the rates of early childbearing: communities whose job markets are open to young women tend to have fewer teenage mothers.[44]

A widespread misconception is that many poor women live on welfare instead of finding a job. In fact, most women on welfare use their grants to supplement the low wages they earn in the work force and to see them through periods of unemployment or poor health.[45] The kinds of jobs they have usually pay very little and provide no benefits; even if they worked full time and year round, their incomes would still be below the poverty level. Recent expansions in the Earned Income Tax Credit made life a little easier for those at the bottom. Now, the cessation of AFDC as an entitlement program and inevitable cutbacks in the Earned Income Tax Credit will make life on the bottom much harder. Their effects on early childbearing are unknown, but they are unlikely to reduce it. Although it is a cherished belief among conservatives that the level of available welfare affects childbearing among teenagers, and among unmarried teens in particular, if this were true the rate of such childbearing would have declined dramatically over the past twenty years as the real value of welfare plummeted.

Society could also do a number of other things that, although they would not reduce early childbearing, would make the children of teenage parents better off, thereby reducing the ranks of disadvantaged and discouraged people at risk of being the next generation's teenage parents. These measures, too, have come to seem hopelessly utopian in the current political climate. For example, most other industrialized nations provide high-quality, publicly subsidized daycare for poor children; in the best of all possible worlds, the United States would, too. A national childcare and preschool system would ideally be part of the public schools, as is the case in France. Daycare workers would be trained like teachers and paid at similar levels. In this way, children born to young or poor parents would be challenged and educated from their earliest years. As things stand now, most poor mothers rely on a relative to provide daycare for their children. But this family-oriented system might actually motivate teens to have babies at an early age, since a young mother's claim on her female kin—usually her own mother—seems much more reasonable if she is sixteen than if she is twenty-four. If she knows that someone other than her mother will be able to help care for her children, she may wait a few years before having her first baby.

The political scientist Hugh Heclo once noted, speaking of antipoverty policies, that what Americans want they can't have, and what they can have they don't want. This dictum seems particularly apt in connection with early pregnancy and childbearing. Americans want teenagers to wait until they are "mature" before they have sex, to wait until they are "ready" before they get pregnant, and to wait until they are married and financially secure before they have children. But there is no consensus on what it means to be "mature," out-of-wedlock births are common throughout the industrialized world, and a great many teenagers will be poor throughout their lives and hence never really "ready" to be parents. Society could conceivably become so punitive and coercive that poor teenagers would be discouraged from ever having babies, but only a few countries such as China have been able to impose this kind of control. It's even doubtful that the draconian welfare-reform policies proposed by the Republicans will make much of a difference. Since teenagers who live in states with generous benefits do not have more out-of-wedlock babies than teens in states with low benefits, and since out-of-wedlock childbearing has been increasing as welfare benefits decline, a radical reduction in welfare benefits for teenagers will probably have a negligible overall effect. As we have seen, myriad factors affect the way in which young people make decisions about sexual activity, relationships, and childbearing; whether or not they are eligible to receive a welfare check is unlikely to alter their behavior. Most will continue to have babies, hoping that things will somehow work out and that their families will rearrange scarce resources to provide for the newcomers.

The more one knows about early pregnancy and childbearing, the more skeptical one becomes that they correlate with poverty in any simple way. Poverty is not exclusively or even primarily limited to single mothers; most single mothers are not teenagers; many teenage mothers have husbands or partners; and many pregnant teenagers do not become mothers. The rates of pregnancy and childbearing among teenagers *are* a serious problem. But early childbearing doesn't make young women poor; rather, poverty makes women bear children at an early age. Society should worry not about some epidemic of "teenage pregnancy" but about the hopeless, discouraged, and empty lives that early childbearing denotes. Teenagers and their children desperately need a better future, one with brighter opportunities and greater rewards. Making the United States the kind of country in which—as in most European countries—early childbearing is rare would entail profound changes in public policy and perhaps even in American society as a whole. Such measures would be costly, and some of them would fail.

Any observer of the current scene would have to conclude that these days the chances of implementing costly social programs are extremely small.

Americans seem bent on making the lives of teenage parents and their children even harder than they already are. Society has failed teenage parents all along the line—they are people for whom the schools, the health care system, and the labor market have been painful and unrewarding places. Now, it seems, young parents are being assigned responsibility for society's failures. Michelle and her baby have never needed help more, yet never have Americans been less willing to help and more willing to blame.

APPENDIX

The Demography of Teenage Pregnancy

Given the rapidity and force with which the issue of early pregnancy came onto the American public-policy agenda, we might logically conclude that the renewed interest in teenagers and their sexual and reproductive lives reflected some dramatic changes in teens' behavior. Some aspects of teens' behavior did change, while others did not, and still others changed in ways that were at odds with the "story" constructed by advocates and the media. Many of the published data surrounding early pregnancy were interpreted in ways that reflected an array of anxieties about teenagers, rather than a firm grasp of what was really happening.

For example, as far back as 1988 two out of three Americans thought that early pregnancy was becoming more prevalent (Harris Poll, "Teenage Pregnancy, Sex Education and Birth Control," May 4, 1988). But since 1960, with the exception of the past few years, *births* to adolescents have been declining. Birthrates among teens have been surprisingly stable for most of this century, with the exception of the baby boom years. When "teenage pregnancy" first appeared on the public policy agenda in the 1970s, therefore, births among teens (like all births) were on a downward trend from their baby boom highs.

Table 1 shows that although there has been an upturn in births in the past few years, even this upturn is within historical range. At this writing it is hard to tell whether this is just random variation or the beginning of a new trend.

Fertility among teens has always been remarkably similar to the fertility rates of older women, going up when those rates go up, and going down when they go down. The similarities are most marked with those women who are just a little older: twenty to twenty-four. But fertility in the U.S. population as a whole tends to respond to large, society-wide forces. Teenagers are not a group unto themselves.

Table 1. Birthrates per thousand women aged fifteen to nineteen, 1920–1990.

Year	Rate
1920	62.6
1930	56.7
1940	53.5
1950	79.5
1960	91.0
1965	73.3
1970	69.7
1975	55.6
1980	53.0
1985	51.0
1990	59.9

Source: 1920–1970: R. Heuser, *Fertility Tables for Birth Cohorts by Color, United States, 1917–1973,* p. 16, Table 3a: "Central Birth Rates for All Women by Age and Birth Order." 1975–1990: National Center for Health Statistics, *Advance Report of Final Natality Statistics, Monthly Vital Statistics Report* 41, no. 9, supplement (1990): Table 4, "Total Fertility Rates and Birth Rates by Age of Mother and Race."

Table 2. Abortion rate, pregnancy rate, and birthrate among teens, per thousand women aged fifteen to nineteen, 1972–1990.

Year	Abortion rate	Pregnancy rate[a]	Birthrate
1972	19	95	62.0
1975	31	101	55.6
1980	43	111	53.0
1985	44	109	51.0
1990	41	117	59.9

a. Contains an estimate for miscarriage: 20 percent of all live births and 10 percent of all abortions.

Source: Abortion rates, 1972–1985: Stanley Henshaw and Jennifer Van Vort, *Abortion Factbook* (New York: Alan Guttmacher Institute, 1992), pp. 172–173. Abortion rate, 1990: Stanley Henshaw, *U.S. Teenage Pregnancy Statistics* (New York: Alan Guttmacher Institute, 1993). Pregnancy rates: Alan Guttmacher Institute, *Sex and America's Teenagers* (New York: Alan Guttmacher Institute, 1994). Births: National Center for Health Statistics, *Advance Report of Final Natality Statistics, Monthly Vital Statistics Reports,* vols. 23–41.

To be sure, fertility among teens, although stable and quite similar to the fertility of older women, did reflect a significant change in the period after 1960. The legalization of abortion in 1973 created a new demographic measure, the "pregnancy rate," which added together the abortion rate and the rate of live births. (This figure does not include an estimate for miscarriages.) Teenagers increasingly turned to newly legal abortion in order to end their pregnancies;

Table 3. Estimated pregnancy rates by age, 1976–1988.

Year	Age					
	15–19	20–24	25–29	30–34	35–39	40 and over
1976	101.4	166.1	150.7	82.3	35.3	9.9
1982	108.8	181.9	163.4	97.6	37.5	8.8
1984	106.5	178.0	159.6	100.3	40.0	8.3
1986	105.6	179.5	160.7	103.9	42.2	8.5
1988	110.8	185.3	166.7	109.7	47.2	9.6

Source: Stephanie Ventura et al., "Trends in Pregnancies and Pregnancy Rates, United States, 1980–1988," *Monthly Vital Statistics Reports, Vital Statistics of the United States* 41, no. 6, supplement (November 16, 1992): 9. Figures include an estimate for miscarriage.

thus, a soaring abortion rate led to an increase in this newly defined pregnancy rate, even in the face of a declining birthrate (see Table 2).

But higher abortion rates were common among women of every age. American women as a group turned to abortion as a way of managing unintended or unwanted pregnancies. In fact, the real "epidemic" of pregnancy, once it was measured in this new way, occurred among women just a little older: those aged twenty to twenty-four (see Table 3).

The rising rate of abortion among women of all ages concealed the fact that some additional trend was having a tremendous impact on the data. Although estimates vary, it is clear that substantially more teenage women were sexually involved in 1990 than in 1960. Depending on which estimates are used, the number of sexually active teenagers almost *doubled* during this thirty-year period, as shown in Table 4. Sexual activity also became more common among young men (Table 5).

Yet pregnancy rates did not double, which in principle they should have. All of the demographic rates considered so far are calculated on a base per thousand women, but the real proportion of those women genuinely at risk of pregnancy, abortion, and childbearing changed dramatically because increasing numbers of them were sexually involved. Since more and more women were choosing abortion and since women overall were using contraception more effectively, the increase in pregnancy rates fell far short of the expected doubling. Table 6 shows the falling pregnancy rate among sexually active teens.

Still another aspect of teenage fertility in the 1970s and 1980s was cause for worry. Increasingly, teenagers began to give birth to their babies out of wedlock: among all babies born to teen mothers, the proportion that were born out of wedlock increased steadily in the 1960s and 1970s, and these proportions were very different for white and African American teens. By 1990, 56 percent of all

Table 4. Rates of premarital sexual activity for women by exact ages fifteen, seventeen, nineteen, and twenty-one.

		Percent sexually active			
Age in 1988	Birthdate	By 15	By 17	By 19	By 21
15–17	1971–73	13.9	—	—	—
18–20	1968–70	10.0	39.5	—	—
21–23	1965–67	9.8	34.0	61.4	68.7
24–26	1962–64	8.4	30.3	57.4	72.0
27–29	1959–61	7.4	30.2	58.2	73.8
30–32	1956–58	5.6	24.3	53.3	68.1
33–35	1953–55	5.1	22.3	50.3	62.9
36–38	1950–52	3.5	18.8	38.7	56.1
39–41	1947–49	3.4	12.6	29.2	57.9
42–44	1944–46	4.0	12.6	26.2	38.0

Source: James Trussell and Barbara Vaughan, "Selected Results Concerning Sexual Behavior and Contraceptive Use from the 1988 National Survey of Family Growth and the 1988 National Survey of Adolescent Males," Princeton University, Office of Population Research Working Paper 91-12, September 1991.

Table 5. Percent of never-married metropolitan-area men who have ever had sex, 1979 and 1988.

Age	1979	1988
17.5	55.7	71.9
18.5	66.0	70.6
19.5	77.5	65.6

Source: 1979 National Survey of Young Men, and 1988 National Survey of Adolescent Males. Reported in Trussell and Vaughan, "Selected Results Concerning Sexual Behavior and Contraceptive Use," p. 15.

Table 6. Pregnancy rates for teenagers, among sexually experienced women and all women per thousand women aged fifteen to nineteen, 1972–1990.

	Pregnancy rate for teens	
Year	Sexually active women	All women
1972	254	95
1975	243	101
1980	247	111
1985	212	109
1990	207	117

Source: Alan Guttmacher Institute, *Sex and America's Teenagers,* p. 41.

Table 7. Distribution of out-of-wedlock births by age of mother, 1970–1990 (in percent).

| | Year | | | |
Age	1970	1975	1980	1990
Under 15	2	1	1	1
15–19	48	40	33	30
20–24	32	36	36	35
25–29	10	15	18	20
30–34	5	6	8	10
35 and over	3	2	3	5

Source: Monthly Vital Statistics Report, Advance Report on Final Natality Statistics, 1990, vols. 23–41.

births to white teenagers and 91 percent of all births to African American teenagers were out of wedlock.

Although most babies born to teens are born out of wedlock, most babies born out of wedlock are *not* born to teens. Having babies out of wedlock is becoming more common among women of all ages (see Table 7).

The proportion of babies born out of wedlock is somewhat misleading, because a proportion is a ratio where both the denominator and numerator can vary independently. In the case of out-of-wedlock births, the numerator is births out of wedlock, while the denominator is all births (that is, births both in and out of marriage). Thus, much of the historical increase in the *proportion* of out-of-wedlock births in recent years has had a great deal to do with declining marital fertility, not increasing nonmarital fertility, and this was particularly true of African Americans. The dramatically declining rate of African American marital fertility made the relatively stable nonmarital fertility loom as a larger and larger proportion of all African American births.

Still, rates of nonmarital fertility among teens *were* increasing. What is less commonly appreciated is that they changed by race, and not in the direction dictated by conventional wisdom. Although the rates of out-of-wedlock births among African Americans have historically been far higher than the rates among whites, in the period after 1960 whites (and especially white teenagers) began to close the gap, as shown in Table 8.

Age at first birth is increasingly mediated by class. In the baby boom years, rich and poor women had children early. In fact, women who waited until their mid-twenties were considered elderly first-time mothers. In the 1980s and 1990s, however, affluent women began postponing their first birth until later, leaving poorer women behind (see Table 9).

Table 8. Rates of out-of-wedlock births per thousand teenage women, by race of child.

Year	All races	White	Black
1970	22.4	10.9	96.9
1975	23.9	12.0	93.5
1980	27.5	15.9	90.3
1985	31.4	20.3	89.3
1990	42.5	29.5	110.1

Source: Monthly Vital Statistics Report, Advance Report on Final Natality Statistics, 1990, vol. 41, no. 9, supplement (February 25, 1993): 34–35.

Table 9. Family formation by class, as percent of all women aged fifteen to nineteen.

	Mother's education[a]		
	Less than high school	High school graduate	More than high school
Neither married nor gave birth as a teen	54	73	92
Married as a teen; did not give birth	17	16	5
Marital birth	18	7	3
Nonmarital birth	10	4	1

a. Means the education of the mother of the teenage woman, and is used as a proxy for class.
Source: Tabulations for the author by Sara McLanahan, Princeton University, using the 1988 National Survey of Family Growth.

Relatively few "babies" were having babies, as is clear from Table 10.

At the same time that poor people were staying with early motherhood, another trend began to emerge in American society: postponed motherhood, or motherhood later than the traditional pattern of having babies in the late teenage years and early twenties (see Table 11).

Taken all together, the demography of teenage pregnancy reveals how complex statistical data are, and the fact that different conclusions can be reached using the same figures.

Table 10. Births to teens, 1991, by age.

Age	Number	Percent
Under 15	12,014	2.3
Ages 15–17	188,226	35.4
Ages 18–19	331,351	62.3

Source: Advance Report on Final Natality Statistics, 1991.

Table 11. Birthrates for women over thirty, 1980–1990.

| Year | Age | | |
	30–34	35–39	Over 40
1980	61.9	19.8	3.9
1983	64.9	22.0	3.9
1985	69.1	24.0	4.0
1987	72.1	26.3	4.4
1990	80.8	31.7	5.5

Source: Monthly Vital Statistics Report, Advance Report on Final Natality Statistics, 1990, vols. 23–41.

NOTES

1. The Problem and Its Human Face

1. David and his mother are real people, but their names and personal characteristics have been changed to protect their privacy. The Eileen Sullivan Daycare Center, likewise referred to here under a pseudonym, is funded by the school district and by the state. Located in a medium-sized community in the western United States, it is a reasonably typical program designed to help teenagers with problems relating to pregnancy and parenting.

2. National Center for Health Statistics, *Advance Report of Final Natality Statistics* 43, no. 5 (1992), Supplement October 25, 1994. For more information about out-of-wedlock births in the United States and their distribution among teens and nonteens, see Appendix 1.

3. Alan Guttmacher Institute, *Sex and America's Teenagers* (New York: Alan Guttmacher Institute, 1994), p. 53. Mike Males, "School Age Pregnancy: Why Hasn't Prevention Worked?" *Journal of School Health* 63, no. 10 (1993): 429–432.

4. The notions of "race" and "ethnicity" also vary within groups, and may even vary from situation to situation within a person's lifetime. See William Peterson, "Politics and the Measurement of Ethnicity," in William Alonso and Paul Starr, eds., *The Politics of Numbers* (New York: Russell Sage, 1987), esp. p. 189. The first census of 1790 counted free white males and females, "all other free persons" (indentured servants and a few free blacks), and "slaves." From 1790 to 1840 there were no specific directives, and classification was presumably left up to the census taker. Between 1840 and 1910 there were various efforts to subdivide the category of black Americans (into mulattos, quadroons, octoroons, and so on). But until the mid-1960s, government survey and research documents typically examined only two categories of people:

whites and "nonwhites." In 1990 the U.S. Census reported a total population of approximately 250 million people, of which 85 percent were white, 12 percent black, and 3 percent "other races" (including Native Americans, Asian Americans, and Pacific Islanders). But research data on these other races are still scarce.

5. Virtually all of the statistics reported in this book have been compiled from these two sources. The National Center for Health Statistics gathered the data on "vital statistics" used for the numerator, and the Bureau of the Census collected the population data used for the denominator. Yet their systems of racial coding differ. For example, whereas the Bureau of the Census allows people to classify themselves and their children, the Center for Health Statistics defines "race" as synonymous with "national origin" and follows a complex set of rules governing the assignment of race of newborn based on race of parent. When only one parent is "white," the child is assigned the other parent's race or national origin. When neither parent is "white," the child is assigned the father's race or national origin—unless one of the parents is Hawaiian, in which case the child is "always assigned to Hawaiian." When information concerning race or national origin is lacking, the child is "allocated electronically" on the basis of previous records. But this system has changed over time: prior to 1964 all births for which race or national origin was unstated were classified as white. Births reported as white or "Hispanic" (an ethnic category) are coded as white, despite the fact that the extent to which Hispanic Americans identify themselves as white varies greatly. When it comes to marriage registration (and the Center for Health Statistics records only licenses to marry, not actual marriages), a different system is used: optional categories are listed (black, white, American Indian, etc.), and the code is often entered by a clerk. In short, the concept of race is extremely unstable and imprecise—a fact that readers should keep in mind throughout this book.

6. This "discourse," which refers to young women in trouble as ignorant but not bad, is very old. In 1910 reformer Annie Allen compared such young women to a baby who "may wreck a railroad train and not even be naughty." She emphasized that "choice—volition—must enter into a wrong deed before the doer can be called wicked. A person must intend not only his act, but the consequences of his act before he can be held accountable." She admitted frankly that "these girls are generally silly and ignorant; if they were not they would not get into trouble." But she maintained that this was the worst that could be said of them. "Very few of them are malicious or even defiant; they seldom have any desire to be mischievous or to do harm of any serious sort to any one." Annie W. Allen, "How to Save Girls Who Have Fallen," *The Survey* 24, no. 1 (1910): 692.

7. For explorations of this point, see Paula England, "The Separative Self: Androcentric Bias in Neoclassical Economics," in Marianne A. Ferber and Julie A. Nelson, eds., *Beyond Economic Man: Feminist Theory and Economics*

(Chicago: University of Chicago Press, 1993), pp. 37–53. See also Nancy Folbre, *Who Pays for the Kids? Gender and the Structure of Constraint* (London: Routledge, 1994).

8. The classic exposition of this cultural shift is Barbara Welter, "The Cult of True Womanhood, 1820–1860," *American Quarterly* 18, no. 2, part 1 (1966): 151–174. For further variations on the theme, see Ann Douglas, *The Feminization of American Culture* (New York: Knopf, 1977); and Christopher Lasch, *Haven in a Heartless World: The Family Besieged* (New York: Basic Books, 1972). In this context, the literary theorist Jane Tompkins makes a most interesting point—namely, that the vitality of the Western as a literary genre comes from the fact that it represents for the male reader a resounding rejection of the "feminized" culture of the late nineteenth century. See Jane Tompkins, *West of Everything: The Inner Life of Westerns* (New York: Oxford University Press, 1992).

9. Following Arlie Hochschild, who argues that women these days must work a "second shift" at home after a long day at work, one could argue that women are required to work a second *moral* shift as well, doing all the emotional caretaking of home, family, and society after they have expended much energy in the competitive world of the marketplace. See Arlie Hochschild with Anne Machung, *The Second Shift: Working Parents and the Revolution at Home* (New York: Viking, 1989). For a particularly insightful view of how women "care" in ways that are invisible both to themselves and others, see Marjorie Devault, *Feeding the Family: The Organization of Caring as Gendered Work* (Chicago: University of Chicago Press, 1991).

10. As we will see in Chapter 6, these are hopes—not expectations—of a better life. To put this in the starkest terms: for most teenage mothers, having a child represents very little in the way of losses and brings at least the potential that things might change for the better. Early motherhood occurs mostly among the discouraged and disadvantaged, and rarely forces a successful young woman off the path to a rewarding life.

11. A cartoon in the *New Yorker* (September 3, 1979, p. 83) highlights this contradiction. It shows an affluent executive standing next to a desk, shaking the hand of his young child. The boy says, "Forget I'm your son, Dad. Give it to me straight." Father: "You're fired. Sorry, son. We're downsizing this family and we're going to have to let you go."

12. The phrase "at the margin" comes from the mathematical notion that changes in the value of a variable within a function ($f[x]$) can make a difference. The size of the difference, however, depends on the mathematical function—if it's even possible to model something as complex as joint and contingent decisions related to engaging in sex, using contraception, and having an abortion, all in the light of welfare policies. The difficulty of modeling this relationship, and of predicting the complex way in which welfare-policy changes may affect sexual and reproductive behavior, is suggested by the fact that the real value of welfare has declined considerably since 1973. (Some analysts put

the decline, in real terms, on the order of 25 percent.) During this period the overall birthrate among teenagers did not change greatly, but the proportion of out-of-wedlock births did, and in exactly the opposite direction from what we would expect if rational economic calculations had been at play.

13. This image leaves it up to the young woman to interrupt the sexual embrace in order to "be responsible." Yet for the reasons hinted at here and examined in later chapters, young women are subject to a cultural handicap that assigns them virtually all of the responsibility for preventing pregnancy but relatively little power to do so.

14. For the argument that abortion is a highly controversial issue precisely because it encapsulates in essential form a range of cultural and social conflicts, see Kristin Luker, *Abortion and the Politics of Motherhood* (Berkeley: University of California Press, 1984).

15. Charles Murray, *Losing Ground: American Social Policy, 1950–1980* (New York: Basic Books, 1984).

16. U.S. Bureau of the Census, *General Population Characteristics, United States, 1990* (Washington, D.C.: Government Printing Office, 1992), p. 34; National Center for Health Statistics, *Advance Report of Final Natality Statistics* 43, no. 5 (1992), Supplement October 25, 1994, p. 48, Table 14, "Number, Rate, and Ratio of Births to Unmarried Women by Age and Race of Mother, United States, 1992."

17. In 1990 there were 349,970 births to women aged fifteen to nineteen (360,615 if births to those younger than fifteen are considered). Of these, 199,896 (204,053 including those under fifteen) were to whites, 139,442 (145,682) to blacks, and 10,910 to women of other races. See National Center for Health Statistics, *Advance Report of Final Natality Statistics* 41, no. 9 (1990), Supplement February 25, 1993, Table 16.

18. Charles Murray, "The Coming White Underclass," *Wall Street Journal,* October 29, 1993. It was William Julius Wilson who formulated the notion of the "declining significance of race"; see Wilson, *The Truly Disadvantaged: The Inner City, the Underclass, and Public Policy* (Chicago: University of Chicago Press, 1987).

19. Roper Poll, 1986, in *Public Opinion Online,* LEXIS, Market Library, R-Poll File, Accession no. 0126650 (eight out of ten Americans surveyed thought teen pregnancy was a major problem); Riter Research Poll for the National Association of Private Psychiatric Hospitals, 1988, in *Public Opinion Online,* LEXIS, Market Library, R-Poll File, Accession no. 0109142 (a survey of people who knew a child or teen coping with unwanted pregnancy); Harris, 1985, in *Public Opinion Online,* LEXIS, Market Library, R-Poll File, Accession no. 0071940 (84 percent of the respondents said teenage pregnancy was a serious problem); Gordon Black for *USA Today,* 1987, LEXIS, Market Library, R-Poll File, Accession no. 0183794 (72 percent of those polled said teenage pregnancy was a very important problem); Riter Poll, 1988, LEXIS,

Market Library, R-Poll File, Accession no. 0109089 (71 percent said teenage pregnancy was an extremely serious or very serious problem); Hart, 1987, LEXIS, Market Library, R-Poll File, Accession no. 0075049 (44 percent said that they would like to see a great deal more attention paid to the issue in election campaigns); Harris, 1986, LEXIS, Market Library, R-Poll File, Accession no. 0072806 (47 percent said they were very interested in the issue).

20. In 1992, among women of all races, 505,415 babies were born to women aged fifteen to nineteen; 287,866 (56.9 percent) were born to women aged eighteen to nineteen. See National Center for Health Statistics, *Advance Report of Final Natality Statistics* 43, no. 5 (1992), Supplement October 25, 1994, p. 33.

21. Prior to the baby boom years (1946–1964), the birthrate among teenagers was roughly 50–60 per thousand. At the peak of the boom, it rose to 97 per thousand. See Robert L. Heuser, *Fertility Tables for Birth Cohort by Color: United States, 1917–1973*, DHEW Publication (HRA)76–1152 (Rockville, Md.: National Center for Health Statistics, 1976); National Center for Health Statistics, *Advance Report of Final Natality Statistics* 38, no. 3 (1987), Supplement June 29, 1989, pp. 1–5.

22. Heuser, *Fertility Tables for Birth Cohort by Color: United States, 1917–1973*; National Center for Health Statistics, *Advance Report of Final Natality Statistics* 38, no. 3 (1987), Supplement June 29, 1989, pp. 1–5.

23. Larry Bumpass and James A. Sweet, "Children's Experience in Single-Parent Families: Implications of Cohabitation and Marital Transition," *Family Planning Perspectives* 21, no. 6 (November–December, 1989): 256–260.

24. U.S. Congress, House Committee on Ways and Means, "Overview of Entitlement Programs, 1994" (Green Book), 103rd Congress, 2nd sess., July 15, 1994, p. 325.

25. U.K. Office of Population Censuses and Surveys, *Birth Statistics: Review of the Registrar General on Births and Patterns of Family Building in England and Wales, 1992* (London: HMSO, 1994), p. 49, Table 9.6, "Live Births: Country of Birth of Mother, Occurrence Inside/Outside Marriages and Previous Liveborn Children, 1982–1992."

26. United Nations Department of International Economic and Social Affairs, "Adolescent Reproductive Behavior: Evidence from Developed Countries," *Population Studies* 1, no. 109 (1988).

27. Ibid., p. 23; Elise F. Jones, Jacqueline Forrest, Noreen Goldman, Stanley Henshaw, Richard Lincoln, Jeannie Rosoff, Charles F. Westoff, and Deirdre Wulf, *Teenage Pregnancy in Industrialized Countries* (New Haven: Yale University Press, 1986).

28. *Ordway v. Hargraves,* 323 F. Supp. 1155 (1971). Title IX of the Educational Amendments of 1972 also outlawed such policies. That teenagers who get pregnant and have babies are already different will be discussed at length in Chapter 5.

29. Here and throughout this book, the word "sex" means heterosexual sex, since

same-sex sexuality is not implied in pregnancies and births among teenagers. But the fact that homosexuality is gaining public acceptance and visibility is closely related to the transformations examined in the pages that follow.

2. Bastardy, Fitness, and the Invention of Adolescence

1. David Flaherty, "Law and the Enforcement of Morals in Early America," *Perspectives in American History* 5 (1971): 225–226.
2. See National Center for Health Statistics, *Advance Report of Final Natality Statistics* 38, no. 3 (1987), Supplement June 29, 1989; and 43, no. 5 (1992), Supplement October 25, 1994.
3. For an overview, see John D'Emilio and Estelle Freedman, *Intimate Matters: A History of Sexuality in America* (New York: Harper and Row, 1988), pp. 22–34; John Demos, *A Little Commonwealth: Family Life in Plymouth Colony* (London: Oxford University Press, 1970), pp. 152–153.
4. The financial burden that an unmarried mother and child presented to poor villages loomed so large in community thinking that the English would sometimes drive a pregnant woman in the throes of labor from town to town, on the grounds that the town in which she eventually gave birth would be the one financially responsible for her and her newborn child. See G. R. Quaife, *Wanton Wenches and Wayward Wives: Peasants and Illicit Sex in Early Seventeenth Century England* (New Brunswick, N.J.: Rutgers University Press, 1979), p. 102. For a discussion of similar cases in the U.S., where towns would "warn off" pregnant women, see Arthur Calhoun, *A Social History of the American Family*, vol. 1 (New York: Barnes and Noble, 1960), p. 139.
5. D'Emilio and Freedman, *Intimate Matters*, pp. 27–32.
6. Daniel Scott Smith, "The Long Cycle in American Illegitimacy and Prenuptial Pregnancy," in Peter Laslett et al., eds., *Bastardy and Its Comparative History: Studies in the History of Illegitimacy and Marital Nonconformism in Britain, France, Germany, Sweden, North America, Jamaica, and Japan* (Cambridge, Mass.: Harvard University Press, 1980), pp. 362–378.
7. John Demos, *Little Commonwealth*, p. 159. See also Lorena S. Walsh, "'Till Death Do Us Part': Marriage and Family in Seventeenth-Century Maryland," in Thad W. Tate and David L. Ammerman, eds., *The Chesapeake in the Seventeenth Century* (Chapel Hill: University of North Carolina Press, 1979), pp. 126–152; D'Emilio and Freedman, *Intimate Matters*, p. 10; Daniel Scott Smith, "The Long Cycle in American Illegitimacy," p. 370; Daniel Scott Smith and Michael S. Hindus, "Premarital Pregnancy in America, 1640–1971: An Overview and an Interpretation," *Journal of Interdisciplinary History* 5 (1975): 537–570; Robert V. Wells, "Illegitimacy and Bridal Pregnancy," in Laslett et al., eds., *Bastardy and Its Comparative History*, pp. 355–356; David Flaherty, "Law and the Enforcement of Morals"; Laurel Thatcher Ulrich, *Good Wives: Image and Reality in the Lives of Women in Northern New England, 1650–1750* (New York: Knopf, 1982), p. 31. Puritan communities

distinguished three categories of people: the married, the unmarried, and the betrothed. (Betrothed people were those who had publicly announced their intention to marry.) Puritan punishments distinguished between fornication among the unmarried and fornication among the betrothed; the fine for an early baby conceived by a betrothed couple was only a quarter of the fine imposed on the unmarried.

8. Flaherty, "Law and the Enforcement of Morals," p. 231. See also Demos, *Little Commonwealth*, p. 152.

9. R. V. Wells, "Illegitimacy and Bridal Pregnancy," p. 354.

10. Michael Grossberg, *Governing the Hearth: Law and Family in Nineteenth Century America* (Chapel Hill: University of North Carolina Press, 1985), pp. 211–217; Demos, *Little Commonwealth*, pp. 140–141.

11. Arthur C. Calhoun, *A Social History of the American Family*, vol. 1, p. 314.

12. Robert V. Wells, "Illegitimacy and Bridal Pregnancy," p. 358; see also Grossberg, *Governing the Hearth*, pp. 127–132.

13. Robert V. Wells, *Revolutions in Americans' Lives: A Demographic Perspective on the History of Americans, Their Families, and Their Society* (Westport, Conn.: Greenwood Press, 1982), p. 59.

14. Michael Grossberg, *Governing the Hearth*, p. 203.

15. Barbara Hobson, *Uneasy Virtue: The Politics of Prostitution and the American Reform Tradition* (New York: Basic Books, 1987), p. 31. R. V. Wells, "Illegitimacy and Bridal Pregnancy," p. 356; William Nelson, "Emerging Notions of Modern Criminal Law in the Revolutionary Era: An Historical Perspective," *N.Y.U. Law Review* 42 (1967): 455–457. By 1817 the Connecticut Supreme Court could declare, in a case concerning bastardy, that the "sin" of fornication was no longer of public concern. It noted that there was "no public wrong . . . to be redressed; no offender punished; but a sum of money for the infant's maintenance is all which the statute contemplates." *Hinman v. Taylor,* 2 Conn. 357, 362 (1817).

16. On the fact that illegitimacy may have been declining, see Smith, "Long Cycle," p. 363.

17. For a historical view with particular emphasis on Catholic canon law, see Jack Goody, *The Development of Family and Marriage in Europe* (New York: Cambridge University Press, 1983).

18. Grossberg, *Governing the Hearth*, pp. 69–71. Americans believed that Britons' concern with "legitimate" marriages, and hence their greater willingness to create "illegitimate" children, was an aristocratic pretension having more to do with the need to protect inheritances than with the need to protect children.

19. Ibid., pp. 202–207. On the very important role of courts in creating American social policy in the nineteenth century, see Steven Skowronek, *Building the New American State: The Expansion of National Administrative Capacities, 1877–1920* (New York: Cambridge University Press, 1982).

20. This intersection of gender, class, and racial ideology, which led to the rise

of movements devoted to the welfare of children and women, is a rich field of feminist inquiry. See, for example, Barbara Epstein, *The Politics of Domesticity* (Middletown: Wesleyan University Press, 1981); Ruth Bordin, *Women and Temperance: The Quest for Power and Liberty, 1873–1900* (Philadelphia: Temple University Press, 1981); Mary Ryan, *Cradle of the Middle Class: The Family in Oneida County, New York, 1790–1865* (New York: Cambridge University Press, 1981); Ruth Rosen, *The Lost Sisterhood: Prostitution in America, 1900–1918* (Baltimore: Johns Hopkins University Press, 1982); Estelle B. Freedman, *Their Sisters' Keepers: Women's Prison Reform in America, 1830–1930* (Ann Arbor: University of Michigan Press, 1981); Nancy A. Hewitt, *Women's Activism and Social Change* (Ithaca: Cornell University Press, 1984); Regina Kunzel, *Fallen Women, Problem Girls: Unmarried Mothers and the Professionalization of Social Work, 1890–1945* (New Haven: Yale University Press, 1993); Joanne J. Meyerowitz, *Women Adrift: Independent Wage Earners in Chicago, 1880–1930* (Chicago: University of Chicago Press, 1988); Constance Nathanson, *Dangerous Passage: The Social Control of Women's Sexuality in Adolescence* (Philadelphia: Temple University Press, 1991).

21. Otto Wilson, *Fifty Years' Work with Girls, 1883–1933: A Story of the Florence Crittenton Homes* (Alexandria, Va.: National Florence Crittenton Mission, 1933), pp. 1–16. For the transformation of these homes, see Kunzel, *Fallen Women, Problem Girls*, pp. 14–17. Kunzel argues that unwed mothers had much more going for them as promising targets of reform than did the larger pool of "fallen women" more generally: they needed a place to stay out of the public eye, had few other options, tended to be more compliant, and, it was hoped, would be more receptive to the desired moral uplift.

22. Kunzel, *Fallen Women*, pp. 14–19; Wilson, *Fifty Years' Work with Girls,* p. 48; Linda Gordon, "Black and White Visions of Welfare: Women's Welfare Activism, 1890–1945," *Journal of American History* 78 (1991): 559–590; W. E. B. DuBois, ed., *Efforts for Social Betterment*, pp. 102–103, cited in Kunzel, *Fallen Women, Problem Girls,* p. 13.

23. Joan Brumberg, "'Ruined' Girls: Changing Community Responses to Illegitimacy in Upstate New York, 1890–1920," *Journal of Social History* 18 (1984): 247–272.

24. Grossberg, *Governing the Hearth*, p. 231.

25. Wilson, *Fifty Years' Work with Girls,* p. 15.

26. *Piccinim et al. v. Connecticut Light and Power Company,* 106 Atlantic 330.

27. U.S. Children's Bureau, *Illegitimacy as a Child Welfare Problem,* Bureau Publications no. 66 (Washington, D.C.: Government Printing Office, 1920), p. 35. The Children's Bureau initiated "maternalist" policies in the United States. For overviews of the rich vein of feminist scholarship in this area, see Linda Gordon, ed., "The New Feminist Scholarship on the Welfare State," in *Women, the State, and Welfare* (Madison, Wis.: University of Wisconsin Press, 1990), pp. 9–35; Theda Skocpol, *Protecting Soldiers and Mothers: The Po-*

litical Origins of Social Policy in the United States (Cambridge, Mass.: Harvard University Press, 1993), pp. 480–524; and Robyn Muncy, *Creating a Female Dominion in American Reform, 1890–1935* (New York: Oxford University Press, 1991).

28. Emma Lundberg, "The Child Mother as a Delinquency Problem," *Proceedings of the National Conference of Social Work* (1926): 10.

29. For an overview of the professionalization of social problems, see Thomas L. Haskell, *The Emergence of Professional Social Science: The American Social Science Association and the Nineteenth-Century Crisis of Authority* (Urbana: University of Illinois Press, 1977); and Mary O. Furner, *Advocacy and Objectivity: A Crisis in the Professionalization of American Social Science, 1865–1905* (Lexington, Ky.: University Press of Kentucky, 1975). For a discussion of this topic that stresses the issue of gender, see Barbara Melosh, *"The Physician's Hand": Work, Culture and Conflict in American Nursing* (Philadelphia: Temple University Press, 1982). For the specific argument with respect to unwed mothers, see Kunzel, *Fallen Women*.

30. W. I. Thomas, *The Unadjusted Girl, with Cases and Standpoint for Behavior Analysis* (Boston: Little, Brown, 1923).

31. Sara B. Edlin, *The Unmarried Mother in Our Society: A Frank and Constructive Approach to an Age-Old Problem* (New York: Farrar, Straus and Young, 1954), p. 12. This change in viewpoint, which is the main focus of Regina Kunzel's book, is all the more remarkable in that Sara Edlin was a committed socialist.

32. Leontine Young, *Out of Wedlock: A Study of the Problems of the Unmarried Mother and Her Child* (New York: McGraw Hill, 1954), p. 8.

33. Constance Nathanson, in contrast to Brumberg, argues that adoption was not seen as the appropriate remedy until the 1930s. Earlier, she argues, ideologies of "redemptive motherhood" prescribed that children be kept with their (unwed) mothers, so that the experience would help the women overcome the sin of sexual promiscuity. See Nathanson, *Dangerous Passage*. Kunzel, in *Fallen Women*, supports this view. Certainly, early advocates of the Children's Bureau fought for state laws forbidding the separation of mother and child, and in some cases worked for laws that mandated breast feeding for a specified period of time.

34. G. Stanley Hall, *Adolescence: Its Psychology and Its Relation to Physiology, Anthropology, Sociology, Sex, Crime, Religion and Education* (New York: Appleton, 1904).

35. Lawrence Cremin, *American Education: The National Experience, 1783–1876* (New York: Harper and Row, 1980), pp. 178–179. Starting in the 1830s, the "common school" provided free, basic education to children. The term comes from Horace Mann, who used it to signal the notion that children of all backgrounds would have an education in common. See Lawrence Cremin, *The American Common School: An Historic Conception* (New York: Teacher's College, Columbia University, 1951).

36. Howard P. Chudacoff, *How Old Are You? Age Consciousness in American Culture* (Princeton: Princeton University Press, 1989), p. 22.

37. Demos, *Little Commonwealth*, p. 148.

38. Chudacoff, *How Old Are You?* p. 9. Likewise, Joseph Kett notes that "in pre-industrial America the language of age had a nebulous quality"; see Kett, *Rites of Passage: Adolescence in America, 1790 to the Present* (New York: Basic Books, 1977), p. 11.

39. Kett, *Rites of Passage*, p. 90.

40. Grossberg, *Governing the Hearth*, p. 105.

41. Ibid., pp. 106–107.

42. The classic work is David J. Pivar, *Purity Crusade: Sexual Morality and Social Control, 1868–1900* (Westport, Conn.: Greenwood Press, 1973); see esp. pp. 104–105.

43. Pivar, *Purity Crusade*, pp. 139–146; Bordin, *Women and Temperance*, pp. 110–111; Epstein, *Politics of Domesticity*.

44. Benjamin deCosta, "Age of Consent Laws, 1886," *The Philanthropist* (February 1886).

45. Pivar, *Purity Crusade*, pp. 140–141.

46. Annual Minutes of the WCTU, 21st meeting, 1894, p. 85; See also Pivar, *Purity Crusade*, pp. 143–145; Epstein, *Politics of Domesticity*, p. 125. Bordin notes that in 1886 the age of consent was ten in twenty states, and as low as seven in one state. Bordin, *Women and Temperance*, p. 110.

47. See, for example, Sydney A. Halpern, *American Pediatrics: The Social Dynamics of Professionalism, 1880–1980* (Berkeley: University of California Press, 1988); and Patricia J. Campbell, *Sex Education Books for Young Adults, 1892–1979* (New York: R. R. Bowker, 1979). For another view, as well as an account of the creation of the Society for the Prevention of Cruelty to Children, see Thomas E. Cone, *History of American Pediatrics* (Boston: Little, Brown, 1979), p. 100.

48. Hall, *Adolescence*, p. 135. For the classic history, see Kett, *Rites of Passage*, esp. pp. 215–244; and John Demos and Virginia Demos, "Adolescence in Historical Perspective," *Journal of Marriage and the Family* 31 (1969): 632–638.

49. Grossberg, *Governing the Hearth*, p. 142.

50. Stephen Schlossman, *Love and the American Delinquent* (Chicago: University of Chicago Press, 1977); Anthony M. Platt, *The Child Savers: The Invention of Delinquency* (Chicago: University of Chicago Press, 1969).

51. Steven Schlossman and Stephanie Wallach, "The Crime of Precocious Sexuality: Female Juvenile Delinquency in the Progressive Era," *Harvard Educational Review* 48 (1978): 70.

52. Meta Chesney-Lind calls this the "sexualization of female deviance." Chesney-Lind found that, by the 1960s, three-quarters of all arrested girls within the juvenile justice system were being charged, directly or indirectly, with sexual offenses. This surprising fact—that girls were usually punished more

harshly than boys in earlier historical periods—is noted in Schlossman and Wallach, "Crime of Precocious Sexuality"; and in Mary Ellen Odem, "Delinquent Daughters: The Sexual Regulation of Female Minors in the United States, 1880–1920" (Diss., University of California, Berkeley, 1989). Meta Chesney-Lind, "Guilty by Reason of Sex: Young Women and the Juvenile Justice System," in Barbara Raffel Price and Natalie Sokoloff, eds., *The Criminal Justice System and Women* (New York: Clark Boardman, 1982). She argues that during the Progressive Era the sexuality of adolescent girls came to be viewed as deviant. As reformer Annie Allen put it, "What society has most to dread and reprobate in a boy is crime; what it has to dread in a girl is sexual irregularity." Annie W. Allen, "How to Save Girls Who Have Fallen," *The Survey* 24, no. 1 (1910): 691.

53. Demos, *Little Commonwealth*, p. 155.

54. Brigham, *The Compact with the Charter and Laws of the Colony of New Plymouth*, cited in Demos, *Little Commonwealth*, p. 154.

55. Grossberg, *Governing the Hearth*, p. 114.

56. Bernard Farber, *Kinship and Class: A Midwestern Study* (New York: Basic Books, 1971), pp. 39–66; Grossberg, *Governing the Hearth*, pp. 110–113.

57. Grossberg, *Governing the Hearth*, pp. 136–139. For his statement that racism runs like a "fault line" through American family jurisprudence, see p. 126.

58. Stanton is cited in William Leach, *True Love and Perfect Union: The Feminist Reform of Sex and Society* (New York: Basic Books, 1980), pp. 31–32.

59. See Linda Gordon, "Why Nineteenth Century Feminists Did Not Support 'Birth Control' and Twentieth Century Feminists Do: Feminism, Reproduction, and the Family," in Barrie Thorne and Marilyn Yalom, eds., *Rethinking the Family: Some Feminist Questions* (Boston: Northeastern University Press, 1992), pp. 40–53.

60. Charles E. Rosenberg, "The Therapeutic Revolution: Medicine, Meaning and Change in Nineteenth-Century America," *Perspectives in Biology and Medicine* 20 (1977): 485–506. On voluntary motherhood, see Linda Gordon, "Why Nineteenth Century Feminists Did Not Support 'Birth Control.'"

61. John N. Hurty, "The Sterilization of Criminals and Defectives," *Social Diseases* 3 (1912): 4.

62. Rudolf J. Vecoli, "Sterilization: A Progressive Measure," *Wisconsin Magazine of History* 43 (1960): 190–202; J. H. Landman, "Appendix A: A Chronologic Presentation of the Various Sexual Sterilization Statutes in the U.S.," in Landman, *Human Sterilization: The History of the Sexual Sterilization Movement* (New York: Macmillan, 1932), pp. 291–293.

63. Harry C. Sharpe, "Vasectomy as a Means of Preventing Procreation in Defectives," *Journal of the American Medical Association* 53 (1909): 1897.

64. Landman, *Human Sterilization*, pp. 112–121.

65. *Buck v. Bell*, 274 US 200, 207 (1927).

66. Landman, *Human Sterilization*, p. 84 and Appendix A.

67. Stephen Jay Gould, "Carrie Buck's Daughter," *Natural History* 7 (1984):

14–18. The decision about Vivien, Carrie's daughter, was made when the child was only a few months old, and was based on a very superficial observation by a social worker who thought she seemed less advanced than the child of a friend. In fact, Vivien Buck, who died at the age of eight, was performing normally in school at the time of her death. Carrie Buck continued to do crossword puzzles until her death. For the data on the role of "sexual license" as grounds for sterilization, see Daniel Kevles, *In The Name of Eugenics: Genetics and the Uses of Human Heredity* (New York: Basic Books, 1981), p. 108.

68. Landman, *Human Sterilization,* p. 289. Vecoli, "Sterilization: A Progressive Measure"; Kevles, *In The Name of Eugenics.*

69. Thomas B. Littlewood, *The Politics of Population Control* (Notre Dame, Ind.: University of Notre Dame Press, 1977), pp. 107–112. *Relf v. Weinberger,* 372 F. Supp. 1196 (D.D.C. 1974).

70. Paul Popenoe, "Some Eugenic Aspects of Illegitimacy," *Journal of Social Hygiene* 9 (1923): 517. Popenoe was also a staunch advocate of eugenic sterilization. By his estimate, approximately ten million "socially inadequate" Americans were in need of sterilization. See Popenoe, "Number of Persons Needing Sterilization," *Journal of Heredity* 19 (1928): 405–410. Landman describes Popenoe's work with the Human Betterment Foundation of Pasadena, and credits him for the fact that by the early 1930s well over half of the nation's documented eugenic sterilizations had been performed in California. Landman, *Human Sterilization,* p. 57.

71. D'Emilio and Freedman note that this was true for a wide range of sexual transgressions in colonial America. With respect to out-of-wedlock pregnancy, they note cases in which men convicted of fornication became town constables, town clerks, selectmen, and even representatives to the General Court, and in which women were permitted to marry and to join the church. In all cases, however, this was contingent upon public confession and repentance. *Intimate Matters,* p. 23.

72. For a more general discussion of this transformation in the view of human behavior, see David Garland, *Punishment and Welfare: A History of Penal Strategies* (Brookfield, Vt.: Gower, 1985).

73. For the view that teenage mothers are victims, see Mike Males, "In Defense of Teenaged Mothers," *Progressive* 58, no. 8 (August 1994): 23, which notes, "Many teen mothers are victimized by adults."

74. This point is covered at some length in Chapter 5, but an early awareness of the role of poverty, rather than youth, in the medical problems associated with early childbearing can be found in Jane Menken, "Teenage Childbearing: Its Medical Aspects and Implications for the United States Population," in *Demographic and Social Aspects of Population Growth,* ed. Westoff and Parke (Washington, D.C., 1972). For a more recent review, see Carolyn Makinson, "The Health Consequences of Teenage Fertility," *Family Planning Perspectives* 17, no. 3 (May–June 1985); and U.S. Congress, Office of Technology

Assessment, *Adolescent Health, Vol. II: Background and the Effectiveness of Certain Selected Prevention and Treatment Programs* (Washington, D.C., 1991), pp. 334–340. For an update on the most recent material, see Christine Bachrach and Karen Carver, "Outcomes of Early Childbearing: An Appraisal of Recent Evidence—NICHD," Center for Population Research, 1992 (mimeo).

75. Irwin Garfinkel and Sara McLanahan, *Single Mothers and Their Children: A New American Dilemma* (Washington, D.C.: Urban Institute Press, 1986). For more detailed data by race, see Larry Bumpass and R. Kelly Raley, "Redefining Single-Parent Families: Cohabitation and Changing Family Reality," *Demography* 32 (1995): 97–109.

76. Since early and out-of-wedlock childbearing has been so insistently linked to poverty, it probably bears repeating here that out-of-wedlock childbearing is more common among people who were poor long before they became pregnant.

77. Sara McLanahan and Gary Sandefur, *Growing Up with a Single Parent: What Hurts, What Helps* (Cambridge, Mass.: Harvard University Press, 1994).

3. Poverty, Fertility, and the State

1. Rev. S. W. Dike, *Perils to the Family: An Address Delivered before the Evangelical Alliance Conference at Washington, D.C., Dec. 8, 1887* (New York: Evangelical Alliance for the United States, 1888).

2. *Annual Reports of the President and Treasurer of Harvard College, 1901–1902,* cited in David M. Kennedy, *Birth Control in America: The Career of Margaret Sanger* (New Haven: Yale University Press, 1970), p. 44; Lydia Commander, *The American Idea* (New York: Barnes, 1907), p. 198; U.S. Immigration Commission, *Report,* 61st Congress, 2nd sess., 1911, pp. 749–753. The hearings noted that immigrant families became smaller in later generations; birthrates among second-generation immigrants approached those of the native-born. Theodore Roosevelt, *The Foes of Our Own Household* (New York: George H. Doran, 1917), p. 257; Alfred Henry Louis, ed., *A Compilation of the Messages and Speeches of Theodore Roosevelt* (Washington, D.C.: Bureau of National Literature and Art, 1906), p. 548.

3. Kristin Luker, "Abortion in the Nineteenth Century: A Domestic Technology," in J. Zimmerman, ed., *The Technological Woman* (New York: Praeger, 1983).

4. Linda Gordon, perhaps the preeminent historian of birth control in America, has pointed out that worries over race suicide were only one part of an "organic worldview" that linked together the sinfulness of contraception, the need for a growing population, race suicide, and the rebellion of women against their "natural" role. See Linda Gordon, *Woman's Body, Woman's Right: Birth Control in America* (New York: Penguin, 1990), pp. 136–158, esp. p. 137. In this early round of discussion, Gordon notes (p. 154), "race"

meant both the human race and the white race, despite the unacknowledged fact that black birthrates were also dropping.

5. Until surprisingly recently, the postal system was the only way that information and products could circulate, outside of small, local exchanges among people who knew one another. Once contraceptive supplies and information had been banned from the mail, individuals, their physicians, and their pharmacists were unable to buy supplies or learn about ways of preventing parenthood. At least in theory, periodicals—ranging from popular magazines to medical journals—couldn't even carry articles about contraception or abortion, since all printed matter went through the mail. The Comstock Law, 17 Stat. 599 (1873), was particularly effective because it targeted the mail—one of the few genuinely federal (that is, national) parts of the government; in so doing, it made the circulation of contraceptive supplies and information a federal offense. Hugh Heclo has pointed out that until the early years of the twentieth century, the only significant interaction between Americans and the state occurred when they mailed a letter or called a policeman; see Heclo, *Modern Social Politics in Britain and Sweden: From Relief to Income Maintenance* (New Haven: Yale University Press, 1974), p. 1. Stephen Skowronek notes that land offices and customs houses, too, were the sites of such interaction: see Skowronek, *Building a New American State: The Expansion of National Administrative Capacities, 1877–1920* (Cambridge: Cambridge University Press, 1982). Twenty-two states added force to the federal statute by passing "little Comstock laws," which typically made the sale, distribution, and in one case the use of contraception illegal. Furthermore, because the Comstock laws defined texts concerning contraception and abortion as "obscene," all but two of the states that lacked little Comstock laws could prosecute the authors and disseminators of such texts under existing obscenity laws. Abraham Stone and Harriet F. Pilpel, "The Social and Legal Status of Contraception," *North Carolina Law Review* 22 (1944): 212–225; Kennedy, *Birth Control in America*, p. 218; C. Thomas Dienes, *Law, Politics and Birth Control* (Urbana, Ill.: University of Illinois Press, 1972), p. 43. Physicians later won special exemptions from these laws.

6. Hugh Hodge, *Foeticide, or Criminal Abortion: A Lecture Introductory to the Course on Obstetrics and the Diseases of Women and Children* (Philadelphia: Lindsay and Blakiston, 1869), pp. 32–33.

7. Andrew Nebinger, *Criminal Abortion: Its Extent and Prevention* (Philadelphia: Collins, 1870), pp. 15–16.

8. For an overview, see James C. Mohr, *Abortion in America: The Origins and Evolution of National Policy, 1800–1900* (New York: Oxford University Press, 1978), pp. 74–82; Gordon, *Woman's Body*, pp. 51–60; Kristin Luker, *Abortion and the Politics of Motherhood* (Berkeley: University of California Press, 1984), p. 19. Abortions in nineteenth-century America were available from private clinics, and it was possible to buy over-the-counter patent medicines that promised to bring on menstruation in cases where it had been "delayed."

For those too timid or too embarrassed to seek help from their local pharmacist, advertisements for such abortifacients were common in newspapers, even in those as august as the *New York Times*. Family-oriented and church-sponsored newspapers carried such advertisements as well. See Mohr, *Abortion in America,* pp. 47–65.

9. Ansley J. Coale and Melvin Zelnik, *New Estimates of Fertility and Population in the United States* (Princeton: Princeton University Press, 1963), p. 36; Colin Forster and G. S. L. Tucker, *Economic Opportunity and White American Fertility Ratios, 1800–1860* (New Haven: Yale University Press, 1972); Yasukichi Yasuba, *Birth Rates of the White Population in the United States, 1800–1860: An Economic Study* (Baltimore: Johns Hopkins Press, 1962). Data on the African American population are much harder to come by, but available evidence shows roughly similar trends. See Reynolds Farley, *Growth of the Black Population* (Chicago: Markham, 1970).

10. *Bours v. United States,* 229 F. 960 (7th Cir. 1915). Physicians had remarkably broad latitude in their ability to perform abortions. See Luker, *Abortion and the Politics of Motherhood,* pp. 45–54.

11. Gordon, *Woman's Body,* p. 258; Kennedy, *Birth Control,* pp. 83–88. Interestingly, the original version of the Comstock Law had included a doctor's exemption; it was dropped in the final reading, and no one seems to know why. See Stone and Pilpel, "Social and Legal Status," p. 219.

12. *People v. Sanger,* 222 N.Y. 192, 118 N.E. 637 (1918).

13. *Youngs Rubber Corporation v. C. I. Lee & Co., Inc.,* 45 F. 2d 103 (2d Cir. 1930). The court held that the producers of Trojans, a leading brand of condoms, could sue a competitor for using its trademark, despite the anticipated defense that since both parties were engaged in illegal activity under the Comstock Law, no such protection existed.

14. *United States v. One Package,* 86 F. 2d 737, 739 (2d Cir. 1936).

15. David Kennedy notes that in principle the Second Circuit's opinion held only for that circuit; as a practical matter, however, *Youngs Rubber* and *One Package* (along with a similar case known as *Davis et al. v. United States,* 62 F. 2d 473, 6th Cir., 1933) in effect created a therapeutic exemption at the federal level. See Kennedy, *Birth Control,* pp. 245–257. At the state level, both Massachusetts and Connecticut disagreed. In *Commonwealth v. Allison,* 227 Mass. 57, 116 N.E. 265, 266 (1917), the Massachusetts Supreme Court ruled that the anticontraceptive law was a reasonable exercise of the state's police powers and that even scientific treatises on contraception were obscene. In 1940, however, in a case concerning condoms, it required the prosecution to prove that the condoms in question were intended to be used for contraception rather than the prevention of disease. (See Stone and Pilpel, "Social and Legal Status," p. 223.) Connecticut, in contrast, steadfastly refused to amend its little Comstock law, which was unique in that it forbade the use of contraception. And the Connecticut Supreme Court consistently declined to grant any therapeutic exemption within the law, counseling abstinence instead.

See Mary L. Dudziak, "Just Say No: Birth Control in the Connecticut Supreme Court before *Griswold v. Connecticut*," *Iowa Law Review* 73 (1990): 915–939; and, for the definitive account, David Garrow, *Liberty and Sexuality: The Right to Privacy and the Making of "Roe v. Wade"* (New York: Macmillan, 1994), pp. 1–269.

16. Ellen Chesler, *Woman of Valor: Margaret Sanger and the Birth Control Movement in America* (New York: Doubleday, 1992), p. 231; Lawrence Lader, *The Margaret Sanger Story and the Fight for Birth Control* (Garden City, N.Y.: Doubleday, 1955), p. 219.

17. The reasoning of the Connecticut courts was that if the state wanted a medical exemption for contraception, the legislature should pass one; such proposals were routinely debated (and defeated) in every legislative session until the *Griswold* decision. Garrow, *Liberty and Sexuality,* pp. 94–159. Birth control reformers were stymied in their attempts to get federal courts to bring Connecticut and Massachusetts into line with *Youngs Rubber* and *One Package,* since the U.S. Supreme Court routinely concluded that the Connecticut cases did not pose federal questions. There was a particularly vexing obstacle in Connecticut: in order to have standing to challenge the state's little Comstock Law, a physician would have to commit a felony and be tried and convicted—but no doctor was willing to do this. Thus, it was difficult to claim a harm sufficient to persuade the U.S. Supreme Court that there was a case to be adjudicated. Garrow, *Liberty and Sexuality,* pp. 131–195. Mrs. Sanger was never successful in her attempts to pass federal legislation granting formal permission to physicians to prescribe birth control. See Kennedy, *Birth Control in America,* pp. 172–217; Gordon, *Woman's Body,* pp. 264–266; Chesler, *Woman of Valor,* pp. 269–286.

18. James Reed, *The Birth Control Movement and American Society: From Private Vice to Public Virtue* (Princeton: Princeton University Press, 1978), pp. 106–107; Gordon, *Woman's Body;* Chesler, *Woman of Valor,* pp. 230–231. On the ways in which women's social class related to their use of birth control, see Marie Kopp, *Birth Control in Practice* (New York: Robert McBride, 1933); Raymond Pearl, "The Differential Birth Rate," *Birth Control Review* 9 (1925): 278–300.

19. For an overview of this literature, see Luker, *Abortion and the Politics of Motherhood,* pp. 260–262, App. 2.

20. Edwin M. Gold et al., "Therapeutic Abortion in New York City: A Twenty Year Review," *American Journal of Public Health* 55 (1965): 964–972.

21. Stone and Pilpel, "Social and Legal Status," p. 216. On the enthusiasm for providing birth control to poor blacks, see Kennedy, *Birth Control in America,* p. 259. The provision of birth control in the South drew on the philanthropic work of Dr. Clarence Gamble. See Reed, *The Birth Control Movement,* pp. 225–277. On the racial debate within Margaret Sanger's organization, see Carole McCann, *Birth Control Politics in the United States, 1916–1945* (Ithaca: Cornell University Press, 1994), pp. 135–173.

22. On the higher fertility rates of those on relief, see Kennedy, *Birth Control in America*, p. 258. On the role of the Federal Emergency Relief Administration (FERA), see ibid., p. 258. On the Farm Security Administration, see Reed, *The Birth Control Movement*, p. 266. According to Gordon, no FERA administrator would admit for the record that birth control information was being provided *(Woman's Body*, p. 315). Reformers continually decried the fact that birth control was available to the rich but not the poor, but these protests were ignored. See, for example, records of the 1934 hearings on a bill to amend the Comstock Law—a bill warning of the dangers of limiting birth control to the upper classes, especially in view of the high cost of relief (Kennedy, *Birth Control in America*, p. 239); and Jonathan Daniels, "Birth Control and Democracy," *The Nation*, November 1, 1941, p. 429.

23. Reed, *The Birth Control Movement*, pp. 266–268. Today HEW is known as the Department of Health and Human Services, or DHHS.

24. Ibid., p. 377. Gruening later became a liberal senator from Alaska and is known, among other things, for his negative vote on the Gulf of Tonkin resolution.

25. Planned Parenthood, "Anatomy of a Victory" (New York, 1959, mimeo); James Finn, "Controversy in New York," *Commonweal*, Sept. 12, 1958, p. 583.

26. For the Chicago case, see Thomas Littlewood, *The Politics of Population Control* (Notre Dame: Notre Dame University Press, 1977), pp. 25–43. For the Pennsylvania case, see Dienes, *Law, Politics and Birth Control*, pp. 277–281.

27. For an overview, see Josh Gamson, "Rubber Wars: Struggles over the Condom in the United States," *Journal of the History of Sexuality* 1 (1990): 262–282; and Rebecca Cook, "State Laws Regulating Condoms," in Myron Redford et al., *The Condom: Increasing Utilization in the United States* (San Francisco: San Francisco Press, 1974), pp. 59–70.

28. See Dudziak, "Just Say No," pp. 927–931; Dienes, *Law, Politics and Birth Control*, pp. 116–147.

29. The Pill had a paradoxical impact on abortion: as people start to take very high levels of control for granted, they become less tolerant of "mistakes." See Luker, *Abortion and the Politics of Motherhood*, p. 112.

30. The IUD, introduced later, likewise reduced the risk of pregnancy to a very low level. U.S. Bureau of the Census, "Table 32: Fertility Indicators, 1970," *Current Population Reports*, Series P-23, no. 36, p. 53.

31. For an overview of this great migration, see Carole Marks, *Farewell—We're Good and Gone* (Bloomington: Indiana University Press, 1989). For a powerfully written (but analytically flawed) account, see Nicholas Lemann, *The Promised Land: The Great Black Migration and How It Changed America* (New York: Knopf, 1991). Lemann argues that some of the patterns examined here (particularly the tendency among African Americans to bear children out of wedlock) have their origins in "sharecropper culture." For a more analytic

account of the way in which public policies have influenced poverty and birth patterns among African Americans, see Gary Orfield, "Race and the Liberal Agenda: The Loss of the Integrationist Dream, 1965–1975," in Margaret Weir, Ann Shola Orloff, and Theda Skocpol, eds., *The Politics of Social Policy in the United States* (Princeton: Princeton University Press), 1988, pp. 313–355.

32. For a historiographic overview, see Linda Gordon, "The New Feminist Scholarship on the Welfare State," in Linda Gordon, ed., *Women, Welfare and the State* (Madison: University of Wisconsin Press, 1990), esp. pp. 9–35; and Theda Skocpol, *Protecting Soldiers and Mothers: The Political Origins of Social Policy in the United States* (Cambridge, Mass.: Harvard University Press, 1993). The account presented here draws very heavily on the work of Jill Quadagno, *The Transformation of Old Age Security: Class and Politics in the American Welfare State* (Chicago: University of Chicago Press, 1988). For an elegant summary of her position with respect to the New Deal, see Jill Quadagno, *The Color of Welfare: How Racism Undermined the War on Poverty* (New York: Oxford University Press, 1994), pp. 17–31.

33. An excellent overview of the original 1935 Social Security Act can be found in Linda Gordon, *Pitied But Not Entitled: Single Mothers and the History of Welfare* (New York: Free Press, 1994), pp. 4–6. See also Emma Lundberg, *Unto the Least of These* (New York: Appleton Century, 1947); and Winifred Bell, *Aid to Dependent Children* (New York: Columbia University Press, 1965).

34. See Gordon, *Pitied But Not Entitled,* pp. 15–35; Theda Skocpol, *Protecting Soldiers and Mothers,* p. 465.

35. Helen Slessarav, "From Mothers' Pensions to Aid to Dependent Children: The Legalization of Women's Traditional Role as Childbearer," cited in Irwin Garfinkel, *Child Support Assurance: An Extension of Social Security* (New York: Russell Sage, 1992); Gordon, *Pitied But Not Entitled,* pp. 19–20.

36. Quadagno, *The Transformation of Old Age Security.*

37. See Gordon, *Pitied But Not Entitled,* pp. 287–305.

38. U.S. Social Security Administration, *Annual Statistical Supplement,* 1966, p. 113, and 1988, p. 334.

39. U.S. Bureau of the Census, "Households by Detailed Marital Status, Age and Sex of Head, 1947," *Current Population Reports,* Series P-2, no. 16 (Washington, D.C.: Government Printing Office, 1947), p. 8; U.S. Bureau of the Census, "One Parent Family Groups, by Race, Hispanic Origin and Marital Status of Householder or Reference Persons: 1988, 1980, and 1970," *Current Population Reports,* Series P-23, no. 162 (Washington, D.C.: Government Printing Office, 1988); U.S. Bureau of the Census, "Table 11, One Parent Family Groups by Marital Status, Sex, Race, and Hispanic Origin of Parent: March, 1990," *Current Population Reports,* Series P-20, nos. 446–450 (Washington, D.C.: Government Printing Office, 1990, 1991).

40. Quadagno, *The Transformation of Old Age Security.* Since the South was, for all practical purposes, a one-party region, southern legislators had seniority

on committees that Franklin Roosevelt had to win over in order to pass the Social Security Act. See Quadagno, *The Color of Welfare,* pp. 19–25, which includes a brief summary of Quadagno's earlier argument.

41. For example, agricultural workers were not covered in the original Social Security legislation, and domestic workers were not covered until 1950. (Even now, few domestic workers are actually covered.) As late as 1960, about 9.5 percent of employed African American men and 9.0 percent of employed African American women were agricultural workers, and an astonishing 35.1 percent of all employed African American women were private household workers. U.S. Department of Labor, Bureau of Labor Statistics, "Table C-6: Employed Persons by Occupation Group and Sex, 1957–1960," *Special Labor Force Report 14: Labor Force and Employment in 1960* (Washington, D.C.: Government Printing Office, 1961), p. a-24.

42. U.S. Bureau of the Census, "One Parent Family Groups, 1988, 1980, 1970."

43. Universal health care was not, of course, part of the original act. Rather, in still another political compromise, private agencies such as employers or unions were permitted to provide health insurance as a benefit tied to employment. On the connection between health care and the labor market, see Paul Starr, *The Social Transformation of American Medicine: The Rise of a Sovereign Profession and the Making of a Vast Industry* (New York: Basic Books, 1982); and Beth Stevens, "Blurring the Boundaries: How the Federal Government Has Influenced Welfare Benefits in the Private Sector," in Weir et al., eds., *The Politics of Social Policy,* pp.123–148. On the language of "excess" fertility, see Carole McCann, *Birth Control Politics in the United States, 1916–1945* (Ithaca: Cornell University Press, 1994).

44. In 1963, for example, Congress worded a foreign-aid bill so as to include language encouraging family planning. See Reed, *Birth Control Movement,* p. 378. For an overview, see Phyllis Piotrow, *World Population Crisis: The United States Response* (New York: Praeger, 1973).

45. Dienes, *Law, Politics and Birth Control,* p. 255; Littlewood, *The Politics of Population Control,* pp. 44–68.

46. Sar A. Levitan, *The Great Society's Poor Law: A New Approach to Poverty* (Baltimore: Johns Hopkins University Press, 1969), pp. 207–208. As we shall see in Chapter 6, the issue of wanting or not wanting a pregnancy or a baby is more complex than it seems at first glance. The original wording of this question built on the assumption that the woman was an older woman who had had all the children she wanted.

47. Levitan, *Great Society's Poor Law,* p. 207; Arthur Campbell, "The Role of Family Planning in the Reduction of Poverty," *Journal of Marriage and the Family* 30 (1968): 236–245; Reed, *The Birth Control Movement,* p. 379.

48. Campbell, "The Role of Family Planning," pp. 237–240; Littlewood, *The Politics of Population Control,* pp. 18–22. Interestingly, this campaign on behalf of the "five million" poor women had an earlier counterpart: a Sanger-sponsored campaign in 1944 in favor of contraceptive services for "thirteen

million" African American women. Later, of course, came the campaign to provide "eleven million" teenagers with services. For an overview of the 1944 campaign, see McCann, *Birth Control Politics in the United States*, pp. 135–173.

49. See, for example, Robert Haveman, "The War on Poverty and the Poor and Nonpoor," *Political Science Quarterly* 102, no. 1 (1987): 65–78; Michael B. Katz, *The Undeserving Poor: From the War on Poverty to the War on Welfare* (New York: Pantheon, 1990); U.S. Congress, Joint Economic Committee, Subcommittee on Monetary and Fiscal Policy, *War on Poverty—Victory or Defeat?* 99th Congress, 1st sess., June 20, 1985; David Zarefsky, *President Johnson's War on Poverty: Rhetoric and History* (University, Ala.: University of Alabama Press, 1986).

50. Littlewood, *The Politics of Population Control*, pp. 40–42; Levitan, *Great Society's Poor Law*, pp. 209–210: U.S. Congress, Senate Committee on Labor and Public Welfare, *Amendments to the Economic Opportunity Act of 1964*, 89th Congress, 2nd sess., p. 98.

51. Littlewood, *The Politics of Population Control*, pp. 40–42.

52. Ibid., pp. 54–55. Estimating the exact amount of funding for contraception is difficult, since many programs provided low-cost birth control.

53. Public Law 91-572.

54. Littlewood, *The Politics of Population Control*, pp. 54–55.

55. Ibid., pp. 53–54.

56. Cited in Levitan, *Great Society's Poor Law*, p. 209.

57. Reed, *The Birth Control Movement*.

58. Jeannie Rosoff, "The Future of Federal Support for Family Planning Services and Population Research," *Family Planning Perspectives* 5, no. 1 (1973): 7–18.

59. Franklin Zimring, *The Changing Legal World of Adolescence* (New York: Free Press, 1992). Interestingly, at the present time the only type of medical care that adolescents can consent to concerns their sexuality and reproductive behavior. Depending on the state in which they live, young people can consent to be treated for venereal disease, to receive contraceptive services, and to have an abortion. Public policy holds that in these cases, encouraging treatment outweighs the need for parental consent. See Eva W. Paul, Harriet F. Pilpel, and Nancy F. Wechsler, "Pregnancy, Teenagers and the Law," *Family Planning Perspectives* 8, no. 1 (1976): 16–21.

60. Littlewood, *The Politics of Population Control*, pp. 63–64.

61. William Mosher and Charles Westoff, "Trends in Contraceptive Practice," Tables 4–9.

62. William F. Pratt, William D. Mosher, Christine A. Bachrach, and Marjorie C. Horne, "Understanding U.S. Fertility: Findings from the National Survey of Family Growth, Cycle III," *Population Bulletin* 39 (1984): 1–43.

63. Ibid., pp. 31–33, Table 14.

64. Calculated from U.S. National Center for Health Statistics, "Table 1: Wanted

and Unwanted Births Reported by Mothers 15–44 Years of Age, United States, 1973," *Vital and Health Statistics: Advance Data,* no. 9, August 10, 1977, p. 4. An increasing number of American women solved their "family planning" needs, once they had all the children they wanted, by undergoing sterilization; poor women, especially, made this choice because Medicaid paid for the procedure. In 1965 slightly more than one in ten married couples included a person who had been sterilized; by 1973 the proportion had risen to almost one in four, and by 1982 it was close to half. (See National Center for Health Statistics, "Wanted and Unwanted Childbearing: United States, 1973–1982.") Although overall rates of sterilization were roughly similar for both blacks and whites, African American men were substantially less likely to have had vasectomies than white men, and African American women were more likely to have had tubal ligations than white women. Charles Westoff and Elise Jones report figures that are slightly different but still within this range. See Westoff and Jones, "Contraception and Sterilization in the United States, 1965–1975," *Family Planning Perspectives* 9, no. 4 (1977): 153–157. Unlike sterilizations performed in earlier years, especially on unmarried women, these sterilizations appear to have been voluntary, encouraged by new regulations that were implemented after revelations of misuse. Health, Education, and Welfare officials instituted elaborate safeguards to protect people whose sterilizations were funded by Medicaid—safeguards that included mandatory waiting periods, informed-consent procedures, and a ban on sterilizations performed during childbirth or on "mentally incompetent" individuals. (See 43 Fed. Reg. 52146, 52416–52175 [1978].) Consequently, the poor women who were undergoing sterilization in rapidly increasing numbers were probably doing so out of genuine preference in most cases.

65. Melvin Zelnik and John Kantner, "Sexual and Contraceptive Experience of Young Unmarried Women in the United States, 1971 and 1976," *Family Planning Perspectives* 9, no. 2 (1977): 55–71.

66. This important point is made in Nathanson, *Dangerous Passage.* Note also that these surveys, much like the National Survey of Family Growth, provided demographic evidence for reformers who wanted to extend public services such as birth control to teenagers.

67. Marion Howard, *Multi-Service Programs for Pregnant School Girls* (Washington, D.C.: Children's Bureau, U.S. Department of Health, Education, and Welfare, 1968).

68. John Willmarth and Leroy Olsen, "Teen-age Marriages and Unwed Pregnant Girls," *The Clearing House* (November 1964): 173; Jerry Kelley, "The School and Unmarried Mothers," *Children* 10 (1963): 60.

69. In 1950 there were only three developed countries—Hungary, Yugoslavia, and the United States—in which more than 10 percent of teenagers were married. See U.N. Department of International Economic and Social Affairs, "Adolescent Reproductive Behavior: Evidence from Developed Countries," *Population Studies* 1, no. 109 (1988): 40.

70. Sidney Marland, cited in Howard, *Multi-Service Programs for Pregnant School Girls.*

71. The *Reader's Guide to Periodic Literature* shows that from 1970 to 1975, "school-age mothers" were the subject of one to five articles yearly.

72. See, for example, H. F. Pilpel and N. F. Wechsler, "Birth Control, Teenagers and the Law," *Family Planning Perspectives* 1, no. 1 (1969): 29. In 1970 about half of all unwed mothers were teenagers; see National Center for Health Statistics, *Advance Report of Final Natality Statistics,* 1970.

73. Paul B. Cornely, quoted in Commission on Population Growth and the American Future, *Population and the American Future* (Washington, D.C.: Government Printing Office, 1972), p. 148.

74. Alan Cranston, quoted in Commission on Population Growth and the American Future, *Population and the American Future,* p. 151.

75. Zimring, *Changing Legal World of Adolescence;* Parnell J. T. Callahan, *Legal Status of Young Adults under Twenty-one: Your Rights and Duties* (New York: Oceana Publications, 1958); Irving J. Sloane, *Youth and the Law: Rights, Privileges and Obligations* (New York: Oceana, 1974); Alan N. Sussman, *The Rights of Young People: The Basic ACLU Guide to a Young Person's Rights* (New York: Avon, 1977); Harriet F. Pilpel and Nancy F. Wechsler, "Birth Control, Teenagers and the Law: A New Look, 1971," *Family Planning Perspectives* 3, no. 3 (1971): 37–45.

76. H. F. Pilpel and N. F. Wechsler, "Birth Control, Teenagers and the Law," p. 29.

77. U.S. House of Representatives, Select Committee on Population, *Fertility and Contraception in the United States,* 95th Congress, 2nd sess., 1978.

78. For a discussion of the racial differences that characterize births among teenagers, see Wendy Baldwin, "Adolescent Pregnancy and Childbearing: Growing Concerns for Americans," *Population Bulletin* 31 (1976). Rates of out-of-wedlock births are from National Center for Health Statistics, "Trends in Illegitimacy, United States, 1940–1965," *Vital and Health Statistics,* Series 21, no. 15, February 1968; and National Center for Health Statistics, "Advanced Natality Statistics, 1974," *Monthly Vital Statistics Report,* vol. 24, no. 11, supp. 2, February 1976.

79. *Griswold v. Connecticut,* 381 U.S. 479, 482 (1964).

80. *Eisenstadt v. Baird,* 405 U.S. 440 (1972).

81. *Carey v. Population Services International,* 431 U.S. 678 (1977).

82. Shelby Hargrave Cook, "The Unresolved Crisis: The Federal Government's Search for an Adolescent Pregnancy Policy," (Diss., University of Maryland, 1986), p. 10. I am indebted to Cook for much of the information in this section; she provides one of the most detailed and carefully researched accounts of the policies under consideration here. See also Littlewood, *The Politics of Population Control,* p. 63.

83. Cook, "The Unresolved Crisis," p. 11; Littlewood, *Politics of Population Control,* pp. 133–143.

84. Cook, "The Unresolved Crisis," p. 41.

85. For example, the House report noted that "the problems of teenage pregnancy have become critical"; and the Senate report claimed that "teenage pregnancy has become an issue of major concern." House Report no. 1191, 95th Congress, 2nd sess. (1978), p. 31; Senate Report no. 822, 95th Congress, 2nd sess. (1978), p. 27. Both documents draw on materials from House Select Committee on Population, *Fertility and Contraception in the U.S.* (1978).

86. Originally there were two plaintiffs in *Roe:* "Jane Roe," a single woman, and "the Does," a married couple. A physician, James Hauberk Halberd, was permitted to intervene (i.e., join) in Roe's case. The Does were denied standing, leaving Roe (with Halberd as intervenor) as the only plaintiff.

87. *Planned Parenthood of Central Missouri v. Danforth,* 428 U.S. 52, 74 (1976).

88. Ibid., p. 75.

89. *Belotti v. Baird,* 443 U.S. 622 (1979). Rhonda Copelon makes the point that this bypass may well be considered a "judicial shaming ceremony," at least insofar as the young woman is concerned. Still, the point made in the text holds: the Supreme Court was willing to dilute the parental rights of parents by creating a mechanism for overriding their preferences. Rhonda Copelon, "From Privacy to Autonomy: The Conditions for Sexual and Reproductive Freedom," in Marlene Gerber Fried, *From Abortion to Reproductive Freedom: Transforming a Movement* (Boston: South End Press, 1990), pp. 27–44.

90. U.S. Select Committee on Population, "Fertility and Contraception in the United States," pp. 84–85; Jeannie Rosoff, "The Future of Federal Support for Family Planning Services and Population Research," *Family Planning Perspectives* 5, no. 1 (1973): 8. Other programs also contained statutory references to family planning; these included Title IV-A of the Social Security Act, Title III of the Public Health Service Act (Migrant Health Programs and Community Health Centers), Title XIII of the Public Health Service Act, Title II of the Economic Opportunity Act, and Section 701(a)3 of the Comprehensive Employment and Training Act. See Jeannie Rosoff, "Summary and Analysis of Federal Laws and Policies Relating to Family Planning, Contraception, Voluntary Sterilization and Abortion," in U.S. Department of Health, Education, and Welfare, *Family Planning, Contraception, Voluntary Sterilization and Abortion* (Washington: Government Printing Office, 1978), p. 4.

91. U.S. Senate, *The Adolescent School-Age Mother and Child Care Act,* 94th Congress, 1st sess., Senate Report no. 29, p. 4.

92. Ibid., p. 20.

93. See, for example, the objections of Louis Hellman, head of the Department of Health, Education, and Welfare, recorded in U.S. Senate, *Hearing before the Subcommittee on Health of the Committee on Labor and Public Welfare, U.S. Senate, 94th Congress, to Enact the National School-Age Mother and Child Health Acts of 1975,* pp. 33–34.

94. One of my informants says that the idea of trying to reduce the incidence of

pregnancy among teenagers was originally proposed in Sargent Shriver's short-lived presidential campaign. Still, it is significant that the successful Democratic candidate, Jimmy Carter, took up the issue.

95. U.S. Senate, Committee on Human Resources, *Hearings on S. 2910*, 95th Congress, 2nd sess., 1978 (hearings on the Adolescent Health, Services, and Pregnancy Prevention and Care Act); Maris Vinovskis, *An "Epidemic" of Adolescent Pregnancy? Some Historical and Policy Considerations* (New York: Oxford University Press, 1988).

96. Vinovskis, *An "Epidemic" of Adolescent Pregnancy?*, p. 23.

97. One large group in this array, consisting of married women who give birth before the age of twenty, in fact disappears from public debate. To the extent that these women represent a concern, it was folded into the older concern about women who start families "too young" and was subsumed into discussions of poverty, which came to focus on young unmarried teens who have babies.

98. *Congressional Record*, 94th Congress, 2nd sess., 1976, vol. 122, part 17: 20410–20413.

99. Chairman Harrison Williams presenting the charge to the committee, U.S. Congress, Hearings on S. 2910, p. 1. Although not detailed in this chapter, virtually the same arguments were made on the House side of this debate. See U.S. Congress, Subcommittee on Health and the Environment of the Committee on Interstate and Foreign Commerce, Hearing on H.R. 12146, June 28, 1978; the hearing included supportive statements from such disparate groups as the American Academy of Pediatrics, American Citizens Concerned for Life, the March of Dimes, and the U.S. Catholic Conference.

100. U.S. Congress, Hearings on S. 2910, p. 19.

101. Ibid., p. 99.

102. Ibid., p. 100.

103. Alan Guttmacher Institute, *Organized Family Planning Services in the United States, 1981–1983* (New York: Alan Guttmacher Institute, 1984); A. Torres and J. D. Forrest, "Family Planning Clinic Services in the United States, 1983," *Family Planning Perspectives* 17 (1985); Melvin Zelnik, M. A. Koenig, and Y. J. Kim, "Source of Prescription Contraceptives and Subsequent Pregnancy among Women," *Family Planning Perspectives* 16 (January–February): 6–13.

104. Sexual activity among teens, part of a widespread pattern of changing sexual mores in the United States since the early twentieth century, is becoming more common throughout the industrialized world. It has continued to increase despite the fact that the Reagan administration dramatically curtailed federal funding for family planning services.

105. If we use education as a rough proxy for social class, it is clear that couples from the less educated segments of the population were the first to begin cohabiting in large numbers. See L. L. Bumpass, J. A. Sweet, and A. J. Cherlin, "The Role of Cohabitation in Declining Rates of Marriage," *Journal*

of Marriage and the Family 53 (1991): 913–927. Contrary to stereotype, blacks were underrepresented in this new phenomenon, perhaps as a result of the same factors that made marriage increasingly rare in the African American community. See M. Belinda Tucker and Claudia Mitchell-Kernan, "Trends in African-American Family Formation: A Theoretical and Statistical Overview," in Tucker and Mitchell-Kernan, eds., *The Decline in Marriage among African-Americans* (New York: Russell Sage, 1995), pp. 3–26.

106. The phrase "babies having babies" seems to have been popularized by Marian Wright Edelman and the Children's Defense Fund. Founded in 1973, the CDF took on the issue of early pregnancy in 1983 and held its first annual conference on the topic in 1985. Although the CDF was effective in shaping public discussion on the issue, it did not focus on the problem until the late 1980s, after pregnancy among teens had become an item on the public-policy agenda. See Betty Cuniberti, "Madison Avenue Enters Battle against Teenage Pregnancy," *Los Angeles Times,* March 6, 1986, "View" section, p. 1; Nadine Brozan, "Success in Preventing Teen-Age Pregnancy," *New York Times,* March 14, 1987, p. 56.

107. Advocates were not aware of this point, or did not think it meaningful, or (what is most likely) were hard put to explain in simple terms why a rate that did not increase even more was a public-policy success of significant proportions.

108. See Michele McKeegan, *Abortion Politics: Mutiny in the Ranks of the New Right* (New York: Free Press, 1992).

109. Cook, *Unresolved Crisis,* pp. 40–41.

110. Ibid., pp. 49–53; *Harris v. McRae,* 448 U.S. 297 (1980).

111. *H.L. v. Matheson,* 450 U.S. 398 (1981). The state laws are described in Patricia Donovan, *Our Daughters' Decisions: The Conflict in State Laws on Abortion and Other Issues* (New York: Alan Guttmacher Institute, 1992).

112. Cook, *Unresolved Crisis,* pp. 38–42.

113. Ibid., pp. 51–52.

114. 47 Fed. Reg. 7699, 7699–7700 (1982).

115. *National Family Planning and Reproductive Health Association v. Department of Health and Human Services,* Civil Action 83–0180, U.S.D.Ct., February 23, 1982 (injunction); March 2, 1983 (decision).

116. *Adolescent Family Life Act: Statutes at Large,* 95, Public Law 97-35 (1981); *Public Health Service Amendment,* 578–592.

117. Public Law 95-626, p. 3595.

118. Public Law 97-35, 95 Stat., pp. 579–580.

119. Ibid., p. 588.

120. *H.L. v. Matheson,* 450 U.S. 398 (1981); *Akron v. Akron Center for Reproductive Health, Inc.,* 462 U.S. 416 (1983); *Planned Parenthood of Kansas City, Mo., Inc. v. Ashcroft,* 462 U.S. 476 (1983); *Hodgson v. Minnesota,* 110 S. Ct. 2926 (1991); and *Ohio v. Akron Center for Reproductive Health,* 110 S. Ct. 2972 (1990).

121. *Hodgson v. Minnesota; Ohio v. Akron Center for Reproductive Health.*
122. Nathanson, *Dangerous Passage.* In real life this division is less neat than it appears, and grew blurrier over time. Middle-class girls became more likely to have children out of wedlock, and poor and black girls opted for abortion. Both patterns caused concern among antiabortionists and among middle-class parents confronted with pregnant, unmarried daughters who were determined to have their babies.

4. Constructing an Epidemic

1. For example, see William Bennett, *The Index of Leading Cultural Indicators: Facts and Figures on the State of American Society* (New York: Simon and Schuster, 1994).
2. Although much of the rhetoric on the Right is about "children," conservatives and even many liberals think of pregnancy among teenagers as something fundamentally affecting "girls" or young women. The issue is usually framed in such a way that half of the people involved—namely, young men—are excluded, and this selectivity is an enormous handicap in the effort to find a solution. As we will see, thinking about the problem in terms of two sexes rather than one opens up a number of new possible solutions.
3. For an overview, see U.S. House of Representatives, 99th Congress, Select Committee on Children, Youth and Families, "Teen Pregnancy: What Is Being Done? A State-by-State Look" (Washington, D.C.: Government Printing Office, 1986); Charles Stewart Mott Foundation, *A State-by-State Look at Teenage Childbearing in the United States* (Flint, Mich.: Charles Stewart Mott Foundation, 1991); Gloria Magat, ed., *Adolescent Pregnancy: Still News in 1989* (New York: Grantmakers Concerned with Adolescent Pregnancy, Women and Foundations/Corporate Philanthropy, 1989); Junior League, *Teenage Pregnancy: Developing Life Options* (New York: Association of Junior Leagues, 1988). For the National Urban League's program with Kappa Alpha Psi, see Cheryl Hayes, ed., *Risking the Future: Adolescent Sexuality, Pregnancy, and Childbearing* (Washington, D.C.: National Academy Press, 1987), vol. 1, p. 178.
4. Prior to the mid 1970s, pregnant teenagers were treated by the media as a subset of "school-age mothers" or of the larger set of "unwed mothers." See *Reader's Guide to Periodic Literature, 1968–1994.* A tabulation of these stories by title and content has been compiled by Kristin Luker.
5. In 1955, out of every thousand adolescent women of all races, 90 gave birth. By 1975 the rate had fallen until it was approximately equal to that of 1915: 60 per thousand. And by 1985 it had declined even further, to only 50 per thousand. Interestingly, the fertility of teenagers has always been remarkably similar to that of older women; the birthrates for both groups rise and fall in tandem. (The similarities are most marked, of course, between the rates for teens and the rates for women who are just a little older—twenty to twenty-

228

four.) Clearly, the fertility of American women tends to respond to large, society-wide forces. See National Center for Health Statistics, *Advance Report of Final Natality Statistics* (Hyattsville, Md.: Public Health Service, various years).

6. Robert L. Heuser, *Fertility Tables for Birth Cohorts by Color: United States, 1917–1973,* DHEW Publication no. (HRA) 76–11182 (Rockville, Md.: National Center for Health Statistics, 1976); National Center for Health Statistics, *Advance Report of Final Natality Statistics, 1987* (Rockville, Md.: National Center for Health Statistics, 1989), vol. 38, no. 3. Even the post-1988 upturn in birthrates among teenagers is still within the range of historical fluctuation, although whether this will continue to be so is uncertain.

7. In 1973, among teenage women of all races, 60 out of every thousand gave birth and 21 per thousand had abortions; thus, a total of 81 out of every thousand were becoming pregnant. In 1980, in contrast, the rate of live births was 52 per thousand and the abortion rate had more than doubled, to 44 per thousand; the pregnancy rate had thus increased to 96 per thousand.

8. For an overview, see *Statistical Abstract of the United States* (Washington, D.C.: Government Printing Office, 1993), Table 101, "Births to Unmarried Women, by Race of Child and Age of Mother, 1970–1990"; U.S. Center for Health Statistics, *Vital Statistics of the United States,* various years; idem, *Monthly Vital Statistics,* various years.

9. This is has led to a set of new social practices unanticipated by Emily Post. People now speak of "my baby's father" or "my baby's mother." One proud father even placed a notice in his local paper announcing that his fiancée had just given birth to their baby (I am indebted to Sheldon Messinger for this information). In the late 1980s commentators did begin to take note of the rising rate of out-of-wedlock births in general; but even within this broader context, experts and the media still focused on teenage mothers.

10. Larry Bumpass and James A. Sweet, "Children's Experience in Single-Parent Families: Implications of Cohabitation and Marital Transition," *Family Planning Perspectives* 21 (November–December): 256–260.

11. In 1986 polls revealed that more than 84 percent of Americans considered pregnancy among teenagers a "major" problem facing the country. Harris poll for PPFA, 1985. See also Roper Report 86-3, 1986 R37XE.

12. Some people, among them demographers such as Phillips Cutwright and polemicists such as Charles Murray, argue that the proportion or ratio of out-of-wedlock births is much more important than the rate. In demographic terms, a "rate" is an event that is standardized over a specified population for a particular period of time. Thus, the birthrate is defined as the number of births (the numerator) per thousand women aged fifteen to forty-four (the denominator) in a year. But many commentators speak of the "illegitimacy rate" or the "abortion rate" when what they really have in mind is a proportion or ratio, a figure that compares two sets of *events* rather than an event to a population. What many people call the "illegitimacy rate" is really a measure

that compares the number of out-of-wedlock births (the numerator) to the total number of births (the denominator). The problem here is that there can be wide fluctuations in *both* of the events being charted, and these fluctuations can lead to dramatic changes in the measure. (Populations fluctuate, too, of course, but much less sharply.) The illegitimacy *rate* (the number of out-of-wedlock births per thousand unmarried women aged fifteen to forty-four) went from 25.4 in 1970 to 43.8 in 1990, an increase of about 70 percent, while the illegitimacy *ratio* (the proportion of out-of-wedlock births to legitimate births) went from 11 percent to 28 percent of all births during that same period, an increase of more than 250 percent. The dramatically larger increase in the ratio, compared to the increase in the rate, was due to an increase in the propensity of American women to bear children out of wedlock, and, simultaneously, a declining propensity to bear children in wedlock. Among African Americans, virtually all of the increase in the illegitimacy ratio was due to declining marital fertility (the denominator), and in fact illegitimacy rates for African American women declined for most of the 1970–1990 period. As Cutright says, what the majority of a cohort is doing matters. Still, commentators tended to emphasize troubling statistics (changes in the proportion of babies born out of wedlock) over more comforting ones (such as the decreases in the incidence of pregnancy per sexually experienced woman and in the rate of out-of-wedlock births among African Americans).

13. One could make the case that this *was* the real story: the fact that birthrates among very young women had not changed much. Since the period of childhood had gradually lengthened in the course of the nineteenth and twentieth centuries, one would have expected a reduction in births to very young women. Birthrates among fourteen-year-olds for the calendar years 1925–1990 were as follows:

1925	3.9 per thousand
1930	3.8
1935	3.7
1940	3.8
1945	3.9
1950	5.8
1955	6.1
1960	6.0
1965	5.2
1970	6.6
1975	7.1
1980	6.5
1985	6.2
1990	7.8

Source for 1925–1970: Heuser, *Fertility Tables for Birth Cohorts by Color,* "Central Birth Rates for All Women during Each Year 1917–73 by Age and Live-Birth Order for Each Cohort from 1888 to 1959," p. 37, Table 4a. Source for 1975–1990: *Vital Statistics of the United States: Natality,* "Central Birth Rates by Live-Birth Order, Current Age of Mother, and Color for Women in Each Cohort," p. 1-32, Table 1-16 (1975); p. 1-42, Table 1-18 (1980); p. 1-36, Table 1-18 (1985); p. 1-45, Table 1-19 (1990).

14. The classic example is Stanley Cohen, *Folk Devils and Moral Panics* (Oxford: Basil Blackwell, 1987). For another view, one that is more in line with the position presented here, see John Kingdon, *Agendas, Alternatives, and Public Policies* (Boston: Little, Brown, 1984).

15. This does not imply that stories told by advocates are necessarily right. Indeed, as in this case, advocates typically confront contradictory data and must strive to make sense of them long before the whole pattern of the phenomenon is clear. On the issue of pregnancy among teenagers, advocates and policymakers were wrong in several important respects, and their errors had profound implications for social policy.

16. Rosalind Petchesky has made the astute point that social scientists often speak of "revolutions" when only white and middle-class behavior has changed. See Petchesky, *Abortion and Women's Choice: The State, Sexuality and Reproductive Freedom* (Boston: Northeastern University Press, 1990).

17. John D'Emilio and Estelle Freedman, *Intimate Matters: A History of Sexuality in America* (New York: Harper and Row, 1988).

18. Calculated from Sandra L. Hofferth, Joan R. Kahn, and Wendy Baldwin, "Premarital Sexual Activity among U.S. Teenage Women over the Past Three Decades," *Family Planning Perspectives* 19, no. 2 (1987): 46–53.

19. Alfred Kinsey et al., *Sexual Behavior in the Human Female* (Philadelphia: W. B. Saunders, 1953), p. 336, Table 78.

20. Melvin Zelnik, "Sexual Activity among Adolescents: Perspectives of a Decade," in E. R. McAnarney, ed., *Premature Adolescent Pregnancy and Parenthood* (New York: Grune and Stratton, 1983); Melvin Zelnik and F. K. Shah, "First Intercourse among Young Americans," *Family Planning Perspectives* 15 (1983): 64–70.

21. American Institute of Public Opinion (AIPO), Gallup Poll, July 1969 (sex before marriage); idem, May 1969 (nudes in magazines); idem, May 1969 (Broadway shows). See Mayer, *Changing American Mind,* p. 385.

22. William G. Mayer, *The Changing American Mind: How and Why American Public Opinion Changed between 1960 and 1988* (Ann Arbor: University of Michigan Press, 1992), p. 385.

23. Floris W. Wood, *An American Profile: Opinions and Behavior, 1972–1989* (New York: Gale Research, 1990), p. 597.

24. These laws were the modern-day remnants of the ones that women reformers had campaigned for in the nineteenth century. When they were challenged in 1981 as a form of reverse discrimination (because a boy under the age of consent was charged with criminal sanctions for having sex with a girl his own age), they were legitimated by the Supreme Court—as a remedy for pregnancy among teenagers! The Court's reasoning was that statutory-rape penalties would discourage teenage men from having sex, just as the risk of

pregnancy would discourage young women. Overall, a most curious case. It shows how profoundly the concept of an "epidemic" of teenage pregnancy had permeated judicial thinking at the highest levels. See *Michael M. v. Superior Court of Sonoma County,* 101 S. Ct. 1200 (1981).

25. Yankelovich, Skelly, and White, poll reported in *Public Opinion Online,* LEXIS, Market Library, R-Poll File, Accession no. 0132089 (1977). National Opinion Research Center, poll reported in *Public Opinion Online,* LEXIS, Market Library, R-Poll File, Accession no. 0092411 (1994).

26. Estimated from James Trussell and Barbara Vaughan, "Selected Results Concerning Sexual Behavior and Contraceptive Use from the 1988 National Survey of Family Growth and the 1988 National Survey of Adolescent Males," Office of Population Research Working Paper Series, Princeton University, working paper no. 91–12 (September 1991).

27. See Melvin Zelnik and John Kantner, "Sexual Activity, Contraceptive Use and Pregnancy among Metropolitan Area Teenagers, 1971–1979," *Family Planning Perspectives* 12 (1980): 230; Kathleen Ford, *Sex and Pregnancy in Adolescence* (Beverly Hills, Calif.: Sage, 1981).

28. Hofferth et al., "Premarital Sexual Activity," p. 49; Jacqueline D. Forrest and Susheela Singh, "The Sexual and Reproductive Behavior of American Women, 1982–1988," *Family Planning Perspectives* 22 (1990): 206–214; Trussell and Vaughan, "Selected Results Concerning Sexual Behavior."

29. Robert Hatcher and his colleagues estimate that the average interval between menarche (first menstruation) and marriage is 13.5 years for all teens. See Robert A. Hatcher et al., *Contraceptive Technology* (New York: Irvington, 1994), p. 131. On menarche, see Phyllis B. Eveleth, "Timing of Menarche: Secular Trend and Population Differences," in Jane Lancaster and Beatrix Hamburg, eds., *School-Age Pregnancy and Parenthood: Biosocial Dimensions* (New York: Aldine, 1986), pp. 39–52. See also J. D. Forrest, "Timing of Reproductive Life Stages," *Obstetrics and Gynecology* 82 (1993): 105–111; and A. F. Saluter, "Marital Status and Living Arrangements," *Current Population Reports,* Series P-20, no. 461 (March 1991). Saluter gives estimates for the length of time between first *intercourse* and marriage. Data on *male* sexual maturity are scattered and contradictory.

30. Melvin Zelnik and John Kantner, "Sexual and Contraceptive Experience of Young Unmarried Women in the United States, 1971 and 1976," *Family Planning Perspectives* 9 (1977): 55–73. See also K. Kost and J. D. Forrest, "American Women's Sexual Behavior and Exposure to Sexually Transmitted Diseases," *Family Planning Perspectives* 24 (1992): 244–254; and Trussell and Vaughan, "Selected Results."

31. J. D. Forrest and S. Singh, "The Sexual and Reproductive Behavior of American Women, 1982–1988," *Family Planning Perspectives* 22 (1990): 206–214; Trussell and Vaughan, "Selected Results Concerning Sexual Behavior and Contraceptive Use."

32. According to the Kinsey data, which are not nationally representative and in

which middle-class people are overrepresented, in the 1940s and 1950s 18 percent of women who obtained only a grade school education (education being a proxy for class) had been sexually active before marriage and prior to the age of fifteen, compared to only 1 percent of the women who went on to college or graduate school. See Kinsey et al., *Sexual Behavior in the Human Female,* p. 295.

33. For an overview of the social construction of symbolic boundaries, see Michele Lamont and Marcel Fournier, *Cultivating Differences: Symbolic Boundaries and the Making of Inequality* (Chicago: University of Chicago Press, 1992), pp. 1–17.

34. Ira Reiss, *Premarital Sexual Standards in America* (New York: Free Press, 1960).

35. Harris Poll for PPFA, 1985; Yankelovich/Time/CNN, 1990; General Social Survey, 1983, (access to birth control information); Contemporary American Family, September 18, 1981, p. 9F (access to birth control devices). In the language of rational-choice theory, adults' preferences on how to deal with sexual activity among teens are "nontransitive."

36. ABC–Washington Post Poll, 1990; Yankelovich/Time/CNN, 1990; Gallup Poll, *Newsweek,* February 1987.

37. Harris Poll for PPFA, 1985; "Speaking of Kids: A National Survey of Children and Parents," September 17, 1990; Gordon S. Black, *U.S.A. Today,* June 1986.

38. Yankelovich, 1978, Health Survey.

39. Louis Harris for PPFA, 1985.

40. Larry Bumpass, "What's Happening to the Family: Interactions between Demographic and Institutional Change," *Demography* 27, no. 4 (1990): 483–498. For a lucid overview, see Irwin Garfinkel and Sara McLanahan, *Single Mothers and Their Children: A New American Dilemma* (Washington, D.C.: Urban Institute Press, 1986). For more detailed data by race, see Larry Bumpass and R. Kelly Raley, "Redefining Single-Parent Families: Cohabitation and Changing Family Reality," *Demography* 32 (1995): 97–109.

41. Respondents were asked whether they thought having children out of wedlock should be illegal—as it still was in many jurisdictions, where eighteenth-century bastardy laws remained on the books (see Chapter 2). Data are from a poll conducted by Harris/Roper for Virginia Slims. On the magnitude of these shifts in public opinion, see Mayer, *Changing American Mind.*

42. *Time,* July 9, 1965. As is so often the case, the human facts here are more complex and tragic than they appear at first glance. The child, a girl, had been born to a mental patient after the woman had been raped; the child's grandfather had sued for negligence on behalf of his daughter and granddaughter. He claimed that the child, because she had been born a bastard, had been deprived of "property rights . . . [and] a normal childhood and home life." But the point here is that *Time,* the plaintiffs, and the judge who permitted the case to go to trial did not a priori reject the idea that being born out of wedlock was a tort for which remedy could be sought.

43. Alex Poinsett, "A Despised Minority," *Ebony,* August 1966, p. 48.
44. Crosby and Logan, "Continuing Education for Unwed Mothers," *Scholastic Teacher,* February 1968, p. 15; reprinted in *Time,* February 10, 1968, p. 65.
45. Elizabeth Keiffer, "Diary of an Unwed Mother," *Good Housekeeping,* May 1968, p. 86.
46. Richard Meryman, "An Unwed Mother Gives Up Her Baby," *Life,* June 14, 1968, pp. 88–97.
47. Anonymous, "I Am an Unwed Mother," *Seventeen,* November 1968, pp. 128, 205.
48. "The Case of the Pregnant School Girl," *Reader's Digest,* September 1970. At least one author has claimed that *Reader's Digest* was liberal on sexual matters, though conservative in other realms. See John Heidenry, *Theirs Was the Kingdom: DeWitt and Lila Acheson Wallace and the Story of the Reader's Digest* (New York: Norton, 1993). Whether the sentiments quoted here were liberal or conservative in their day depends on one's viewpoint.
49. My own suspicion is that the legalization of abortion in 1973 ironically made it permissible for women to have children out of wedlock. After 1973, women who had unwanted pregnancies clearly did not have to give birth—another option was available to them. It was the underlying social and economic forces, however, that led increasing numbers of women to exercise this option. Japan, after all, has had legalized abortion since the end of World War II and has very low (albeit increasing) levels of extramarital childbearing.
50. "In Trouble: The Story of an Unwed Woman's Decision to Keep Her Child," *Atlantic,* March 1970.
51. Edward Kiester, "The Bitter Lessons Too Many of Our Schools Are Teaching Pregnant Teenagers," *Today's Health,* June 1972, p. 56.
52. Ibid., p. 54.
53. See *Ordway v. Hargraves,* 323 F. Supp. 1155 (1971), in which the Court held that young unmarried women who were pregnant and also students had the right to continue their schooling.
54. "Single Motherhood," *Time,* September 6, 1971.
55. See "Unmarried Parent: Is Martha Doing Right?," *Senior Scholastic,* October 1972, p. 101; Cokie Roberts and Steven Roberts, "Having a Baby Is a Very Alone Thing," *Seventeen,* January 1973; "Opinion: When a Single Girl Becomes Pregnant," *Mademoiselle,* March 1971.
56. Patricia Pope, "One Hand to Hold," *Ladies' Home Journal,* October 1983, p. 62; M. Guido, "School Board Gives Teacher a Scarlet A," *Ms. Magazine,* April 1983, p. 23.
57. "A Question of Role Models," *Newsweek,* January 27, 1986, p. 107. When I spoke with a representative of the Girls' Clubs in 1993, I learned that this unwed mother had not been able to use the courts to get her job back, as had the white women whose cases had attracted the attention of the public media. Now known as Girls, Inc., the Girls' Club organization was founded in 1945 and today has 250,000 members nationwide. Supported by the United Way,

Girls' Clubs run programs for girls aged six to eighteen, focusing on leadership, sports, adventure, "life skills," and "self-reliance." Girls, Inc., is often a public advocate on issues affecting girls and young women.

58. The term "hollowing out" was first used in this sense by Frank Levy. He has examined different estimates of the Gini index, as well as other measures, such as the variance of the natural log of earnings (VLN), the coefficient of variation, and the Theil Entropy Index. All of these measure different patterns of inequality and yield results consistent with the arguments in this chapter. See Frank Levy and Richard Murnane, "U.S. Earnings Levels and Earnings Inequality: A Review of Recent Trends and Proposed Explanations," *Journal of Economic Literature* 30 (1992): 1333-1382. For another overview of this process, see Nan Maxwell, *Income Inequality in the United States, 1947-1985* (New York: Greenwood, 1990). For figures based on net worth rather than income, see Arthur B. Kennickell and R. Louise Woodburn, "Estimation of Household Net Worth Using Model-Based and Design-Based Weights: Evidence from the 1989 Survey of Consumer Finances," Federal Reserve Board (April 1992). The figures show a roughly similar trend: the Gini coefficient (based on the Survey of Consumer Finances) increased from .777 in 1983 to .793 in 1989.

59. Malcolm Sawyer, "Income Redistribution in OECD Countries," OECD Occasional Studies, Paris (July 1976); John Coder, Lee Rainwater, and Timothy Smeeding, "Inequality among Children and Elderly in Ten Modern Nations: The U.S. in International Context," Paper presented at the meetings of the American Economic Association, December 1988; Gordon Green et al., "International Comparisons of Earnings Inequality for Men in the 1980s," *Review of Income and Wealth* 38 (1992): 1-15; U.S. Census Bureau, "Studies in the Distribution of Income," *Current Population Reports,* Series P-60, no. 183 (1992).

60. The income structure in the United States is very volatile, of course, and people are constantly moving up and down the income ladder. Here I am referring to relative movements over time.

61. Claudia Goldin and Robert Margo, "The Great Compression: The Wage Structure in the United States at Mid-Century," *Quarterly Journal of Economics* 107 (1992): 1-34. See also Claudia Goldin, *Understanding the Gender Gap: An Economic History of American Women* (New York: Oxford, 1990). Increases in the Gini index, therefore, although they are significant, simply widen what is already a rather large divide.

62. Frank Levy and Richard Michel, *Economic Future of American Families: Income and Wealth Trends* (Washington, D.C.: Urban Institute, 1991), p. 35.

63. This figure is adjusted for fringe benefits; see Levy and Michel, *Economic Future,* p. 8, Table 21.

64. Ibid., pp. 9-10; Gary Burtless, ed., *A Future of Lousy Jobs? The Changing Structure of U.S. Wages* (Washington, D.C.: Brookings Institute, 1990).

65. For a poignant example of how these economic changes affect people's lives,

see Katharine Newman, *Declining Fortunes: The Withering of the American Dream* (New York: Basic Books, 1993).

66. U.S. Bureau of the Census, "Poverty in the United States, 1991," *Current Population Reports,* Series P-60, no. 181; Eugene Smolensky et al., "The Declining Significance of Age in the United States," in John Palmer, Timothy Smeeding, and Barbara Torrey, eds., *The Vulnerable* (Washington, D.C.: Urban Institute Press, 1988).

67. Many of these trends were already visible by the late 1960s and were probably not "caused" in any direct, uncomplicated way by declining real wages. But the decline in real wages probably made these trends steeper and more widespread than they would otherwise have been.

68. Cynthia Taeuber, *Statistical Handbook on Women in America* (Phoenix, Ariz.: Oryx Press, 1991), p. 299.

69. U.S. Bureau of the Census, "Household and Family Characteristics," *Current Population Reports,* Series P-20, various years. Since analysts tend to focus on the vital statistics concerning legal marriage, nonspecialists often assume that the terms "unmarried mother" and "single mother" are interchangeable. However, increases in what the demographers call "cohabitation" (and what everyone else calls "living together") have to some extent offset the decline in marriage. See L. L. Bumpass, J. A. Sweet, and A. J. Cherlin, "The Role of Cohabitation in Declining Rates of Marriage," *Journal of Marriage and the Family* 53, no. 4 (1991): 913–927.

70. Gordon Green, Paul Ryscavage, and Edward Welniak, "Factors Affecting Black-White Income Differentials: A Decomposition," *Current Population Reports,* issue on consumer income, Series P-60–183.

71. Ellwood and Crane, *Journal of Economic Perspectives* 4 (Fall 1990).

72. Green et al., "Factors Affecting Black-White Income Differentials," pp. 31–32.

73. Paul Ryscavage, Gordon Green, and Edward Welniak, "The Impact of Demographic, Social, and Economic Change on the Distribution of Income," *Current Population Reports,* Series P-60–183, p. 14.

74. The term "cultural capital" was coined by the French sociologist Pierre Bourdieu. It refers to the cultural and social skills that affluent parents pass on to their children and that aid the children on tests that are ostensibly based on "merit." See Pierre Bourdieu and Jean-Claude Passeron, *The Inheritors: French Students and Their Relation to Culture* (Chicago: University of Chicago Press, 1979).

75. Arlie Hochschild, *The Second Shift: Inside the Two-Job Marriage* (New York: Viking, 1989).

76. For an example of how families used sexual choices as an explanation for their children's downward mobility, see Newman, *Declining Fortunes.*

77. Charles Murray, *Losing Ground: Social Policy, 1950–1980* (New York: Basic Books, 1984); David Ellwood, *Poor Support: Poverty in the American Family* (New York: Basic Books, 1988).

78. This framing of the problem admittedly begs a second question—namely, why teenagers don't wait until they are married to have children, so that a husband rather than welfare could support them and their babies. The answer to this is complex and draws on all three of the revolutions cited here: the new sexual mores, the increase in childbearing outside marriage, and the dramatic changes in the world economy. See Chapter 6 for a detailed discussion of this issue.

79. See Gary Burtless, ed., *A Future of Lousy Jobs? The Changing Structure of U.S. Wages* (Washington, D.C.: Brookings Institute, 1990).

80. Alan Guttmacher Institute, *Sex and America's Teenagers* (New York: Alan Guttmacher Institute, 1994), p. 58.

81. Robert Moffitt, "Incentive Effects of the U.S. Welfare System: A Review," *Journal of Economic Literature* 30 (1992): 1–61.

5. Choice and Consequence

1. John Kingdon, *Agendas, Alternatives, and Public Policies* (New York: Harper Collins, 1984), p. 99. The same official noted that these teenagers receive poor medical care and are malnourished, but he still claimed that their age was the primary cause of the problem.

2. Calculated from data compiled by the National Center for Health Statistics, from Victor Showers, *World Facts and Figures* (New York: John Wiley, 1990), and from the *Demographic Yearbook*. National rankings according to infant mortality rates in the late 1980s are as follows:

Ranking	Country	Rate
1	Andorra	3.7
2	Monaco	3.8
8	Switzerland	6.9
11	Taiwan	7.5
13	Antigua	7.7
15	Canada	7.9
22	Netherlands	8.2
27	East Germany	9.2
29	U.S.: total	10.4
22	U.S. whites only	8.2
27	U.S.: mothers older than 20	9.0
14	U.S.: mothers with some college education	7.9

3. There is a considerable literature on the way in which childbearing affects the health of teenagers. The best overview is Donna M. Strobino, "The Health and Medical Consequences of Sexuality and Pregnancy: A Review of the Literature," in *Risking the Future: Adolescent Sexuality, Pregnancy, and Childbearing*, vol. 2: *Working Papers and Statistical Appendix*, ed. Sandra L. Hofferth and Cheryl D. Hayes (Washington, D.C.: National Academy Press,

1987), pp. 93–122. See also Carolyn Makinson, "The Health Consequences of Teenage Fertility," *Family Planning Perspectives* 17, no. 3 (May–June 1985): 132–139. Comparative statistics need to be compiled on married and unmarried women, since the data suggest that marriage may have an independent effect on some of the factors of interest here, such as the rate at which teenage mothers drop out of school.

4. For a lucid overview see Hayes, *Risking the Future,* vol. 1, pp. 125–128; detailed statistics can be found in Sandra Hofferth, "Social and Economic Consequences of Teenage Childbearing," in *Risking the Future,* vol. 2, ed. Hofferth and Hayes, pp. 123–144. For a more recent review of the literature, see U.S. Congress, Office of Technology Assessment, *Adolescent Health,* vol. 2: *Background and the Effectiveness of Certain Selected Prevention and Treatment Programs* (Washington, D.C.: Government Printing Office, 1991), pp. 334–340. For an update on recent material, see Christine Bachrach and Karen Carver, "Outcomes of Early Childbearing: An Appraisal of Recent Evidence—NICHD," Center for Population Research, 1992 (mimeo).

5. The best initial overview of this literature is Hayes, *Risking the Future,* vol. 1, pp. 132–134. For an overview from the vantage point of those doing research on poverty, see Michael Katz, *The Undeserving Poor: From the War on Poverty to the War on Welfare* (New York: Pantheon, 1989), pp. 215–223.

6. Valerie Polakow, *Lives on the Edge: Single Mothers and Their Children in the Other America* (Chicago: University of Chicago Press, 1993).

7. This is what economists call "selection bias." If (to take one classic example) users of the Pill differ from users of other forms of contraception in substantial ways—age, class, number of sexual partners—then whatever differences are later observed between Pill users and, say, condom users are likely to be related in large part to these preexisting differences, not to the contraceptive method itself.

8. *People,* October 24, 1994, p. 38. In fact, poor people tend to have poor children. As early as 1964, long before "teenage pregnancy" was assigned a leading role in the drama, people recognized this simple fact. "A poor individual of a poor family has a high probability of staying poor," noted the President's Council of Economic Advisors in that year. See *Economic Report of the President, 1964,* pp. 69–70.

9. On the increased risk that a teenage mother will herself come from a single-parent family, see Cheryl Hayes, ed., *Risking the Future,* vol. 1, pp. 95–121; J. L. Peterson et al., "Starting Early: The Antecedents of Early Premarital Intercourse," Report prepared for the Office of Adolescent Pregnancy and Parenting, Washington, D.C., August 1985; and Susan Newcomer and Richard Udry, "Adolescent Sexual Behavior and Popularity," *Adolescence* 18 (1983): 515–522. This risk applies to both children of divorced parents and children of never-married single parents; see Sara McLanahan and Gary Sandefur, *Growing Up with a Single Parent: What Helps, What Hurts* (Cambridge, Mass.: Harvard University Press, 1994), p. 67. On the correlation between early pregnancy and poor performance in school, see Allan F. Abrahamse,

Peter A. Morrison, and Linda Waite, *Beyond Stereotypes: Who Becomes a Single Mother?* (Santa Monica, Calif.: Rand Corporation, 1988); B. L. Devaney and K. S. Hubley, "The Determinants of Adolescent Pregnancy and Childbearing," Report prepared for the National Institute of Child Health and Human Development, U.S. Department of Health and Human Services (Washington, D.C.: Government Printing Office, 1981); J. B. Jones and S. Phillilber, "Sexually Active but not Pregnant," *Journal of Youth and Adolescence* 12, no. 3 (1983): 235–251; Peterson et al., "Starting Early." On the risk that a teenage mother will come from a family in which there has been a divorce or breakup, see McLanahan and Sandefur, *Growing Up with a Single Parent,* p. 70. On the effect of divorce and breakup on out-of-wedlock childbearing, see Lawrence Wu and Brian Martinson, "Family Structure and the Risk of a Premarital Birth," *American Sociological Review* 58, no. 2 (1993): 210–232. On "concentration effects" (that is, the extent to which coming from a bad neighborhood influences a young person's behavior) see the citations in note 24, below.

10. Author's calculations from National Center for Health Statistics, *Advance Report of Final Natality Statistics* (Washington, D.C.: U.S. Department of Health and Human Services, various years).

11. Jane Menken, "The Health and Demographic Consequences of Adolescent Pregnancy and Childbearing," in Catherine Chilman, ed., *Adolescent Pregnancy and Childbearing: Findings from Research* (Washington, D.C.: U.S. Department of Health and Human Services, 1980); Elizabeth McArney et al., *Premature Adolescent Pregnancy and Parenthood* (New York: Grune and Stratton, 1983), pp. 109–193; I. B. Taylor et al., "Teenage Mothering: Admission to Hospital and Accidents during the First Five Years," *Archive of Disease in Childhood* 58, no. 6 (1983): 6–11.

12. Some researchers assume that race alone is a reasonable proxy for poverty, while others argue that even middle-class blacks suffer stress due to what is conventionally called racism. This is a philosophical issue that sociologists are currently debating; see, for example, William J. Wilson, *The Declining Significance of Race: Blacks and Changing American Institutions* (Chicago: University of Chicago Press, 1980). But some medical research suggests that there may indeed be independent effects due to racism—effects that cannot be a function simply of poverty. At least one innovative study of blood pressure suggests that the prevalence of hypertension among blacks is partly a result of the stress of living in a society charged with racial hostility and that this effect occurs across the class spectrum. See M. J. Klag et al., "The Association of Skin Color with Blood Pressure in U.S. Blacks with Low Socioeconomic Status," *Journal of the American Medical Association* 265, no. 5 (February 1991): 599–602.

13. Menken, "The Health and Demographic Consequences of Adolescent Pregnancy and Childbearing," pp. 177–206.

14. On the way in which poverty and minority-group status affect the age at which a person first has intercourse, see James Trussell and Barbara Vaughan,

"Selected Results Concerning Sexual Behavior and Contraceptive Use from the 1988 National Survey of Family Growth and the 1988 National Survey of Adolescent Males," Office of Population Research (Sept. 1991); F. L. Sonenstein et al., "Levels of Sexual Activity among Adolescent Males in the United States," *Family Planning Perspectives* 23, no. 4 (July–August 1991): 162–167. On the way in which youth, poverty, and minority-group status make it increasingly unlikely that a person will use contraceptives, see L. S. Zabin et al., "The Risk of Adolescent Pregnancy in the First Months of Intercourse," *Family Planning Perspectives* 11, no. 4 (1979): 215–222; L. S. Zabin et al., "Why They Delay: A Study of Teenage Family Planning Clinic Patients," *Family Planning Perspectives* 13 (1981): 205–217; M. Zelnik and J. F. Kantner, "Sexual Activity, Contraceptive Use and Pregnancy among Metropolitan Area Teenagers," *Family Planning Perspectives* 12, no. 5 (1980): 230–237.

15. Hayes, *Risking the Future,* vol. 1, pp. 111–114; D. Hughes, K. Johnson, J. Simons, and S. Rosenbaum, *Maternal and Child Health Data Book: The Health of America's Children* (Washington, D.C.: Children's Defense Fund, 1986); Elizabeth Cooksey, "Factors in the Resolution of Adolescent Premarital Pregnancies," *Demography* 27, no. 2 (May 1990): 207–218; Frank Furstenberg, J. Brooks-Gunn, and S. Philip Morgan, *Adolescent Mothers in Later Life* (Cambridge: Cambridge University Press, 1987).

16. Alan Guttmacher Institute, *Sex and America's Teenagers* (New York: Alan Guttmacher Institute, 1994), p. 58.

17. Cooksey, "Factors in the Resolution of Adolescent Premarital Pregnancies," pp. 207–218.

18. Carol Stack and Linda Burton, "Kinscripts: Nexus of Individual and Families," Paper presented at the joint Berkeley-Stanford Conference on Teenage Pregnancy, Palo Alto, Calif., 1989. See also Linda Burton and Carol Stack, "Conscripting Kin: Reflections on Family, Generation and Culture," in Deborah Rhode, ed., *The Politics of Pregnancy: Adolescent Sexuality and Public Policy* (New Haven: Yale University Press, 1993).

19. Laurie Schwab Zabin and Samuel Clark, "When Urban Adolescents Choose Abortion: Effects on Education, Psychological Status and Subsequent Pregnancy," *Family Planning Perspectives* 21, no. 6 (November–December 1989): 248–255.

20. Joyce Ladner, *Tomorrow's Tomorrow: The Black Woman* (Garden City, N.Y.: Doubleday, 1972), p. 200.

21. Kristin Moore, Margaret Simms, and Charles Betsey, *Choice and Circumstance: Racial Differences in Adolescent Sexuality and Fertility* (New Brunswick, N.J.: Transaction Books, 1986), p. 72.

22. Ibid.

23. Allan Abrahamse, Peter A. Morrison, and Linda Waite, "Teenagers Willing to Consider Single Parenthood: Who Is at Greatest Risk?" *Family Planning Perspectives* 20, no. 1 (January–February 1988): 13–18. Their conclusion is particularly relevant in the context we are discussing here: "These data imply

that for a segment of the population that refuses to consider out-of-wedlock childbearing, single parenthood is not simply an 'accident' but is rather an avoidable outcome. Compared with young women who would consider having a child outside marriage, those who reject the idea appear better able to avoid that outcome, even when their backgrounds alone strongly predispose them toward it" (p. 16). See also Abrahamse et al., *Beyond Stereotypes*.

24. Sociologist William J. Wilson, in his book *The Truly Disadvantaged* (Chicago: University of Chicago Press, 1987), uses the phrase "concentration effects" to describe this pattern. For evidence, see Dennis Hogan and Evelyn Kitagawa, "The Impact of Social Status, Family Structure and Neighborhood on the Fertility of Black Adolescents," *American Journal of Sociology* 90 (1985): 825–855; Abrahamse et al., *Beyond Stereotypes;* Karin Brewster, "Race Differences in Sexual Activity among Adolescent Women," *American Sociological Review* 59 (1994): 408–424; Jonathan Crane, "The Epidemic Theory of Ghettos and Neighborhood Effects on Dropping Out and Childbearing," *American Journal of Sociology* 96 (1991): 1226–1259.

25. Hayes, *Risking the Future,* pp. 111–117.

26. See U.S. Congress, Office of Technology Assessment, *Healthy Children: Investing in the Future* (Washington, D.C.: Government Printing Office, 1988). Note also that due to a loophole in the Pregnancy Discrimination Act of 1978 (PL-95-555) an estimated one-third of all pregnant teenagers are not covered under their parents' private insurance. U.S. Congress, Office of Technology Assessment, *Adolescent Health,* p. 400.

27. One study (of white teenagers in Utah) has concluded that the conventional wisdom is correct: even middle-class white teens face more risks in pregnancy than do older mothers, specifically a higher rate of premature births. Since I am arguing here that the birthrate among teens responds to both socioeconomic and psychosocial factors (those that make an individual "disadvantaged and discouraged"), middle-class status alone may not disprove the selection effect. See A. M. Fraser et al., "The Association of Young Maternal Age with Adverse Reproductive Outcomes," *New England Journal of Medicine* 332, no. 17 (1995): 1113–1117. U.S. Department of Health and Human Services, National Center for Health Statistics, Division of Vital Statistics, "Advance Report of Final Natality Statistics, 1992," Monthly Vital Statistics Report 43, no. 5, supp. (October 25, 1994). This figure includes the approximately 12,000 pregnant teenagers under age fifteen, who are much less likely to get prenatal care than older teens.

28. Office of Technology Assessment, *Adolescent Health,* vol. 2, p. II-339. Makinson, "The Health Consequences of Teenage Fertility."

29. Office of Technology Assessment, *Adolescent Health,* vol. 2, p. II-339; Strobino, "The Health and Medical Consequences of Sexuality and Pregnancy," in *Risking the Future,* vol. 2, ed. Hofferth and Hayes; Kristin Moore et al., "Nonvoluntary Sexual Activity among Adolescents," *Family Planning Perspectives* 21, no. 3 (May–June 1989): 111. Researchers are still uncertain as

to whether the problems associated with very early births are physiological in nature or a result of the fact that very young women are much more socially and economically disadvantaged than other teens.

30. Frederick Jaffe, "View from the United States," in Donald Bogue, ed., *Adolescent Pregnancy* (Chicago: Community and Family Study Center, 1977), p. 22. See also Ronald Rindfuss, Larry Bumpass, and Craig St. John, "Education and Fertility: Implications for the Roles Women Occupy," *American Sociological Review* 45, no. 3 (June 1980): 434.

31. Frank Furstenberg, *Unplanned Parenthood: The Social Consequences of Teenage Parenthood* (New York: Free Press, 1976). See also Frank Furstenberg, J. Brooks-Gunn, and S. Philip Morgan, *Adolescent Mothers in Later Life* (Cambridge: Cambridge University Press, 1987); Harriet Presser, *Role and Fertility Patterns of Urban Mothers* (New York: Columbia University Press, 1976); Sandra Hofferth and Kristin Moore, "Early Childbearing and Later Economic Well-being," *American Sociological Review* 44 (1979): 784–815; J. J. Card and L. L. Wise, "Teenage Mothers and Teenage Fathers: The Impact of Early Childbearing on the Parents' Personal and Professional Lives," *Family Planning Perspectives* 10, no. 4 (1978): 199–205; Rindfuss et al., "Education and Fertility: Implications"; Margaret Marini, "The Transition to Adulthood: Sex Differences in Educational Attainment and Age at Marriage," *American Sociological Review* 43 (August 1978): 483–507; Margaret Marini, "Effects of the Timing of Marriage and First Birth on Fertility," *Journal of Marriage and the Family* 43 (1981): 27–46; H. P. Koo and R. E. Bilsbarrow, *Multivariate Effects of Age at First Birth* (Research Triangle Park, N.C.: Research Triangle, 1979). At least some of the research on the effects of childbearing among teenagers defines "education" as receipt of a formal diploma, but this definition tends to understate the amount of education that teen mothers eventually get. Some researchers have noted that when one assesses education, particularly in the case of teenage mothers, it is important to include the General Equivalency Degree (GED) as a measure, although whether the GED is exactly equivalent to a high school diploma is still subject to debate. F. L. Mott and W. Marsiglio, "Early Childbearing and the Completion of High School," *Family Planning Perspectives* 17, no. 5 (1985): 234–237. For a study which argues both that teenage mothers are more likely to obtain a GED and that the GED is not equivalent to a high school diploma, see V. Joseph Hotz et al., "The Costs and Consequences of Teenage Childbearing for Mothers," in *Kids Having Kids: A Report to the Robin Hood Foundation* (New York: Robin Hood Foundation, 1995).

32. There are, unfortunately, few studies of the way in which early childbearing affects *college* attendance. To look at this question carefully, one would need to compile data on the number of students who went on to college after completing high school and who did so after 1975, when it became illegal to expel pregnant teens and when the government instituted special policies to help keep pregnant students in school. I know of no such studies at the present

time. The data that *People* magazine refers to, as well as the data that the Alan Guttmacher Institute cites in *Sex and America's Teenagers* (p. 60), do not appear to meet these two essential criteria.

33. Hofferth asserts that much of the research on the effects of early childbearing, though of very high quality, is "limited in its sensitivity to complex relationships" ("Social and Economic Consequences of Teenage Childbearing," p. 125). This situation should change as researchers develop longitudinal data bases that are amenable to techniques such as event history analysis.

34. Phillips Cutright, "Timing of First Birth: Does It Matter?" *Journal of Marriage and the Family* 35 (1973): 585; Peter Morrison, Presentation at the Rockefeller Foundation's "Seminar on the Effects of School Dropout on Subsequent Pregnancies and Births" (Minneapolis, 1984), cited in Hofferth, "Social and Economic Consequences of Teenage Childbearing," p. 126. See also Dawn Upchurch and James McCarthy, "The Timing of a First Birth and High School Completion," *American Sociological Review* 55, no. 2 (April 1990): 224–234. Lois Weis and her colleagues found that the majority of girls who dropped out listed reasons other than pregnancy. Lois Weis et al., *Dropouts from School: Issues, Dilemmas, and Solutions* (Albany: State University of New York Press, 1989).

35. On the problem of young women who "drift" away from school, see Abrahamse et al., *Beyond Stereotypes.*

36. David Bloom and James Trussell, "What Are the Elements of Delayed Childbearing and Permanent Childlessness in the United States?" Paper presented at the meetings of the Population Association of America, April 1983; Marini, "The Transition to Adulthood: Sex Differences." As we saw in Chapter 4, many affluent Americans have been persuaded that "babies are having babies" because they themselves have delayed or forgone childbearing in order to invest in education and a career and thus pursue upward mobility.

37. Card and Wise, "Teenage Mothers and Teenage Fathers," pp. 199–205.

38. On the timing of second births, see D. F. Polit and J. R. Kahn, "Early Subsequent Pregnancy among Economically Disadvantaged Teenage Mothers," *American Journal of Public Health* 76, no. 2 (1986): 167–171; and D. S. Kalmuss and P. B. Namerow, "Subsequent Childbearing among Teenage Mothers: The Determinants of a Closely Spaced Second Birth," *Family Planning Perspectives* 26, no. 4 (1994): 149–153. On the fact that teenagers once tended to have larger families than nonteens, see James Trussell and Jane Menken, "Early Childbearing and Subsequent Fertility," *Family Planning Perspectives* 10 (July–August 1978): 209–218; F. F. Furstenberg, Jr., and A. G. Crawford, "Family Support: Helping Teenage Mothers to Cope," *Family Planning Perspectives* 10, no. 6 (1978): 322–333; S. L. Hofferth and K. A. Moore, "Early Childbearing and Later Economic Well-Being," *American Sociological Review* 44, no. 5 (1979): 784–815; L. L. Bumpass, R. R. Rindfuss, and R. B. Janosik, "Age and Marital Status at First Birth and the Pace of Subsequent Fertility," *Demography* 15, no. 1 (1978): 75–86. On the fact

that teenagers are tending to have smaller families, see S. Millman and G. Hendershot, "Early Fertility and Lifetime Fertility," *Family Planning Perspectives* 12 (May–June 1980): 139–149.

39. *Ordway v. Hargraves,* 323 F. Supp. (1971); Title IX of the Educational Amendments of 1972. Title IX not only outlawed summary expulsion of pregnant teens; it also facilitated (and in some cases was interpreted as mandating) special programs to help them get an education, thus reducing the "push" effect that led them to drop out and increasing the "pull" effect that induced them to stay in school.

40. Dawn Upchurch and James McCarthy, "Adolescent Childbearing and High School Completion in the 1980s: Have Things Changed?" *Family Planning Perspectives* 21, no. 5 (September–October 1980): 200.

41. Hayes, *Risking the Future,* vol. 1, p. 126; F. F. Furstenberg and A. G. Crawford, "Family Support: Helping Teenage Mothers to Cope," *Family Planning Perspectives* 10 (November–December 1978): 322–333.

42. There is a great deal of qualitative literature (see text of this chapter for an overview), but researchers have devoted much less attention to determining the specific effects of race. John Ogbu has argued that being a member of a "subordinate minority" (as opposed to a member of an "immigrant minority") can have a powerful influence, yet this insight has not been systematically pursued. A noteworthy exception to this gap in the literature is Kristin Moore, Margaret Simms, and Charles Betsey, *Choice and Circumstance: Racial Differences in Adolescent Sexuality and Fertility,* which uses longitudinal, quantitative data in an imaginative way.

43. Upchurch and McCarthy, "Adolescent Childbearing and High School Completion," p. 201.

44. See Card and Wise, "Teenage Mothers and Teenage Fathers," p. 503.

45. Kristin Moore and Martha Burt, *Private Crisis and Public Cost: Policy Perspectives on Teenage Childbearing* (Washington, D.C.: Urban Institute, 1982); Frank Furstenberg et al., *Adolescent Mothers in Later Life.*

46. Arline T. Geronimus and Sanders Korenman, "The Socioeconomic Consequences of Teenage Childbearing Reconsidered," Paper 90-190, Population Studies Center, University of Michigan, 1990. See also Arline T. Geronimus and Sanders Korenman, "The Socioeconomic Consequences of Teen Childbearing Reconsidered," National Bureau of Economic Research, Working Paper 3701 (Cambridge, Mass.: National Bureau of Economic Research, 1991). For an equally clever study comparing teenagers who had miscarriages with those who gave birth, see V. Joseph Hotz et al., "The Costs and Consequences of Teenage Childbearing for Mothers," pp. 1–130. Hotz found that teenage mothers had lower rates of high school graduation but higher rates of GED completion, and that younger teenage mothers were less likely to graduate than older teen mothers—that is, those who were eighteen or nineteen when they gave birth.

47. For example, see Saul Hoffman, Michael Foster, and Frank Furstenberg,

"Reevaluating the Costs of Teenage Childbearing (Comment)," *Demography* 30, no. 1 (1993): 1–13; Greg Duncan and Saul Hoffman, "Teenage Welfare Receipt and Subsequent Dependence among Black Adolescent Mothers," *Family Planning Perspectives* 22, no. 1 (1990): 16–20. For another study that queries the validity of the Geronimus-Korenman sample, see Kristin Moore, *Teenage Childbearing: No Problem?* (Washington, D.C.: Child Trends, 1991).

48. Kristin Moore and Sandra Hofferth, "Factors Affecting Early Family Formation: A Path Model," *Population and Environment* 3, no. 1 (1980): 73–98.

49. Upchurch and McCarthy, "The Timing of a First Birth," p. 229.

50. Gordon Berlin and Andrew Sum, *Toward a More Perfect Union: Basic Skills, Poor Families, and Our Economic Future* (New York: Ford Foundation, 1988).

51. In the studies that looked at pairs of sisters, this was an even more daunting problem. The number of pairs of sisters who meet the criterion (that one sister be a teenage mother and the other not) is small, and the explanatory power of such studies is thus limited.

52. For an ethnographic account of how schools "produce" dropouts, see Michele Fine, *Framing Dropouts: Notes on the Politics of an Urban Public High School* (Albany: State University of New York Press, 1991). For a heart-rending journalistic account of how these forces play out in young women's lives, see Peggy Orenstein, *School Girls: Young Women, Self Esteem and the Confidence Gap* (New York: Doubleday, 1994). On the way in which schools systematically fail young women, see Myra Sadker and David Sadker, *Failing at Fairness: How America's Schools Cheat Girls* (New York: Scribner's, 1994). The issue of gender and schooling is more complex than it appears at first glance: although young women may face subtle pressures that make it harder for them to compete, they still are more likely to graduate from high school than are young men.

53. Martha Burt, *Estimates of Public Costs for Teenage Childbearing* (Washington, D.C.: Center for Population Options, 1986).

54. U.S. Congressional Budget Office, *Sources of Support for Adolescent Mothers* (Washington, D.C.: Government Printing Office, 1990), p. 55.

55. U.S. House of Representatives, Committee on Ways and Means, *Overview of Entitlement Programs* (Green Book) (Washington, D.C.: Government Printing Office, 1994), p. 366, Table 10-11.

56. Robert Moffitt, "Incentive Effects of the U.S. Welfare System: A Review," *Journal of Economic Literature* 30 (1992): 1-61.

57. U.S. House of Representatives, Committee on Ways and Means, *Overview of Entitlement Programs,* p. 325, Table 10-1.

58. Moffitt, "Incentive Effects of the U.S. Welfare System."

59. U.S. House of Representatives, Committee on Ways and Means, *Overview of Entitlement Programs,* p. 1111; Moffitt, "Incentive Effects of the U.S. Welfare System," p. 4.

60. K. A. Moore and S. Caldwell, "The Effect of Government Policies on Out-of-Wedlock Sex and Pregnancy," *Family Planning Perspectives* 9, no. 4

(1977): 164–169; D. Ellwood and M. J. Bane, *The Impact of AFDC on Family Structure and Living Arrangements* (Cambridge, Mass.: Harvard University Press, 1984); K. A. Moore, *Policy Determinants of Teenage Childbearing: Final Report to the National Institute of Child Health and Human Development* (Washington, D.C.: Urban Institute, 1980); B. Field, "A Socio-Economic Analysis of Out-of-Wedlock Birth among Teenagers," in K. Scott, T. Field, and E. G. Robertson, eds., *Teenage Parents and Their Offspring* (New York: Grune and Stratton, 1981); B. Janowitz, "Why Do Projections of the Cost of Family Planning Differ So Widely?" *Studies in Family Planning* 24, no. 1 (1993): 62–65.

61. Constance Sorrentino, "The Changing Family in International Perspective," *Monthly Labor Review* 113, no. 3 (1990): 41–58; U.S. Department of Health, Education, and Welfare, Social Security Administration, "The Relation of Social Security Spending Expenditures of GNP in Forty-Five Countries," *Social Security Bulletin* 28, no. 30 (1965).

62. There is a very large literature on this effect. See Phillips Cutright, "Illegitimacy: Myths, Causes and Cures," *Family Planning Perspectives* 3 (January 1971): 26–48. See also notes 63 and 65, below.

63. H. Ross and Isabel Sawhill, *Time of Transition: The Growth of Families Headed by Women* (Washington, D.C.: Urban Institute, 1975); Harriet Presser, "Early Motherhood: Ignorance or Bliss?" *Family Planning Perspectives* 6, no. 8 (1974): 14; Kristin Moore and S. Caldwell, "The Effect of Government Policies on Out-of-Wedlock Sex and Pregnancy," *Family Planning Perspectives* 9 (July–August 1977); David Ellwood and Mary Jo Bane, *The Impact of AFDC on Family Structure and Living Arrangements.*

64. Irwin Garfinkel and Sara McLanahan, *Single Mothers and Their Children* (Washington, D.C.: Urban Institute Press, 1986), pp. 124–127.

65. Robert Plotnik, "Marriage and Out-of-Wedlock Childbearing; Evidence from the 1990s," *Journal of Marriage and the Family* 53, no. 3 (1990): 735–746; Shelley Lundberg and Robert Plotnik, "Effects of State Welfare, Abortion and Family Planning Policies on Premarital Childbearing by White Adolescents," *Family Planning Perspectives* 22, no. 6 (1990): 246–251; Saul Duncan and Greg Hoffman, "Teenage Welfare Receipt and Subsequent Dependence among Black Adolescent Mothers," *Family Planning Perspectives* 22, no. 1 (1989): 16–20; Saul Duncan and Greg Hoffman, "Welfare Benefits, Economic Opportunities and Out-of-Wedlock Births among Black Teenage Girls," *Demography* 27, no. 4 (1990): 519–535.

66. Alan Guttmacher Institute, *Sex and America's Teenagers,* p. 61.

67. On the effects of marriage, see Elizabeth Thomson, Thomas L. Hanson, and Sara McLanahan, "Family Structure and Child Well-Being: Economic Resources versus Parental Behaviors," *Social Forces* 73, no. 1 (September 1994): 221–242; and Lynne Casper, Sara McLanahan, and Irwin Garfinkel, "The Gender-Poverty Gap: What We Can Learn from Other Countries," *American Sociological Review* 59, no. 4 (August 1994): 594–606.

68. W. Baldwin and V. S. Cain, "The Children of Teenage Parents," *Family*

Planning Perspectives 12, no. 1 (1980): 34–43; Moore et al., *Choice and Circumstance;* F. F. Furstenberg et al., "The Children of Teenage Mothers: Patterns of Early Childbearing in Two Generations," *Family Planning Perspectives* 22, no. 2 (1990): 54–61. On abuse and neglect: E. M. Kinard and L. V. Klerman, "Teenage Parenting and Child Abuse: Are They Related?" *American Journal of Orthopsychiatry* 50, no. 3 (1980): 481–488; O. Sahler, "Adolescent Parenting: Potential for Child Abuse and Neglect?" *Pediatric Annals* 9 (1980): 67–75.

69. Furstenberg et al., *Adolescent Mothers in Later Life.*

70. C. D. Hayes, ed., *Risking the Future: Adolescent Sexuality, Pregnancy and Childbearing* (Washington, D.C.: National Academy Press, 1987). Note that Furstenberg did control for background differences.

71. Arline T. Geronimus, Sanders Korenman, and Marianne M. Hillemeier, "Does Young Maternal Age Adversely Affect Child Development? Evidence from Cousin Comparisons in the United States," *Population and Development Review* 20, no. 3 (September 1994): 585–611.

72. Furstenberg, *Unplanned Parenthood;* Furstenberg et al., *Adolescent Mothers in Later Life,* p. 99.

73. Furstenberg et al., *Adolescent Mothers in Later Life,* p. 8.

6. Why Do They Do It?

1. In this chapter I examine every ethnographic account I could find concerning the way in which teenagers think about their pregnancies. By "ethnographic account" I mean the sort of narrative produced by a researcher who observes or interviews young people in a naturalistic setting and then renders their life experience, often in their own words. Most such narratives are doctoral dissertations (the problem of early pregnancy having spawned its own research genre), although a few are published—usually journalistic—accounts. The notes in this chapter cite a number of both types. For other journalistic accounts, see Leon Dash, *When Children Want Children: The Urban Crisis of Teenage Childbearing* (New York: William Morrow, 1989); and Sharon Thompson, "Pregnant on Purpose: Choosing Teenage Motherhood," *Village Voice,* December 23, 1986.

2. Donna Ewy and Rodger Ewy, *Teen Pregnancy—The Challenges We Faced, The Choices We Made: Teens Talk to Teens about What It's Really Like to Have a Baby* (New York: Signet, 1984), p. 135.

3. Ibid., p. 142.

4. Dash, *When Children Want Children,* p. 72.

5. Ewy and Ewy, *Teen Pregnancy,* p. 212.

6. Kathleen Thornton, "Comprehensive Evaluation of a Teen Pregnancy and Parenting Program" (Diss., University of Pennsylvania, 1992), p. 196.

7. Elaine Kaplan, "The Lure of Motherhood" (Diss., University of California at Berkeley, 1988). Kaplan is just the most recent scholar to have made this point. For lists of her predecessors, see Frank Furstenberg, *Unplanned Par-*

enthood (New York: Free Press, 1976); and Joyce Ladner, *Tomorrow's Tomorrow: The Black Woman* (Garden City, N.Y.: Doubleday, 1971).

8. For an overview, see Larry Bumpass and James A. Sweet, "Children's Experience in Single-Parent Families: Implications of Cohabitation and Marital Transition," *Family Planning Perspectives* 21, no. 6 (1989): 256–260. On visits by divorced fathers and never-married fathers, see Sara McLanahan and Gary Sandefur, *Growing Up with a Single Parent: What Hurts, What Helps* (Cambridge, Mass.: Harvard University Press, 1994), p. 97. On child support payments, see U.S. Census Bureau, "Child Support and Alimony," *Current Population Reports,* 1990, 1972. On the willingness of never-married fathers to live with or spend time with their children, see David Eggebeen et al., "Patterns of Adult Male Coresidence among Young Children of Adolescent Mothers," *Family Planning Perspectives* 22, no. 5 (September–October 1990): 219–223; Janet Hardy et al., "Fathers of Children Born to Young Mothers," *Family Planning Perspectives* 21, no. 4 (July–August 1989): 159–165; and Robert Lerman and Theodora Ooms, *Young Unwed Fathers* (Philadelphia: Temple University Press, 1993).

9. Manufacturing jobs, especially unionized ones, are declining at the same time that service jobs, particularly those that were traditionally female, are increasing. Much the same process occurred during the Depression, when, despite cultural caveats that women should not work, many jobs existed in the service sector yet men would not cross invisible gender barriers to take them.

10. The term "stalled revolution" is from Arlie Hochschild, *The Second Shift: Inside the Two-Job Marriage* (New York: Viking, 1989).

11. Arland Thornton, "Changing Attitudes towards Family Issues in the United States," *Journal of Marriage and the Family* 51 (1989): 873–893; Frances Goldsheider and Linda Waite, *No Families, New Families: The Transformation of the American Home* (Berkeley: University of California Press, 1991).

12. Laurie Ann McDade, "Community Responses to Teenage Pregnancy and Parenting: An Ethnography of a Social Problem" (Diss., Rutgers University, 1987), p. 105.

13. Sandy K. Dunn, "Fertility Decision Making among Young Mothers" (Diss., University of Florida, 1985), p. 201.

14. Brenda Schwab, "Someone to Always Be There: Teenage Childbearing as an Adaptive Strategy in Rural New England" (Diss., Brandeis University, 1983), p. 132.

15. McDade, "Community Responses," p. 287.

16. Ibid., p. 276.

17. The analogy between drug use and sexual activity among teens is made in William Galston, "A Liberal Democratic Case for the Two Parent Family," *Responsive Community* 1, no. 1 (Winter 1990–1991): 14–26. The plea for "a little virginity" was made in a full-page advertisement purchased by the conservative advocacy group Focus on the Family. The ad, which appeared in 1991 and 1992, ran in newspapers nationwide, including the *Los Angeles*

Times, the *New York Times,* the *Chicago Tribune,* the *Wichita Eagle,* and the *St. Louis Post-Dispatch.* Unfortunately, the much-vaunted campaign against drug use among teens has had at best only temporary success. See U.S. General Accounting Office, "Teenage Drug Use," Report to the Select Committee on Narcotic Abuse and Control, U.S. House of Representatives, January 1991; and Department of Health and Human Services, Public Health Service, "Survey Results on Drug Use from the *Monitoring the Future* Study" (Ann Arbor: University of Michigan, 1992). This is to say not that public campaigns to persuade people to change their behavior are useless, but that such campaigns typically have only sporadic and limited success.

18. Dash, *When Children Want Children,* pp. 124–125.
19. Ewy and Ewy, *Teen Pregnancy,* p. 243.
20. Ibid., p. 243.
21. Ibid., p. 251.
22. Kaplan, "The Lure of Motherhood," p. 146.
23. Katharine G. Herr, "An Ethnographic Study of Adolescent Pregnancy in an Urban High School" (Diss., Ohio State University, 1988), p. 146.
24. Mary S. Nelums, "Antecedents to Teenage Pregnancy" (Diss., University of Illinois at Chicago, 1989), p. 63.
25. Jill Taylor, "Development of Self, Moral Voice, and the Meaning of Adolescent Motherhood" (Diss., Harvard University, 1989), p. 84.
26. Constance Willard Williams, "An Acceptable Life: Pregnancy and Childbearing from the Black Teen Mother's Perspective" (Diss., Brandeis University, 1989), p. 99.
27. Dash, *When Children Want Children,* p. 68.
28. Nelums, "Antecedents to Teenage Pregnancy," p. 63.
29. Herr, "An Ethnographic Study," p. 127.
30. Ibid., p. 154.
31. Daniel Scott Smith, "The Long Cycle in American Illegitimacy and Prenuptial Pregnancy," in Peter Laslett et al., eds., *Bastardy and Its Comparative History* (Cambridge, Mass.: Harvard University Press, 1980).
32. Ira Reiss, *Premarital Sexual Standards in America* (New York: Free Press, 1960). See also Ira Reiss and Gary Lee, *Family Systems in America* (New York: Holt, Rinehart and Winston), p. 133.
33. United Nations, Department of International Economic and Social Affairs, "Adolescent Reproductive Behavior: Evidence from Developed Countries," *Population Studies* 1, no. 109 (1988): 47. Elise Jones et al., *Teenage Pregnancy in Industrialized Countries* (New Haven: Yale University Press, 1989), pp. 21–36.
34. United Nations, "Adolescent Reproductive Behavior," p. 49.
35. Kenji Hayashi, "Adolescent Sexual Activities and Fertility in Japan," *Bulletin of the Institute for Public Health* 32 (1983): 88–94, Table 9; and Kenji Hayashi, "Sex Education in Japan," *Acta Paediactrica Japonica* 27 (1985): 349–354.

36. On variations in contraceptive policies in European countries, see United Nations, "Adolescent Reproductive Behavior"; and Elise Jones et al., *Teenage Pregnancy in Industrialized Countries*. On federal funding see Leighton Ku, *Financing of Family Planning Services in Publicly Supported Family Planning Services in the United States* (Washington, D.C.: Urban Institute and Child Trends, Inc., 1993).

37. *Current Population Survey* (1991), Table 143, "Marriage Rates and Median Age at First Marriage." In 1988 the median age at first marriage was 23.7 for women and 25.5 for men.

38. Perhaps they *should* be considered a problem. Although there may be a selection effect (that is, teens who choose to marry may be different in significant ways from those who do not), married teens are more likely to drop out of school, more likely to drop out of the job market, and more likely to have a second child soon after the first. If the marriage ends after the first child is born (and marriages among teenagers tend to be even more fragile than is usual nowadays), the married teen mother is, ironically, more disadvantaged than her unmarried peer because wives in general fare badly after divorce.

39. Jacqueline D. Forrest and Susheela Singh, "The Sexual and Reproductive Behavior of American Women, 1982, 1988," *Family Planning Perspectives* 22 (1990): 206–214.

40. Ibid., p. 209.

41. Calculated from Sandra Hofferth and Cheryl Hayes, eds., *Risking the Future: Adolescent Sexuality, Pregnancy, and Childbearing*, vol. 2: *Working Papers and Statistical Appendix* (Washington, D.C.: National Academy Press, 1987), pp. A-62, A-63.

42. This is shown most clearly in Alan Guttmacher Institute, *Sex and America's Teenagers* (New York: Alan Guttmacher Institute, 1994), p. 41, Figure 30: "Decline and Rise in Pregnancy Rates."

43. Hofferth and Hayes, eds., *Risking the Future*, vol. 2, pp. A-62, A-63; National Center for Health Statistics, *Advance Report of Final Natality Statistics*, vols. 23–42, Supplements 1974 to 1994.

44. On the fact that people who are older when they first have intercourse are more adept at using contraceptives, see John Kantner and Melvin Zelnik, "Sexual Experience of Young Unmarried Women in the United States," *Family Planning Perspectives* 4 (1972): 9–18; Melvin Zelnik and John Kantner, "Sexual and Contraceptive Experience of Young Unmarried Women in the United States, 1971 and 1976," *Family Planning Perspectives* 9 (1977): 55–71; Laurie Zabin and S. D. Clark, "Why They Delay: A Study of Teenage Family Planning Clinic Patients," *Family Planning Perspectives* 13 (1981): 205–217. On the fact that women with higher educational aspirations are more inclined to use contraceptives, see Zelnik et al., *Sex and Pregnancy in Adolescence* (Beverly Hills, Calif.: Sage, 1981); R. F. Wertheimer and K. A.

Moore, *Teenage Childbearing: Public Sector Costs,* Final Report on Contract no. NO1-HD-92822, submitted to the Center for Population Research, National Institute of Child Health and Human Development (Washington, D.C.: Urban Institute, 1982); George Cvetkovich and Barbara Grote, "Psychosocial Development and the Social Problems of Teenage Illegitimacy," in Catherine S. Chilman, ed., *Adolescent Pregnancy and Childbearing: Findings from Research* (Washington, D.C.: U.S. Department of Health and Human Services, 1980).

45. Larry Bumpass and James Sweet, "Children's Experience in Single-Parent Families: Implications of Cohabitation and Marital Transitions," *Family Planning Perspectives* 21, no. 6 (1989): 256–260. See also Larry Bumpass, "Children and Marital Disruptions: A Replication and Update," *Demography* 21 (1984): 71.

46. Melvin Zelnik, "Sexual Activity among Adolescents: Perspective of a Decade," in Elizabeth McAnarney, ed., *Premature Adolescent Pregnancy and Parenthood* (New York: Grune and Stratton, 1983), pp. 29–32; Alan Guttmacher Institute, *Sex and America's Teenagers,* p. 29.

47. A. Torres and S. Singh, "Contraceptive Practice among Hispanic Adolescents," *Family Planning Perspectives* 18 (1989): 193–194.

48. Ibid. See also James Trussell and Barbara Vaughan, "Selected Results Concerning Sexual Behavior and Contraceptive Use from the 1988 National Survey of Family Growth and the 1988 National Survey of Adolescent Males," Office of Population Research, Working paper no. 91-12 (September 1991).

49. Based on an analysis of the 1988 National Survey of Family Growth; see Jane Mauldon and Kristin Luker, "Contraception at First Sex: The Effects of Sex Education," Working paper no. 206, Graduate School of Public Policy, University of California, Berkeley, 1994. On class, see Alan Guttmacher Institute, *Sex and America's Teenagers,* p. 34.

50. K. Kost and J. Forrest, "American Women's Sexual Behavior and Exposure to Risk of Sexually Transmitted Diseases," *Family Planning Perspectives* 24 (1992): 100–106.

51. M. M. Koenig and Melvin Zelnik, "The Risk of Premarital First Pregnancy among Metropolitan American Teenagers: 1976 and 1979," *Family Planning Perspectives* 14 (1982): 239–248.

52. Kristin Moore, Christine Winquist, and James L. Peterson, "Involuntary Sexual Activity among Adolescents," *Family Planning Perspectives* 21 (1989): 110–114. The data come from the National Survey of Children, in which a nationally representative group of children ranging in age from seven to eleven were interviewed several times between 1976 and 1987, by which time they ranged in age from eighteen to twenty-two. It is not clear from the data whether the interviewees were reporting sexual coercion by men or women; other limited data suggest that regardless of the sex of the victim, the person

doing the coercing is most often male. See E. Laumann et al., *The Social Organization of Sexuality: Sexual Practices in the United States* (Chicago: University of Chicago Press, 1994), p. 336.

53. See Susan Estrich, *Real Rape: How The Legal System Victimizes Women Who Say No* (Cambridge, Mass.: Harvard University Press, 1987).

54. See Ira Reiss, *Premarital Sexual Standards in America: A Sociological Investigation of the Relative Social and Cultural Integration of American Sexual Standards* (Glencoe: Free Press, 1964).

55. Religious teenagers are less likely to engage in sex, but teenagers who are sexually active become less religious. See A. Thornton and D. Camburn, "Religious Participation and Adolescent Sexual Behavior and Attitudes," *Journal of Marriage and the Family* 51 (1989): 641–653.

56. Based on calculations by Jane Mauldon and Kristin Luker, using data from the National Survey of Family Growth. See Mauldon and Luker, "Contraception at First Sex," p. 27.

57. K. Kost and J. D. Forrest, "American Women's Sexual Behavior and Exposure to Risk of Sexually Transmitted Disease," *Family Planning Perspectives* 24 (1992): 248; Alan Guttmacher Institute, *Sex and America's Teenagers,* p. 32.

58. McDade, "Community Responses," p. 264.

59. Kaplan, "The Lure of Motherhood," p. 101.

60. Ewy and Ewy, *Teen Pregnancy,* p. 264.

61. Sharon Thompson, "Search for Tomorrow: On Feminism and the Reconstruction of Teen Romance," in Carole S. Vance, ed., *Pleasure and Danger: Exploring Female Sexuality* (Boston: Routledge & Kegan Paul, 1984).

62. Alan Guttmacher Institute, *Sex and America's Teenagers,* p. 53. Data are from the 1988 National Maternal and Infant Health Survey.

63. Zelnik and Kantner, "Sexual and Contraceptive Experience of Young Unmarried Women"; Zabin and Clark, "Why They Delay"; J. P. Hornick et al., "Premarital Contraceptive Usage among Male and Female Adolescents," *Family Coordinator* 28 (1979): 181–190; E. W. Freeman et al., "Adolescent Contraceptive Use: Comparisons of Male and Female Attitudes and Information," *American Journal of Public Health* 70 (1980): 790–797.

64. Zabin and Clark, "Why They Delay."

65. For an overview, see Sandra Hofferth, "Contraceptive Decision-Making among Adolescents," in Hofferth and Hayes, eds., *Risking the Future,* vol. 2, pp. 56–77.

66. For instance, calculations from the 1988 National Survey of Family Growth suggest that 58 percent of black teens are on the Pill, compared to 45 percent of white teens. Mauldon and Luker, "Contraception at First Sex."

67. Michelle Fine, personal communication.

68. Dash, *When Children Want Children,* p. 11.

69. Ibid., p. 164.

70. McDade, "Community Responses," p. 263.

71. Thornton, "Comprehensive Evaluation," p. 168.

72. Kaplan, "The Lure of Motherhood," p. 140.
73. Ibid.
74. Schwab, "Someone to Always Be There," pp. 182–183.
75. Ewy and Ewy, *Teen Pregnancy,* p. 24.
76. Alan Guttmacher Institute, *Sex and America's Teenagers,* p. 43. Data are for unmarried teens under age nineteen and are from the 1988 National Maternal and Infant Health Survey.
77. Prior to 1982, only married women were interviewed, although in the two previous cycles (1973 and 1976) unmarried mothers were included if their children were living with them. Thus, we have data on unmarried women only for 1982 and 1988. Among married women aged nineteen and under, 33 percent reported that their pregnancies resulted in intended births.
78. Linda B. Williams and William F. Pratt, *Wanted and Unwanted Childbearing in the United States, 1973–1988* (Hyattsville, Md.: National Center for Health Statistics, 1990), p. 2.
79. Linda B. Williams and William F. Pratt, "Number of Children Born in the Last Five Years to Never-Married Women 15–44 Years of Age and Percent Distribution by Wantedness Status, according to Age and Race of Mother: United States, 1982 and 1988." Note that births are aggregated over the five-year span.
80. Ibid., p. 5, Table 4.
81. In 1988 a number of pregnant women aged fifteen to nineteen were asked if their pregnancy was accidental. Those who said yes included 93 percent of the teenagers from high-income homes, 83 percent of those from poor homes, and 79 percent of those from low-income homes. Among older women this pattern is inverted. See Alan Guttmacher Institute, *Sex and America's Teenagers,* p. 82, no. 163.
82. For an overview, see Cheryl Hayes, ed., *Risking the Future: Adolescent Sexuality, Pregnancy, and Childbearing* (Washington, D.C.: National Academy Press, 1987), vol. 1, pp. 112–113; See also Allan F. Abrahamse, Peter A. Morrison, and Linda Waite, *Beyond Stereotypes: Who Becomes A Single Teenage Mother?* (Santa Monica, Calif.: Rand Corporation, 1988); J. Evans et al., "Teenagers: Fertility Control Behavior and Attitudes before and after Abortion, Childbearing, or Negative Pregnancy Test," *Family Planning Perspectives* 8 (1976): 192–200; M. Eisen et al., "Factors Discriminating Pregnancy Resolution Decisions of Unmarried Adolescents," *Genetic Psychology Monographs* 108 (1983): 69–95; Zelnik et al., *Sex and Pregnancy in Adolescence;* R. W. Blum and M. D. Resnick, "Adolescent Sexual Decision-Making: Contraception, Pregnancy, Abortion and Motherhood," *Pediatric Annals* 11 (1982): 797–805.
83. See Rachel Benson Gold, *Abortion and Women's Health* (New York: Alan Guttmacher Institute, 1990); Alan Guttmacher Institute, *Sex and America's Teenagers,* p. 82.
84. M. Eisen and G. Zellman, "Factors Predicting Pregnancy Resolution Decision

and Satisfaction of Unmarried Adolescents," *Genetic Psychology* 108 (1983): 69–95; R. Rosen, "Adolescent Pregnancy Decision-Making: Are Parents Important?" *Adolescence* 15 (1980): 43–54.

85. Ewy and Ewy, *Teen Pregnancy,* p. 213.

86. Kaplan, "The Lure of Motherhood," p. 143.

87. Eisen and Zellman, "Factors Predicting Pregnancy Resolution Decision and Satisfaction of Unmarried Adolescents"; R. W. Blum and M. D. Resnick, "Adolescent Sexual Decision-Making: Contraception, Pregnancy, Abortion and Motherhood," *Pediatric Annals* 11 (1982): 797–805.

88. Gold, *Abortion and Women's Health,* p. 25; S. K. Henshaw, J. D. Forrest, and J. Van Vort, "Abortion Services in the United States, 1984 and 1985," *Family Planning Perspectives* 19 (1987): 63.

89. Carol Korenbrot et al., "Trends in Rates of Live Births and Abortions Following State Restrictions on Public Funding of Abortion," *Public Health Reports* 105 (1990): 555–562; Centers for Disease Control, "Effects of Restricting Federal Funds for Abortion: Texas," *Morbidity and Mortality Weekly Reports* (1980); James Trussell et al., "The Impact of Restricting Medicaid Financing for Abortion," *Family Planning Perspectives* 12 (1980): 120–130; G. L. Rubin, I. Gold, and W. Cates, "Response of Low-Income Women and Abortion Facilities to Restriction of Public Funds," *American Journal of Public Health* 69 (1979): 948–950.

90. People who believe that life begins at conception regard *all* abortions as reprehensible: for them, the argument that abortion becomes more objectionable as the fetus develops is irrelevant and false. However, a very large sector of the American public, possibly the majority, believes that the rights and wrongs of abortion must be weighed in context, and that the context includes the stage of gestation. According to this view, an embryo that is a day old has less standing than one of twelve weeks, which in turn has less standing than one of six months. The much-criticized framework presented in *Roe v. Wade,* in which the permissibility of abortion diminishes in each succeeding trimester of a pregnancy, captures something important about many people's intuitions. Thus, the *Roe* decision is not on a "collision course with itself," as Justice Sandra Day O'Connor seems to think. See Kristin Luker, *Abortion and the Politics of Motherhood* (Berkeley: University of California Press, 1984). On the abortion rates of married teens, see S. K. Henshaw, "Abortion Trends in 1987–1988: Age and Race," *Family Planning Perspectives* 24 (1992): 85–86.

91. S. K. Henshaw and K. Kost, "Parental Involvement in Minors' Abortion Decisions," *Family Planning Perspectives* 24 (1992): 196–207.

92. M. O'Connell and C. Rogers, "Out-of-Wedlock Births, Premarital Pregnancies and Their Effect on Family Formation and Dissolution," *Family Planning Perspectives* 16 (1984): 58.

93. Ibid.

94. Ibid., p. 160. See also Elizabeth Cooksey, "Factors in the Resolution of

Adolescent Premarital Pregnancies," *Demography* 27, no. 2 (May 1990): 207–218.

95. William Marsiglio, "Adolescent Fathers in the United States: Their Initial Living Arrangements, Marital Experience, and Educational Outcomes," *Family Planning Perspectives* 19 (1987): 240.

96. Bumpass and Sweet, "Children's Experience in Single-Parent Families."

97. On the declining marriageability of African American men, see William J. Wilson, *The Truly Disadvantaged: The Inner City, the Underclass and Public Policy* (Chicago: University of Chicago Press, 1987). On attitudinal factors, see Arland Thornton, "Changing Attitudes towards Separation and Divorce: Causes and Consequences," *American Journal of Sociology* 90 (1985): 856–872. On women's increasing economic independence, the best source is Gary Becker, *A Treatise on the Family* (Cambridge, Mass.: Harvard University Press, 1991). For studies that try to weigh the "availability" thesis and the "women's economic independence" thesis, see R. D. Mare and C. Winship, "Socioeconomic Change and the Decline in Marriage for Blacks and Whites," in Christopher Jencks and Paul Petersen, eds., *The Urban Underclass* (Washington, D.C.: Brookings Institution, 1991), pp. 175–202; D. T. Lichter et al., "Race and the Retreat from Marriage: A Shortage of Marriageable Men?" *American Sociological Review* 57 (1992): 781–799; and D. T. Lichter et al., "Local Marriage Markets and the Marital Behavior of Black and White Women," *American Journal of Sociology* 96 (1991): 843–867.

98. Williams, p. 163.

99. Schwab, "Someone to Always Be There," p. 134.

100. Ewy and Ewy, *Teen Parenthood*, p. 217.

101. Ibid., p. 164.

102. Ibid., p. 216.

103. Schwab, "Someone to Always Be There," p. 156.

104. Ewy and Ewy, *Teen Pregnancy*, pp. 216–217.

105. Dash, *When Children Want Children*, p. 217.

106. Sara McLanahan and Lynne Caspar, "The American Family in 1990: Growing Diversity and Inequality." See also M. Belinda Tucker and Claudia Mitchell-Kernan, eds., *The Decline in Marriage among African Americans* (New York: Russell Sage, 1995).

107. Ibid., Table 1.3.

108. *Vital Statistics of the United States*. Code is for race of child.

109. Some historians argue that in the early 1900s ideologies of "redemptive motherhood" encouraged—and in some cases insisted—that women keep their babies. See Constance Nathanson, *Dangerous Passage: The Social Control of Sexuality in Women's Adolescence* (Philadelphia: Temple University Press, 1991); Regina Kunzel, *Fallen Women, Problem Girls: Unmarried Mothers and the Professionalization of Social Work, 1890–1945* (New Haven: Yale University Press, 1993); Rickie Solinger, *Wake Up Little Susie: Single Pregnancy and Race before "Roe v. Wade"* (New York: Routledge, 1992).

110. See Winifred Bell, *Aid to Dependent Children* (New York: Columbia University Press, 1965); and Solinger, *Wake Up Little Susie.*

111. C. A. Bachrach, "Adoption Plans, Adopted Children, and Adoptive Mothers," *Journal of Marriage and the Family* 48 (1986): 243; C. A. Bachrach, K. S. Stolley, and K. A. London, "Relinquishment of Premarital Births: Evidence from National Survey Data," *Family Planning Perspectives* 24 (1992): 26.

112. What remains is the Voluntary Cooperative Information System, run by a nonprofit social agency called the American Public Welfare System. It collects data on a voluntary basis from agencies that handle adoptions; but since many adoptions are not arranged through agencies, the data are very incomplete. See Hayes, ed., *Risking the Future.*

113. Bachrach, "Adoption Plans, Adopted Children, and Adoptive Mothers."

114. Ibid.

115. See L. J. Grow, "Today's Unmarried Mothers: The Choices Have Changed," *Child Welfare* 58 (1979): 363.

116. Ewy and Ewy, *Teen Pregnancy,* p. 22.

117. Schwab, "Someone to Always Be There," p. 187.

118. Ewy and Ewy, *Teen Pregnancy,* p. 221.

119. These are both worrisome outcomes, but not necessarily for the traditional reasons. Since American society has not been able to reach a consensus on abortion, abortions are expensive and politically controversial; women who seek them are subject to harassment and intimidation. Very few people would claim that abortion is a good first choice. The real problem in American society is the extent to which men seem to have retreated from a commitment to their children, both within and outside marriage. To the extent that marriage creates ties between men and children, a child born out of wedlock is at a comparative disadvantage.

120. A quick way to see this is to examine the *Statistical Abstract of the United States* for 1994. Table 113, "Abortions by Selected Characteristics, 1973–1988," shows that teenagers in 1988 had about 25 percent of all abortions in that year; women aged twenty to twenty-four had 33 percent; women aged twenty-five to twenty-nine had 22 percent; and women over twenty-nine had the remaining 20 percent. Thus, abortions were spread throughout the reproductive life span. Likewise, Table 101, "Births to Unmarried Mothers, by Race of Child and Age of Mother, 1970–1990," demonstrates that in 1990 teens had 30 percent of all births out of wedlock; women aged twenty to twenty-four had 35 percent; women aged twenty-five to twenty-nine had 20 percent; and women over thirty had 15 percent. Again, births out of wedlock, like abortions, occurred throughout the reproductive life cycle. *Statistical Abstract of the United States* (Washington, D.C.: Government Printing Office, 1994).

121. National Center for Health Statistics, *Monthly Vital Statistics Report,* 41, 6, Supp. November 16, 1992. Figures on abortions are from S. K. Henshaw and J. Van Vort, eds., *Abortion Factbook, 1992 Edition: Readings, Trends and State and Local Data to 1988* (New York: Alan Guttmacher Institute, 1992).

122. As a point of comparison: in the 1985–1987 period, abortion rates per thousand women aged fifteen to forty-four ranged from 10.2 in Canada, to 13.2 in France, to 14.2 in England and Wales, to 18.6 in Japan, to 19.8 in Sweden. The United States has no official rate, since data are not routinely reported to Vital Statistics. Two "surveillance" reports, however, one from the Center for Disease Control and the other from the Alan Guttmacher Institute, are thought to give reasonably reliable estimates. In 1985 the Center for Disease Control estimated that the abortion rate for American women aged fifteen to forty-four was 23.8; the Guttmacher Institute estimated it at 28.0. Although reports from more recent years suggest a small drop in the abortion rate, the point is still clear: American women of all ages have many more abortions than their European peers. See Stanley Henshaw and Evelyn Morrow, *Induced Abortion: A World Review—1990 Supplement* (New York: Alan Guttmacher Institute, 1990), pp. 32–58, esp. Table 2, "Number of Illegal Abortions, Abortion Rates and Abortion Ratios: Selected Area, Years and Characteristics."

123. U.K. Office of Population Censuses and Surveys, *Birth Statistics: England and Wales* (London: HMSO, 1994), Table 9.6.

124. U.S. Bureau of the Census, "Marital Status and Living Arrangements, 1990," *Current Population Reports,* Series P-20, no. 450 (1991), p. 1, Table A.

125. Ibid.

126. Andrew Cherlin, *Marriage, Divorce, Remarriage* (Cambridge, Mass.: Harvard University Press, 1992).

127. Larry Bumpass, "What's Happening to the Family: Interactions between Demographic and Institutional Change," *Demography* 27: 483–498.

128. William J. Wilson, *The Truly Disadvantaged,* pp. 81–90.

129. National Center for Health Statistics, *Advance Report of Final Marriage Statistics,* vol. 40, no. 4, Supp. August 26, 1991.

130. Mercer Sullivan, "Patterns of AFDC Use in a Comparative Ethnographic Study of Young Fathers and Their Children in Three Low Income Neighborhoods," Paper prepared for the Office of the Assistant Secretary for Planning and Evaluation, U.S. Department of Health and Human Services, 1990.

131. Scott J. South and Glenna Spitze, "Housework in Marital and Nonmarital Households," *American Sociological Review* 59, no. 3 (1994): 327–348; Sarah Fenstermaker Berk and Anthony Shih, "Contributions to Household Labor: Comparing Wives' and Husbands' Reports," in Berk, ed., *Women and Household Labor* (Beverly Hills, Calif.: Sage), pp. 191–227.

132. Arlie Hochschild, *The Second Shift* (New York: Avon Books, 1989).

133. U.S. Department of Commerce, "Child Support and Alimony," *Current Population Reports,* Special Studies, Series P-23, no. 167.

134. Sara McLanahan and Gary Sandefur, *Growing Up with a Single Parent: What Hurts, What Helps* (Cambridge, Mass: Harvard University Press, 1994), p. 97. (Data are from the National Survey of Families and Households.)

135. Valerie Oppenheimer, *The Female Labor Force in the United States: Demographic and Economic Factors Governing Its Growth and Composition* (West-

port, Conn.: Greenwood Press, 1976); Suzanne Bianchi and Daphne Spain, *American Women in Transition* (New York: Russell Sage, 1986).

136. Grace K. Baruch and Rosalind Barnett, "Correlates of Fathers' Participation in Family Work: A Technical Report," Working paper no. 196 (Wellesley, Mass.: Wellesley College Center for Research on Women, 1983), pp. 80–81.

137. See Ruth Sidel, *On Her Own: Growing Up in the Shadow of the American Dream* (New York: Penguin, 1990).

138. Lawrence Stone, *The Family, Sex and Marriage in England, 1500–1800* (London: Weidenfeld and Nicholson, 1977).

139. United Nations, Department of International Economic and Social Affairs, "Adolescent Reproductive Behavior: Evidence from Developed Countries," *Population Studies* 1, no. 109 (1988).

140. Family and Medical Leave Act, Public Law 103-3 (1993).

141. See Arline Geronimus and Sanders Korenman, "The Socioeconomic Consequences of Teenage Childbearing Reconsidered," Paper no. 90-190, Population Studies Center, University of Michigan, 1990.

142. Unless, of course, their postponing leads them to be much more affluent than they would otherwise be. The point here is that this is a risky bet. What if you postpone having a baby and don't become affluent? Given that infertility treatment is only rarely covered by insurance, a woman must be affluent indeed to afford it.

143. Peter Neumann, S. Gharib, and Milton Weinstein, "The Cost of a Successful Delivery with In Vitro Fertilization," *New England Journal of Medicine* 331, no. 4 (1994): 239–244.

144. National Center for Health Statistics, *Advance Report of Final Natality Statistics: Monthly Vital Statistics Report*, vol. 43, no. 5, Supp. October 25, 1994 (1992). Because the phenomenon of late childbearing is both new and largely unremarked, the exact costs and consequences of it are unknown. For changes in the distribution of first-time mothers by age, see Stephanie Ventura, "Trends and Variations in First Births to Older Women, 1970–86," *Vital Health Statistics* 21, no. 47 (1989). The data on the effects of maternal age are also complex: a woman who is having her first child at age forty is obviously in a different risk group from one who is having her fifth—or fifteenth. For an overview, see Michael B. Aldous and M. Bruce Edmonson, "Maternal Age at First Childbirth and Risk of Low Birth Weight and Preterm Delivery in Washington State," *Journal of the American Medical Association* 270, no. 21 (December 1993): 2574; A. Friede et al., "Older Maternal Age and Infant Mortality in the United States," *Obstetrics and Gynecology* 72 (1988): 152–157; K. S. Lee et al., "Maternal Age and Incidence of Low Birth Weight at Term: A Population Study," *American Journal of Obstetrics and Gynecology* 158 (1988): 84–89; and G. S. Berkowitz et al., "Delayed Childbearing and the Outcome of Pregnancy," *New England Journal of Medicine* 322 (1990): 659–664.

145. Ibid.

146. Gordon Berlin and Andrew Sum, *Toward a More Perfect Union: Basic Skills, Poor Families and Our Economic Future* (New York: Ford Foundation, 1988).

7. Teenage Parents and the Future

1. For public opinion on welfare, see Blackside Polls, Inc., for Public Broadcasting System. See also Times Mirror Poll, July 12–25, 1994, reported in "Compassion for the Poor Is Declining, Poll Finds," *New York Times,* September 21, 1995.

2. The Republican Party has proposed the Personal Responsibility Act, which prohibits AFDC payments to unmarried mothers under eighteen and permits states to withhold AFDC from unmarried mothers under twenty-one. Ed Gillespie and Bob Schellhas, eds., *Contract with America: The Bold Plan by Representative Newt Gingrich, Representative Dick Armey and the House Republicans to Change the Nation* (New York: Times Books, 1994), p. 66. See also House Republican Conference, *Legislative Digest,* September 27, 1994, p. 16. One reading of this proposal ("The Real Welfare Reform Act," H.R. 4566) is that all children born to unmarried mothers under twenty-one (and under twenty-five after 1998) would be barred *forever* from receiving welfare benefits. As I have argued throughout this book, poor women have their babies young, so this is an extraordinarily clever strategy to limit the social safety net by excluding large numbers of children *for life* under the guise of reducing "teenage pregnancy." See also Kathleen Sylvester, *Preventable Calamity: Rolling Back Teen Pregnancy* (Washington, D.C.: Progressive Policy Institute, 1994).

3. Gillespie and Schellhas, eds., *Contract with America,* p. 75.

4. Jill McLean Taylor, "Development of Self, Moral Voice, and the Meaning of Adolescent Motherhood: The Narratives of Fourteen Adolescent Mothers" (Diss., Harvard University, 1989), pp. 79, 130.

5. Constance Willard Williams, "An Acceptable Life: Pregnancy and Childbearing from the Black Teen Mother's Perspective" (Diss., Brandeis University, 1989), pp. 136–137.

6. Brenda Schwab, "Someone to Always Be There: Teenage Childbearing as an Adaptive Strategy in Rural New England" (Diss., Brandeis University, 1983), p. 186.

7. Ibid., p. 188.

8. Virginia Hunter, "Impact of Adolescent Parenthood on Black Teenage Mothers and Their Families" (Diss., UCLA, 1982), p. 134.

9. Kathleen Thornton, "Comprehensive Evaluation of a Teen Pregnancy and Parenting Program" (Diss., University of Pennsylvania, 1992), p. 171.

10. Laurie Ann McDade, "Community Responses to Teenage Pregnancy and Parenting: An Ethnography of a Social Problem" (Diss., Rutgers University, 1987), p. 281.

11. Ibid., p. 285.

12. U.S. House of Representatives, Committee on Ways and Means, *Overview of Entitlement Programs,* 103rd Congress, 2nd session (Washington, D.C.: Government Printing Office, 1994), pp. 365–367, Tables 10–11.

13. For an elegant summary of the numbers, see Katherine Edin and Christopher Jencks, "The Real Welfare Problem," *American Prospect* 1, no. 1 (1990).

14. For an overview, see Judith Gueron and Edward Pauly, *From Welfare to Work* (New York: Russell Sage, 1991).

15. Jill Quadagno, *The Transformation of Old Age Security: Class and Politics in the American Welfare State* (Chicago: University of Chicago Press, 1988).

16. For evidence that Americans really have become more "me-centered" (and simultaneously less committed to the notion of "duty" to others, including spouses and children), see Joseph Veroff, *The Inner American: A Self-Portrait from 1957 to 1976* (New York: Basic Books, 1981). For evidence that this may in fact indicate a change in fundamental values across the globe (or at least throughout the First World), see Ronald Inglehart, *Culture Shift in Advanced Industrial Society* (Princeton: Princeton University Press, 1990).

17. Melvin Zelnik, M. A. Koenig, and Y. J. Kim, "Source of Prescription Contraceptives and Subsequent Pregnancy among Women," *Family Planning Perspectives* 16 (1984): 6–13. See also Alan Guttmacher Institute, *Sex and America's Teenagers,* p. 34.

18. A. Torres and J. D. Forrest, "Family Planning Clinic Services in the United States, 1983," *Family Planning Perspectives* 17, no. 1 (1985): 30–35; Alan Guttmacher Institute, *Organized Family Planning Services in the United States, 1981–1983* (New York: Alan Guttmacher Institute, 1984); M. Chamie, S. Eisman, J. D. Forrest, M. Orr, and A. Torres, "Factors Affecting Adolescents' Use of Family Planning Clinics," *Family Planning Perspectives* 14 (1982): 126–139; R. Levine and L. Tsolflias, "Publicly Supported Family Planning in the U.S.: Use in the 1980s," Henry J. Kaiser Foundation, 1994.

19. U.S. Department of Health and Human Services, Public Health Service, Center for Disease Control, "Use of Family Planning Services in the United States, 1982–1988," *Advance Data from Vital and Health Statistics,* vol. 184 (Hyattsville, Md.: National Center for Health Statistics, 1990).

20. Levine and Tsolflias, "Publicly Supported Family Planning in the U.S."

21. Torres and Forrest, "Family Planning Clinic Services"; Levine and Tsolflias, "Publicly Supported Family Planning in the U.S."

22. Leighton Ku, "Financing of Family Planning Services in Publicly Supported Family Planning Services in the United States" (Washington, D.C.: Urban Institute and Child Trends, Inc., 1993).

23. R. B. Gold, *Abortion and Women's Health* (New York: Alan Guttmacher Institute, 1990).

24. Michael Imber, "Toward a Theory of Curricular Reform: An Analysis of the First Campaign for Sex Education," *Curriculum Inquiry* 12 (1982): 339–362.

25. Benjamin C. Gruenberg, *High Schools and Sex Education* (Washington, D.C.: Government Printing Office, 1940).

26. U.S. Senate, Committee on Labor and Human Resources, *Reauthorization of the Adolescent Family Life Demonstration Projects Act of 1981: Hearing before the Subcommittee on Family and Human Services of the Committee on Labor and Human Resources*, 98th Congress, 2nd sess., 1984.

27. Freya L. Sonenstein and Karen J. Pittman, "The Availability of Sex Education in Large City School Districts," *Family Planning Perspectives* 16 (1984): 19–25.

28. Calculations by Jane Mauldon and Kristin Luker, based on the 1988 National Survey of Family Growth. See Jane Mauldon and Kristin Luker, "Contraception at First Sex: The Effects of Sex Education," Working paper no. 206, Graduate School of Public Policy, University of California at Berkeley, 1994.

29. William Marsiglio and F. L. Mott, "The Impact of Sex Education on Sexual Activity, Contraceptive Use and Premarital Pregnancy among American Teenagers," *Family Planning Perspectives* 18, no. 4 (1986): 151–162.

30. Ibid.

31. L. C. Ku, F. Sonenstein, and J. Pleck, "Factors Affecting First Intercourse among Young Men," *Public Health Reports* 108 (1993): 680–694.

32. Frank Furstenberg et al., "Sex Education and Sexual Experience among Adolescents," *American Journal of Public Health* 75, no. 11 (1985): 1331–1332.

33. Deborah A. Dawson, "The Effects of Sex Education on Adolescent Behavior," *Family Planning Perspectives* 18 (1986): 162–170. Melvin Zelnik and Y. J. Kim, "Sex Education and Its Association with Teenage Sexual Activity, Pregnancy and Contraceptive Use," *Family Planning Perspectives* 14 (1982): 117–126. Kirby et al., "School-Based Programs to Reduce Sexual Risk Behaviors," pp. 339–359.

34. Lana D. Muraskin with Paul Jargowsky, *Creating and Implementing Family Life Education in New Jersey* (Alexandria, Va.: National Association of State Boards of Education, 1985).

35. Marsiglio and Mott, "The Impact of Sex Education Programs," pp. 151–162.

36. Mauldon and Luker, "Contraception at First Sex."

37. Respect, Inc. For an overview, see Colleen Kelly Mast, *Love and Life: A Christian Sexual Morality Guide for Teens* (San Francisco: Ignatius Press, 1986).

38. S. E. Weed and J. A. Olsen, "Evaluation Report of the Sex Respect Program: Results for the 1988–1989 School Year," Office of Adolescent Pregnancy Programs, Office of Population Affairs, Department of Health and Human Services; S. Christopher and M. Roosa, "An Evaluation of an Adolescent Pregnancy Prevention Program: Is 'Just Say No' Enough?" *Family Relations* 39 (1990): 68–72; M. Roosa and S. Christopher, "Evaluation of an Abstinence-Based Adolescent Pregnancy Prevention Program: A Replication," *Family Relations* 39 (1990): 363–367.

39. Kirby, "School-Based Programs to Reduce Sexual Risk Behaviors," pp. 339–359.

40. Mauldon and Luker, "Contraception at First Sex."
41. Even in affluent communities boys and young men seem much less interested in preventing pregnancy, and this is a real problem.
42. C. Mallar et al., *Evaluation of the Economic Impact of the Job Corps Program* (Princeton, N.J.: Mathematica, 1978).
43. R. J. Olsen and G. Farkas, *The Effects of Economic Opportunity and Family Background on Adolescent Fertility among Low Income Blacks* (Rockville, Md.: U.S. Department of Health and Human Services, 1987).
44. Elaine McCrate, "Employment Opportunities and Teenage Childbearing," Paper delivered at first annual meeting of the Women's Policy Institute, Washington, D.C., May 1989.
45. Katherine Edin and Christopher Jencks, "The Real Welfare Problem," *American Prospect* (1990): 31–50.

SELECTED BIBLIOGRAPHY

Abrahamse, Allan F. "Teenagers Willing to Consider Single Parenthood: Who Is at Greatest Risk?" *Family Planning Perspectives* 20, no. 1 (January–February 1988): 13–18.

———; Peter A. Morrison; and Linda J. Waite. *Beyond Stereotypes: Who Becomes a Single Teenage Mother?* Santa Monica, Calif.: Rand Corporation, 1988.

Alan Guttmacher Institute. *Eleven Million Teenagers: What Can Be Done about the Epidemic of Adolescent Pregnancies in the United States.* New York: Planned Parenthood Federation of America, 1976.

——— *Sex and America's Teenagers.* New York: Alan Guttmacher Institute, 1994.

Anderson, Elijah. *Streetwise: Race, Class, and Change in an Urban Community.* Chicago: University of Chicago Press, 1990.

Bachrach, C. A. "Adoption Plans, Adopted Children, and Adoptive Mothers." *Journal of Marriage and the Family* 48, no. 2 (May 1986): 243–253.

Baldwin, Wendy H. "Adolescent Pregnancy and Childbearing: Growing Concerns for Americans." *Population Bulletin* 31, no. 2 (September 1977): 3–31.

——— "The Children of Teenage Parents." *Family Planning Perspectives* 12, no. 1 (January–February 1980): 34–39, 42–43.

Becker, Gary A. *A Treatise on the Family.* Cambridge, Mass.: Harvard University Press, 1991.

Bell, Winifred. *Aid to Dependent Children.* New York: Columbia University Press, 1965.

Berlin, Gordon, and Andrew Sum. *Toward a More Perfect Union: Basic Skills, Poor Families, and Our Economic Future.* New York: Ford Foundation, 1988.

Bianche, Suzanne, and Daphne Spain. *American Women in Transition.* New York: Russell Sage Foundation, 1986.

Blake, Judith. "The Teenage Birth Control Dilemma and Public Opinion." *Science* 180, no. 87 (May 1973): 708–712.

Blum, R. W., and M. D. Resnick. "Adolescent Sexual Decision-Making: Contraception, Pregnancy, Abortion and Motherhood." *Pediatric Annals* 11, no. 10 (October 1982): 797–805.

Bolton, Frank G. *The Pregnant Adolescent: Problems of Premature Parenthood.* Beverly Hills: Sage Publications, 1980.

Brewster, Karin. "Race Differences in Sexual Activity among Adolescent Women." *American Sociological Review* 59, no. 3 (June 1994): 408–424.

———; J. O. G. Billy; and William R. Grady. "Social Context and Adolescent Behavior: The Impact of Community on the Transition to Sexual Activity." *Social Forces* 71, no. 3 (March 1993): 713–740.

Bumpass, Larry. "Children and Marital Disruption: A Replication and Update." *Demography* 21, no. 1 (February 1984): 71–82.

——— "What's Happening to the Family: Interactions between Demographic and Institutional Change." *Demography* 27, no. 4 (November 1990): 483–498.

——— and James A. Sweet. "Children's Experience in Single-Parent Families: Implications of Cohabitation and Marital Transition." *Family Planning Perspectives* 21, no. 6 (November–December 1989): 256–260.

Burt, Martha. "Estimates of Public Costs for Teenage Childbearing." Washington, D.C.: Center for Population Options, 1986.

Campbell, Arthur A. "The Role of Family Planning in the Reduction of Poverty." *Journal of Marriage and the Family* 30, no. 2 (1968): 236–245.

Card, Josefina J., and Lauress Wise. "Teenage Mothers and Teenage Fathers: The Impact of Early Childbearing on the Parents' Personal and Professional Lives." *Family Planning Perspectives* 10, no. 4 (July–August 1978): 199–205.

Casper, L. M.; S. S. McLanahan; and I. Garfinkle. "The Gender-Poverty Gap: What We Can Learn from Other Countries." *American Sociological Review* 59, no. 4 (August 1994): 594–605.

Chamie, Mamie, et al. "Factors Affecting Adolescents' Use of Family Planning Clinics." *Family Planning Perspectives* 14, no. 3 (May–June 1982): 126–139.

Cherlin, Andrew. *Marriage, Divorce, Remarriage.* Cambridge, Mass.: Harvard University Press, 1992.

Chudacoff, Howard. *How Old Are You? Age Consciousness in American Culture.* Princeton: Princeton University Press, 1989.

Cook, Shelby H. "The Unresolved Crisis: The Federal Government's Search for an Adolescent Pregnancy Policy, 1970–1985." Diss., University of Maryland, 1986.

Cooksey, Elizabeth C. "Factors in the Resolution of Adolescent Premarital Pregnancies." *Demography* 27, no. 2 (May 1990): 207–218.

Cooper, J. "Births Outside Marriage: Recent Trends and Associated Demographic and Social Changes." *Population Trends* 63 (Spring 1991): 8–18.

Crane, Jonathan. "The Epidemic Theory of Ghettos and Neighborhood Effects on Dropping Out and Teenage Childbearing." *American Journal of Sociology* 96, no. 5 (March 1991): 1226–1259.

Darabi, Katherine, and Vilma Ortiz. "Childbearing among Young Latino Women in the United States." *American Journal of Public Health* 77, no. 1 (1987): 25–28.

Dash, Leon. *When Children Want Children: The Urban Crisis of Teenage Childbearing.* New York: William Morrow, 1989.

Davis, Sally. "Pregnancy in Adolescents." *Pediatric Clinics of North America* 36, no. 3 (June 1989): 665–680.

Dawson, Deborah A. "The Effects of Sex Education on Adolescent Behavior." *Family Planning Perspectives* 18, no. 4 (July–August 1986): 162–170.

D'Emelio, John, and Estelle Friedman. *Intimate Matters: A History of Sexuality in America.* New York: Harper and Row, 1988.

Dryfoos, Joy G. "School-Based Health Clinics: A New Approach to Preventing Adolescent Pregnancy?" *Family Planning Perspectives* 17, no. 2 (March–April 1985): 70–75.

———— *Adolescents at Risk: Prevalence and Prevention.* New York: Oxford University Press, 1990.

Dudziak, Mary L. "Just Say No: Birth Control in the Connecticut Supreme Court before *Griswold v. Connecticut.*" *Iowa Law Review* 75, no. 4 (May 1990): 915–939.

Duncan, Greg J., and Willard Rodgers. "Longitudinal Aspects of Childhood Poverty." *Journal of Marriage and the Family* 50 (November 1988): 1007–1021.

Duncan, Greg J., and Saul Hoffman. "Teenage Welfare Receipt and Subsequent Dependence among Black Adolescent Mothers." *Family Planning Perspectives* 22, no. 1 (January–February 1990): 16–20.

———— "Welfare Benefits, Economic Opportunities, and Out-of-Wedlock Births among Black Teenage Girls." *Demography* 27, no. 4 (November 1990): 519–535.

Eisen, M., and G. Zellman. "Factors Predicting Pregnancy Resolution Decision Satisfaction of Unmarried Adolescents." *Journal of Genetic Psychology* 145, no. 2 (December 1984): 231–239.

Ellwood, David. *Poor Support: Poverty in the American Family.* New York: Basic Books, 1988.

———— and M. J. Bane. *The Impact of AFDC on Family Structure and Living Arrangements.* Cambridge, Mass.: Harvard University Press, 1984.

Farley, Reynolds, and Albert Hermalin. *Growth of the Black Population: A Study of Demographic Trends.* Chicago: Markham, 1970.

———— "Family Stability: A Comparison of Trends between Blacks and Whites." *American Sociological Review* 36, no. 1 (February 1971): 1–17.

Fine, Michelle. "Sexuality, Schooling and Adolescent Females: The Missing Discourse of Desire." *Harvard Educational Review* 58, no. 1 (February 1988): 29–53.

———— *Framing Dropouts: Notes on the Politics of an Urban Public High School.* Albany: State University of New York Press, 1991.

Flaherty, David H. "Law and the Enforcement of Morals in Early America." *Perspectives in American History* 5 (1971): 225–226.

Forrest, Jacqueline D., and Richard Fordyce. "U.S. Women's Contraceptive Attitudes and Practice: How Have They Changed in the 1980s?" *Family Planning Perspectives* 20, no. 3 (May–June 1988): 112–118.

Forrest, Jacqueline D., and Susheela Singh. "The Sexual and Reproductive Behavior of American Women, 1982–1988." *Family Planning Perspectives* 22, no. 5 (September–October 1990): 206–214.

Funiciello, Teresa. *Tyranny of Kindness: Dismantling the Welfare System to End Poverty in America.* New York: Atlantic Monthly Press, 1993.

Furstenberg, Frank, Jr. *Unplanned Parenthood: The Social Consequences of Teenage Childbearing.* New York: Free Press, 1976.

———; J. A. Levine; and J. Brooks-Gunn. "The Children of Teenage Mothers: Patterns of Early Childbearing in Two Generations." *Family Planning Perspectives* 22, no. 2 (March–April 1990): 54–61.

Furstenberg, Frank, Jr.; J. Brooks-Gunn; and S. Philip Morgan. "Race Differences in the Timing of Adolescent Intercourse." *American Sociological Review* 52 (August 1987): 511–518.

Furstenberg, Frank, Jr.; J. Brooks-Gunn; and S. Philip Morgan. *Adolescent Mothers in Later Life.* Cambridge: Cambridge University Press, 1987.

Furstenberg, Frank, Jr.; K. A. Moore; and J. L. Peterson. "Sex Education and Sexual Experience among Adolescents." *American Journal of Public Health* 75, no. 11 (November 1985): 1331–1332.

Geronimus, Arline T. "Clashes of Common Sense: On the Previous Child-Care Experience of Teenage Mothers-to-Be." *Human Organization* 51, no. 4 (1992): 318–329.

Geronimus, Arline T., and Sanders Korenman. "The Socioeconomic Consequences of Teen Childbearing Reconsidered." Research Report 90-190, Population Studies Center, University of Michigan, September 1990.

——— "The Socioeconomic Consequences of Teen Childbearing Reconsidered." *Quarterly Journal of Economics* 107, no. 4 (1992): 1187–1214.

——— "Maternal Youth or Family Background? On the Health Disadvantages of Infants with Teenage Mothers." *American Journal of Epidemiology* 137, no. 2 (1993): 213–225.

Gillespie, Ed, and Bob Schellhas, eds. *Contract with America: The Bold Plan by Rep. Newt Gingrich, Rep. Dick Armey and the House Republicans to Change the Nation.* New York: Times Books, 1994.

Gold, Rachel Benson. *Abortion and Women's Health: A Turning Point for America?* New York: Alan Guttmacher Institute, 1990.

Gordon, Linda. *Woman's Body, Woman's Right: Birth Control in America.* New York: Penguin, 1990.

——— *Pitied But Not Entitled: Single Mothers and the History of Welfare.* New York: Free Press, 1994.

Gosney, E. S., and Paul Popenoe. *Sterilization for Human Betterment: A Summary of Results of 6,000 Operations in California, 1909–1929.* New York: Macmillan, 1931.

Green, Gordon; Paul Ryscavage; and Edward Welniak. "Studies in the Distribution of Income." *Current Population Reports,* P-60-183.

Grossberg, Michael. *Governing the Hearth: Law and the Family in Nineteenth-Century America.* Chapel Hill: University of North Carolina Press, 1985.

Gruenberg, Benjamin C. *High Schools and Sex Education.* Public Health Service Report 7. Washington, D.C.: Government Printing Office, 1939.

Gueron, Judith, and Edward Pauly. *From Welfare to Work.* New York: Russell Sage Foundation, 1991.

Hall, G. Stanley. *Adolescence: Its Psychology and Its Relations to Physiology, Anthropology, Sociology, Sex, Crime, Religion and Education.* New York: D. Appleton, 1905.

Hardy, Janet B.; Anne K. Duggan; Katya Masnyk; and Carol Pearson. "Fathers of Children Born to Young Urban Mothers." *Family Planning Perspectives* 21, no. 4 (July–August 1989): 159–163, 187.

Harris, Katherine. "Teenage Mothers and Welfare Dependency: Working Off Welfare." *Journal of Family Issues* 12, no. 4 (December 1991): 492–518.

———— "Work and Welfare among Single Mothers in Poverty." *American Journal of Sociology* 99, no. 2 (September 1993): 317–352.

Hayes, Cheryl D., ed. *Risking the Future: Adolescent Sexuality, Pregnancy, and Childbearing.* Washington, D.C.: National Academy Press, 1987.

Henshaw, Stanley K. "Characteristics of U.S. Women Having Abortions, 1982–1983." *Family Planning Perspectives* 19, no. 1 (January–February 1987): 5–9.

———— "Characteristics of U.S. Women Having Abortions, 1987." *Family Planning Perspectives* 23, no. 2 (March–April 1991): 75–81.

Henshaw, Stanley K., and Jennifer Van Vort. *Abortion Services in the United States: Each State and Metropolitan Area.* New York: Alan Guttmacher Institute, 1988.

———— "Abortion Services in the United States, 1987 and 1988." *Family Planning Perspectives* 22, no. 3 (May–June 1990): 102–108, 142.

Henshaw, Stanley K., and Lynn Wallisch. "The Medicaid Cutoff and Abortion Services for the Poor." *Family Planning Perspectives* 16, no. 4 (July–August 1984): 171–172, 177–180.

Henshaw, Stanley K., et al. *Teenage Pregnancy in the United States: The Scope of the Problem and State Responses.* New York: Alan Guttmacher Institute, 1989.

Heuser, Robert L. *Fertility Tables for Birth Cohort by Color: United States, 1917–1973.* DHEW Publication (HRA)76-11182. Rockville, Md.: National Center for Health Statistics, 1976.

Hindus, Michael. "Premarital Pregnancy in America, 1640–1971: An Overview and an Interpretation." *Journal of Interdisciplinary History* 5 (July 1975): 537–570.

Hochschild, Arlie. *The Second Shift: Working Parents and the Revolution at Home.* New York: Viking, 1989.

Hofferth, Sandra L. "A Comment on 'Social Determinants of Age at First Birth.'" *Journal of Marriage and the Family* 46, no. 1 (February 1984): 7–8.

———— and Kristin A. Moore. "Early Childbearing and Later Economic Well-Being." *American Sociological Review* 44, no. 5 (October 1979): 784–815.

———; J. R. Kahn; and W. Baldwin. "Premarital Sexual Activity among U.S. Teenage Women over the Past Three Decades." *Family Planning Perspectives* 19, no. 2 (March–April 1987): 46–53.

Hogan, Dennis P., and Evelyn Kitagawa. "The Impact of Social Status, Family Structure and Neighborhood on the Fertility of Black Adolescents." *American Journal of Sociology* 90, no. 4 (January 1985): 825–855.

Hogan, Dennis P., et al. "Social and Environmental Factors Influencing Contraceptive Use among Black Adolescents." *Family Planning Perspectives* 17, no. 4 (July–August 1985): 165–169.

Jencks, Christopher. *Rethinking Social Policy: Race, Poverty, and the Underclass*. Cambridge, Mass.: Harvard University Press, 1992.

Jones, Elise F., et al. *Teenage Pregnancy in Industrialized Countries*. New Haven: Yale University Press, 1986.

Kahn, J. R.; R. Rindfuss; and D. K. Guilkey. "Adolescent Contraceptive Method Choices." *Demography* 27, no. 3 (1990): 323–335.

Kalmuss, N., et al. "Adoption versus Parenting among Young Pregnant Women." *Family Planning Perspectives* 23, no. 1 (January–February 1991): 17–23.

Katz, Michael. *The Undeserving Poor: From the War on Poverty to the War on Welfare*. New York: Pantheon Books, 1989.

Kennedy, David. *Birth Control in America: The Career of Margaret Sanger*. New Haven: Yale University Press, 1970.

Kingdon, John. *Agendas, Alternatives, and Public Policies*. New York: Harper Collins, 1995.

Kirby, Douglas. "The Effects of School Sex Education Programs: A Review of the Literature." *Journal of School Health* 50, no. 10 (December 1980): 559–563.

——— et al. "Reducing the Risk: Impact of a New Curriculum on Sexual Risk-Taking." *Family Planning Perspectives* 23, no. 6 (November–December 1991): 253–263.

——— et al. "School-Based Programs to Reduce Sexual Risk Behaviors: A Review of Effectiveness." *Public Health Reports* 109, no. 3 (May–June 1994): 339–360.

Klepinger, D. H.; S. Lundberg; and R. D. Plotnick. "Adolescent Fertility and the Educational Attainment of Young Women." *Family Planning Perspectives* 27, no. 1 (January–February 1995): 23–28.

Kost, K., and J. D. Forrest. "American Women's Sexual Behavior and Exposure to Risk of Sexually Transmitted Disease." *Family Planning Perspectives* 24, no. 6 (November–December 1992): 244–254.

Ku, L. C. "Financing of Family Planning Services." In *Publicly Supported Family Planning Services in the United States*. Sponsored by the Henry J. Kaiser Family Foundation. Washington, D.C.: Urban Institute and Child Trends, 1993.

Ku, L. C; F. Sonenstein; and J. Pleck. "Factors Influencing First Intercourse for Teenage Men." *Public Health Reports* 108, no. 6 (November–December 1993): 680–694.

——— "The Association of AIDS Education and Sex Education with Sexual

Behavior and Condom Use among Teenage Men." *Family Planning Perspectives* 24, no. 3 (May–June 1992): 100–106.

Landman, J. H. *Human Sterilization: The History of the Sexual Sterilization Movement.* New York: Macmillan, 1932.

Laslett, Peter, et al., eds. *Bastardy and Its Comparative History.* Cambridge, Mass.: Harvard University Press, 1980.

Levine, Ruth, and Lynn Tsolflias. "Publicly-Supported Family Planning in the U.S.: Use in the 1980s." Report prepared for the Henry J. Kaiser Foundation, 1994.

Levy, Frank. *Dollars and Dreams: The Changing American Income Distribution.* New York: Norton, 1988.

Lindenman, Constance. *Birth Control and Unmarried Young Women.* New York: Springer, 1974.

Littlewood, Thomas B. *The Politics of Population Control.* Notre Dame: University of Notre Dame Press, 1977.

Lombardo, Paul A. "Eugenic Sterilization in Virginia: Aubrey Strode and the Case of *Buck v. Bell.*" Diss., University of Virginia, 1982.

Lundberg, Emma O. "Children of Illegitimate Birth, and Measures for Their Protection." Publication 166, U.S. Department of Labor, Children's Bureau, 1926.

———— "Unmarried Mothers in the Municipal Court of Philadelphia." Bureau of Municipal Research of Philadelphia, Philadelphia Municipal Court Survey Series, Thomas Skeleton Harrison Foundation, 1933.

Lundberg, Shelly, and Robert Plotnick. "Testing the Opportunity Cost Hypothesis of Adolescent Premarital Childbearing." Working Paper 8, Russell Sage Foundation, 1990.

———— "Effects of State Welfare, Abortion and Family Planning Policies on Premarital Childbearing among White Adolescents." *Family Planning Perspectives* 22, no. 6 (November–December 1990): 246–275.

———— "Adolescent Premarital Childbearing: Do Economic Incentives Matter?" *Journal of Labor Economics* 13, no. 2 (April 1995): 177–200.

MacCorquodale, Patricia L. "Gender Roles and Premarital Contraception." *Journal of Marriage and the Family* 46, no. 1 (February 1984): 57–63.

Maciak, Barbara J., et al. "Pregnancy and Birth Rates among Sexually Experienced U.S. Teenagers: 1974, 1980, and 1983." *Journal of the American Medical Association* 258, no. 15 (October 1987): 2069–2071.

Marini, Margaret Mooney, and Burton Singer. "Women's Educational Attainment and the Timing of Entry into Parenthood." *American Sociological Review* 49, no. 4 (August 1984): 491–511.

Marsiglio, William. "Adolescent Fathers in the United States: Their Initial Living Arrangements, Marital Experience and Educational Outcomes." *Family Planning Perspectives* 19, no. 6 (November–December 1987): 240–251.

———— and Frank L. Mott. "The Impact of Sex Education on Sexual Activity, Contraceptive Use and Premarital Pregnancy among American Teenagers." *Family Planning Perspectives* 18, no. 4 (July–August 1986): 151–162.

Mayer, William. *The Changing American Mind: How and Why American Public*

Opinion Changed between 1960 and 1988. Ann Arbor: University of Michigan Press, 1992.

McLanahan, Sara S., and Gary Sandefur. *Growing Up with a Single Parent: What Hurts, What Helps*. Cambridge, Mass.: Harvard University Press, 1994.

McLanahan, Sara S., et al. "Sex Differences in Poverty, 1950–1980." *Signs* 15, no. 1 (Fall 1989): 102–122.

Mead, Lawrence. *Beyond Entitlement: The Social Obligations of Citizenship*. New York: Free Press, 1986.

——— *New Politics of Poverty: The Non-Working Poor in America*. New York: Basic Books, 1992.

Menken, Jane. "Teenage Childbearing: Its Medical Aspects and Implications for the United States Population." In Westoff and Parke, eds., *Demographic and Social Aspects of Population Growth*. Washington, D.C., 1972.

——— "The Health and Demographic Consequences of Adolescent Pregnancy and Childbearing." In C. Chilman, ed., *Adolescent Pregnancy and Childbearing: Findings from Research*. Washington, D.C.: U.S. Department of Health and Human Services, 1980.

Moffitt, Robert. "Incentive Effects of the U.S. Welfare System: A Review." *Journal of Economic Literature* 30 (March 1992): 1–61.

Mohr, James. *Abortion in America: The Origins and Evolution of National Policy, 1800–1900*. New York: Oxford University Press, 1978.

Moore, Kristin A., and Linda J. Waite. "Early Childbearing and Educational Attainment." *Family Planning Perspectives* 9, no. 5 (September–October 1977): 220–225.

Moore, Kristin A., and Martha R. Burt. *Private Crisis, Public Cost*. Washington, D.C.: Urban Institute Press, 1982.

Moore, Kristin A., and Richard F. Wertheimer. "Teenage Childbearing and Welfare: Preventive and Ameliorative Strategies." *Family Planning Perspectives* 16, no. 6 (November–December 1984): 285–289.

Moore, Kristin A., and Steven B. Caldwell. "The Effect of Government Policies on Out-of-Wedlock Sex and Pregnancy." *Family Planning Perspectives* 9, no. 4 (July–August 1977): 164–169.

Moore, Kristin A., et al. *Teenage Motherhood: Social and Economic Consequences*. Washington, D.C.: Urban Institute, 1979.

Moore, Kristin A.; Christine Winquist; and James L. Peterson. "Nonvoluntary Sexual Activity among Adolescents." *Family Planning Perspectives* 21, no. 3 (May–June 1989): 110–114.

Morrison, Peter A., et al. "Teenage Parenthood: A Review of Risks and Consequences." Paper presented at the National Institute of Education, Santa Monica, Calif., 1981.

Mosher, William D., and James W. McNally. "Contraceptive Use at First Premarital Intercourse: United States, 1965–1988." *Family Planning Perspectives* 23, no. 3 (May–June 1991): 108–116.

Murray, Charles. *Losing Ground: American Social Policy, 1950–1980.* New York: Basic Books, 1984.

Nathanson, Constance. *Dangerous Passage: The Social Control of Sexuality in Women's Adolescence.* Philadelphia: Temple University Press, 1991.

—— and Marshall H. Becker. "Family and Peer Influence on Obtaining a Method of Contraception." *Journal of Marriage and the Family* 48, no. 3 (August 1986): 513–525.

O'Connell, Martin, and Carolyn C. Rogers. "Out-of-Wedlock Births, Premarital Pregnancies and Their Effect on Family Formation and Dissolution." *Family Planning Perspectives* 16, no. 4 (July–August 1984): 157–162.

Olson, Lucy. "Social and Psychological Correlates of Pregnancy Resolution among Adolescent Women: A Review." *American Journal of Orthopsychiatry* 50, no. 3 (July 1980): 432–445.

Ooms, Theodora. *Teenage Pregnancy in a Family Context: Implications for Policy.* Philadelphia: Temple University Press, 1981.

Orr, Margaret Terry. "Sex Education and Contraceptive Education in U.S. Public High Schools." *Family Planning Perspectives* 14, no. 6 (November–December 1982): 304–313.

Pivar, David. *Purity Crusade: Sexual Morality and Social Control, 1868–1900.* Westport, Conn.: Greenwood Press, 1973.

Plotnick, Robert. "Welfare and Out-of-Wedlock Childbearing: Evidence from the 1980s." *Journal of Marriage and the Family* 52, no. 3 (August 1990): 735–746.

Popenoe, Paul, and E. S. Gosney. *Twenty-Eight Years of Sterilization in California.* Pasadena: Human Betterment Foundation, 1938.

Population Council. "The United States: The Pill and the Birth Rate, 1960–1965." *Studies in Family Planning* 20 (June 1967).

Pratt, William F., et al. "Understanding U.S. Fertility: Findings from the National Survey of Family Growth, Cycle III." *Population Bulletin* 39, no. 5 (December 1984): 3–40.

Presser, Harriet. "Early Motherhood: Ignorance or Bliss?" *Family Planning Perspectives* 6, no. 1 (Winter 1974): 8–14.

Quadagno, Jill. "Theories of the Welfare State." *Annual Review of Sociology* 13 (1987): 109–128.

—— *The Transformation of Old Age Security: Class and Politics in the American Welfare State.* Chicago: University of Chicago Press, 1988.

—— *The Color of Welfare: How Racism Undermined the War on Poverty.* New York: Oxford University Press, 1994.

Reed, James. *The Birth Control Movement and American Society: From Private Vice to Public Virtue.* Princeton: Princeton University Press, 1978.

Reichelt, Paul A. "Public Policy and Public Opinion toward Sex Education and Birth Control for Teenagers." *Journal of Applied Social Psychology* 16, no. 2 (1986): 95–106.

Reiss, Ira L. *Premarital Sexual Standards in America: A Sociological Investigation of the Relative Social and Cultural Integration of American Sexual Standards.* Glencoe, Ill.: Free Press, 1960.

Rindfuss, Ronald R., et al. "Education and Fertility: Implications for the Roles Women Occupy." *American Sociological Review* 45, no. 3 (June 1980): 431–447.

——— "Disorder in the Life Course: How Common and Does It Matter?" *American Sociological Review* 52, no. 6 (December 1987): 785–801.

Robinson, Bryan E. *Teenage Fathers.* Lexington, Mass.: Lexington Books, 1988.

Rogers, James L., et al. "Impact of the Minnesota Parental Notification Law on Abortion and Birth." *American Journal of Public Health* 81, no. 3 (March 1991): 294–298.

Roosa, M. W., and F. S. Christopher. "Evaluation of an Abstinence-Only Adolescent Pregnancy Prevention Program: A Replication." *Family Relations* 39, no. 4 (October 1990): 363–367.

Rosen, R. "Adolescent Pregnancy Decision-Making: Are Parents Important?" *Adolescence* 15, no. 57 (Spring 1980): 43–54.

Rubin, G. L.; J. Gold; and W. Cates, Jr. "Response of Low-Income Women and Abortion Facilities to Restriction of Public Funds for Abortion; A Study of a Large Metropolitan Area." *American Journal of Public Health* 69, no. 9 (September 1979): 948–950.

Scharf, Kathleen Rudd. "Funding for Pregnant Adolescents: A Legislative History." In Max Sugar, ed., *Adolescent Pregnancy.* New York: Spectrum, 1984.

Schlossman, Steven, and Stephanie Wallach. "The Crime of Precocious Sexuality: Female Juvenile Delinquency in the Progressive Era." *Harvard Educational Review* 48, no. 1 (February 1978): 65–94.

Shah, Farida; Melvin Zelnik; and John F. Kantner. "Unprotected Intercourse among Unwed Teenagers." *Family Planning Perspectives* 7, no. 1 (January–February 1975): 39–44.

Singh, Susheela. "Adolescent Pregnancy in the United States: An Interstate Analysis." *Family Planning Perspectives* 18, no. 5 (September–October 1986): 210–220.

Skocpol, Theda. *Protecting Soldiers and Mothers: The Political Origins of Social Policy in the United States.* Cambridge, Mass.: Harvard University Press, 1992.

Skolnick, Arlene, *Embattled Paradise: The American Family in an Age of Uncertainty.* New York: Basic Books, 1991.

Skrownek, Stephen. *Building a New American State: The Expansion of National Administrative Capacities, 1877–1920.* Cambridge: Cambridge University Press, 1982.

Smith, Daniel Scott. "The Long Cycle in American Illegitimacy and Prenuptial Pregnancy." In Peter Laslett et al., eds., *Bastardy and Its Comparative History.* Cambridge: Cambridge University Press, 1980.

Smith, Herbert L., and Philips Cutright. "Thinking about Change in Illegitimacy Ratios: United States, 1963–1983." *Demography* 25, no. 2 (May 1988): 235–247.

Smith-Rosenberg, Carroll. *Disorderly Conduct: Visions of Gender in Victorian America*. New York: Knopf, 1985.

Sonenstein, Freya L., and Karen J. Pittman. "The Availability of Sex Education in Large City School Districts." *Family Planning Perspectives* 16, no. 1 (January–February 1984): 19–25.

Sonenstein, Freya L., et al. "Levels of Sexual Activity among Adolescent Males in the United States." *Family Planning Perspectives* 23, no. 4 (July–August 1991): 162–167.

Stone, Abraham. "The Social and Legal Status of Contraception." *North Carolina Law Review* 22 (1944): 212–225.

Sullivan, Mercer L. "Patterns of AFDC Use in a Comparative Ethnographic Study of Young Fathers and Their Children in Three Low-Income Neighborhoods." Paper prepared for the Office of the Assistant Secretary for Planning and Evaluation, U.S. Department of Health and Human Services, June 1990.

—— *The Male Role in Teenage Pregnancy and Parenting: New Directions for Public Policy*. New York: Vera Institute of Justice, 1990.

Taylor, B.; J. Wadsworth; and N. R. Butler. "Teenage Mothering, Admission to Hospital, and Accidents during the First Five Years." *Archives of Disease in Childhood* 58, no. 1 (January 1983): 6–11.

Thorton, Arland. "Changing Attitudes toward Family Issues in the United States." *Journal of Marriage and the Family* 51, no. 4 (November 1989): 873–893.

Torres, Aida. "The Effects of Federal Funding Cuts on Family Planning Services, 1980–1983." *Family Planning Perspectives* 16, no. 3 (May–June 1984): 134–138.

—— and J. D. Forrest. "Family Planning Clinic Services in the United States, 1983." *Family Planning Perspectives* 17, no. 1 (January–February 1985): 30–35.

Torres, Aida, and S. Singh. "Contraceptive Practice among Hispanic Adolescents." *Family Planning Perspectives* 18, no. 4 (July–August 1986): 193–194.

Trussell, J. T. "Economic Consequences of Teenage Childbearing." *Family Planning Perspectives* 8, no. 4 (July–August 1976): 184–190.

—— "Teenage Pregnancy in the United States." *Family Planning Perspectives* 20, no. 6 (November–December 1988): 262–272.

—— and B. Vaughan. "Selected Results Concerning Sexual Behavior and Contraceptive Use from the 1988 National Survey of Family Growth and the 1988 National Survey of Adolescent Males." Office of Population Research Working Paper 91-12, Princeton University, 1991.

Trussell, J. T., et al. "The Impact of Restricting Medicaid Financing for Abortion." *Family Planning Perspectives* 12, no. 3 (May–June 1980): 120–123, 127–130.

Udry, J. R., and J. O. G. Billy. "Initiation of Coitus in Early Adolescence." *American Sociological Review* 52, no. 6 (December 1987): 841–855.

Ulrich, Laurel Thatcher. *Good Wives: Image and Reality in the Lives of Women in Northern New England, 1650–1750*. New York: Knopf, 1982.

United Nations. Department of International Economic and Social Affairs. "Adolescent Reproductive Behaviour: Evidence from Developed Countries." *Population Studies* 1, no. 109 (1988).

Upchurch, Dawn, and James McCarthy. "Adolescent Childbearing and High School Completion in the 1980s: Have Things Changed?" *Family Planning Perspectives* 21, no. 5 (September–October 1989): 199–202.

———— "The Timing of a First Birth and High School Completion." *American Sociological Review* 55, no. 2 (April 1990): 224–234.

U.S. Centers for Disease Control. "Effects of Restricting Federal Funds for Abortion: Texas." *Morbidity and Mortality Weekly Reports,* June 6, 1980.

U.S. Congress. "Report on the Family Planning Services and Population Research Act of 1970." U.S. Code, Congressional and Administrative News 3, 1970.

———— Subcommittee on Children, Youth and Families. *Teen Pregnancy: What Is Being Done? A State-by-State Look.* Washington, D.C.: Government Printing Office, 1986.

———— Office of Technology Assessment. *Adolescent Health, Volume II: Background and the Effectiveness of Selected Prevention and Treatment Services.* OTA-H-466. Washington, D.C.: Government Printing Office, 1991.

U.S. House of Representatives. Committee on Ways and Means. *Overview of Entitlement Programs.* Green Book. Washington, D.C.: Government Printing Office, 1994.

U.S. Public Health Service. "Trends in Illegitimacy: United States, 1940–1965." *Vital and Health Statistics* 1, series 1 (Program and Collection Procedures), no. 15 (March 1968): 1–90.

U.S. Senate. *Hearing before the Subcommittee on Health of the Committee on Labor and Public Welfare, U.S. Senate, 94th Congress, to Enact the National School-Age Mother and Child Health Acts of 1975.* Washington, D.C.: Government Printing Office, 1975.

———— Committee on Labor and Human Resources. *Reauthorization of the Adolescent Family Life Demonstration Projects Act of 1981: Hearing before the Subcommittee on Family and Human Services of the Committee on Labor and Human Resources, United States Senate, 98th Congress, 2nd Session, April 24 and 26, 1984.* Washington, D.C.: Government Printing Office, 1985.

Veccoli, Rudolf J. "Sterilization: A Progressive Measure." *Wisconsin Magazine of History* (Spring 1960): 190–202.

Ventura, Stephanie J. "Trends in Teenage Childbearing: United States, 1970–1981." *Vital and Health Statistics* 41, series 21 (September 1984).

Veroff, Joseph. *The Inner American: A Self-Portrait from 1957 to 1976.* New York: Basic Books, 1981.

Vinovskis, Maris. *An "Epidemic" of Adolescent Pregnancy? Some Historical and Policy Considerations.* New York: Oxford University Press, 1988.

Ward, Martha. *Poor Women, Powerful Men: America's Great Experiment in Family Planning.* Boulder, Colo.: Westview, 1986.

Watson, Amey Brown Eaton. "Illegitimacy: Philadelphia's Problem and the Development of Standards of Care." Diss., Bryn Mawr College, 1923.

Weis, Lois. "High School Girls in a De-Industrializing Economy." In Lois Weis, ed., *Class, Race and Gender in American Education.* Albany: State University of New York Press, 1988.

Weisman, Carol S., et al. "Adolescent Women's Contraceptive Decision Making." *Journal of Health and Social Behavior* 32, no. 2 (June 1991): 130–144.

Wells, R. V. "Illegitimacy and Bridal Pregnancy in Colonial America." In Peter Laslett et al., eds., *Bastardy and Its Comparative History.* Cambridge, Mass.: Harvard University Press, 1980.

Wertheimer, Richard, and Kristin Moore. *Teenage Childbearing, Public Sector Costs: A Final Report.* Washington, D.C.: Urban Institute, 1982.

Westoff, Charles F. "Contraceptive Paths toward the Reduction of Unintended Pregnancy and Abortion." *Family Planning Perspectives* 20, no. 1 (January–February 1988): 4–13.

Westoff, Charles F., and Norman Ryder. "Duration of Use of Oral Contraception in the United States, 1960–65." *Public Health Reports* 83, no. 4 (April 1968): 277–287.

———— "United States: Methods of Fertility Control, 1955, 1960, and 1965." *Studies in Family Planning* 17 (February 1967): 1–5.

Wiebe, Robert H. *The Search for Order, 1877–1920.* New York: Hill and Wang, 1967.

Williams, Linda B., and William F. Pratt. "Wanted and Unwanted Childbearing in the United States, 1973–1988." In *Advance Data from Vital and Health Statistics.* Hyattsville, Md.: National Center for Health Statistics, 1990.

Wilson, William Julius. *The Truly Disadvantaged: The Inner City, the Underclass, and Public Policy.* Chicago: University of Chicago Press, 1987.

Wong, Yin-Ling Irene, et al. "Single-Mother Families in Eight Countries: Economic Status and Social Policy." *Social Service Review* 67, no. 2 (June 1993): 177–197.

Zabin, Laurie Schwab, and Samuel Clark, Jr. "Why They Delay: A Study of Teenage Family Planning Clinic Patients." *Family Planning Perspectives* 13, no. 5 (September–October 1981): 205–207, 211–217.

Zabin, Laurie Schwab; M. B. Hirsch; and M. R. Emerson. "When Urban Adolescents Choose Abortion: Effects on Education, Psychological Status and Subsequent Pregnancy." *Family Planning Perspectives* 21, no. 6 (November–December 1989): 248–255.

Zabin, Laurie Schwab; M. B. Hirsch; and J. A. Boscia. "Differential Characteristics of Adolescent Pregnancy Test Patients: Abortion, Childbearing, and Negative Test Groups." *Journal of Adolescent Health Care* 11, no. 2 (March 1990): 107–113.

Zabin, Laurie Schwab, et al. "The Risk of Adolescent Pregnancy in the First Months of Intercourse." *Family Planning Perspectives* 11, no. 4 (July–August 1979): 215–222.

———— "Adolescent Sexual Attitudes and Behavior: Are They Consistent?" *Family Planning Perspectives* 16, no. 4 (July–August 1984): 181–185.

Zellman, Gail L. *The Response of the Schools to Teenage Pregnancy and Parenthood.* Report prepared for the National Institute of Education. Santa Monica, Calif.: Rand Corporation, 1981.

—— "Public School Programs for Adolescent Pregnancy and Parenthood: An Assessment." *Family Planning Perspectives* 14, no. 1 (January–February 1982): 15–21.

Zelnik, Melvin, and John Kantner. "Sexual and Contraceptive Experience of Young Unmarried Women in the United States, 1971 and 1976." *Family Planning Perspectives* 9, no. 2 (March–April 1977): 55–56, 58–63, 67–71.

—— "Sexual Activity, Contraceptive Use and Pregnancy among Metropolitan-Area Teenagers, 1971–1979." *Family Planning Perspectives* 12, no. 5 (September–October 1980): 230–231, 233–237.

—— and Kathleen Ford. *Sex and Pregnancy in Adolescence.* Beverly Hills: Sage Publications, 1981.

Zelnik, Melvin, and Y. J. Kim. "Sex Education and Its Association with Teenage Sexual Activity, Pregnancy and Contraceptive Use." *Family Planning Perspectives* 14, no. 3 (May–June 1982): 117–126.

Zelnik, Melvin, and Farida Shah. "First Intercourse among Young Americans." *Family Planning Perspectives* 15, no. 2 (March–April 1983): 64–70.

Zelnik, Melvin; M. A. Koenig; and Y. J. Kim. "Sources of Prescription Contraceptives and Subsequent Pregnancy among Young Women." *Family Planning Perspectives* 16, no. 1 (January–February 1984): 6–13.

INDEX